JESUS CHRIST AS [
IN THE GOSPEL OF MARK

This study contributes to the debate over the function of Davidic sonship in the Gospel of Mark. In contrast to William Wrede's paradigm, Max Botner argues that Mark's position on Jesus' ancestry cannot be assessed properly through isolated study of the name "David" (or the patronym "son of David"). Rather, the totality of Markan messiah language is relevant to the question at hand. Justification for this paradigm shift is rooted in observations about the ways in which ancient authors spoke of their messiahs. Botner shows that Mark was participant to a linguistic community whose members shared multiple conventions for stylizing their messiahs, Davidic or otherwise. He then traces how the evangelist narratively constructed his portrait of Christ via creative use of the Jewish scriptures. When the *Davidssohnfrage* is approached from within this sociolinguistic framework, it becomes clear that Mark's Christ is indeed David's son.

MAX BOTNER is Assistant Professor of New Testament at Grand Rapids Theological Seminary. His work has been published in the *Journal for Biblical Literature*, the *Journal for Theological Studies*, the *Journal for the Study of the Pseudepigrapha*, and the *Catholic Biblical Quarterly*. He is also a coeditor of the forthcoming volume, *Atonement: Sin, Sacrifice, and Salvation in Jewish and Christian Antiquity*.

SOCIETY FOR NEW TESTAMENT STUDIES

MONOGRAPH SERIES

General Editor: Edward Adams, Kings College, London

174

JESUS CHRIST AS THE SON OF DAVID IN THE GOSPEL
OF MARK

Jesus Christ as the Son of David in the Gospel of Mark

MAX BOTNER

Grand Rapids Theological Seminary

CAMBRIDGE
UNIVERSITY PRESS

CAMBRIDGE
UNIVERSITY PRESS

University Printing House, Cambridge CB2 8BS, United Kingdom

One Liberty Plaza, 20th Floor, New York, NY 10006, USA

477 Williamstown Road, Port Melbourne, VIC 3207, Australia

314-321, 3rd Floor, Plot 3, Splendor Forum, Jasola District Centre, New Delhi - 110025, India

79 Anson Road, #06-04/06, Singapore 079906

Cambridge University Press is part of the University of Cambridge.

It furthers the University's mission by disseminating knowledge in the pursuit of education, learning and research at the highest international levels of excellence.

www.cambridge.org
Information on this title: www.cambridge.org/9781108702140
DOI: 10.1017/9781108569835

First published 2019
First paperback edition 2020

A catalogue record for this publication is available from the British Library

Library of Congress Cataloging in Publication data
Names: Botner, Max, 1985– author.
Title: Jesus Christ as the son of David in the Gospel of Mark / Max Botner,
    Grand Rapids Theological Seminary, Michigan.
Description: 1 [edition]. | New York : Cambridge University Press, 2019. |
    Series: Society for New Testament studies monograph series ; 174 |
    Includes bibliographical references and index.
Identifiers: LCCN 2018047995 | ISBN 9781108477208 (hardback) |
    ISBN 9781108702140 (pbk.)
Subjects: LCSH: Bible. Mark–Criticism, interpretation, etc. |
    Jesus Christ–Person and offices–Biblical teaching.
Classification: LCC BS2585.52 .B68 2019 | DDC 226.3/06–dc23
LC record available at https://lccn.loc.gov/2018047995

ISBN 978-1-108-47720-8 Hardback
ISBN 978-1-108-70214-0 Paperback

For Jessica

ὁ συνεργός μου εἰς τὴν βασιλείαν τοῦ θεου

And in loving memory of Pennie D. Rhein Botner (1945–2008)

quae me multos annos fleverat ut oculis tuis viverem

– Augustine,
Confessions, 9.12.3

CONTENTS

ACKNOWLEDGMENTS

This book is a lightly revised version of my doctoral dissertation, *How Can Mark's Christ Be David's Son?* As such, there are a number of people whom I wish to thank and who deserve credit for whatever success its argument may find. First and foremost, I am deeply grateful to my doctoral advisor, Elizabeth Shively, who proved to be an expert guide throughout the dissertation process. She is a model of scholarly excellence and leadership to which I will always aspire. I am also indebted to my examiners, David Moffitt and Matthew Novenson, both of whom pushed me to tighten points of my argument. Their careful and incisive comments greatly improved the book.

Among the many advantages of studying at the University of St. Andrews is the support of wonderful colleagues. In particular, my scholarship was greatly aided during my time working as a research assistant for Professor N. T. Wright. Tom has been an incredible mentor and advocate both during and after the completion of my doctoral studies. Other members of the St. Mary's faculty who deserve special recognition are Madhavi Nevader, who graciously commented on large portions of my writing, along with Jim Davila, Scott Hafemann, and Bill Tooman, each of whom were timely conversation partners along the way. I would be remiss not to extend my thanks to my fellow St. Andrews postgraduates, too, especially Kai Akagi, Garrick Allen, Justin Duff, and Simon Dürr.

The argument of this book has also been enhanced by a number of individuals outside my home department at St. Andrews – namely, Helen Bond, George Brooke, Susan Docherty, Crispin Fletcher-Louis, Peter Rodgers, Anthony Stiff, and Steven Tyra. Matthew Novenson kindly shared with me a prepublication draft of the third chapter of his recent monograph, *The Grammar of Messianism:*

An Ancient Jewish Political Idiom and Its Users (2017). Both Paul Trebilco and the anonymous reviewer from Studiorum Novi Testamenti Societas rendered helpful feedback on points of presentation and style. Without a doubt, these brilliant colleagues have covered a multitude of infelicities; any remaining issues with the book are my responsibility alone.

I had the opportunity to present parts of the book in a number of professional settings and colloquia, including the University of St. Andrews New Testament Seminar, the British New Testament Conference, the Annual Meeting of the Society of Biblical Literature, the International Meeting of the Society of Biblical Literature, and the Annual Meeting for the Institute of Biblical Research. I am grateful to Oxford University Press, the Society of Biblical Literature, and SAGE Publications, respectively, for their permission to use material I previously published in their journals. A section of Chapter 1 appeared in a slightly different form in "What Has Mark's Christ to Do with David's Son? A History of Interpretation," *Currents in Biblical Research* 16 (2017): 50–70. Parts of Chapter 4 appeared in different forms in "The Messiah Is 'the Holy One': ὁ ἅγιος τοῦ θεοῦ as a Messianic Title in Mark 1:24," *Journal of Biblical Literature* 136 (2017): 419–435, and in "Has Jesus Read What David Did? Probing Problems in Mark 2:25–26," *Journal of Theological Studies* (2018): 484–499.

Revision and editing of the book were completed during my time as a lecturer in the New Testament Department at Goethe-Universität Frankfurt am Main. I am grateful to Stefan Alkier and the rest of the New Testament faculty and my colleagues in the LOEWE research group – above all, Christian Wiese and Nina Fischer – for their warm hospitality and rich vision for *Religionswissenschaft*. It is my pleasure to publish this book within the framework of the Hessian Ministry for Science and Art Funded by the LOEWE research hub "Religiöse Positionierung: Modalitäten und Konstellationen in jüdischen, christlichen und islamischen Kontexten" at Goethe-Universität Frankfurt am Main/Justus-Liebig-Universität Gießen. Thanks are also due to Beatrice Rehl and the rest of the fine team at Cambridge University Press for making each stage of the publication process seamless.

Finally, I would like to express my deepest gratitude to my family. My father has long been a supporter of my academic pursuits, esoteric though they may be. My three children, Ava, Noah, and Olivia, have been a constant source of joy and encouragement. Their smiling faces and laughter whisper – at times even shout – of God's love. Most importantly, I could not have completed this book without the sacrificial love and support of my wife, Jessica, and my mother, Pennie – who insisted during her last days, in October 2008, that I had a book or two in my future. I dedicate this book to these two remarkable women.

ABBREVIATIONS

For all primary sources, I follow the abbreviations prescribed in the second edition of *The SBL Handbook of Style* (Atlanta: SBL, 2014).

AB	Anchor Bible
AcBib	Society of Biblical Literature Academia Biblica
ACW	Ancient Christian Writers
AGJU	Arbeiten zur Geschichte des antiken Judentums und des Urchristentums
ANESSup	Ancient Near Eastern Studies Supplement Series
ArBib	The Aramaic Bible
BBR	*Bulletin for Biblical Research*
BCOTWP	Baker Commentary on the Old Testament Wisdom and Psalms
BDAG	Danker, Frederick W., Walter Bauer, William F. Arndt, and F. Wilbur Gingrich. *Greek-English Lexicon of the New Testament and Other Early Christian Literature.* 3rd ed. Chicago: University of Chicago Press, 2000 (Danker–Bauer–Arndt–Gingrich)
BDF	Blass, Friedrich, Albert Debrunner, and Robert W. Funk. *A Greek Grammar of the New Testament and Other Early Christian Literature.* Chicago: University of Chicago Press, 1961.
BECNT	Baker Exegetical Commentary on the New Testament
BETL	Bibliotheca Ephemeridum Theologicarum Lovaniensium
BHS	*Biblia Hebraica Stuttgartensia.* Edited by K. Elliger and W. Rudolph. Stuttgart, 1983.
Bib	*Biblica*
BibInt	*Biblical Interpretation*

BibInt	Biblical Interpretation Series
BibS(F)	Biblische Studien (Freiburg, 1895–)
BibS(N)	Biblische Studien (Neukirchen, 1951–)
BNTC	Black's New Testament Commentaries
BR	*Biblical Research*
BWA(N)T	Beiträge zur Wissenschaft vom Alten (und Neuen) Testament
BZ	*Biblische Zeitschrift*
BZNW	Beihefte zur Zeitschrift für die neutestamentliche Wissenschaft
CahRB	Cahiers de la Revue biblique
CBET	Contributions to Biblical Exegesis and Theology
CBQ	*Catholic Biblical Quarterly*
CBQMS	Catholic Biblical Quarterly Monograph Series
CBR	*Currents in Biblical Research*
CC	Continental Commentaries
CCSL	Corpus Christianorum: Series Latina
CGTC	Cambridge Greek Testament Commentary
CNT	Commentaire du Nouveau Testament
ConBNT	Coniectanea Biblica: New Testament
ConBOT	Coniectanea Biblica: Old Testament Series
CSEL	Corpus Scriptorum Ecclesiasticorum Latinorum
CTQ	*Concordia Theological Quarterly*
DJD	Discoveries in the Judean Desert
DSD	*Dead Sea Discoveries*
EJL	Society of Biblical Literature Early Judaism and Its Literature Series
EKKNT	Evangelisch-katholischer Kommentar zum Neuen Testament
FAT	Forschungen zum Alten Testament
FB	Forschung zur Bibel
FRLANT	Forschungen zur Religion und Literatur des Alten und Neuen Testaments
FTS	Frankfurter Theologische Studien
GNT	Grundrisse zum Neuen Testament
HNT	Handbuch zum Neuen Testament
HThKNT	Herders Theologischer Kommentar zum Neuen Testament
HTR	*Harvard Theological Review*
HTS	Harvard Theological Studies

HUCM	Monographs of the Hebrew Union College
ICC	International Critical Commentary
Imm	*Immanuel*
JBL	*Journal of Biblical Literature*
JJS	*Journal of Jewish Studies*
JPS	Jewish Publication Society
JPSTC	Jewish Publication Society Torah Commentary Series
JQR	*Jewish Quarterly Review*
JR	*Journal of Religion*
JSHJ	*Journal for the Study of the Historical Jesus*
JSJ	*Journal for the Study of Judaism in the Persian, Hellenistic, and Roman Periods*
JSJSup	Supplements to the Journal for the Study of Judaism
JSNT	*Journal for the Study of the New Testament*
JSNTSup	Journal for the Study of the New Testament Supplement Series
JSOTSup	Journal for the Study of the Old Testament Supplement Series
JSP	*Journal for the Study of the Pseudepigrapha*
JSPSup	Journal for the Study of the Pseudepigrapha Supplement Series
JSQ	*Jewish Studies Quarterly*
JSS	*Journal of Semitic Studies*
JTI	*Journal of Theological Interpretation*
JTS	*Journal of Theological Studies*
KEK	Kritisch-exegetischer Kommentar über das Neue Testament
LCL	Loeb Classical Library
LD	Lectio Divina
LHBOTS	The Library of Hebrew Bible/Old Testament Studies
LNTS	The Library of New Testament Studies
LXX	Septuagint
MT	Masoretic Text
NA[28]	*Novum Testamentum Graece*, Nestle-Aland, 28th edn.
NICNT	New International Commentary on the New Testament
NIGTC	New International Greek Testament Commentary
NovT	*Novum Testamentum*

NovTSup	Novum Testamentum Supplement Series
NTS	*New Testament Studies*
OTP	*Old Testament Pseudepigrapha*. Edited by James H. Charlesworth. 2 vols. New York: Doubleday, 1983, 1985.
OtSt	*Oudtestamentische Studiën*
PAAJR	*Proceedings of the American Academy of Jewish Research*
RB	*Revue biblique*
RBS	Resources for Biblical Study
RevQ	*Revue de Qumran*
SANT	Studien zum Alten und Neuen Testaments
SBLDS	Society of Biblical Literature Dissertation Series
SBLGNT	The Greek New Testament: SBL Edition.
SBLMS	Society of Biblical Literature Monograph Series
SBS	Stuttgarter Bibelstudien
SBT	Studies in Biblical Theology
SC	Sources chrétiennes
SCS	Septuagint and Cognate Studies
SEÅ	*Svensk exegetisk årsbok*
SNTSMS	Society for New Testament Studies Monograph Series
SP	Sacra Pagina
STDJ	Studies on the Texts of the Desert of Judah
StPB	Studia Post-Biblica
SUNT	Studien zur Umwelt des Neuen Testaments
SVTP	Studia in Veteris Testamentari Pseudepigraphica
SymS	Society of Biblical Literature Symposium Series
THKNT	Theologischer Handkommentar zum Neuen Testament
TS	Texts and Studies
TSAJ	Texte und Studien zum antiken Judentum
UBS⁵	*The Greek New Testament*, United Bible Societies, 5th edn.
VC	*Vigiliae Christianae*
VT	*Vetus Testamentum*
VTSup	Supplements to Vetus Testamentum
WBC	Word Biblical Commentary
WUNT	Wissenschaftliche Untersuchungen zum Neuen Testament

YJS	Yale Judaica Society
ZAW	*Zeitschrift für die alttestamentliche Wissenschaft*
ZNW	*Zeitschrift für die neutestamentliche Wissenschaft und die Kunde der älteren Kirche*
ZTK	*Zeitschrift für Theologie und Kirche*

1

THE SON OF DAVID AND THE CHRIST OF MARK

Beyond an Interpretive Impasse

Wir haben nicht ganz wenig Zeugnisse, dass die Davids-
sohnschaft Jesu in den ersten Jahrhunderten von gewissen
Seiten bestritten worden ist.
    – William Wrede, *Vorträge und Studien*, 171

[T]he pull of the use of Psalm 110:1 as a proof-text for Jesus'
Davidic sonship elsewhere in and beyond the New Testament is strong on many Markan readers and interpreters . . .
From the point of view of Matthew, Luke, Romans, and 2
Timothy, this aspect of the Markan narrative might be
mystifying, but reading this text through those is not the
best way to make sense of it . . . [M]any readers and commentators resolve (or dissolve?) the mystery . . . by reading
Mark's Gospel against a strong background belief in Jesus
as the Son of David that they bring with them to the
narrative, a Christian belief that is simply assumed to be in
all "Christian" materials.
    – Elizabeth Struthers Malbon, *Mark's Jesus*, 160

The Synoptic evangelists Matthew, Mark, and Luke present their
audiences with a puzzle. While teaching in the temple courts around
the time of the Passover festival, days before his crucifixion, Jesus
openly disputes the premise that the messiah is the son of David by
appealing to an ancient oracle in which David calls the messiah
"my lord" (citing Ps 110:1). The upstart from Nazareth presses his
interlocutors, "David himself calls him lord; how then can he be
his son?" (Mark 12:37 pars.). The answer is not at once obvious. Is
the point of the *Davidssohnfrage* ("son-of-David question") to deny
the premise that the messiah would be a descendant of David? Or
does the question assume the premise in order to say something more
about the messiah? Current wisdom suggests that the answer

depends, at least in part, on *which* Jesus is asking the question. That is, while interpreters generally agree that the evangelists Matthew and Luke circumvent a negative answer to the *Davidssohnfrage* – a denial that the messiah would be a descendant of David – the same cannot be said for the evangelist Mark. In fact, many are convinced that he guides his audience to precisely the opposite conclusion: his messiah is manifestly *not* the son of David.

The ostensive dissonance between the Gospel of Mark and its Synoptic counterparts on the question of the messiah's ancestry is governed by the most basic of interpretive principles. "[A]ny interpretation given of a certain portion of a text can be accepted if it is confirmed by, and must be rejected if it is challenged by, another portion of the same text. In this sense the internal textual coherence controls the otherwise uncontrollable drives of the reader."[1] Gospels scholars accordingly take it for granted that the meaning of the *Davidssohnfrage* – a certain portion of a text – is conditioned by the larger narrative – the remaining portions of the same text – in which the question is situated. (Indeed, part of the problem with extracting the question from its Synoptic context and recontextualizing it in an alternative *Sitz im Leben* is that there are no controls for the "drives of the reader."[2]) The consensus of Gospels research is that whereas

---

[1] Umberto Eco et al., *Interpretation and Overinterpretation*, ed. Stefan Collini (Cambridge: Cambridge University Press, 1992), 65. Ambrose offers an ancient example of this interpretive principle when he inquires, "This too must be considered, since he resists those who say that the Christ is the son of David: How did the blind man merit healing by confessing that he is the son of David? How did the children with loud shouts proclaiming, 'Hosanna to the son of David,' render glory to God? But they [the scribes] are not resisted, in this instance [the *Davidssohnfrage*], because they claim he is the son of David, but because they do not believe he is the son of God [*Illud quoque considerandum, quia reprehendit eos qui Christum Dauid filium dicunt, et quomodo caecus ille Dauid filium confitendo meruit sanitatem? Quomodo pueri dicentes osanna filio Dauid praecelsae praedicationis deo gloriam deferebant? Sed non reprehenduntur hoc loco quia Dauid filium confitentur, sed quia non credunt filium dei*]" (*Exp. Luc.* 10.2; Dom Gabriel Tissot, ed., *Ambroise de Milan Traité sur L'Évangile de S. Luc.*, 2 vols., SC 45 and 52 [Paris: Cerf, 1956–1958], 2:158). While textual coherence for the bishop of Milan is at least the twofold witness of Matthew and Luke, the basic guideline that one's interpretation of a portion of a narrative must cohere with one's interpretation of the rest of that narrative is analogous to the way modern scholars approach the *Davidssohnfrage*.

[2] Gerhard Schneider chronicles modern scholarship's fascination with the "real" *Sitz* of the *Davidssohnfrage* ("Die Davidssohnfrage [Mark 12,35–37]," *Bib* 53 [1972]: 65–90). There is evidence to suggest that the *Davidssohnfrage* may have circulated outside of its Synoptic context (cf. Barn. 12:10–11), and isolated treatment of this tradition, in conjunction with sweeping attacks on Davidic messiahship in general, seems to have serviced *adversus Iudaeos* and Marcionite polemics (cf. Tertullian,

the Matthean and Lukan narratives discard one possible interpretation of the *Davidssohnfrage*, a denial of the Christ's Davidic ancestry, the Markan narrative leaves this interpretive option squarely on the table. At best, the evangelist is circumspect about the idea of Davidic sonship; at worst, he finds it antithetical to his gospel message.

This book sets out to scrutinize the state of the question on Davidic sonship in the Gospel of Mark. I contend that the framework within which modern scholarship has assessed this issue, at least from Wrede onwards, is arbitrary when compared to the ways in which ancient authors constructed their messiahs. These were participants of a linguistic community whose members recognized multiple conventions for characterizing their messiahs, Davidic or otherwise. Markan scholars, by contrast, tend to assume that ancient discourse about messiahs is reducible to names and titles, and so they invariably attempt to answer Mark's *Davidssohnfrage* through isolated study of pericopae with the name David. My proposal is that the evangelist's language about his Christ should be evaluated on the terms of his own linguistic community, as nothing short of a "creatively biblical linguistic act."[3]

The present chapter establishes the rationale for my argument. A survey of the secondary literature demonstrates that Markan scholarship has long reduced the *Davidssohnfrage* to the insular study of passages with the name David. The proposed antidote to this misguided approach is an intervention along sociolinguistic lines: How did participants in ancient messianic discourse communicate what they meant by the term "messiah"? Do these writers make use of certain conventions when constructing their messiahs? How does son-of-David language feature within this field of discourse? And so forth. The answer to Mark's *Davidssohnfrage*, I will argue, lies neither in our capacity to reconstruct the *Sitz im Leben* of the evangelist's community nor in our aptitude to discern the veiled wink of an implied author, but in our commitment to read the Gospel as the product of a competent language user of a particular ancient linguistic community.

Marc. 4.36; Origen, *Comm. Jo.* 10.19; inter alia); as discussed, e.g., in William Wrede, *Vorträge und Studien* (Tübingen: Mohr Siebeck, 1907), 171–173.

[3] To borrow an apt phrase from Matthew V. Novenson, *Christ among the Messiahs: Christ Language in Paul and Messiah Language in Ancient Judaism* (New York: Oxford University Press, 2012), 62. I explore the significance of Novenson's work on messiah language in Section 1.2.1.

1.1   Contesting David's Son: The Problem of Messianism and the Christology of Mark

Étienne Trocmé speaks for a large swathe of interpreters when he claims, "'Christ'– and the cognate titles 'Son of David' and 'King of the Jews' – is to say the least ambiguous in the eyes of the evangelist … It carries no special stress, even though it is not as drastically rejected as some think."[4] Although Trocmé ultimately falls in line with what Wrede calls the "orthodox" position on Davidic sonship,[5] there are, as he alludes, "some" who would want to go further. Indeed, for these interpreters the evangelist is not ambiguous on this issue at all; rather, he regards it as fundamentally incompatible with sound Christology. The following *Forschungsgeschichte* attempts to elucidate why "some" – in fact, quite a few – interpreters have arrived at the conclusion that the Christ of Mark cannot be the son of David.

1.1.1   Shaping the Son-of-David Debate: From Reimarus to Wrede

Every student of ancient messianism and early Christology remains indebted to the work of Hermann Samuel Reimarus. While previous skeptics had already begun to assail the notion that the historical Jesus could be aligned with the second person of the Trinity, Reimarus was the first to do so by locating him within the milieu of early Judaism.[6] In particular, he contended that "to be called 'Son of God' and 'Christ the Messiah' meant one and the same thing,"[7] concluding that the *Davidssohnfrage* discloses the messiah's

---

[4] Étienne Trocmé, "Is There a Marcan Christology?" in *Christ and Spirit in the New Testament*, eds. Barnabas Lindars and Stephen S. Smalley (Cambridge: Cambridge University Press) 3–14, here 7. This section represents and develops material from Max Botner, "What Has Mark's Christ to Do with David's Son? A History of Interpretation," *CBR* 16.1 (2017): 50–70. © The 2017. Reprinted by permission of SAGE Publications. https://doi.org/10.1177/1476993X17717838.

[5] Wrede, *Vorträge*, 168.

[6] Werner Georg Kümmel, for example, traces Reimarus's debt to the English Deists (*The New Testament: The History of the Investigation of Its Problems*, trans. S. McLean Gilmour and Howard C. Clark [Nashville: Abingdon, 1972], 90). Unlike the Deists, however, Reimarus ruthlessly wielded the category of messianism, as he understood it, as a weapon against orthodox Christianity.

[7] Hermann Samuel Reimarus, *Fragments*, ed. Charles H. Talbert, trans. Ralph S. Fraser (London: SCM press, 1971), 83. The so-called *Wolfenbütteler Fragmente* were published posthumously by Gotthold Ephraim Lessing in 1974 and 1977.

superiority "only insofar as he as Messiah is to establish a kingdom for which all the dead, including David himself, would be awakened by God."[8] Moreover, he reasoned that if the historical Jesus was in fact the long-awaited son of David, he would have had but one option: he must cast off the Roman yoke and usher in an earthly political kingdom of God.[9]

The reception of Reimarus's proposal was mixed. On the one hand, many scholars, particularly those in the German-speaking world, followed his attempt to interpret christological categories within the framework of early Judaism, irrespective of doctrines and creeds.[10] "Son of God" was thus routinely treated as a messianic epithet, cognate with "son of David" and "messiah."[11] On the other hand, virtually no one was willing to follow Reimarus's assertion that the historical Jesus capitulated to the political expectations facing any would-be messiah. Instead, *Neutestamentler* lined up in droves to argue that Jesus eschewed the messianic spirit of his time, often adducing the *Davidssohnfrage* as evidence that the harbinger of Enlightenment morality discarded the baggage of the son-of-David label.[12]

The year 1901 witnessed the publication of William Wrede's *Das Messiasgeheimnis* and Albert Schweitzer's *Das Messianitäts- und Leidensgeheimnis*. As Schweitzer would conclude several years later,

---

[8] Ibid., 87.　　[9] Ibid., 138.

[10] Note, in particular, Heinrich Julius Holtzmann's declaration that "[k]ein namhafter protestantischer Theologe vertritt heute noch die Zweinaturenlehre der Symbole" (*Das messianische Bewusstein Jesu: Ein Beitrag zur Leben-Jesu-Forschung* [Tübingen: Morh Siebeck, 1907], 100).

[11] See, e.g., Bernhard Weiss, *Biblical Theology of the New Testament*. 2 vols., trans. David Eaton and James E. Duguid (Edinburgh: T&T Clark, 1882–1883 [German 1873]), 1: 78–81, 2:283–286; Ezra P. Gould, *A Critical and Exegetical Commentary on the Gospel according to St. Mark*, ICC (Edinburgh: T&T Clark, 1896), 12; Julius Wellhausen, *Das Evangelium Marci* (Berlin: Georg Reimer,1903), 6–7; Heinrich Julius Holtzmann, *Lehrbuch der neutestamentlichen Theologie*, 2 vols. (Tübingen: Mohr Siebeck, 1911), 1: 336–337, 340, 352.

[12] This had long been the de facto position of critical scholarship by the time Wrede wrote his important essay "Jesus als Davidssohn," in 1904 (*Vorträge*, esp. 148, 168). See, e.g., Johannes Weiss, *Jesus' Proclamation of the Kingdom of God*, trans. Richard Hyde Hiers and David Larrimore Holland (Philadelphia: Fortress, 1971 [German 1892]), 83, 102–103; Wellhausen, *Das Evangelium Marci*, 104; Holtzmann, *Das messianische Bewusstein*, 27 n. 4. According to Weiss, Jesus exchanged one messianic idea for another: "Jesus turned away from the Davidic conception of the Messiah to a loftier image of the Messiah. For Jesus, the proper form in which the figure of the Messiah was to be thought of was the Son of man of Daniel and *Enoch*" (*Jesus' Proclamation*, 116). This line anticipates what one finds in Bousset, *inter alios* (see Section 1.1.2).

the viability of Jesus research had reached a crossroad: either one must follow Wrede's skepticism (*konsequenter Skeptizimus*) or one must embrace the profoundly un-Germanic eschatological world of early Judaism (*konsequente Eschatologie*) – "*Tertium non datur!*"[13] While the Schweitzer–Wrede split was primarily over the viability of the so-called quest for the historical Jesus, it had implications for Markan Christology as well. Whereas Schweitzer was persuaded that Mark's Jesus – with slight, albeit necessary, augmentation from Matthew's – fit within the broader messianic expectations of early Judaism, Wrede concluded that this construct belonged not to "the actual life of Jesus" (*das wirkliche Leben Jesu*), but to "the history of dogma" (*die Dogmengeschichte*).[14]

Wrede reaches a similar conclusion in his programmatic essay "Jesus als Davidssohn."[15] After acknowledging that Davidic descent appears to be at the bedrock of early Christian tradition (cf. Rom 1:3), he devotes the first half of his study to examining whether this or any other piece of evidence for Davidic descent can be traced back to Jesus.[16] As one might imagine, he is suspicious that it can, and so shifts course to his real interest, "die Geschichte der

---

[13] The full passage reads: "Es gibt entweder die eschatologische Lösung, die dann mit einem Schlag die unabgeschwächte, unzusammenhängende und widerspruchsvolle Markusdarstellung als solche zur Geschichte erhebt, oder die literarische, die jenes Dogmatisch-Fremdartige als Eintrag des Urevangelisten in die Überlieferung von Jesus betrachtet und damit zugleich die Messianität aus dem historischen Leben Jesu tilgt. *Tertium non datur.*" (Albert Schweitzer, *Geschichte der Leben-Jesu-Forschung*, [Tübingen: Mohr Siebeck 1913; repr. 2 vols., München: Siebenstern Taschenbuch 1966], 388; English translation: *The Quest of the Historical Jesus: A Critical Study of Its Progress from Reimarus to Wrede*, trans. W. Montgomery and F. C. Burkitt (Mineola, NY: Dover [German 1906]), 335. The first edition of Schweitzer's remarkable *oeuvre* was published under the title *Von Reimarus zu Wrede: Eine Geschichte der Leben-Jesu-Forschung* (Tübingen: Mohr Siebeck, 1906).

[14] The full statement reads: "Deshalb bleibt es wahr: als Gesamtdarstellung bietet das Evangelium keine historische Anschauung mehr vom wirklichen Leben Jesu. Nur blasse Reste einer solchen sind in eine übergeschichtliche Glaubensauffassung übergegangen. Das Markusevangelium gehört in diesem Sinne in die Dogmengeschichte" (*Das Messiasgeheimnis in den Evangelien: Zugleich ein Beitrag zum Verständnis des Markusevangeliums* [Göttingen: Vandenhoeck & Ruprecht,1901], 131; English translation: *The Messianic Secret*, trans. J. C. G. Greig; [Cambridge: James Clarke & Co., 1971]), 131.

[15] Wrede, *Vorträge*, 147–177.

[16] Ibid., 149–166. Although the first section comprises an impressive assessment of the evidence, its length is primarily the result of Wrede's sense that he needed to redress the objections leveled by Kawerau against the lecture he delivered on April 18, 2004 in Breslau at the opening of the Protestant-Theological Section of *Der Vaterländischen Gesellschaft für Schlesische Kultur*. As he confesses at the outset, "Handelte es sichlediglich um den historischen Wert der neutestamentlichen Tradition vom

Davidssohnschaft Jesu in der ältesten Christenheit."[17] Here, Wrede contends that the *Davidssohnfrage* provides demonstrable evidence that Jesus's Davidic descent was roundly rejected by some of the earliest Christians, most notably the author of the second-century Epistle of Barnabas (Barn. 12:10–11).

By emphasizing a disjunction between the "Jewish" idea of a mundane messiah and the "Christian" idea of divine sonship *sensu metaphysico*, Pseudo-Barnabas captured what Wrede perceived to be the "plain meaning" of Mark 12:35–37.[18] He concludes his study by tracing this disjunction back to Paul's concept of the preexistent son who travels "vom Himmel her zum Himmel hin," rendering Jesus's humanity, and therefore his status *as a descendant of David*, "nur noch den Schatten einer Würde."[19]

Wrede's approach to Davidic sonship in the Gospels sets a clear agenda for subsequent research. According to the Breslau professor, "Die Erklärung kann nur gesucht werden in der Art, wie Nachrichten verschiedener Herkunft in diesem Evangelium [i.e., Mark] zusammengeflossen sind."[20] That is to say, one attempts to identify an evangelist's position on this "Jewish" desideratum by isolating instances of genealogical material, titles, and scriptural proof texts containing the name David. In the case of Matthew's Gospel, Wrede felt that there was simply too much counterevidence to conclude that the evangelist adopted the "plain meaning" of the *Davidssohnfrage*.[21] Yet, in the case of Mark's, he concluded that the paucity of evidence in support of Davidic sonship opens up the possibility that the evangelist agreed with the premise of this tradition: according to one highly idiosyncratic interpretation of Psalm 110, the messiah cannot be David's son. The one piece of evidence that gave Wrede pause was a tradition in which Jesus is twice heralded "son of David"

Davididen Jesus, so hätte das Thema: Jesus als Davidssohn, *weing Reiz für mich*" (148, my emphasis).

[17] Ibid., 166–177.

[18] "Jesus ist Davids Sohn wird verworfen als die jüdische These, wobei aber daran zu bedenken ist, dass diese jüdische These auch von Christen akzeptiert wurde. Das tritt fast überall in der Polemik hervor. Barnabas spricht vom Irrtum der Sünder. Und auch Markus lässt Jesus sagen: Die Schriftgelehrten behaupten, dass der Christus Davids Sohn sei. Es ist also ein jüdischer Satz" (*Vorträge*, 176).

[19] Ibid., 177.   [20] Ibid., 176.

[21] Wrede claims, quite strikingly, "Ob Matthäus selbst geglaubt hat, die beiden Prädikate Davids Sohn und Gottes Sohn doch miteinander reimen zu können, was ich aus bestimmten Gründen annehmen möchte, ist einerlei" (*Vorträge*, 174). One would think the ease with which Matthew can "die beiden Prädikate ... miteinander reimen" would be directly relevant to the subject at hand.

(cf. Mark 10:47–48).[22] "Wie ist neben dem allen unsere Perikope innerhalb des Markus zu begreifen?" Wrede asks. His answer: "[D]ie Frage ist nicht leicht."[23] Full stop.

Although no one from this period was particularly interested in *Markan* Christology, the landmark studies of Reimarus and Wrede clearly set the terms of the debate. Reimarus opened up a Pandora's Box that continues to haunt New Testament studies to this day: Does the confession of Jesus as the messiah of early Judaism undermine the Christ of the church's creeds? Many have approached Reimarus's challenge that "son of God" means "messiah" rather than "second person of the Trinity" as if it demands participation in a zero-sum game. This may explain why many conservative scholars, who were in fact much closer to Reimarus and Schweitzer on the question of the historical Jesus, eagerly embraced the Wrede-an premise that son-of-God language *in Mark* no longer has anything to do with the anointed king of the Jewish scriptures.[24] Indeed, it was not until Donald Juel's dissertation (publ. 1977) that Markan scholarship was compelled, once again, to consider the possibility that divine sonship language is a subset of messiah language (see Section 2.4.4.1).[25] Reimarus also aided scholars of various ideological commitments to unite on another front: no one wanted Jesus to be the son of David if that entailed associating him with the militant, ethnocentric messianism of his time.

Wrede was not persuaded by the so-called "liberal" solution, however, and so he popularized the notion that the *Davidssohnfrage* represented the rejection of Jesus's Davidic ancestry not simply, or

<hr>

[22] Ibid., 176.   [23] Ibid.

[24] See, e.g., Adolf Schlatter, *Markus: Der Evangelist für die Griechen* (Stuttgart: Calwer 1935, 30), 230; A. E. J. Rawlinson, *St Mark: With Introduction, Commentary, and Additional Notes*, 4th edn. (London: Methuen, 1936), l–li; M.-J. Lagrange, *Évangile selon Saint Marc, with Corrections and Additions*, 6th edn. (Paris: Librairie Lecoffre, 1942), CXVII–CXLIX, 11; Vincent Taylor, *The Gospel According to St. Mark: The Greek Text with Introduction, Notes, and Indexes* (London: Macmillan, 1952), 120–121.

[25] Daniel Johansson observes a similar shift in research on Markan Christology c. 1970 ("The Identity of Jesus in the Gospel of Mark: Past and Present Proposals," *CBR* 9 [2010]: 364–393, at 371). His survey suggests that the dichotomy between "messiah" and "divine" Christologies persists in current scholarship (372–375). Consider, for example, Phillip Davis's diagnosis of the problem with (what he perceives to be) Jack Dean Kingsbury's unsatisfactory account of Markan Christology: "[U]nfortunately, Kingsbury himself is all too quick to resort to Old Testament and Jewish ideas when he turns to the task of interpretation" ("Mark's Christological Paradox," *JSNT* 35 [1989]: 3–18, at 17 n. 27).

even necessarily, at the level of the historical Jesus, but at the earliest stratum of the tradition.[26] "Wir haben nicht ganz wenig Zeugnisse [including and especially the Gospel of Mark], dass die Davids-sohnschaft Jesu in den ersten Jahrhunderten von gewissen Seiten bestritten worden ist." Not only did he convince subsequent generations to set out on a quest for the community responsible for producing this tradition; he also set the agenda for what would count as evidence that an early tradent accepted, rejected, or augmented its Christology. The vast majority of subsequent scholarship, whether consciously or unwittingly, has adopted the Wredean position that primitive traditions with the name David constitute the only evidence of relevance to Mark's *Davidssohnfrage*.

1.1.2 Sidelining David's Son: The *Religionsgeschichtliche Schule*

Building on Wrede's project the *religionsgeschichtliche Schule* sought to trace the development of christological concepts from their Palestinian origins into the wider Greco-Roman world.[27] The paragon of this approach is Wilhelm Bousset's *Kyrios Christos*.[28] According to Bousset, the messianic idea oscillated between two poles: while the majority of first-century Jews anticipated the arrival of a mundane messiah son of David, Jewish apocalyptic imagination had forged the notion of a transcendent messiah son of man.[29] Thus, he poses the question, "Did it [the Palestinian community] adopt the earthly political ideal of the Messiah as the Son of David or that strange transcendent ideal of the Messiah, or perhaps even in essence a blending of the two pictures of the Messiah?"[30]

---

[26] Wrede's disagreement with what he called "die liberale Hauptauffassung" was just that it could not be traced back to the historical Jesus but, rather, belonged to the primitive theologizing of some early community, which, for one reason or another, rejected the notion that Jesus was born of the Davidic line.
[27] Wrede was, of course, part of the original group of plucky young scholars who met in Göttingen in the 1880s and widely became known as *die religionsgeschichtliche Schule*. Yet, unlike his contemporary Wilhelm Bousset and subsequent generations of *religionsgeschichtliche Forscher*, he showed little interest in locating cultural parallels to early Christianity in Greco-Roman and mystery religions (see Robert Morgan, *The Nature of New Testament Theology: The Contributions of William Wrede and Adolf Schlatter*, SBT 25 [London: SCM, 1973], 10–11). It is only in this sense that my survey distinguishes his scholarship from that of the *Schule*.
[28] Wilhelm Bousset, *Kyrios Christos: A History of the Belief in Christ from the Beginnings of Christianity to Irenaeus*, trans. John E. Steely (Nashville: Abingdon, 1971 [German, 1921]).
[29] Ibid., 31–32.   [30] Ibid., 32.

Bousset answers his question by turning to the Synoptic Gospels. These documents indicate, as Wrede had demonstrated, that "the primitive community people were at best indifferent and even distrustful toward the ideal of the Son of David."[31] Rejection of the populist son-of-David strand of messianism left the Palestinian community with only one viable alternative:

> The first community of the disciples of Jesus viewed him as the Messiah, in that they, half-consciously rejecting the Son-of-David ideal, adapted to him the Jewish apocalyptic figure of the Son of Man. From this point all previously made observations draw their inner unity: the complete subsidence of the title of the Son of David, the polemic against the idea of Christ's being a son of David, the less frequent use of the name Christ, the dominance of the Son-of-Man title ... The messianic faith of the primitive community could be formed after the death of Jesus in no other form than that of the ideal of a transcendent Messiah. The hope that Jesus as an earthly man would take over the role on earth of the king from David's tribe was once and for all shattered.[32]

Bousset was less certain about how son-of-God language fit within this scheme. While the title is ostensively indebted to scriptural idioms about the Davidic king, he felt that it had "a much too mythical ring" to align with the Christology of the Palestinian community.[33] And so he posited that "an early influencing of primitive Christian messianology of Deutero-Isaiah," represented by the designation παῖς μου, "my servant," must lie beneath the divine designation of Jesus as υἱὸς μου, "my son."[34] This in turn implies that divine sonship language, as it stands in the Synoptic Gospels, has "nothing more to do with Jewish-primitive Christian messianology."[35]

Although he was not concerned with Markan Christology as such, Bousset's account of Jewish messianism provides an explanation for why Palestinian Christians may have retained an apocalyptic form of

---

[31] Ibid., 35, 81.   [32] Ibid., 49.
[33] Ibid., 93. He also concluded that the title "son of God" could not have been derived from biblical language, since "the Old Testament and the messianic faith of late Judaism did not know" it *as a title* (96). I address this objection in Chapter 2.
[34] Ibid., 96–97.   [35] Ibid., 97.

messianism, even if they were convinced that the hope for the son of David had been nailed to the cross of Christ.[36] Moreover, his proposal that a servant Christology lies behind the Synoptics' son-of-God Christology soon came to be accepted as the context in which one could still conceive of Jesus's baptism as a messianic event (cf. Mark 1:9–11 and pars.).[37] How this affected subsequent accounts of Markan Christology would vary, though one of its consequences was the prolonged assumption that Christian divine sonship language transposes Jewish messianism into the realm of "Greek" or "Gnostic" mythology.

Rudolf Bultmann found fewer vestiges of the Palestinian community's faith in the Synoptic Gospels than did Bousset. While he detected a trace of the "Hellenistic-Jewish" notion that Jesus became the messiah at his resurrection in the transfiguration account (cf. Mark 9:7 and pars.),[38] Bultmann concluded that messianism was largely superfluous to Mark's interests. The evangelist's principal objective, rather, was *"the union of the Hellenistic kerygma about Christ,* whose essential content consists of the Christ myth as we learn of it in Paul (esp. Phil 2:6ff.; Rom 3:24) with the *tradition of the*

---

[36] Bousset's bipolar iteration of the messianic idea articulates the dominant approach to Jewish messianism, at least through the mid-twentieth century; see also Sigmund Mowinckel, *He That Cometh: The Messiah Concept in the Old Testament and Later Judaism,* trans. G. W. Anderson (Nashville: Abingdon, 1955 [1951]; repr., Grand Rapids, MI: Eerdmans, 2005), 280–450. This approach was widely accepted by New Testament scholars (e.g., Rudolf Bultmann, *The History of the Synoptic Tradition,* trans. John Marsh [Oxford: Blackwell, 1963 {German 1921}], 137; Ferdinand Hahn, *Titles of Jesus in Christology: Their History in Early Christianity,* trans. Harold Knight and George Ogg [London: Lutterworth, 1969 {German 1963}], 147; Reginald Fuller, *The Foundations of New Testament Christology* [London: Lutterworth, 1965], 23–43) and continues to shape how some interpreters account for Markan Christology (e.g., William R. Telford, *The Theology of the Gospel of Mark* [Cambridge: Cambridge University Press, 1999], 35–36; M. Eugene Boring, *Mark: A Commentary,* NTL [Louisville: Westminster John Knox, 2006], 348).

[37] See esp. Joachim Jeremias, "παῖς θεοῦ," in volume 5 of *Theological Dictionary of the New Testament,* ed. Gerhard Kittel and Gerhard Friedrich, trans. Geoffrey W. Bromiley, 10 vols. (Grand Rapids, MI: Eerdmans), 654–717; see also Barnabas Lindars, *New Testament Apologetic* (London: SCM, 1961), 139–152; Oscar Cullmann, *The Christology of the New Testament,* trans. Shirley C. Guthrie and Charles A. M. Hall (Philadelphia: Westminster, 1963 [German 1957]), 66; Hahn, *Titles,* 336–341; Fuller, *Foundations,* 169; Fritzleo Lentzen-Deis, *Die Taufe Jesu nach den Synoptikern: Literarkritische und gattungsgeschichtliche Untersuchungen,* Frankfurter Theologische Studien 4 (Frankfurt: Knecht, 1970), 186.

[38] Rudolf Bultmann, *New Testament Theology,* 2 vols., trans. Kendrick Grobel (New York: Scribner's Sons [German 1951, 1955]; repr., Waco, TX: Baylor University Press, 2007), 50.

story of Jesus."[39] Mark weds his disparate christological traditions
together in the title (the) son of God, by which he intends
the Hellenistic concept of the "divine man," θεῖος ἀνήρ.[40] The
Davidssohnfrage represents an early protest piece against the tradition that Jesus was a descendant of David.[41] Whether or not this
tradition reflects *Mark's* position Bultmann does not say.

Benjamin Wiser Bacon, however, exemplifies how "the union of
the Hellenistic kerygma about Christ ... with the tradition of the
story of Jesus" might influence the evangelist's christological inclin-
ations. According to the prodigious Yale scholar, "This nationalistic
[i.e., Davidic] type of Messiah is explicitly repudiated by Paul;
considerately and tactfully in Rom. 1:3 f., more peremptorily in II
Cor. 5:16 as 'a Christ after the flesh.'"[42] He continues several pages
later, "[Mark] presupposes factors identical with some presupposed
by Paul, and in almost the same relation. Mark manifestly knows the
Son of David Christology, though his attitude toward it is even
more hostile than Paul's."[43] The *Davidssohnfrage* not only indicates
that the messiah need not sprout from David's seed; it unmasks
such yearnings as the wiles of the Devil (cf. Mark 8:33).[44] "Mark
has small respect for the little caliphate at Jerusalem," Bacon concludes, "He has perhaps even less respect for the Son of David
Christology."[45]

Bacon thus goes beyond the likes of Wrede, Bousset, and
Bultmann in situating Davidic sonship within Mark's christological
program. Whereas Wrede stops short of ascribing the "plain meaning" of the *Davidssohnfrage* to the evangelist, Bacon interprets
the language of Davidic filiation as an indication of blindness to
the ways of God (cf. Mark 10:46–52; 11:1–11).[46] In so doing, he
anticipates an interpretive trend that would reach its apex with

---

[39] Bultmann, *History*, 347–348, his emphasis. Martin Dibelius draws many of the
same conclusions, though he seems less interested than Bultmann in locating Hellenistic parallels (*From Tradition to Gospel*, trans. Betram Lee Woolf [London: James
Clark & Co., 1971 {German 1919}], 93–95, 230, 273–279).
[40] Bultmann, *New Testament Theology*, 130–131. Most interpreters now would
question the explanatory power of the θεῖος-ἀνήρ construct (see esp. Carl Holladay,
*Theios Anēr in Hellenistic Judaism: A Critique of the Use of This Category in New
Testament Christology*, SBLDS 40, [Missoula, MT: Scholars Press, 1977]), though
some continue to defend its utility (e.g., Heikki Räisänen, *The "Messianic Secret" in
Mark's Gospel*, trans. C. M. Tuckett [Edinburgh: T&T Clark, 1990], 64–65).
[41] Bultmann, *History*, 137; Bultmann, *New Testament Theology*, 49–50.
[42] Benjamin Wiser Bacon, *The Gospel of Mark: Its Composition and Date* (New
Haven, CT: Yale University Press, 1925), 222.
[43] Ibid., 225.   [44] Ibid.   [45] Ibid., 226.   [46] Ibid., 225.

the development of *redaktionsgeschichtlich* proposals for why the evangelist was compelled to confront a pernicious "Jewish" Christology.

1.1.3 "Get Behind Me Satan!" *Redaktionsgeschichte* and "Corrective" Christology

If previous generations had been largely content to treat Mark as a collection of stratified traditions, *Redaktionsgeschichte* marked a new phase in which scholars attempted to discern how the evangelist qua theologian arranged and manipulated his material.[47] Of particular interest to the redaction critics were the ways in which the evangelist handled the various christological titles at his disposal. Johannes Schreiber's 1961 article, "Die Christologie des Markusevangeliums," offers a parade example of this approach. Schreiber's thesis is that Mark's central christological title, (the) son of God, does not signify a θεῖος ἀνήρ, as Bultmann had thought, but the savior figure of the Gnostic redeemer myth (*der gnostische Erlösermythus*).[48] He concludes that the evangelist rejected the titles messiah and son of David and severely attenuated the apocalyptic title the son of man,[49] a proposal that lends support to the Bultmannian dogma that the author of the Second Gospel is a Hellenistic Christian of the Pauline sphere whose aim was to wrest the Christ away from the misguided messianology of the Jerusalem *Urgemeinde*.[50]

Werner Kelber, too, is convinced that son of God "emerges victorious" over the other christological titles.[51] In fact, he is more

---

[47] The dawn of *Redaktionsgeschichte* in Markan scholarship is typically associated with Willi Marxsen's iconic study, *Mark the Evangelist: Studies on the Redaction History of the Gospel*, translated James Boyce et al. (Nashville: Abingdon, 1969 [German 1956]); see, e.g., Seán P. Kealy, *Mark's Gospel: A History of Its Interpretation: From Its Beginning until 1979* (New York: Paulist, 1982), 160–165.

[48] Johannes Schreiber, "Die Christologie des Markusevangeliums," *ZTK* 58 (1961): 154–183, at 158.

[49] Ibid., 164–166.

[50] Ibid., 178. As far as I can tell, Schreiber has not changed his position on this issue; see *Die Markuspassion: Eine redaktionsgeschichtliche Untersuchung*, BZNW 68 [Berlin: de Gruyter, 1993], 238–240). Joseph Tyson, who also thought Mark was a Pauline theologian, argued that the disciples' obduracy functions to repudiate a son-of-David Christology ("The Blindness of the Disciples in Mark," *JBL* 80 [1961]: 261–268).

[51] Werner Kelber, *The Kingdom in Mark: A New Place and a New Time* (Philadelphia: Fortress, 1974), 80–81, following Philipp Vielhauer, *Aufsätze zum Neuen Testament* (München: Chr. Kaiser, 1965), 199–214.

decisive than his predecessors, aside from perhaps Bacon, in his approach to the *Davidssohnfrage*, proposing to read the narrative progression of Mark 10:46–12:37 as the evangelist's calculated deconstruction of Davidic messianism:

> Mark dissociates the acclamation from Jerusalem and places it into an anti-Jerusalem, anti-Davidic context. One can almost detect a progressive exposure of the inadequacy of the title as Jesus approaches the seat of Davidic hopes: the confession of Blind Bartimaeus at Jericho, the wrong acclamation at the outskirts, and Jesus' personal rejection in the temple.[52]

Mark's aim "is to break the myth of Davidic messianism and to dissociate the Kingdom from the temple,"[53] in order to reorient his community to Galilee. This gospel message was of great urgency, Kelber argues, since the Markan community had just witnessed the collapse of the "Peter-Christians," a group of "apocalyptically incited Jewish Christians," who, anticipating "the restoration of the 'Kingdom of our father David,'" joined their fellow Judeans in "the final battle against the armies of Satan [i.e., the Romans]."[54]

Theodore Weeden believes that Mark's message was equally exigent, but for quite another reason: the evangelist wrote for a community that had been bombarded by "heretical" missionaries claiming apostolic authority.[55] The first half of the Gospel (1:1–8:29), climaxing in Peter's messianic confession, articulates the christological commitments of this heretical enclave. This, in turn, provides a foil for the latter half of the Gospel (8:30–16:8), wherein Jesus takes up the evangelist's own *theologica crucis*. Norman Perrin basically agrees with Weeden's assessment but suggests that the evangelist "uses Christ and Son of God to establish rapport with his readers, and Son of Man to interpret and give content to those titles."[56] He also believes that the titles messiah and son of David are problematic for Mark, though he concedes, "I have no firm opinion

---

[52] Ibid., 96.   [53] Ibid., 105.   [54] Ibid., 137.

[55] Theodore J. Weeden, "The Heresy that Necessitated Mark's Gospel," *ZNW* 59 (1968): 145–158; repr., ed. William R. Telford, *The Interpretation of Mark*, 2nd edn. (Edinburgh: T&T Clark, 1995), 89–104.

[56] Norman Perrin, "The Christology of Mark: A Study in Methodology," *JR* 51 (1971): 173–187; repr., ed. William R. Telford, *The Interpretation of Mark*, 2nd edn. (Edinburgh: T&T Clark, 1995), 125–140, at 137.

with regard to the function of the Son of David pericope in the Gospel of Mark."[57]

Paul Achtemeier agrees with Perrin that son of man is Mark's preferred christological title,[58] and with Schreiber and Kelber that the evangelist staunchly repudiates Davidic ancestry.[59] He avers that the *Davidssohnfrage* represents the only unequivocal statement on Davidic sonship in the Gospel. (In every other instance where David is mentioned [cf. 2:23–27; 10:46–52; 11:1–11], Mark intentionally bypasses opportunities to clarify that Jesus is a descendant of David).[60] "The point then," Achtemeier concludes, "appears to be the growing denial of Jesus as son of David, rather than a growing affirmation of that fact."[61]

While there is nothing inherent to *Redaktionsgeschichte* that necessitates locating conflicting Christologies in Mark,[62] the assumption that the evangelist writes to correct a misguided "Jewish" Christology predominates much of the secondary literature from the 1960s and 1970s. The line from Wrede through the form critics and *religionsgeschichtliche Schule* to the redaction critics is not difficult to trace: christological titles, evaluated in the ongoing development of early Christian dogma, function as receptacles of christological ideas drawn from different cultural spheres. As a good Pauline theologian of the Hellenistic sphere, Mark has no patience for a "Jewish" Christ according to the flesh and so only incorporates a son-of-David Christology, already prevalent in the Jewish-Christian sphere, in order to repudiate it. To those yearning for the advent of the son of David, the evangelist's answer is simple: "Get behind me Satan!"[63]

---

[57] Ibid., 131–132; see also Ernest Best, *Disciples and Discipleship: Studies in the Gospel according to Mark* (Edinburgh: T&T Clark, 1986), 34.

[58] Paul J. Achtemeier, "'He Taught Them Many Things': Reflections of Marcan Christology," *CBQ* 42 (1980): 465–481.

[59] Paul J. Achtemeier, "'And He Followed Him': Miracles and Discipleship in Mark 10:46–52," *Semeia* 11 (1978): 115–145.

[60] Ibid., 126–131.   [61] Ibid., 127.

[62] Some of the most influential commentaries during this period manage to be thoroughly *redaktionsgeschichtlich* without concluding that Mark's aim is to correct poor Christology; see, e.g., Eduard Schweizer, *The Good News According to Mark*, trans. Donald H. Madvig (Louisville: John Knox, 1970 [German 1967]); Rudolf Pesch, *Das Markusevangelium*, 2 vols., HThKNT 2 (Freiburg: Herder, 1976–1977).

[63] Each of the previously discussed reconstructions of Mark's *Sitz im Leben* involves an oppositional group (represented by the Twelve) whose ideology is funded by the "triumphalist" spirit of Davidic messianism. By and large, however, the notion that the disciples function as a cipher for such an oppositional community has been abandoned. This is due, in part, to the impact of Clifton Black's landmark critique of *Redaktionsgeschichte* in Markan scholarship (*The Disciples According to Mark: Markan*

1.1.4   The Character Witness of a Blind Man: Narrative Approaches to Markan Christology

The studies examined thus far have been primarily interested in Mark's Gospel as (1) a source for reconstructing the historical Jesus (e.g., Reimarus), (2) evidence for a particular strand of early Christology (e.g., Wrede), or (3) a window into the christological and social debates of the Markan community (e.g., redaction critics). In this section, I examine whether the turn toward narrative criticism has shifted the ways in which interpreters assess the question of Davidic sonship in Mark. One would anticipate that a method aimed at counteracting the *formsgeschichtlich* portrait of Mark as a "scissors-and-paste-man"[64] and the *redaktionsgeschichtlich* portrait of the evangelist as a "creative genius" might bring fresh perspective to the son-of-David debate. Before doing so, however, I need to clarify briefly what I mean by "narrative criticism."

Mark Allan Powell has recently suggested that narrative criticism, particularly in Markan scholarship, is best understood as a general "reading strategy" that interpreters deploy to various hermeneutical and ideological ends.[65] Among those who make use of narrative critical tools, he detects three distinct groups: (1) *author-oriented* narrative critics attempt to discern the evangelist's aims through careful attention to the narrative;[66] (2) *text-oriented* narrative critics are concerned primarily with the effect of the narrative on the implied audience, although they also make judgments about the perspective of the implied author;[67] and (3) *reader-oriented* narrative

---

Redaction in Current Debate, JSNTSup 27 [Sheffield: Sheffield Academic Press, 1989; repr., Grand Rapids, MI: Eerdmans, 2012]) and, in part, to a burgeoning consensus that the tools of narrative criticism (e.g., Robert Tannehill, "The Disciples in Mark: The Function of a Narrative Role," JR 57 [1977]: 386–405; Elizabeth Struthers Malbon, *In the Company of Jesus: Characters in Mark's Gospel* [Louisville: Westminster John Knox, 2000], 41–69) as well as the insights drawn from studies on orality (e.g., Joanna Dewey, *The Oral Ethos of the Early Church: Speaking, Writing, and the Gospel of Mark*, Biblical Performance Criticism Series 8 [Eugene, OR: Cascade, 2013], 111–114) are better suited to evaluate the multifaceted role of the Twelve.

[64] So Janice Capel Anderson and Stephen D. Moore, "Introduction: The Lives of Mark," in *Mark & Method: New Approaches in Biblical Studies*, eds. Janice Capel Anderson and Stephen D. Moore, 2nd edn. (Minneapolis, MN: Fortress, 2008), 1–27, at 7.

[65] Mark Allan Powell, "Narrative Criticism: The Emergence of a Prominent Reading Strategy," in *Mark as Story: Retrospect and Prospect*, eds. Kelly R. Iverson and Christopher W. Skinner, RBS 65 (Atlanta, GA: Society of Biblical Literature, 2011), 19–43.

[66] Ibid., 26–32.   [67] Ibid., 33–36.

critics endeavor "to read texts from the perspective of any posited reader,"[68] an umbrella category that covers not only a broad range of reading strategies but also those who wish to explore Mark's narrative "in performance." My review will focus on three scholars who represent well the diverse interests of Markan narrative critics: Eugene M. Boring (author-oriented), Elizabeth Struthers Malbon (text-oriented), and Richard Horsley (reader/audience-oriented).[69]

1.1.4.1 Author-Oriented Narrative Criticism: Boring's Narrative Christology

In his 2006 commentary, M. Eugene Boring treats Mark's Gospel as a seamless narrative written to communities of Christians in Syria or Galilee during the turbulent years of the Jewish War (c. 66–72 CE).[70]

---

[68] Ibid., 39.

[69] The notion that Mark's Gospel rejects Davidic sonship tout court remains one of the dominant interpretations of the *Davidssohnfrage*, irrespective of the interpreter's methodological commitments. A representative list of scholars who arrive at this conclusion is as follows: Dieter Lührmann, *Das Markusevangelium*, HNT 3 (Tübingen: Mohr Siebeck, 1987), 208–209; George Macrae, "Messiah and Gospel," in *Judaisms and Their Messiahs at the Turn of the Christian Era*, eds. Jacob Neusner et al. (Cambridge: Cambridge University Press, 1987), 169–185, at 174; Ched Myers, *Binding the Strong Man: A Political Reading of Mark's Story of Jesus* (New York: Orbis, 1988), 290–322; Herman Waetjen, *A Reordering of Power: A Socio-Political Reading of Mark's Gospel* (Minneapolis, MN: Fortress, 1989), 194–195; R. G. Hamerton-Kelly, "Sacred Violence and the Messiah: The Markan Passion Narrative as a Redefinition of Messianology," in *The Messiah: Developments in Earliest Judaism and Christianity*, ed. James H. Charlesworth (Minneapolis, MN: Fortress, 1992), 461–493, at 477; Cilliers Breytenbach, "Das Markusevangelium, Psalm 110,1 und 118,22f.: Folgetext und Prätext," in *The Scriptures in the Gospels*, ed. C. M. Tuckett, BETL 131 (Leuven: Leuven University Press, 1997), 197–222, at 205–208; Martin Karrer, *Jesus Christus im Neuen Testament*, GNT 11 (Göttingen: Vandenhoeck & Ruprecht, 1998), 58, 188–190, 195–196; Telford, *Theology*, 35–41, 113, 154–155; Richard A. Horsley, *Hearing the Whole Story: The Politics of Plot in Mark's Gospel* (Louisville: Westminster John Knox, 2001); Francis J. Moloney, *The Gospel of Mark: A Commentary* (Peabody, MA: Hendrickson, 2002), 209, 244; Boring, *Mark*, 19, 256, 304–307, 313–316, 347–349; Elizabeth Struthers Malbon, *Mark's Jesus: Characterization As Narrative Christology* Waco, TX: Baylor University Press, 2009; eadem, "The Jesus of Mark and the 'Son of David,'" in *Between Author & Audience in Mark: Narration, Characterization, and Interpretation*, ed. Elizabeth Struthers Malbon, New Testament Monographs 23 (Sheffield: Sheffield Phoenix Press, 2009), 162–185; C. Clifton Black, *Mark*, ANTC (Nashville: Abingdon Press, 2011), 260–261; Michael Peppard, *The Son of God in the Roman World: Divine Sonship in Its Social and Political Context* (Oxford: Oxford University Press, 2011), 125–126; David Rhoads, Joanna Dewey, and Donald Michie, *Mark as Story: An Introduction to the Narrative of a Gospel*, 3rd edn. (Minneapolis, MN: Fortress, 2012), 110, 149.

[70] Boring, *Mark*, 14–20.

"Christology," Boring contends, "is the generative and driving force of the Markan narrative,"[71] which he describes as follows,

> Mark uses a broad spectrum of titles, designations, and imagery to communicate the significance of Jesus. All are derived from tradition and influenced by their previous biblical, religious, and cultural contexts; none are created by Mark himself. Titles are important, but their meaning can be explicated only in terms of the Markan narrative. Mark's Christology functions as narrative Christology, and cannot be grasped by cataloging and explicating the traditional meaning(s) of various titles, as though each title were a univocal theological package. Thus each title and image must be examined with regard both to its traditional connotations and function in the Markan narrative.[72]

One detects here a much-needed correction of the idealism endemic to the titular Christologies of the *Schule* and redaction critics. Mark's christological titles, Boring rightly maintains, are not conduits of ideas produced by different cultural spheres of Christianity; they have a particular meaning within a particular context – Mark's narrative.

Yet when it comes to assessing the *Davidssohnfrage*, Boring seems to revert back to the well-trodden assumptions of his predecessors. First, reminiscent of Kelber, he argues that "[t]he events of 66–70 . . . *had made it impossible* to believe in *Jesus* as Messiah in traditional Davidic terms."[73] Second, channeling Bousset, he contends that what is at stake in the *Davidssohnfrage* "is the general image and mission associated with messianic faith: Son of David empowered by God to bring the kingdom 'from below,' or suffering Son of Man

---

[71] Ibid., 248.

[72] Ibid., 248–249; see also Robert C. Tannehill's seminal essay, "The Gospel of Mark as Narrative Christology," *Semeia* 16 (1980): 57–96.

[73] Ibid., 348, my emphasis. Boring's reconstructed *Sitz im Leben* is largely indebted to Joel Marcus ("The Jewish War and the *Sitz im Leben* of Mark," *JBL* 111 [1992]: 441–462). Yet Marcus nowhere suggests that the events of the war made it impossible to affirm Jesus as the son of David. On the contrary, he concludes that Mark's Christ is David's son, even if this designation does not express everything the evangelist wants to say about Jesus (*The Way of the Lord: Christological Exegesis of the Old Testament in the Gospel of Mark* [Louisville: Westminster John Knox, 1992], 130–152; "Jewish War," 457; *Mark 8–16: A New Translation with Notes and Commentary*, AB 27 [New Haven, CT: Yale University Press, 2009], 846–851).

who will return from heaven to establish God's kingdom 'from above.'"[74] Third, he recapitulates the Wredean line that there is minimal evidence in Mark to offset the "plain meaning" of the *Davidssohnfrage*.[75] On the few occasions when the Gospel does broach the topic of Davidic sonship, the evangelist provides evidence that the audience is supposed to reject this idea. Bartimaeus's cry, "son of David have mercy on me" (10:47–48), cannot be trusted, for instance, because it comes from a blind man who is seated beside the way, the place where the sown word falls prey to the clutches of Satan (cf. 4:4, 15).[76] Just as Jesus demands Peter repent of his devilish desire for the Davidic messiah (cf. 8:31–33), so he liberates blind Bartimaeus to see a world beyond his son-of-David myopia.

1.1.4.2 Text-Oriented Narrative Criticism: Malbon's Christology as Characterization

No scholar has done more to bring the fruit of narrative criticism to bear on interpretation of Mark's Gospel than Elizabeth Struthers Malbon.[77] Her 2009 monograph, *Mark's Jesus: Characterization as Narrative Christology*, assesses the *Davidssohnfrage* within an impressive account of Mark's multilayered narrative Christology, including: (1) "what Jesus does" (*enacted Christology*), (2) "what other characters say to and about Jesus" (*projected Christology*), (3) "what Jesus says in response to other characters" (*deflected Christology*), (4) "what Jesus says instead of what other characters and the narrator say" (*refracted Christology*), and (5) "what other characters do that mirrors what Jesus says and does" (*reflected Christology*).[78] Malbon's proposal is that the interpreter should reason inductively from these different categories to the perspective of the implied author.[79]

---

[74] Ibid., 348, cf. 349.   [75] Ibid., 256.   [76] Ibid., 305.

[77] For an overview of her approach, see Elizabeth Struthers Malbon, "Narrative Criticism: How Does the Story Mean?" in *Mark & Method: New Approaches in Biblical Studies*, eds. Janice Capel Anderson and Stephen D. Moore, 2nd edn. (Minneapolis, MN: Fortress, 2008), 29–57. Following Seymour Chatman (*Story and Discourse: Narrative Structure in Fiction and Film* [Ithaca, NY: Cornell University Press], 148), she approaches Mark by bracketing off the "real" author/audience to focus on the communicative pairs "internal" to the narrative: (1) the implied author/ audience, and (2) the narrator/narratee ("Narrative Criticism," 32–33).

[78] Reproduced from Malbon, *Mark's Jesus*, 18.

[79] For the wider implications of this approach, see ibid., 256–257.

The primary observation Malbon's approach adds to the debate on the *Davidssohnfrage* is that the three characters whose perspectives come closest to the position of the implied author (i.e., the narrator, the Markan Jesus, and the heavenly voice [God]) never affirm the title son of David.[80] She also detects the following pattern in the sequence of pericopae covering the controversy cycle in the temple: "(1) a positive evaluation of what one scribe says and does [12:28–34], (2) a negative evaluation of what scribes generally say [12:35–37], (3) a negative evaluation of what scribes generally do [12:38–40], (4) a positive evaluation of what one poor widow, of the type victimized by the scribes, does [12:41–44]."[81] Beyond these observations, Malbon's assessment of the *Davidssohnfrage* adheres closely to the Wredean script. She insists there is a "plain meaning" of Mark 12:35–37 and develops her case for an anti-Davidic interpretation by isolating pericopae with the name David.[82] Everything, therefore, hangs on her interpretation of Mark 10:46–52. Whereas some mistakenly interpret the Markan Jesus's decision to heal Bartimaeus as his approval of the title son of David, Malbon insists that he ignores the title, and that the blind man subsequently shirks it once he receives his sight.[83]

The problem with David and his line, according to Malbon, has preciously little to do with "high" or "low" Christology, exalted or mundane messiahs, but with the Markan narrative's pervasive rejection of the concept of human kingship, what she refers to as "the kingship model."[84] Malbon muses, "Perhaps the Markan Gospel is as antikingship in its orientation as the antimonarchical strand of tradition in the David stories in the Hebrew Bible!"[85] While it is difficult to know exactly what she means by "the kingship model" (there are, in fact, multiple models of kingship in the Hebrew Bible),[86] her proposal undoubtedly appeals to a *traditionsgeschichtlich* paradigm. That is, she seems to suggest that the implied author rejects the concept of kingship because he is inspired by a strand of the scriptural traditions that Hebrew Bible scholars often classify as "antimonarchical." This should remind us that

---

[80] Ibid., 167.   [81] Ibid., 164.   [82] Ibid., 87–92, 99–101, 159–169.
[83] Malbon, "The Jesus of Mark," 182.   [84] Malbon, *Mark's Jesus*, 121.
[85] Ibid.
[86] See, e.g., Gary N. Knoppers, "David's Relation to Moses: The Contexts, Content and Conditions of the Davidic Promises," in *King and Messiah in Israel and the Ancient Near East: Proceedings of the Oxford Old Testament Seminar*, ed. John Day, LHBOTS 270 (Sheffield: Sheffield Academic Press, 1998), 72–90.

every interpretation of Mark – even one that prizes data "internal" to the narrative – involves significant decisions about the historical and cultural contexts informing the evangelist and his audience.[87]

1.1.4.3 Reader/Audience-Oriented Narrative Criticism: Horsley's Eclipse of Christology

In *Hearing the Whole Story: The Politics of Plot in Mark's Gospel*, Richard Horsley expounds Mark's Gospel as "the grounding history of origins of (one branch of) that Jesus movement as a renewal movement of the people of Israel and other subject peoples over against the Jerusalem rulers and Roman imperial rule."[88] Based on the evangelist's social location, Horsley surmises that the traditions informing Mark's portrait of Jesus must have been prophetic or messianic "scripts," rather than the "scriptures" of the scribal elite.[89] ("Scripts," according to Horsley, are oral traditions about charismatic prophets and revolutionary anointed kings, which must be distinguished sharply from the "imperial royal ideology" represented in the Psalms and the Prophets).[90] It follows, therefore, that Mark's community could not be interested in written texts such as Psalms 2 and 110 or in the scribal fantasy of a future son of David.[91] Rather, the options available to the community launched by Jesus's ministry were either to risk association with other violent revolutionary movements and their leaders or to remember Jesus of Nazareth as a prophet of covenant renewal. Not surprisingly, his followers opted for the latter.

Horsley represents a class of Anglophone scholars that has provided a fresh response to the "problem" of messianism. For these

---

[87] Malbon would seem to agree with this point, at least in principle (*Mark's Jesus*, 168 n. 62).

[88] Horsley, *Hearing*, 23.

[89] Ibid., 37. Mark appears to be sui generis among early Christian literature in that this document preserves a "people's history" rather than the ideology of the scribal elite. Elsewhere, however, Horsley suggests that the logia-source Q is similar to Mark in this regard (*Text and Tradition in Performance and Writing*, Biblical Performance Criticism 9 [Eugene, OR: Cascade, 2013], 143).

[90] Ibid., 236–253. This approach to messianism is developed in Richard A. Horsley and John S. Hanson, *Bandits, Prophets & Messiahs: Popular Movements in the Time of Jesus*, 2nd edn. (Harrisburg, PA: Trinity, 1999), 88–134.

[91] Ibid., 251; see also Richard A. Horsley, "'Messianic' Figures and Movements in First-Century Palestine," in *The Messiah: Developments in Earliest Judaism and Christianity*, ed. James H. Charlesworth (Minneapolis, MN: Fortress, 1992), 276–295, esp. 294–295.

interpreters, the issue at stake in divorcing Mark's Jesus from David's son is not only to avoid associating him with Jewish "particularism" and "militarism," but also to establish him as the antithesis of imperial ideology so that he might speak a word afresh to a world under the shadow of Western imperialism.[92] Stephen Moore is exactly right when he observes, "implicit in Horsley's reading of Mark is the notion that this gospel, properly understood, is consistently anti-imperial in thrust, and hence a solid basis for theological critique of hegemonic ideologies and institutions, whether those of ancient Rome or the contemporary United States."[93] This is indeed what appears to be at stake for Horsley, among others, in the *Davidssohnfrage*: by rejecting the premise that the messiah would be the son of David, Mark repudiates the repressive ideology of empire.

Yet one wonders whether anti-imperial critics of Mark's Gospel have been rigorous enough in their application of postcolonial theory. As Homi Bhabha notes, colonized groups tend to resist their colonizers through a process of "colonial mimicry," a far more subtle phenomenon than what we find in the anti-imperial readings of Mark currently on offer.[94] And as Stephen Moore and Tat-siong Benny Liew argue, each in his own way, the Markan Christ is manifestly a divinely appointed ruler over the cosmos – a totalizing claim, if there ever was one.[95] In fact, Moore and Liew agree that the quintessential icon of imperialism in Mark is not the son of David but the glorified son of man.[96] Their scholarship thus problematizes the assumption that one solves the "problem" of messianism by

[92] See also Myers, *Binding*; Waetjen, *Reordering*; Rhoads, Dewey and Michie, *Mark as Story*.

[93] Stephen D. Moore, *Empire and Apocalypse: Postcolonialism and the New Testament*, The Bible in the Modern World 12 (Sheffield: Sheffield Phoenix Press, 2006), 12.

[94] Bhabha describes colonial mimicry as "the desire for a reformed, recognizable Other, *as a subject of a difference that is almost the same, but not quite.* Which is to say, that the discourse of mimicry is constructed around an *ambivalence*; in order to be effective, mimicry must continually produce its slippage, its excess, its difference … mimicry emerges as the representation of a difference that is itself a process of disavowal. Mimicry is, thus the sign of a double articulation; a complex strategy of reform, regulation and discipline, which 'appropriates' the Other as it visualizes power" (*The Location of Culture* [London: Routledge, 1994], 122, his emphasis).

[95] See Tat-siong Benny Liew, *Politics of Parousia: Reading Mark Inter(con)textually*, BibInt 42 (Leiden: Brill, 1999); Tat-siong Benny Liew, "Tyranny, Boundary, and Might: Colonial Mimicry in Mark's Gospel." *JSNT* 73 (1999): 7–31; Moore, *Empire*, 24–44.

[96] Liew, "Tyranny," 22–23; Moore, *Empire*, 40–41.

shifting the image of an earthly messiah son of David to a heavenly messiah son of man – not to mention it thoroughly deconstructs the notion that a purge of all things Davidic suddenly transforms the Second Gospel into an anti-imperial manifesto.

1.1.5 Summary: Many Approaches, Three Common Claims

Despite the diversity of the group surveyed earlier, every scholar who argues that the Christ of Mark cannot be the son of David justifies this claim by appealing to one or more of the following arguments:

(1)   *The Davidssohnfrage is Mark's answer to the "problem" of Jewish messianism.* The problem to which the evangelist is responding is either the militaristic and particularistic nature of messianism or, in some recent iterations, the ideology of empire.

(2)   *The plain meaning of the Davidssohnfrage is that the Christ cannot be the son of David.* This argument is logically prior to the others. The moment one concedes the possibility that the *Davidssohnfrage* is not a straightforward rejection of Davidic sonship she loses a stable basis from which she may scrutinize the "ambiguous" evidence in the rest of the Gospel.

(3)   *There is no clear counterevidence in Mark to offset the plain meaning of the Davidssohnfrage.* This argument is integrally related to the previous one. Jesus's Davidic status is not in question, for example, in the Gospels of Matthew and Luke, since each evangelist is believed to have offered sufficient counterevidence to ward off a negative appraisal of the *Davidssohnfrage* (cf. Matt 22:41–46; Luke 20:41–44). How one determines what counts as counterevidence against the plain meaning of the *Davidssohnfrage* is, therefore, of immense importance. And, on this point, Wrede continues to set the agenda: the only data that count are genealogical material, scriptural proof texts, and titles containing the name David. This decision ineluctably fixes Mark 10:46–52 as the *crux interpretum* for adjudicating the evangelist's position on Davidic sonship. And as long as the testimonies of a blind man and an unwieldy parochial crowd are thrown out of the court as inadmissible, all one has to go on, so the argument runs, is Jesus's "plain" statement that the Christ cannot be the son of David.

1.2   Rescuing the Son of David: Or, How to Play by Wrede's Rules

Numerous studies attempt to redress some or all of the above claims, but the debate has been waged primarily on Wredean terms. For example, Ferdinand Hahn adopts Wrede's approach but rejects his conclusion. According to Hahn, Mark is contextually closer to Matthew and Luke than to the Epistle of Barnabas and thus belongs among those early Christian texts that reflect a *Zweistufenchristologie*, "two-stage Christology": the belief that Jesus is son of David according to the flesh, son of God and lord according to the resurrection (cf. Rom 1:3–4).[97] Joel Marcus shrewdly commences his treatment of the *Davidssohnfrage* by highlighting its historical peculiarity,

> The apparent denial in Mark 12:35–37 that the Messiah is the son of David, therefore, represents a puzzling piece of christology that is at home neither in first-century Judaism, nor in first-century Christianity, nor in the flow of Mark's story. Altering the wording of Mark 12:35b, then, it might be more correct to ask: How can our author say that the Messiah is *not* the Son of David?[98]

Robert Stein is more trenchant: "If Mark therefore was seeking to teach in this account that Jesus was denying his Davidic descent, he was singularly inept."[99] Hahn, Marcus, and Stein thus offer alternative accounts of the historical data to that of Wrede, which in turn function as counterevidence against the conclusion that Mark would be inclined to agree with the "plain reading" of the *Davidssohnfrage*.

Yet to avoid the charge that they are merely "dissolving the mystery of Mark's Christology,"[100] these scholars recognize that they must also provide evidence that Mark affirms Davidic sonship. That this aspect of the debate has also been thoroughly shaped by Wrede is lucidly illustrated by Christoph Burger's watershed monograph *Jesus als Davidssohn*.[101] Although Burger

---

[97] Hahn, *Titles*, 252.

[98] Marcus, *Way*, 140, his emphasis; see also Joseph Fitzmyer, *Essays on the Semitic Background of the New Testament* (London: Chapman, 1971), 123.

[99] Robert H. Stein, *Mark*, BECNT (Grand Rapids, MI: Baker Academic, 2008), 569.

[100] So Malbon, *Mark's Jesus*, 160.

[101] Christoph Burger, *Jesus als Davidssohn: Eine traditionsgeschichtliche Untersuchung*, FRLANT 98 (Göttingen: Vandenhoeck & Ruprecht, 1970).

eventually arrives at the conclusion that Mark reflects a
Zweistufenchristologie, his procedure is unquestionably that of
Wrede. "Die spärliche Überlieferung zum Davidssohn," Burger
observes, "ist nicht über das Evangelium verstreut, sondern auf
drei zusammenhängende Kapitel konzentriert, die eine geographische und wohl auch theologische Einheit bilden."[102] This
observation suggests that one can arrive at the evangelist's position on Davidic sonship by isolating the section in question, Mark
10:46–12:37. The effect is that the healing of Bartimaeus, treated
as an isolated pericope, becomes load bearing for Burger's interpretation of the *Davidssohnfrage*.[103]

The narrative turn in Markan studies has done little to alter the
interpretive status quo. For example, Jack Dean Kingsbury's
lengthy chapter, "The Christology of Mark: The Davidic
Messiah-King, The Son of God," offers no justification for why
Mark's Christ should be considered "Davidic" prior to the healing
of Barimaeus in 10:46–52.[104] His position that Jesus's decision to
heal Bartimaeus is equivalent to an approval of the title son of
David has failed to convince others (e.g., Malbon). The problem,
then, is clear: every scholar who claims that the Christ of Mark is
the son of David rests his case, almost exclusively, on the plea of a
blind man, "son of David, have mercy on me" (10:47–48). And for
every scholar who claims that Jesus's decision to heal Bartimaeus
indicates that Davidic sonship is being "calmly and unhesitatingly
accepted,"[105] another claims, with equal conviction, that Jesus's
decision to heal is a sign of his compassion for the blind man in
spite of his lack of insight.[106]

---

[102] Ibid., 59.

[103] Ibid., 58–63; see also Vernon K. Robbins, "The Healing of Blind Bartimaeus
(10:46–52) in the Marcan Theology," *JBL* 92 (1973): 224–243; Jack D. Kingsbury,
The Christology of Mark's Gospel (Philadelphia: Fortress, 1983), 102–114; David
M. Hay, *Glory at the Right Hand: Psalm 110 in Early Christianity*, SBLMS 18
(Nashville: Abingdon, 1973; repr., Atlanta, GA: Society of Biblical Literature,
1989), 114; Marcus, *Way*, 140–141; Stephen H. Smith, "The Function of the Son of
David Tradition in Mark's Gospel," *NTS* 42 (1996): 523–539, esp. 527–528; Hans-
Joachim Eckstein, "Markus 10,46–52 als Schlüsseltext des Markusevangeliums,"
ZNW 87 (1996): 33–50, esp. 38–45; Bas M. F. van Iersel, *Mark: A Reader-Response
Commentary*, trans. W. H. Bisscheroux, JSNTSup 164 (Sheffield: Sheffield Academic
Press, 1998), 341, 381–383; Stephen P. Ahearne-Kroll, *The Psalms of Lament in
Mark's Passion: Jesus' Davidic Suffering*, SNTSMS 142 (Cambridge: Cambridge
University Press, 2007), 138–144.

[104] Kingsbury, *Christology*, 47–155.   [105] So Hahn, *Titles*, 252.

[106] E.g., Malbon, *Mark's Jesus*.

Is there a way beyond the interpretive impasse? I suggest that there is and that it has already been anticipated in previous decades of Markan research. In particular, interpreters who attend to the ways in which the evangelist read his scriptures christologically conclude, overwhelmingly, in fact, that the Markan Jesus is indeed the son of David.[107] In so doing, they appear to have intuited, consciously or not, that Wrede was wrong about what should count in the son-of-David debate. Consider, for example, Richard Hays's recent critique of Horsley's *Hearing the Whole Story*: "Horsley badly underestimates the density and hermeneutical sophistication of scripture citation in Mark. Precisely for that reason, Horsley also advocates an interpretation of the Gospel that minimizes Mark's Christology; if the scriptural intertexts in Mark are ignored, a diminished Christology inevitably follows."[108] Hays is undoubtedly correct that an account of Markan Christology must attend to the presence of scriptural intertexts in the narrative. Yet I would argue that what he identifies as a particularity of Markan hermeneutics is, in actuality, an indication that the evangelist's language about his Christ plays by the rules of an ancient Mediterranean language game, what Matthew Novenson calls "the grammar of messianism."[109] If this is correct, then it is not enough simply to tweak our approach to Mark's *Davidssohnfrage*. Rather, we need to rethink the terms of the debate altogether.

---

[107] See Marcus *Way*; Joel Marcus, *Mark 8–16*; Rikki E. Watts, *Isaiah's New Exodus in Mark*, WUNT 2/88 (Tübingen: Mohr Siebeck, 1997; repr., Grand Rapids, MI: Baker Academic, 2000); Ibid., "The Lord's House and David's Lord: The Psalms and Mark's Perspective on Jesus and the Temple," *BibInt* 15 (2007): 307–322; Ibid., "Mark," in *Commentary on the New Testament Use of the Old Testament*, eds. G. K. Beale and D. A. Carson (Grand Rapids, MI: Baker Academic, 2007), 111–249; Craig A. Evans, *Mark 8:27–16:20*, WBC 34B (Nashville: Thomas Nelson, 2001); Robert D. Rowe, *God's Kingdom and God's Son: The Background to Mark's Christology from Concepts of Kingship in the Psalms*, AGJU 50 (Leiden: Brill, 2002); Ahearne-Kroll, *Psalms of Lament*; Adela Yarbro Collins, *Mark: A Commentary*, Hermeneia (Minneapolis, MN: Fortress, 2007); Richard B. Hays, *Echoes of Scripture in Gospels* (Waco, TX: Baylor University Press, 2016).

[108] Hays, *Echoes of Scripture in the Gospels*, 98.

[109] Matthew V. Novenson, *The Grammar of Messianism: An Ancient Jewish Political Idiom and Its Users* (New York: Oxford University Press, 2017). Novenson is exactly right when he claims that "Jewish messianism – of which Christian messianism can be thought of as just an extraordinary well-documented example – always and everywhere involves the interplay of biblical tradition and empirical circumstance" (196). This is an important caveat to Hays's project, which tends to treat the evangelists' portraits of Christ in a vacuum.

1.3 Rethinking the Terms of the Son-of-David Debate: Method and Presuppositions

Although he does not acknowledge it, Wrede's decision about what should count in adjudicating Mark's position on the *Davidssohnfrage* rests on an implicit but far-reaching assumption about the evangelist's linguistic community. Namely, he must assume that competent language users in this linguistic community agree that the only way to communicate that messiahs are Davidic is to use the name David (or the patronym son of David). Assumptions about how language works require constant scrutiny from semiotic and communicative theory; for our purposes, I suggest Umberto Eco's conceptual model of the *encyclopedia* could prove immensely helpful.[110] For Eco, it is essential to recognize that linguistic competence is not limited to "semantic competence" – that is, an awareness of the interrelations and distinctions of the discrete sememes one encounters in a dictionary – but entails facility in the social conventions, presuppositions, shared history, and so forth that comprise the system of conceptual knowledge undergirding linguistic meaning, the encyclopedia.[111]

The explanatory power of Eco's model is that it is able to account for every linguistic utterance as the act of a competent language user selecting words and phrases that evoke certain *frames* or *scripts*

---

[110] Perhaps no one has done more to bring the Peircean semiotic tradition – as mediate through Eco – to bear on New Testament interpretation than Stefan Alkier; see esp. "Intertextualität – Annäherungen an ein texttheoretisches Paradigma," in *Heiligkeit und Herrschaft: Intertextuelle Studien zu Heiligkeitsvorstellungen und zu Psalm 110*, ed. D. Sänger, Biblisch-Theologische Studien 55 (Neukirchen-Vluyn: Neukirchener, 2003), 1–26, as well as his essays in Richard B. Hays, Stefan Alkier, and Leroy A. Huizenga, eds., *Reading the Bible Intertextually* (Waco, TX: Baylor University Press, 2015).

[111] Cf. Alkier, *Neues Testament*, UTB 3404 (Tübingen: Fracke), 146: "Eine Enzyklopädie besteht nicht nur sprachlichem Wissen, sonder auch aus dem Wissen um Höflichkeitsformen, Verhaltensnormen, politischem, religiösem, technischem, geographischem, pratischem Wissen, etc." Eco develops his model of the *encyclopedia* in *A Theory of Semiotics* (Bloomington, IN: Indiana University Press, 1976), 98–114. Although, in theory, the encyclopedia may be likened to "a Global Semantic System" (or "Library of Libraries"), in practice, it depends on the observation that "it is always possible to isolate a cultural framework in which some contextual and circumstantial selections are coded" (112). That is to say, the processes of decoding does not require one to survey every possible usage of a word or phrase, "but only those which are *culturally* and *conventionally* recognized as the more statistically probable" (110, his emphasis; see also Umberto Eco, *Kant and the Platypus: Essays on Language and Cognition*, trans. Alastair McEwen [London: Vintage, 1999], 226–232). Eco applies his model to written texts in *The Role of the Reader: Explorations in the Semiotics of Texts* (Bloomington, IN: Indiana University Press, 1979); see my discussion in Section 1.3.3.

latent in the encyclopedia. So, for example, Eco asks us to consider an instance in which a wife informs her husband, "Honey, there is a man on the lawn near the fence!"[112] Before the husband can respond appropriately, he must first "make some conjecture or abduction about the ad hoc dictionary that both speakers, in that situation, take for granted."[113] Only then can he "reasonably [conjecture] that, by uttering man, his wife was magnifying or *blowing up* certain semantic properties and *narcotizing* some others."[114] If the husband is a competent language user, he will recognize that his wife is "blowing up" the suspicious and potentially nefarious entailments of the lexeme "man," while "narcotizing" those that might suggest the spotting of a "man" in one's yard is an innocuous event. The entire conversation, in other words, presupposes an encyclopedia in which the word "man" has the potential "[to elicit] the retrieval of a given frame such as 'burglars in the night.'"[115]

Like the example of the woman and her husband, Mark the evangelist tells his story about a figure called Χριστός, "Christ," with reference to a particular encyclopedia. As the semantic potential of "man" in Eco's example depends on its capacity to activate frames latent in the couple's encyclopedia, so the semantic potential of "Christ/messiah" depends on the range of its attendant frames in the evangelist's encyclopedia. My present aim, then, is to develop a plausible encyclopedic framework for interpreting Mark's language about his Christ.

1.3.1   Messiah Texts as Examples of Encyclopedic Competence

The surfeit of studies devoted to Jewish messianism over the past decades has problematized the notion of a coherent messianic idea within early Judaism.[116] James Charlesworth aptly sums up the *status quaestionis* when he states, "[t]he complexity of messianic ideas, the lack of a coherent messianology among the documents in the Pseudepigrapha and among the Dead Sea Scrolls, and the frequently contradictory messianic predictions prohibit anything

---

[112] Eco, *Semiotics and the Philosophy of Language* (London: Macmillan Press, 1984), 79.
[113] Ibid.   [114] Ibid.   [115] Ibid.
[116] For the most recent – and indeed devastating – critique of the messianic idea, see Novenson, *The Grammar of Messianism*; and my review thereof in *JSJ* 48 (2017): 591–594.

approximating coherency in early Jewish messianology."[117] Even
a more refined study of messianic ideas (pl.) in just four documents
(i.e., Pss. Sol. 17; 1 En. 37–71; 4 Ezra; 2 Bar.) leads Loren
Stuckenbruck to conclude, "beyond their immediate literary presen-
tations, these compositions resist any attempt to streamline or syn-
thesize their respective ideas, ideas that are integral to the particular
concerns of the authors and their communities."[118] In light of such
diversity, many would echo the sentiments of William Scott Green
that, "[i]n early Jewish literature, 'messiah' is all signifier with no
signified; the term is notable primarily for its indeterminacy."[119]

Against the trend of treating the word messiah as "all signifier with
no signified," Matthew Novenson proposes an alternative sociolinguistic approach. Novenson argues that the meaning of the lexeme
messiah is dependent neither on how many people were expecting
messiah(s) nor on our ability to find common threads running
throughout the various and diverse portraits of messiahs in antiquity
but, as with any other word, on what it signified for members of a

---

[117] James H. Charlesworth, "From Messianology to Christology: Problems and
Prospects," in *The Messiah: Developments in Earliest Judaism and Christianity*, ed.
James H. Charlesworth. (Minneapolis, MN: Fortress, 1992), 3–35, at 28–29. John
Collins detects "four messianic paradigms in Judaism around the turn of the era: king,
priest, prophet, and heavenly messiah or Son of Man." Yet "[t]hese paradigms were
not always distinct," and "permutations and combinations were possible" (*The
Scepter and the Star: Messianism in Light of the Dead Sea Scrolls*, 2nd edn. [Grand
Rapids, MI: Eerdmans 2010], 215). See also the collection of essays in Jacob Neusner,
William Scott Green, and Ernest S. Frerichs, eds., *Judaisms and Their Messiahs at the
Turn of the Christian Era* (Cambridge: Cambridge University Press); and Andrew
Chester, *Messiah and Exaltation: Jewish Messianic and Visionary Traditions and New
Testament Christology*, WUNT 207 (Tübingen: Mohr Siebeck, 2007), esp. 355.

[118] Loren T. Stuckenbruck, "Messianic Ideas in the Apocalyptic and Related
Literature of Early Judaism," in *The Messiah in the Old and New Testaments*, ed.
Stanley E. Porter (Grand Rapids, MI: Eerdmans, 2007), 90–113, here 112. Similarly,
there is no uniform portrait of the Davidic messiah across the literature of the Second
Temple period (so rightly Kenneth E. Pomykala, *The Davidic Dynasty Tradition in
Early Judaism: Its History and Significance for Messianism*, EJL 7 [Atlanta, GA:
Scholars Press, 1995]).

[119] William Scott Green, "Introduction: Messiah in Judaism: Rethinking the Question," in *Judaisms and Their Messiahs at the Turn of the Christian Era*, eds. Neusner
et al. (Cambridge: Cambridge University Press, 1987), 1–13, here 4. Given the state of
the question, it is not surprising that some have proposed replacement labels for
"messiah," such as "agent of God" (Howard Clark Kee, *Community of the New
Age: Studies in Mark's Gospel* [Philadelphia: Westminster, 1977; repr., Macon, GA:
Mercer University Press, 1983]; Howard Clark Kee, "Christology in Mark's Gospel,"
in *Judaisms and Their Messiahs at the Turn of the Christian Era*, eds. Jacob Neusner
et al. [Cambridge: Cambridge University Press, 1987], 187–208), or "positive eschatological protagonist" (Géza Xeravits, *King, Priest, Prophet: Positive Eschatological
Protagonists of the Qumran Library*, STDJ 67 [Leiden: Brill]).

specific linguistic community.[120] Novenson develops his approach through inductive analysis of Jewish and Christian *messiah texts* (i.e., texts containing the lexeme משיח/χριστός and its translation equivalents composed in the period c. 200 BCE to c. 100 CE).[121] He observes, first, that "when one finds the word 'messiah' in an early Jewish or Christian text, one very often finds it in a phrase whose structure itself has precedent in one of the 'messiah' passages in the Jewish scriptures."[122] Two examples of this phenomenon are (a) "the use of 'messiah' as a predicate noun following a copulative verb" (i.e., "X is the messiah"), borrowing from a pattern of speech common to 1–2 Samuel (משיח יהוה הוא; cf. 1 Sam 24:7, 11), and (b) the occurrence of "messiah" in a temporal clause with a verb of "coming" or "appearing," as attested in the book of Daniel, "From the time that the word went out to restore and rebuild Jerusalem *until [the coming of] an anointed ruler* [עד משיח נגיד], there shall be seven weeks" (Dan 9:25).[123] These messianic syntagmata are not allusions to particular scriptures, but "simply part of the linguistic inheritance that comes packaged with the lexeme [messiah]."[124] Second, Novenson finds that "most Jewish and Christian messiah texts also make explicit citation of or allusion to one or more scriptural source texts,"[125] in order "to clarify what the author intends by 'messiah.'"[126] Thus, as a general rule, one could say that the authors of messiah texts "take the word ['messiah'] itself from one set of scriptures and the imagery with which they interpret the word from a different set of scriptures."[127] Third, Novenson discerns that the list of scriptures accounting for the vast majority of citations and

---

[120] Novenson, *Christ among the Messiahs*, 41–47. Novenson works with Saussure's dyadic distinction between "signified" and "signifier," but his linguistic insights are equally valid for Peirce's triadic model of the "sign" (on which, see Charles Sanders Peirce, *Elements of Logic*, vol. 2 of *Collected Papers*, eds. Charles Hartshorne and Paul Weiss, 8 vols. [Cambridge, MA: Harvard University Press, 1932], 228). More recently, Novenson makes use of Wittgenstein's concept of the *Sprachspiel*, "language game" (*Grammar of Messianism*, 11–21).

[121] For Novenson, these include Dan; Pss. Sol.; 1 En. 37–71; 4 Ezra; 2 Bar.; CD; 1QS; 1QSa; 1QM; 1Q30; 4Q252; 4Q270; 4Q375; 4Q376; 4Q377; 4Q381; 4Q382; 4Q458; 4Q521; 11Q13; and the New Testament (*Christ among the Messiahs*, 6 n. 23). He also recognizes that messiahs can be signified by alternative titles such as "branch of David," or "prince of the congregation," as suggested, for example, by the overlapping of משיח, צמח דוד, and נשיא העדה in the Dead Sea Scrolls, on which, see Johannes Zimmermann, *Messianische Texte aus Qumran: Königliche, priesterliche und prophetische Messiasvorstellungen in den Schriftfunden von Qumran*, WUNT 2/104 (Tübingen: Mohr Siebeck, 1998), 46–127.

[122] Novenson, *Christ among the Messiahs*, 53.   [123] Ibid., 54–55.
[124] Ibid., 53.   [125] Ibid., 55.   [126] Ibid., 56.   [127] Ibid., 58.

allusions in messiah texts is remarkably small (i.e., Gen 49:10; Num 24:17; 2 Sam 7:12–13; Isa 11:1–2; Amos 9:11; Dan 7:13–14).[128] He thus concludes, "not only did authors of ancient messiah texts find their messiahs in the Jewish scriptures; they found them in the same particular scriptures."[129]

Treating messianism as a sociolinguistic phenomenon – i.e., messiah language – enables Novenson to appreciate the vast diversity of messiahs in antiquity as the result of competent language users employing the same scriptural resources toward different ideological ends while, at the same time, avoiding the fallacy that the word messiah is devoid of concrete meaning. Two significant corollaries follow from this account: first, every messiah text "should be taken into consideration as evidence of this interpretive practice";[130] and, second, "no one messiah text has a claim to represent 'the messianic idea' in its pristine form over against other messiah texts that do so less adequately ... since every particular messiah text is just one instance of the use of certain scriptural linguistic resources."[131]

My own approach builds on Novenson's in two ways. First, I take it for granted that there is no pristine construct of *the* Davidic messiah against which we can measure Mark's Christ. The common supposition that Mark is ambivalent about Davidic sonship because he does not present his Christ in the same manner as another author cannot hold if every depiction of a messiah is a "creatively biblical linguistic act."[132] Second, I examine messiah texts to determine how ancient authors communicated that their messiahs were "Davidic."[133] Although Novenson never engages Eco's work, his observations about messiah language in antiquity suggest that its users shared an encyclopedia to which any given example of messiah language might provide a point of access. In other words, messiah language is the idiolect of a speech community that not only had access to a common pool of linguistic resources (i.e., the Jewish scriptures), but also shared certain assumptions about the attendant

---

[128] Ibid., 57–58; see also the helpful tables compiled in Gerbern S. Oegema, *The Anointed and His People*, JSPSup 27 (Sheffield: Sheffield Academic Press, 1998), 294–299.

[129] Novenson, *Christ among the Messiahs*, 57.   [130] Ibid., 62.

[131] Ibid., 62–63; cf. Novenson, *Grammar of Messianism.*   [132] Ibid., 62.

[133] Since my research question is primarily concerned with a linguistic system rather than "background" material, it is justifiable to examine texts written over a broad period of time by both Jewish and Christian authors. On the grounds for this approach, see Novenson, *Christ among the Messiahs*, 8–10; Novenson, *Grammar of Messianism*, 21–26.

frames of those resources, a core feature of linguistic competence. My own assumption is that careful attention to how ancient authors employed the Jewish scriptures to characterize their messiahs provides the requisite sociolinguistic context for assessing the contours of Markan messiah language.

1.3.2   Implicit Use of the Jewish Scriptures in Ancient Literature

The argument of this book depends on our ability as modern readers to detect – and indeed to interpret – the use of the Jewish scriptures in ancient literature.[134] Whereas citations are *explicit* uses of the Jewish scriptures (i.e., they are marked by a citation formula or some other distinctive feature), allusions and echoes are *implicit*, and so their plausibility must be established by some predetermined criteria.[135] The criteria I use for establishing the plausibility of implicit scriptural use are those of Richard Hays; by now, these are well known: (1) *availability*, (2) *volume*, (3) *recurrence*, (4) *thematic coherence*, (5) *historical plausibility*, (6) *history of interpretation*, and (7) *satisfaction*.[136]

---

[134] The past decades have been a boon for the study of Mark's use of the Jewish scriptures; see esp. Kee, *Community*; Hans-Jörg Steichele, *Der leidende Sohn Gottes: Eine Untersuchung einiger alttestamentlicher Motive in der Christologie des Markusevangeliums*, Biblische Untersuchungen 14 (Regensburg: Pustet, 1980); Marcus, *Way*; Watts, *Isaiah's New Exodus*; Thomas R. Hatina, *In Search of a Context: The Function of Scripture in Mark's Narrative*, JSNTSup 232 (Sheffield: Sheffield Academic Press, 2002); Ahearne-Kroll, *Psalms of Lament*; Holly J. Carey, *Jesus' Cry from the Cross: Towards a First-Century Understanding of the Intertextual Relationship between Psalm 22 and the Narrative of Mark's Gospel*, LNTS 398 (London: T&T Clark, 2009); Kelli S. O'Brien, *The Use of Scripture in the Markan Passion Narrative*, LNTS 384 (London: T&T Clark, 2011); Hays, *Echoes of Scriptures in the Gospels*, 15–103. While these studies diverge at many points, they offer a compelling cumulative argument that the Jewish scriptures make up an essential part of the encyclopedia informing Mark's narrative world.

[135] I follow Hays's distinction between *allusion* (i.e., "obvious intertextual references") and *echo* (i.e., "subtler [intertextual references]") (*Echoes of Scripture in the Letters of Paul* [New Haven, CT: Yale University Press, 1989], 29). Whereas literary allusion implies a staged process – (1) recognition of a marker in the alluding text, (2) identification of the marker's source, (3) interpretation of the marker in light of the evoked text, and (4) the potential for fresh readings of the alluding text in light the wider context of the evoked text (so Ziva Ben-Porat, "The Poetics of Literary Allusion," *PTL* 1[1976], 105–128, at 110–116) – that requires recognizing an author's intent to evoke a specific text, echo suggests that there is less certainty about intent, and that the surface meaning of the text could be grasped with or without recognition of the proposed echo.

[136] Hays, *Echoes of Scripture in the Letters of Paul*, 29–32. Other lists of criteria for discerning implicit scriptural use are roughly equivalent; e.g., Dale C. Allison, *The New Moses: A Matthean Typology* (Edinburgh: T&T Clark, 1993), 19–23;

Like Hays, I use these criteria not as a set of rules to be applied mechanistically to ancient texts, but as the means by which I can discuss and advocate the plausibility of particular intertextual proposals.[137]

The study of implicit use of scripture will always involve disagreement about the plausibility of particular proposals, but the exercise is hardly arbitrary. Here it is worth quoting Hays in full:

> The identification of allusions and especially echoes is not a strictly scientific matter lending itself to conclusive proof, like testing for the presence or absence of a chemical in the bloodstream. The identification of allusions, rather, is an art practiced by skilled interpreters within a reading community that has agreed on the value of situating individual texts within a historical and literary continuum of other texts (i.e., a canon). The "yes" or "no" judgment about any particular alleged allusion is primarily an *aesthetic* judgment pronounced upon the fittingness of a proposed reading. This does *not* mean, I hasten to add, that such judgments are purely arbitrary ... there are norms and standards internal to the practice, and those who have studied the practice closely should be able to develop significantly convergent

William A. Tooman, *Gog of Magog: Reuse of Scripture and Compositional Technique in Ezekiel 38–39*, FAT 2/52 (Tübingen: Mohr Siebeck, 2011), 27–31, though Tooman's criterion of *inversion*, which he notes is rare in its own right, tends not to feature in the other lists. For a helpful discussion of the different "models of reading Jewish exegetical literature," see Bruce Norman Fisk, *Do You Not Remember? Scripture, Story and Exegesis in the Rewritten Bible of Pseudo-Philo*, JSPSup 37 (Sheffield: Sheffield Academic Press, 2001), 54–108. Michael Fishbane's grounding-breaking study remains essential reading as well (*Biblical Interpretation in Ancient Israel* [Oxford: Clarendon, 1988]).

[137] Paul Foster has recently argued that certain (mis-)appropriations of Hays's approach demonstrate its inability "[to reject] spurious cases of perceived echoes" ("Echoes without Resonance: Critiquing Certain Aspects of Recent Scholarly Trends in the Study of the Jewish Scriptures in the New Testament," *JSNT* 38 [2015]: 96–111, at 104). Foster writes, "perhaps for the perspective of the method, it would be argued that there are no spurious cases, simply more and less plausible readings." One wonders, though, whether this is an actual weakness of Hays's approach or simply the reality facing any interpreter who sets about the task of attempting to detect and interpret the implicit use of intertexts in ancient literature. To this end, it is telling that Foster never defines his criterion of "significant or extensive verbal parallels" (109). Perhaps this is because one cannot predetermine in advance which combinations of features will make any given locution "significant," but only arrives at such a judgment in the act of interpreting that locution in its particular context.

judgments. The ability to recognize – or to exclude – possible allusions is a skill, a reader competence, inculcated by reading communities.[138]

I submit every argument for implicit scriptural use in this study to the sensibility of the guild of "skilled interpreters" who have devoted themselves to the study of the transmission and interpretation of the Jewish scriptures.

1.3.3   Constructing Christ through Narrative

As Powell notes, the act of reading always involves "a strategy for understanding a particular type of literature in a particular way for a particular constituency."[139] My approach to Mark's Gospel broadly coheres with Powell's description of author-oriented narrative criticism in that I examine how the evangelist shapes the significance of "Christ" through a coherent narrative. In so doing, however, I am consciously interpreting the Second Gospel with reference to the "treasury of intertextuality" or encyclopedia governing ancient discourse about messiahs.[140] This move may be likened to what Eco

---

[138] Richard B. Hays, *The Conversion of the Imagination: Paul As Interpreter of Israel's Scriptures* (Grand Rapids, MI: Eerdmans, 2005), 30, his emphasis.

[139] Powell, "Narrative Criticism," 22.

[140] According to Eco, "[every] reader has been 'programmed' to borrow from the treasury of intertextuality" (*Role*, 21). My decision to limit the "treasury of intertextuality" to ancient Jewish literature is in response to the research question at hand and is not intended to disparage the value of situating Mark in a Greco-Roman encyclopedia (see Yarbro Collins, "Mark and His Readers: The Son of God among Greeks and Romans," *HTR* 93 [2000]: 85–100; Michael Peppard, *The Son of God in the Roman World: Divine Sonship in Its Social and Political Context* [Oxford: Oxford University Press, 2011]). It does, however, reflect my conviction that Mark's story belongs squarely within the broader theater of discourse of early Judaism, no matter who we think its target audience was (see, e.g., Menahem Kister, "Plucking on the Sabbath and Christian-Jewish Polemic," *Imm* 24–25 [1990]: 35–51; Daniel Boyarin, "The Talmud in Jesus: How Much Jewishness in Mark's Christ?" in *Envisioning Judaism: Studies in Honor of Peter Schäfer on the Occasion of His Seventieth Birthday*, eds. Ra'anan Boustan et al., 2 vols. [Tübingen: Mohr Siebeck, 2013], 2:941–964). Thus, questions of dating, provenance, and identity of the evangelist, though important in their own right, remain ancillary to my study. Broadly speaking, I find it unwise to be dogmatic about either the Gospel's provenance – whether it was written in Rome (e.g., Martin Hengel, *Studies in the Gospel of Mark*, trans. John Bowden [Minneapolis, MN: Fortress, 1985; repr., Eugene, OR: Wipf and Stock, 2003], 1–30; Brian J. Incigneri, *The Gospel to the Romans*, BibInt 65 [Leiden: Brill, 2003]) or Syria (e.g., Kee, *Community*; Marcus, "Jewish War") – or issues surrounding the identity of its author. For judicious treatments of the pertinent evidence, see C. Clifton Black, *Mark: Images of an Apostolic Interpreter* (Columbia: University of South Carolina

describes as "a kind of interpretive bet."[141] Based on the observations that I have made thus far – namely, (1) that the Jewish scriptures offer the pool linguistic resources for ancient messiah language, (2) that the evangelist tells his story about a particular messiah (cf. 1:1), and (3) that he indicates the Jewish scriptures are central to the significance of his story (cf. 1:2–3) – I am wagering that my reading strategy offers an "economic way" of answering the question, is the Christ of Mark the son of David?[142]

Since this study inquires about a particular referential character – i.e., is the Christ of Mark the son of David? – I make use of the analytic tools available for assessing how narratives construct characters. The literary critic Mieke Bal notes that, from the first, audiences unconsciously engage in a linear process of anticipating and adapting their perceptions of the characters being portrayed.[143] This process is facilitated by the fact that every auditor assesses characters in light of the conventional *frames of reference* she brings with her to the text.[144] So, for example, "[a] *she* cannot, in general, become

---

Press, 1994; repr., Minneapolis, MN: Fortress, 2001), 1–13; Yarbro Collins, *Mark*, 2–6.

[141] Eco, *Interpretation*, 63.

[142] The phrase "economic way" is borrowed from Eco (*Interpretation*, 68). He uses the language of economy as a short-hand for denoting that texts, although they can be read in an endless variety of ways, have their own ways of postulating the "kind of reading competence" necessary to read them in an appropriate fashion (cf. Eco's notion of the "Model Reader" [*Role*, 7–11]).

[143] Mieke Bal, *Narratology: Introduction to the Theory of Narrative*, 2nd edn. (Toronto: University of Toronto Press, 1997). Throughout this study, I use the term "audience/auditors" rather than "readers," since the vast majority of people in the first century would have encountered Mark through oral "performance" (e.g., Justin, 1 *Apol.* 67; Harry Y. Gamble *Books and Readers in the Early Church: A History of Early Christian Texts* [New Haven, CT: Yale University Press, 1995], 84). This should not be taken to suggest, however, that I dichotomize "orality" and "textuality," as some performance critics do (on this issue, see Larry Hurtado, "Oral Fixation and New Testament Studies? 'Orality', 'Performance' and reading Texts in Early Christianity," *NTS* 60 [2014]: 321–340). Rather, the evidence suggests a much more fluid and dialectic relationship between orality and textuality within ancient Jewish (Martin S. Jaffee, *Torah in the Mouth: Writing and Oral Tradition in Palestinian Judaism, 200 BCE–400 CE* [Oxford: Oxford University Press, 2001]) and Christian communities (Eric Eve, *Behind the Gospels: Understanding the Oral Tradition* [London: SPCK, 2013], 1–14).

[144] Bal, *Narratology*, 119–122; see also Meir Sternberg's classic essay on the ways in which readers of biblical literature engage in the process of "gap-filling" (*The Poetics of Biblical Narrative: Ideological Literature and the Drama of Reading* [Bloomington, IN: Indiana University Press, 1987], 186–229); see too Frances M. Young, *Biblical Exegesis and the Formation of Christian Culture* (Peabody, MA: Hendrickson, 2002), 11–12.

either a Catholic priest or a rapist"; or, "sooner or later a miner will be trapped in a shaft that has collapsed ... if he doesn't die of some kind of lung disease."[145] As with Bal's model, Eco's recognizes *frames* as the means by which texts draw on the reader's encyclopedia, guiding her to *blow up* (i.e., *actualize*)[146] certain semantic properties and to *narcotize* others. He likens the reader's encounter with a narrative and the characters therein to an extended "inferential walk," in which the reader continuously develops and adjusts hypotheses based on the ways in which the narrative activates and suppresses frames latent in the encyclopedia.[147]

This, I suggest, offers a model for assessing how Mark's narrative constructs Ἰησοῦς Χριστός. As with other messiah texts, Mark's is nothing less than a "creatively biblical linguistic act;" as with other ancient biographers, the evangelist crafts a narrative to highlight the significance of his subject.[148] And, in fact, these dovetail at the very outset of the Gospel: "the beginning of the gospel of Jesus *Christ* [comes about] *as it is written* in Isaiah the prophet" (1:1–3). The ensuing narrative progressively constructs Christ by selecting frames latent in the encyclopedia, actualizing certain semantic properties, while downplaying others. This model recognizes that narrative order matters for our assessment of the *Davidssohnfrage*, since the audience does not approach 12:35–37 (or, for that matter, 10:46–52) as *tabulae rasae*. It also opens up the possibility for the narrative both to actualize and to deconstruct certain assumptions we as modern

---

[145] Bal, *Narratology*, 123–124, her emphasis. Shared frames provide the opportunity for what Jerome Bruner describes as "breaches of the canonical," i.e., departures from the norm ("The Narrative Construction of Reality," *Critical Inquiry* 18 [1991]: 1–21, at 12). He makes the salient observation that these breaches "are often highly conventional and are strongly influenced by narrative traditions." Mark's most famous "breach of the canonical" is Jesus's insistence that the son of man "*must* undergo great suffering, and be rejected by the elders, the chief priests, and the scribes, and be killed, and after three days rise again" (8:31). In this instance, Mark's breach – i.e., that rejection, suffering, and death are a necessary part of the messiah's story – is mediated through an allusion to a scriptural text about a vindicated Davidic king (Ps 118). One of the points I explore later in this study is Mark's penchant for mediating messianic suffering through a "Davidic" (i.e., "traditional") lens.

[146] Throughout this study I use the term "actualize," one of Eco's preferred terms in *The Role of the Reader*, rather than "blow up," since the latter carries with it connotations that might confuse my readers. I am grateful to Paul Trebilco and the anonymous review at SNTS for alerting me to this issue.

[147] Eco, *Role*, 31–33.

[148] See Richard A. Burridge, *What Are the Gospels? A Comparison with Greco-Roman Biography*, 2nd edn. (Grand Rapids, MI: Eerdmans, 2004).

readers may have about what it means to be a Davidic messiah. In other words, Mark's narrative not only answers the question, is the Christ of Mark the son of David? it also answers the question, how?

1.4 Outline of the Book

The argument of the book will proceed as follows. I begin, in Chapter 2, by interrogating how users of ancient messiah language communicated that a particular messiah was "Davidic." Among other things, I show that Markan language about Jesus Christ adheres to the linguistic conventions his contemporaries used to characterize their messiahs – whether messiahs *like* David or *descendants* of the Davidic line. If, therefore, Mark's Gospel has the linguistic features one would anticipate of a "Davidic" messiah text, how does the evangelist develop their significance narratively? Chapters 3 through 6 set out to answer this question.

In Chapter 3, I argue that Mark introduces his subject Jesus of Nazareth as a messiah with discernible Davidic features. Beyond the broad consensus that the evangelist alludes to Ps 2:7 and Isa 42:1 at Jesus's baptism (1:11), I propose a number of ways in which the language and the themes of the prologue resonate with the opening of David's career in 1 Samuel 16–17. I then take aim, in Chapter 4, at the common caricature of the first half of Mark as being largely void of Davidic/messianic material prior to Peter's "confession." I mount a case that there are, in fact, a significant number of pericopae in this part of the narrative that suggest, to varying degrees, that the Galilean prophet is a messiah like David (cf. 1:21–28; 2:23–28; 3:20–35; 6:30–44).

In Chapter 5, I turn my attention to the section of the Gospel that has dominated the landscape of the son-of-David debate, 10:46–12:37. I argue that this section of the narrative not only affirms the audience's suspicion that this Jesus is a son of David, but also functions to recalibrate messiahship in terms of suffering and vindication. The cry of blind Bartimaeus, "son of David, have mercy on me" (10:47–48), while ambiguous when read in isolation, is lucid when read in light of everything that precedes (1:1–10:45) and immediately follows (11:1–11): according to the evangelist, this charismatic messiah from Nazareth is none other than the rightful heir to the Davidic throne. The trajectory of the ensuing "conflict cycle" (11:27–12:37) then appears to move from resurrection to enthronement, such that the *Davidssohnfrage* explodes the "scribal" notion of what messiahship ought to entail. At stake for the evangelist is neither the question of whether the Christ is the son of David (a point already established in the narrative) nor the "problem" of messianism (a point never addressed in the narrative), but the christological implications of Psalm 110 (109 LXX).

Chapter 6 then explores two aspects of Mark's passion narrative that have received recent attention. First, I respond to Malbon's proposal that the Markan narrative in general and crucifixion account in particular is "antimonarchical." Second, I treat the evangelist's use of Psalm 22 (21 LXX) in his crucifixion account as an example of an early hermeneutical practice in which Christ followers discerned the voice of David's son – Jesus Christ – in the Psalter.

I conclude the book, in Chapter 7, by drawing together the results of my study along with its implications for further research. What I am proposing is fundamental reorientation in how we approach Mark's son-of-David question, one that moves away from outdated, largely Christianizing assumptions about how ancient authors must talk about the Davidic messiah. Mark the evangelist operates just like every other ancient author who happened to be interested in messianism: he read (and reread) his scriptural traditions in light of the empirical circumstances surrounding his messiah, Jesus of Nazareth.

2

THE MAKINGS OF A MESSIAH

Sons of David, Messiahs Like David,
and the Markan Jesus

[N]ot all Jewish leaders are messiahs, not all messiahs
are royal, not all royal messiahs are Davidic, and not all
Davidic messiahs are sons of David
  – Matthew Novenson, *The Grammar of Messianism*, 111

In the preceding chapter, I demonstrated that Markan interpreters
have and continue to operate from an unchecked assumption that
the only materials that count in the son-of-David debate are pericopae containing the name David. As a result, we find ourselves at
an interpretive impasse: participants on both sides of the debate are
convinced that their accounts of Mark 10:46–47 are correct but are
unable to persuade those on the other side. Thus, the primary goal of
this chapter is to challenge the dominant assumption about how son-
of-David language worked in antiquity, to reshuffle the deck, as it
were, so that we might start the game afresh. Following Novenson's
lead, I take a sociolinguistic approach to messiah texts in order to
interrogate the ways in which the members of Mark's linguistic
community signaled that a messiah was "Davidic." In point of fact,
these texts divulge significant information about the linguistic conventions and attendant assumptions of their authors. This, in turn,
allows us to develop a heuristic sociolinguistic map on which we
might plot Markan messiah language. We begin, however, by revisiting a question that Gospels scholars have all too frequently neglected: how exactly do we know when a messiah is Davidic?

2.1   What Makes a Messiah Davidic? The Use of a Label
in Modern Scholarship

Scholars of ancient messianism continue to dispute the criteria by
which one may justifiably label a messiah "Davidic." John Collins,
for example, maintains that the messiah of Israel mentioned in the

Damascus Document and the Community Rule is Davidic, because
this figure appears to hold an eschatological office "comparable to
that of the King Messiah."[1] Kenneth Pomykala, by contrast, points
out that "a specific description of this figure is lacking," and that
"nowhere is davidic status attributed to or implied for the Messiah of
Israel; nor is the davidic tradition invoked."[2] To complicate matters
further, some authors who do invoke "the Davidic tradition," as
Pomykala puts it, appear indifferent with respect to the messiah's
ancestry (e.g., 1 En. 37–71; 2 Bar.).[3] Thus, Novenson is exactly right
when he states, "not all Jewish leaders are messiahs, not all messiahs
are royal, not all royal messiahs are Davidic, and not all Davidic
messiahs are sons of David."[4] In a number of instances, whether one
describes a messiah as "Davidic" is largely a matter of definition.

My approach is to use the label "Davidic" as a heuristic place-
holder for demarcating messiahs who have been characterized by
Davidic scriptural traditions. For our purposes, these are traditions
that ancient authors typically associated with David and his descendants, including: (1) dynastic traditions with the name David
(e.g., Jer 23:5; Ezek 34:23–24; Amos 9:11), (2) oracles concerning

[1] Collins, *Scepter*, 81. Collins posits continuity between texts describing the
messiahs of Aaron and Israel and others describing a descendant of David alongside
an eschatological priest/teacher (e.g., 4Q174). Certainly, it is possible that those who
discussed the messiah of Israel assumed that this figure would be a son of David in the
same way that the writer of the *Temple Scroll*'s "statutes of the king" (11QT[a] LVI–
LIX) may have assumed that the מלך would be a Davidide; see discussion in
Laurence H. Schiffman, "The King, His Guard, and the Royal Council in the Temple
Scroll," *PAAJR* 54 (1987): 237–257, at 256; Steven D. Fraade, "The Torah of the
Kind (Deut 17.14–20) in the Temple Scroll and Early Rabbinic Law," in *The Dead
Sea Scrolls as Background to Postbiblical Judaism and Early Christianity: Papers from
an International Conference at St. Andrews in 2001*, ed. James R. Davila, STDJ 46
(Leiden: Brill, 2003), 25–60, at 30.
[2] Pomykala, *Davidic Dynasty*, 238; see also Laurence H. Schiffman, "Messianic
Figures and Ideas in the Qumran Scrolls," in *The Messiah: Developments in Earliest
Judaism and Christianity*, ed. James H. Charlesworth (Minneapolis, MN: Fortress,
1992), 116–129, at 119–122.
[3] On the use of Davidic scriptural traditions in the Parables of Enoch, see George
W. E. Nickelsburg and James C. VanderKam, *1 Enoch 2: A Commentary on the Book
of 1 Enoch Chapters 37–82*, Hermeneia (Minneapolis, MN: Fortress, 2012). On the use
of Davidic scriptural traditions in 2 Baruch, see Stuckenbruck, "Messianic Ideas,"
111–112; and Matthias Henze, *Jewish Apocalypticism in Late First Century Israel:
Reading Second Baruch in Context*, TSAJ 142 (Tübingen: Mohr Siebeck, 2011), 303.
[4] Novenson, *Grammar of Messianism*, 111. I am grateful for the conversations I had
with Matthew both during and after the writing of my dissertation. He was particularly generous to share a prepublication version of his chapter "Messiahs Born and
Made" (*Grammar of Messianism*, 65–113), the contents of which, it will become clear,
I am largely in agreement.

the Judahite-Davidic line (e.g., Gen 49:9–11; Isa 11:1–10), (3) so-called psalms "of David" and other royal psalms (e.g., Pss 2, 89), and (4) traditions about David's life as recounted by the Deuteronomistic Historian and the Chronicler, respectively.[5] Pomykala is indeed correct that "writers in the early Jewish period ... would be free to use it [sc. the Davidic dynasty tradition] or ignore it, and if they used it, to employ and adapt it for whatever purposes the author chose,"[6] and, therefore, that the most important question one must ask is "*how* early Jewish writers employed and adapted the biblical traditions about davidic figures and the davidic dynasty."[7] By using the label "Davidic," I am acknowledging that a group of ancient authors made conscious decisions to characterize their messiahs with recognizable features of Davidic scriptural traditions, in order to examine *how* each respective author deployed these traditions.

Greater attention to how these authors used their traditions about Israel's ancient monarchs should greatly aid our assessment of Mark's *Davidssohnfrage*. In particular, such an exercise calls into question two assumptions that continue to pervade New Testament scholarship: first, that Mark has only a little son-of-David material and, second, that the only way the evangelist could characterize Jesus as Davidic is by using the name David. Let us take each of these in turn.

---

[5] My definition still leaves some ambiguity as to whether one should refer to the messiah of Israel as "Davidic." Perhaps more significant than labels, though, are the observations, first, that the use of this title draws on a strand of royal theology that sets the king on par with his "brother" Israelites (cf. Num 24:17; Deut 17:14–20) and, second, that it is precisely this strand to which the supporters of a non-Davidide such as bar Kokhba could appeal to legitimate his messianic claim (y. Taʿan. 4:8/27; so rightly Novenson, *Christ among the Messiahs*, 59 n. 107). There is also ambiguity with regard to 4Q246, 4Q251, and 11Q13. A strong case can be made that the epithet ברה די אל, "son of God," in 4Q246 is dependent on scriptural language about the Davidic king (see Section 2.4.4.1). In the cases of 4Q521 and 11Q13, however, there are too many points of uncertainty to label either of these messiahs "Davidic." Collins (*Scepter*, 131–141) may be correct that both are eschatological prophets along the lines of Elijah *redivivus*, although the matter is far from certain (see Lidija Novakovic, *Messiah, the Healer of the Sick: A Study of Jesus As the Son of David in the Gospel of Matthew*, WUNT 2/170 [Tübingen: Mohr Siebeck, 2003], 169–176). The messiah in 11Q13 is identified as the "anointed ruler," משיח־נגיד, of Dan 9:25, who could be interpreted as a royal figure (he was likely a priest), but it seems a stretch to label him "Davidic" (*pace* Paul Rainbow, "Melchizedek as a Messiah at Qumran," *BBR* 7 [1997]: 179–194).
[6] Pomykala, *Davidic Dynasty*, 68.   [7] Ibid., his emphasis.

2.2   Quantifying Davidic Ancestry: The Frequency of Ancestral Claims in Messiah Texts

Christoph Burger's loaded phrase, "[d]ie spärliche Überlieferung zum Davidssohn," articulates the broad consensus that, at best, Mark is hardly interested in the issue of the messiah's ancestry.[8] Yet scholars have rarely stopped to ask the question: how *spärlich* is Mark's son of David material really? The following chart (p. 43) lists the number of times ancient authors linked their messiahs to the Davidic line (excluding, for the moment, the Synoptic Gospels).

In addition, Davidic descent is never mentioned in the following messiah texts: the Community Rule (1QS), the War Scroll (1QM), the Damascus Document (CD), the Rule of the Congregation (1Q28), 4QApocryphon of Moses[b?] (4Q376), the Parables of Enoch (1 En. 37–70), 2 Baruch, James, 1–2 Peter, 1–2 John, and Jude.[9] These documents vary significantly in length (some are highly fragmentary), such that the numbers in my chart offer something more along the lines of a broad sketch than an exacting representation. Nonetheless, insofar as the amount of material devoted to a specific topic accurately correlates to the significance that topic holds for a given author, the list suggests that Mark is just as interested in the question of Davidic ancestry as any other ancient author.

In fact, Mark's engagement with Davidic ancestry only appears *spärlich* when one limits the comparison to the Synoptic Gospels. But such a move is untenable for at least two reasons. First, if one assumes Markan priority, then it is unclear why the Second Gospel should be compared exclusively to texts with which it could not possibly have interacted.[10] Second, it seems likely that Mark's son-of-David material served as a source of inspiration for his earliest interpreters, the evangelists Matthew and Luke (cf. Matt 9:27; 20:30–31; 21:1–11; 22:41–46; Luke 18:38–39; 20:41–44). As John

---

[8] Burger, *Jesus als Davidssohn*, 59.

[9] This list is based on the overlapping of the epithets משיח, צמח דוד, and נשיא העדה in the Scrolls, on which see Zimmermann, *Messianische Texte aus Qumran*, 46–127. One may wish to dispute the inclusion of some of these, e.g., 1QM; 4Q376.

[10] An assumption of Markan priority means we need to be more circumspect about how we assess the questions posed by F. C. Baur: "Warum beginnt Markus ohne eine Vorgeschichte, wie Matthäus und Lukas eine solche haben, warum datirt er den Anfang des Evangeliums so bestimmt von Täufer, warum erzählt er auch die Versuchungsgeschichte nur so summarisch?" (*Das Markusevangelium: Nach seinem Ursprung und Charakter, nebst einem Anhang über das Evangelium Marcion's* [Tübingen: Mohr Siebeck, 1851], 138).

Davidic Ancestry in Messiah Texts (Excluding the Synoptic Gospels)

Text	Number of References	Reference(s)
Psalms of Solomon 17	1	"See, Lord, and raise up for them their king, the son of David [υἱὸν Δαυίδ], to rule over your servant Israel in the time known to you, O God" (17:21)
Isaiah Pesher[a]	1	"[the shoot] of David [דויד] which will sprout in the fi[nal days ...]" (3:18)
Midrash on Eschatology[a]	2	"This (refers to the) branch of David [צמח דויד], who will arise with the Interpreter of the law" (I, 11) [...]. "This (refers to) the booth of David [סוכת דויד] which has fall[en, w]hich he will raise up to save Israel" (1:12–13)
Commentary on Genesis A	1	"Until the messiah of righteousness comes, the branch of David [צמח דויד]" (5:3–4)
Undisputed Letters of Paul	2	"regarding his son, who was descended from David according to the flesh [τοῦ γενομένου ἐκ σπέρματος Δαυίδ κατὰ σάρκα]" (Rom 1:3) "and again Isaiah says, 'there shall be the root of Jesse [ἡ ῥίζα τοῦ Ἰεσσαί], the one who rises to rule the gentiles" (Rom 15:12)
Disputed Letters of Paul	1	"Remember Jesus Christ, raised from the dead, descended from David [ἐκ σπέρματος Δαυίδ], in accordance with my gospel" (2 Tim 2:8)
Hebrews	1	"For it is clear that our Lord arose from Judah [ἐξ Ἰούδα ἀνατέταλκεν]" (7:14)
John	1	"Has not the scripture said that the messiah is descended from David [ἐκ τοῦ σπέρματος Δαυίδ] and comes from Bethlehem, the village where David lived?" (7:42)
Revelation	2	"See, the lion of the tribe of Judah [ὁ λέων ὁ ἐκ τῆς φυλῆς Ἰούδα], the root of David [ἡ ῥίζα Δαυίδ], has conquered" (5:5) "I am the root and descendant of David [ἡ ῥίζα καὶ τὸ γένος Δαυίδ], the bright morning star" (22:16).[a]

[a] The risen Christ refers to himself as "the holy one, the true one, who has the key of David [ὁ ἔχων τὴν κλεῖν τοῦ Δαυίδ]" (Rev 3:7). I discuss this text in Section 4.1.3.

P. Meier observes, "the only clear example of Son-of-David Christology in Matthew that is not derivable from Mark's Gospel or from Matthean redaction is in the infancy narrative."[11] And if infancy narratives and extensive genealogies are requisite features of interest in Davidic ancestry, then it would seem Matthew and Luke alone have the corner on the son-of-David market.

2.3   Qualifying Davidic Ancestry: The Function of Ancestral Claims in Messiah Texts

As shown in the previous chapter, scholars who treat Mark's son-of-David material in an isolated fashion tacitly assume that the only way for the evangelist to communicate that his Christ is Davidic is by using the name David. In practice, however, explicit claims for Davidic ancestry – whether through scriptural citations, allusions, or titles – are almost always accompanied by other distinct features of Davidic traditions.[12] The following chart (p. 45) lists every messiah text containing the lexeme דוד/Δαυίδ as part of a title (second column). Listed alongside these titles (third column) are citations of and allusions to additional Davidic scriptural traditions (n.b.: this list is intended to be illustrative rather than exhaustive).

The chart illustrates that titles such as the branch/son/root of David are hardly the sine qua non of messianic discourse. In fact,

---

[11] John P. Meier, "From Elijah-Like Prophet to Royal Davidic Messiah," in *Jesus: A Colloquium in the Holy Land*, ed. Doris Donnelly (New York: Continuum, 2001), 56. Since scholars tend to compare Mark's son-of-David material to Matthew's, it is worth noting that Matthew's portrait of the son of David is not without its own complications. While Matthew foregrounds Davidic ancestry in a way that Mark does not (cf. Matt 1:1–17), he immediately complicates the matter by suggesting that Jesus was begotten not by human parents but by the holy spirit (Matt 1:20–25; cf. Luke 1:26–38). As a result, Jesus appears to be of Davidic lineage only insofar as he has been "adopted" by Joseph into the Davidic line (see Yigal Levine, "Jesus, 'Son of God' and 'Son of David': The 'Adoption' of Jesus into the Davidic Line," *JSNT* 28 [2006]: 415–442).

[12] Explicit claims for Davidic descent tend to be drawn from the "promise tradition," on which see Dennis C. Duling, "The Promises to David and Their Entrance into Christianity – Nailing Down a Likely Hypothesis," *NTS* 20 (1975): 55–77. This is true not only for citations and allusions, but also for messianic titles: (1) צמח דויד, "branch of David" (4Q161; 4Q174; 4Q252; 4Q285), alluding to Jer 23:5–6 (cf. Jer 33:15); (2) υἱὸς Δαυίδ (בן דוד), "son of David" (Pss. Sol. 17:21; Mark 10:47 pars.), alluding to scriptural traditions in which YHWH promises to raise up a new David or David's seed (e.g., 2 Sam 7:12–14; Jer 30 [LXX 37]:9); and (3) ἡ ῥίζα Δαυίδ, "the root David" (Rev 5:5) and ἡ ῥίζα καὶ τὸ γένος Δαυίδ, "the root and the offspring of David" (Rev 22:16), conflating Isa 11:1/10 (ἡ ῥίζα τοῦ Ιεσσαι) and texts that speak of David's offspring or "seed."

Text	Titles with דוד/Δαυίδ	Additional Davidic Scriptural Traditions
Isaiah Pesher[a]	Branch of David	• prince of the congregation (cf. Ezek 34:24) • Isa 11:1–5
Midrash on Eschatology[a]	Branch of David	• 2 Sam 7:12–14 • Amos 9:11 • Ps 2:1–2
Genesis Commentary A	Branch of David	• Gen 49:10 • messiah of righteousness (cf. Jer 23:5)
Sefer Hamilḥamah	Branch of David	• prince of the congregation (cf. Ezek 34:24) • Isa 11:1
Psalms of Solomon 17	Son of David	• Isa 11:1–5 • Ps 2:9 • righteous king (cf. Ps 72; Jer 23:5; Zech 9:9)
Matthew	Son of David	• Davidic genealogy • Mic 5:2 • Zech 9:9
Luke-Acts	Son of David	• Davidic genealogy • 2 Sam 7:12–14 • Ps 2:2 • Amos 9:11
Revelation	Root of David	• the lion from the tribe of Judah (cf. Gen 49:9) • Isa 11:1–5 • Ps 2:1–2, 9

we could eliminate the material in column 2 and still be confident that scripturally competent language users would conclude that the messiahs portrayed in these texts are Davidic, at least in some sense. Some of these texts would, of course, still retain names and epithets such as David, Judah, and the shoot of Jesse, but that should not distract us from the more salient point: the way ancient authors indicate that their messiahs are Davidic is not through explicit claims for Davidic ancestry alone, but by characterizing their messiahs with a combination of distinct elements, including the use of titles, derived from scriptural sources their linguistic community recognized as presaging a Davidic figure.

This language game worked, to recapitulate Novenson's point, because members of this particular speech community found their messiahs in the same scriptures. Thus, for example, while some writers refer to Isa 11:1–10 by using the locution "the shoot (from the stump) of Jesse" (e.g., 4Q285; Rom 15:12), others could appeal to alternative, equally distinct elements of the oracle. An author might elect to portray his messiah receiving the spirit of YHWH, and thus being filled with YHWH's wisdom and strength (e.g., Pss. Sol. 17:37; 1 En. 49:3); or he might claim that his messiah will "strike the earth with the rod of his mouth" and/or "slay the wicked with the breath of his lips" (e.g., 1Q28b 5:24–25; Pss. Sol. 17:24; 2 Thess 2:8; 4 Ezra 13:10). The key is that this particular linguistic community's encyclopedia contains multiple conventions for suggesting someone is the figure described in Isaiah 11.

Of course, each writer has the freedom to employ these conventions in accordance with his own ideological aims. So, for example, while the vast majority of authors elected to actualize the ancestral pedigree of the figure described in Isaiah 11, some chose to minimize it, even to the point of suggesting that the figure depicted in this oracle is *not* a descendant of David (e.g., 1 En. 37–71; 4QTLevi[a] ar 1:14; T. Levi 18:5–7).[13] In these more extreme instances, however, there can be little doubt that the writers are challenging a common frame of Isaiah 11. Thus, it is hardly surprising to find that, in each instance, this move is nested within a wider strategy aimed at mediating all Davidic traditions through an alternative ancestral line.[14] That such a move is possible should alert us to the flexibility of Davidic scriptural traditions in the language game. But the rules of the game are not arbitrary. On the contrary, attendance to how these writers make particular moves suggests that the rhetoric of characterizing messiahs depends on a theoretic encyclopedia.

---

[13] As noted, e.g., in Pomykala, *Davidic Dynasty*, 242.

[14] E.g., the writer of Aramaic Levi explicates the name of Levi's second son, Kohath, with language drawn from Gen 49:10, an oracle about a future descendant of Judah (ALD 67; versification follows James R. Davila's translation, in volume 1 of *Old Testament Pseudepigrapha: More Noncanonical Scriptures*, eds. Richard Bauckam, James R. Davila, and Alexander Panayotov [Grand Rapids, MI: Eerdmans, 2013]). As Jonas C. Greenfield, Michael Stone, and Esther Eshel observe, "From the use of Gen 49:10 in Kohath's name midrash it emerges very clearly that *ALD* applied Israelite messianic language to the Priestly-Levitical messiah" (*The Aramaic Levi Document: Edition, Translation, Commentary*, SVTP 19 [Leiden: Brill, 2004], 187–188; see also Henryk Drawnel, *An Aramaic Wisdom Text from Qumran: A New Interpretation of the Levi Document*, JSJSup 86 [Leiden: Brill, 2004], 307–308). They go on to note, however, that "*ALD* takes an extreme and unusual position in this matter and tends to attribute to Levi language drawn from the royal context" (188).

Given that explicit claims of Davidic ancestry are nothing more than an optional aspect of messiah language, it seems imprudent to assume that "die spärliche Überlieferung zum Davidssohn" offers the only evidence of relevance to Mark's *Davidssohnfrage*. And yet, as we saw in the previous chapter, it is precisely this assumption that undergirds every negative appraisal of Mark's *Davidssohnfrage*. If, however, Mark behaves anything like the other messiah texts examined earlier, one would expect to find other elements of potential relevance to his *Davidssohnfrage*. One would expect, in particular, to find allusions to the same pool of linguistic resources to which other members of the evangelist's linguistic community turned when they wanted to characterize their messiahs as Davidic.

2.4 Messiah Language in Mark: Variations on a Theme

According to Rikki Watts, the Gospel of Mark contains approximately 70 citations of and allusion to the Jewish scriptures.[15] A cross-check of these intertexts suggests interest in a number of commonly used messianic source texts, including: Ps 2:7 (cf. Mark 1:11; cf. 9:7; 12:6),[16] Dan 7:13–14 (cf. Mark 2:10; 2:28; 8:28; 10:45; 13:26; 14:62),[17] and Gen 49:11 (cf. Mark 11:2–7).[18] While hardly exhaustive, this list offers a convenient point of departure for our assessment of Markan messiah language. I begin by addressing the claim, still persistent in some scholarship, that interest in Daniel's mysterious one like a son of man necessitates a move away from "Davidic" messianism. Next, I examine the potential significance of the evangelist's decision to characterize his Christ as the anointed son of God in Psalm 2. Finally, I widen the lens to sketch additional

---

[15] Watts, "Mark," 111. Lists of citations and allusions can vary significantly depending on the criteria being used; compare, e.g., Kee, *Community*, 45; Hatina, *In Search*, 1; O'Brien, *Use of Scripture*, 20–112.

[16] Watts, "Mark," 122–124, 186–188; see also Marcus, *Way*, 59–77.

[17] Watts, "Mark," 133–138, 184–185, 228, 233–234. On the use of Dan 7:13–14 in Mark, see Adela Yarbro Collins, "The Influence of Daniel on the New Testament," in John J. Collins, *Daniel: A Commentary on the Book of Daniel*, Hermeneia (Minneapolis, MN: Fortress, 1993), 97–98; on the interpretative possibilities of כבר אנש in Dan 7:13, see Collins, *Daniel*, 304–310.

[18] Watts, "Mark," 206. I think it would be difficult to demonstrate definitively that Mark intends to allude to Gen 49:10–11. One can, however, make a case that some scripturally literate first-century readers would conceive of the untying of the colt in terms of this ancient oracle (see my discussion in Section 5.2.1).

instances of messianic discourse in the Second Gospel, including the import of the titles son of God and son of David.

2.4.1   A Challenger to David's Son? Daniel's One like a Son of Man

The evangelist's identification of his Christ as Daniel's one like a son of man has not been without consequence for assessments of Markan Christology, since, as we saw in the previous chapter, Dan 7:13–14 has often been treated as the source of inspiration for an "apocalyptic" form of messianism that stands in direct conflict with a "traditional" or "Davidic" form of messianism.[19] Thus, William Telford concludes, "[w]hile rejecting a Jewish-Christian identification of Jesus as the Davidic Messiah, Mark appears to have accepted with qualifications a traditional Jewish-Christian identification of Jesus as the victorious apocalyptic Son of Man."[20] Boring, too, casts Mark's options in antithetical categories when he asserts, "the issue is whether the Messiah as God's agent will establish God's justice in Davidic terms, as the righteous king empowered by God to bring in God's kingdom ... or whether Christology is conceived in Markan apocalyptic terms;"[21] and again, "the point is how the Christ is understood – as a David-like one who will fulfill Israel's national hopes, or as the transcendent Lord who will come again as Son of Man."[22] The persistence with which this antithesis is espoused by some of the finest New Testament interpreters of our day merits response. In what follows, I examine those texts that characterize messiahs with language and concepts drawn from Dan 7:13–14, namely, the undisputed letters of Paul, Matthew, Luke-Acts, John, Revelation, the Parables of Enoch (1 En. 37–71), and 4 Ezra.[23] Do these texts evince the sort of antithesis Telford and Boring suggest?

The clear answer is no. In at least one place, Paul clearly envisages the enthroned Christ as Daniel's one like a son of man

---

[19] E.g., Bousset, *Kyrios Christos*; Mowinckel, *He That Cometh*.

[20] Telford, *Theology*, 113; so, too, Ernst Lohmeyer, *Das Evangelium des Markus*, KEK 2. 11th edn. (Göttingen: Vandenhoeck & Ruprecht: 1951), 262–263.

[21] Boring, *Mark*, 348.   [22] Ibid., 349.

[23] 4Q246 may offer an early interpretation of Daniel's one like a son of man as a Davidic messiah. For a list of scholars who hold this view, see Adela Yarbro Collins and John J. Collins, *King and Messiah as Son of God* (Grand Rapids, MI: Eerdmans, 2008), 66 n. 87. Since this remains disputed, however, I refrain from treating it in this section (see Section 2.4.4.1).

(cf. 1 Cor 15:23–28).[24] Although Davidic messiahship is not the topic of discussion, it is nonetheless "axiomatic for the argument of the passage."[25] The evangelists Matthew and Luke depict Jesus as both a descendant of David (cf. Matt 1:1; Luke 2:4) and Daniel's one like a son of man (cf. Matt 19:27–28; Luke 12:8–9) without any hint of tension between the two. Further, although distinct from the Synoptic portraits in many ways, John's Christ also emerges as Daniel's one like a son of man (cf., John 3:14; 5:27; 12:23, 34) and a messiah like David.[26] Admittedly, there is debate over whether the evangelist accepts or rejects the notion that the messiah would be a descendant of David (cf. John 7:40–44), and the overall flavor of the Gospel suggests that human ancestry is not of any great concern.[27] Yet, as Margaret Daly-Denton cogently demonstrates, John's messianism appears to be rooted in the conviction that "the 'Davidic' qualities of Jesus are important arguments for Jesus' status as the Christ."[28] For the beloved disciple, the Christ is Davidic not so much by right of birth, at least not explicitly, but by a pervasive association with the language, imagery, and hopes a strand of scriptural traditions attribute to an ideal Davidide.

The Parables of Enoch, Revelation, and 4 Ezra are all apocalypses in genre, but of these, only the Parables spurns Davidic descent.[29]

---

[24] See Yarbro Collins and Collins, *King and Messiah*, 109–110; James A. Waddell, *The Messiah: A Comparative Study of the Enochic Son of Man and the Pauline Kyrios*, Jewish and Christian Texts in Contexts and Related Studies Series 10 (London: T&T Clark, 2011), 186–201; Nickelsburg and VanderKam, *1 Enoch 2*, 74–75.

[25] Novenson, *Christ among the Messiahs*, 146, cf. 143–146.

[26] For a summary treatment of the use of Dan 7:13–14 in the Gospel of John, see Yarbro Collins, "Influence," 100–102; a fuller treatment may be found in Benjamin E. Reynolds, *The Apocalyptic Son of Man in the Gospel of John*, WUNT 2/249 (Tübingen: Mohr Siebeck, 2008).

[27] The evangelist's position toward the crowd's objection that Jesus cannot be ὁ χριστός, since he comes ἐκ τῆς Γαλιλαίας instead of, as the scriptures presage, ἐκ τοῦ σπέρματος Δαυίδ and ἀπὸ Βηθλέεμ, is ambiguous (John 7:42). Some interpreters see this is an instance of dramatic irony and, thus, that John expects his audience to recognize the crowd's ignorance as confirmation that Jesus is indeed from the line of David (e.g., Raymond E. Brown, *The Gospel According to John (i-xii): Introduction, Translation, and Notes*, AB29 [Garden City, NY: Doubleday, 1966; repr. London: Chapman, 1975], 330). Others see the crowd's objection as a veiled rejection of the tradition that Jesus descended from David (e.g., Burger, *Jesus als Davidssohn*, 1971, 158).

[28] Margaret Daly-Denton, *David in the Fourth Gospel: The Johannine Reception of the Psalms*, AGJU 47 (Leiden: Brill, 2000), 313.

[29] Despite its absence from the Qumran library, the emerging consensus is that the Parables represent a "Jewish" work composed sometime in the first century BCE or CE; see Matthew Black, "The Messianism of the Parables of Enoch: Their Date and Contributions to Christological Origins," in *The Messiah: Developments in Earliest*

In its current form, this series of revelatory visions concludes with the ascent of Enoch into heaven, at which time he learns that he is the heavenly figure, the righteous one/chosen one/son of man/messiah, seated on or beside the divine throne (cf. 1 En. 71:14).[30] Debate persists as to whether chapters 70 and 71 constitute later appendices or are integral to the work's original structure, but, in either case, the exalted figure is never identified as a descendant of David.[31] At the same time, though, this figure is manifestly imbued with Davidic traits – for example, the first occurrence of the word messiah takes place within an allusion to Ps 2:2: "For they have denied the Lord of Spirits and his messiah" (1 En. 48:10; cf. 52:4);[32] and, on two separate occasions, he is characterized with language derived from Isa 11:1–5: "And the Lord of Spirits <seated him> on the throne of his glory, and the spirit of righteousness was poured upon him. And the word of his mouth will slay all the sinners, and all the unrighteous will perish from his presence" (1 En. 62:2; cf. 49:3–4).[33] When

---

Judaism and Christianity, ed. James H. Charlesworth (Minneapolis, MN: Fortress, 1992), 145–168; the collection of essays in Gabriele Boccaccini, ed., *Enoch and the Messiah Son of Man: Revisiting the Book of Parables* (Grand Rapids, MI: Eerdmans, 2007); and James H. Charlesworth, "The Date and Provenience of the Parables of Enoch, in *Parables of Enoch: A Paradigm Shift*, eds. James H. Charlesworth and Darrell L. Bock, Jewish and Christian Texts in Context and Related Studies Series 11 (London: T&T Clark, 2013). Even if, however, the final form is late, say, the mid-second century CE, its language about the son-of-man figure is undoubtedly relevant to the study of ancient messianism and early Christology.

[30] The exalted figure is a composite of different scriptural traditions: (1) chosen one (Isa 42:1; 49:1–2), (2) righteous one (Isa 53:11), (3) messiah (Ps 2:2), and (4) (that) son of man (Dan 7:13); see esp. James C. VanderKam, "Righteous One, Messiah, Chosen One, and Son of Man in 1 Enoch 37–71," in *The Messiah: Developments in Earliest Judaism and Christianity*, ed. James H. Charlesworth (Minneapolis, MN: Fortress, 1992), 169–191. There is some dispute over whether all three Ethiopic terms typically translated as "(that) son of man" reference Daniel's one like a son of man; at the very least, the expression (*zekku/zentu*) *walda sab'* (cf. 1 En. 46:2, 3, 46:4; 48:2; etc.) alludes to this figure.

[31] It is inconsequential, for my purposes, whether the identification of Enoch as "that son of man" constitutes a secondary development (so Collins, *Scepter*, 196–205), or is integral to the original work (so VanderKam, "Righteous One," 177–185; Helge S. Kvanvig, "The Son of Man in the Parables of Enoch," in *Enoch and the Messiah Son of Man: Revisiting the Book of Parables*, ed. Gabriele Boccaccini [Grand Rapids, MI: Eerdmans, 2007], 197–210).

[32] All English translations of 1 Enoch follow that of Nickelsburg and VanderKam, *1 Enoch: The Hermeneia Translation* (Minneapolis, MN: Fortress, 2012). For the sake of consistency, I have substituted "messiah" for their "Anointed One."

[33] Cf. Johannes Theisohn, *Der auserwählte Richter: Untersuchungen zum traditionsgeschichtlichen Ort der Menschensohngestalt der Äthiopischen Henoch*, SUNT 12 (Göttingen: Vandenhoeck & Ruprecht, 1975), 138. Other examples could be listed;

we observe how the writer of the Parables uses his scriptures, it becomes apparent, as George Nickelsburg and James VanderKam note, that "[t]he enthroned one in Daniel 7 is identified with the king whose enthronement as God's son authorizes his judgment of the kings of the earth."[34] That is to say, the writer of the Parables agrees with Paul, the evangelists Matthew, Luke, and John, and the seers of Revelation and 4 Ezra that Daniel's one like a son of man is the anointed king of Psalm 2; he just disagrees that this figure needs to be the son of David.

There is, therefore, little basis to the claim that an author's decision to identify the messiah as Daniel's one like a son of man necessarily results in a form of messianism that is anti-Davidic. Quite the contrary: in the vast majority of the texts surveyed, the messiah son of man is explicitly identified as the son of David. Even if, moreover, one assumes that the Parables reflect a broader tradition about a heavenly son of man figure who is disentangled from a human ancestry, Davidic or otherwise, this would not constrain a first-century writer from postulating that this son of man is also the son of David. To this end, it is instructive that the author most likely to have shared source material with the Parables of Enoch begins his Gospel, "An account of the genealogy of Jesus Christ, the *son of David*" (Matt 1:1).[35]

Mark's decision to characterize his Christ as the Danielic son of man cannot, therefore, be marshalled as "evidence" to support the claim that the evangelist is anti-Davidic; if anything, the presence of allusions to Dan 7:13–14 leads one to suspect that the evangelist will also evince interest in Davidic scriptural traditions (e.g., Psalm 2; Isaiah 11). But, of course, what matters most is *how* the evangelist made use of his linguistic resources, the frames his chose to actualize and those he chose to narcotize.

---

see further in Theisohn, *Der auserwählte Richter*; and Nickelsburg and VanderKam, *1 Enoch 2*.

[34] Nickelsburg and VanderKam, *1 Enoch 2*, 119; see also David E. Aune, "From the Idealized Past to the Imaginary Future: Eschatological Restoration in Jewish Apocalyptic Literature," in *Restoration: Old Testament, Jewish, and Christian Literature*, ed. James M. Scott, JSJSup 72 (Leiden: Brill, 2001), 153–154; Yarbro Collins and Collins, *King and Messiah*, 90.

[35] For a comparison of the son-of-man traditions in the Parables and Matthew, see Leslie W. Walck, *The Son of Man in the Parables of Enoch and in Matthew*, Jewish and Christian Texts in Contexts and Related Studies Series 9 (London: T&T Clark, 2011), esp. 226–252.

2.4.2   Markan Use of Davidic Scriptural Traditions: Psalm 2 as a Test Case

The following chart (p. 53) lists Psalm 2 in both its Hebrew and Greek versions. Clauses in **bold** indicate those parts of the oracle to which Mark 1:11 and parallels allude; underlined clauses and phrases indicate those parts which are cited or alluded to in other messiah texts; and a broken underline indicates textual echoes. The allusion to Ps 2:7 at Jesus's baptism (cf. Mark 1:11) and, by extension, at his transfiguration (cf. Mark 9:7), is now widely accepted in Markan scholarship.[36] While interpreters continue to debate the christological implications of these allusions, most would concede that the psalm has messianic connotations within Mark's narrative world.[37] But it remains unclear precisely what these connotations entail. I develop the proposal that there is sufficient evidence in the trove of ancient messiah texts to make plausible deductions about the sort of frames an allusion to Psalm 2 would activate for members of the evangelist's linguistic community.[38]

In addition to the New Testament evidence (on which, see later), three writers of this period elected to construct their messiahs using the language of Psalm 2 (Pss. Sol. 17; 1 En. 37–71; 4 Ezra), with the possibility of a fourth (1QSa).[39] In each case, the writers of these

---

[36] Bousset's once popular suggestion that underneath υἱός μου, "my son," lies the more primitive παῖς μου, "my servant/child," has largely been abandoned (*Kyrios Christos*, 96–97). Recent attempts at undermining the allusion to Ps 2:7 are less convincing (see my discussion in Section 3.4.2).

[37] Eduard Schweizer, *The Good New according to Mark*, trans. Donald M. Madvig (Louisville: John Knox, 1964), 40–41; Steichele, *Der leidende Sohn Gottes*, 135–161; Kingsbury, *Christology*, 60–68; Frank J. Matera, *The Kingship of Jesus: Composition and Theology in Mark 15*, SBLDS 66 (Chico, CA: Scholars Press, 1982), 77–78; Marcus, *Way*, 59–79; Donald Juel, "The Origins of Mark's Christology," in *The Messiah: Developments in Earliest Judaism and Christianity*, ed. James H. Charlesworth (Minneapolis, MN: Fortress, 1992), 449–460, esp. 455–457; Rowe, *God's Kingdom*, 242–262; Watts, "Lord's House," 309–313; Yarbro Collins, *Mark*, 150; O'Brien, *Use of Scripture*, 164–165.

[38] On the interpretation of Ps 2 in the late Second Temple period, see Annette Steudel, "Psalm 2 im antiken Judentum," in *Gottessohn und Menschensohn: Exegetische Studien zu zwei Paradigmen biblischer Intertextualität*, ed. Dieter Sänger, BibS (N) 67 (Neukirchen-Vluyn: Neukirchener, 2004); John J. Collins, "The Interpretation of Psalm 2," in *Echoes from the Caves: Qumran and the New Testament*, ed. Florentino García Martínez, STDJ 85 (Leiden: Brill, 2009) 49–66; Sam Janse, *"You Are My Son": The Reception History of Psalm 2 in Early Judaism and the Early Church*, CBET (Leuven: Peeters, 2009).

[39] I treat the citation of Ps 2:1–2 in 4Q174 separately, since the writer does not interpret the psalm messianically. Moreover, I do not discuss the phrase γενέσθαι αὐτῷ υἱόν in T. Levi 4:2, because the language is closer to 2 Sam 7:14 LXX than Ps 2:7 LXX

MT	LXX
Why do the nations conspire, and the peoples plot in vain? The kings of the earth set themselves, and the rulers take counsel together, against YHWH and his messiah [עַל־יְהוָה וְעַל־מְשִׁיחוֹ], saying, "Let us burst their bonds asunder, and cast their cords from us." He who sits in the heavens laughs; YHWH holds them in derision. Then he will speak to them in his wrath, and terrify them in his fury, saying, "I have set my king on Zion, my holy hill." I will tell of the decree of YHWH: He said to me, "**You are my son**; today I have begotten you. Ask of me, and I will make the nations your inheritance, and the ends of the earth your possession. You shall break them with a rod of iron, and dash them in pieces like a potter's vessel." Now therefore, O kings, be wise; be warned, O rulers of the earth. Serve the Lord with fear, with trembling kiss the son, or he will be angry, and you will perish in the way; for his wrath is quickly kindled. Blessed are all who take refuge in him.	Why are the nations arrogant, and peoples concern themselves with vain thing? The kings of the earth stand side by side and the rulers gathered together in the same place, against the Lord and against his messiah [κατὰ τοῦ κυρίου καὶ κατὰ τοῦ χριστοῦ αὐτό] [Interlude][a] "Let us burst their bonds asunder, and cast their yoke from us." He who resides in the heavens will laugh at them, and the Lord will mock them. "But I was established king by him, on Zion, his holy mountain,[b] by proclaiming the Lord's ordinances: the Lord said to me, '**you are my son**; today I have begotten you. Ask of me, and I will give you nations as your inheritance, and as your possession the ends of the earth. You shall shepherd[c] them with an iron rod, and like a potter's vessel you will shatter them.'" And now, O kings, learn discipline; be instructed, all you who judge the earth. Serve the Lord with fear, and rejoice in him with trembling. Seize upon discipline, lest the Lord become angry and you will perish from the righteous way, when his anger quick blazes out. Blessed are all who trust in him.

[a] Reflecting διάψαλμα; סלה lacking in MT.

[b] LXX takes v. 6 as the beginning of the king's speech: ἐγὼ δὲ κατεστάθην βασιλεὺς ὑπ' αὐτοῦ ἐπὶ Σιων ὄρος τὸ ἅγιον αὐτοῦ, "But I have been made king by him on Zion, his holy mountain" (Ps 2:6). The translator's *Vorlage* may have agreed with the MT's, since נסכתי can be pointed as a *qal* (נָסַכְתִּי; as in the MT) or as a *niphal* (נָסַכְתִּי), and since the first person suffixes may have been mistaken for third person suffixes. What is preserved of Ps 2 from 3QPs and 11QPs[c] agrees with the MT on this point (see Eugene Ulrich, ed., *The Biblical Qumran Scrolls: Transcriptions and Textual Variants*, 3 vols. [Leiden: Brill, 2013], 3:627); the Peshitta also attests to this reading.

[c] LXX reads תרעם, from the root רעה, "to shepherd," rather than רעע, "to shatter," and is followed by the Peshitta. The difference is reflected in early allusions to Psalm 2: e.g., Pss. Sol. 17:23 has ἐκτρῖψαι, "to smash," likely rendering רעע, while Rev 19:15 has ποιμανεῖ, "he will shepherd," reflecting רעה.

texts selected elements of the psalm in accordance with their literary and ideological aims: (1) the poet of Psalms of Solomon 17 weaves together allusions to Ps 2:9 and Isa 11:1–5 to craft an anointed son of David who will purge a defiled Jerusalem of its gentile overlords (cf. Pss. Sol. 17:21–24);[40] (2) the seer of the Parables draws inspiration from the language of Ps 2:2 when he envisages the rebellion of the "kings of the earth" against the "Lord of Spirits and his messiah" (1 En. 48:10);[41] (3) the scribe of 4 Ezra espies a "man from the sea," who is reproached by the assembled nations while standing atop Mount Zion (cf. Ps 2:1–2, 6), before he rebukes and destroys them with the breath of his lips (cf. Isa 11:4) and gathers the exiled tribes of Israel (cf. Isa 11:10–16; 4 Ezra 13:5–13, 32–47);[42] finally, (4) the writer of the Rule of the Congregation may have alluded to Ps 2:7 when he speaks of the time "when [God] begets the messiah with them [אתם המשיח[ת]א[ל]יד[יו אם]" (1QSa 2:11–12).[43]

Although the Midrash on Eschatology[a] (4Q174) lacks a messianic interpretation of Psalm 2, the wider context suggests that the interpreter presupposes a messianic frame. Specialists in early Judaism have been struck, quite understandably, by the observation that the interpreter explicates משיחו, "his messiah," in Ps 2:2 as בחירי ישראל,

---

(text in Marinus Jonge, ed., *The Testament of the Twelve Patriarchs: A Critical Edition of the Greek Text* [Leiden: Brill, 1978], at 29).

[40] On the allusion to Ps 2:9 in Pss. Sol. 17:22–23, see Kenneth R. Atkinson, *An Intertextual Study of the Psalms of Solomon* (Lewiston, NY: Mellon, 2001), 346–347.

[41] Nickelsburg and VanderKam, *1 Enoch 2*, 176.

[42] Michael Stone notes the allusions to Ps 2:6 and Isa 11:4 in Ezra's vision of the man from the sea (*Fourth Ezra: A Commentary on the Book of Fourth Ezra*, Hermeneia [Minneapolis, MN: Fortress, 1990], 403–404); see also Collins, "Interpretation," 62. 2 Baruch 40:1 may also reflect a dual allusion to Ps 2:6 and Isa 11:4: "The last ruler, who will then be left alive when the multitude of his host will be destroyed, will be bound, and they will take him up unto Mount Zion. And my Messiah will reprove him on account of all his evil deeds, and he will assemble and set before him all the deeds of his hosts" (translation in Michael E. Stone and Matthias Henze, *4 Ezra and 2 Baruch: Translation, Introduction, and Notes* [Minneapolis, MN: Fortress, 2013], at 107)

[43] Hebrew text in Dominique Barthélemy and J. T. Milik, eds., *Qumran Cave 1: I*, DJD 1 (Oxford: Clarendon, 1955), 110. There remains dispute as to whether one should read יוליד, "he begets," despite Barthélemy's claim that this reading is "practiquement certaine" (*Qumran Cave 1: I*, 117). One could read יוליך, "he sends," and Emile Puech has raised the possibility that we should read יתג[ל]ה, "est révélé," correcting יועד, "s'adjoint" ("Préséance Sacerdotale et Messie-Roi dans la Règle de la Congrégation [1Qsa ii 11–22]," *RevQ* 16 [1993–1995]: 351–365, here 361). In any case, I am in agreement with Collins ("Interpretation," 64) that "[i]f the reading [יוליד] is correct, it is simply picking up and endorsing the language of the Psalms."

"[the] elect ones of Israel."[44] Yet one wonders if the psalm's function in column 2 exhausts the interpreter's understanding of the text.[45] Such an inference is difficult to square with what he writes about a future descendant of David in the previous column: "[And] YHWH [de]clares to you that [citing 2 Sam 7:12–14] 'he will build you a house. I will raise up your seed after you and establish the throne of his kingdom [for ev]er. I will be a father to him and he will be a son to me.' This (refers to the) branch of David" (4Q174 1:10–11).[46] It is possible that the interpreter saw no connection between the one whom YHWH calls "my son" in Ps 2:7 and the branch of David whom YHWH will make his son à la 2 Sam 7:14. But it seems more plausible that his interpretation of "his messiah" as "the elect of Israel" trades on the scriptural notion that the anointed king is God's son elected to deliver God's elect son/s, Israel.[47] Since the interpreter applies the conflict in Ps 2:1–2 to the period of time in which the sectarians already lived (i.e., "in the last days"),[48] it is less surprising that he aligns his community with the individual whom the psalmist portrays as the focal point of all earthly antagonism directed toward YHWH. This suggests that the writer's corporate midrash on Ps 2:1–2 does not necessarily rule

---

[44] Although משיחו is missing due to a lacuna at the beginning of line 19, the reconstruction is nearly certain. The critical text may be found in John M. Allegro, ed., *Qumrân Cave 4: I (4Q158–4Q186)*, DJD 5 (Oxford: Clarendon, 1968), 53; see also Annette Steudel, *Der Midrasch zur Eschatologie aus der Qumrangemeinde (4QMidrEschat ᵃ·ᵇ): Materielle Rekonstruktion, Textbestand, Gattung und traditionsgeschichtliche Einordnung des durch 4Q174 ("Florilegium") und 4Q177 ("Catena A") reprasentierten Werkes aus den Qumranfunden*, STDJ 13 (Leiden: Brill, 1994), 25, 47.

[45] Contra Janse (*"You Are My Son,"* 54), who, following Steudel ("Psalm 2"), speaks of a "de-messianizing" interpretation of Psalm 2.

[46] Text in Allegro, ed., *Qumrân Cave 4*, 53. The English translation follows Florentino García Martínez and Eibert J. C. Tigchelaar, *The Dead Sea Scrolls Study Edition*, 2 vols. (Leiden: Brill, 1997–1998), 1:353. See discussion in George J. Brooke, *Exegesis at Qumran: 4QFlorilegium in Its Jewish Context*, JSOTSup 29 (Sheffield: JSOT Press, 1985), 158–159.

[47] I develop this point further in my essay, "'Whoever Does the Will of God' (Mark 3:35): Mark's Christ As the Model Son," in *Son of God: Divine Sonship in Jewish and Christian Antiquity*, eds. Garrick V. Allen et al. (University Park: Pennsylvania State University Press, 2019), 106–117. The Davidic branch's role in 4Q174 is reminiscent of a traditional royal function: he will "take office in order to deliver Israel" (1:13); "to deliver," ישע, in this context, has to do with deliverance from Israel's enemies, who are the same enemies currently scheming against the "elect of Israel," according to the pesher on Ps 2.

[48] On the phrase אחרית הימים, in the Dead Sea Scrolls, see Annette Steudel, "אחרית הימים in the Texts from Qumran," *RevQ* 16 (1993): 225–246.

out an "individual/messianic" interpretation of the psalm, if and when the appropriate time should arrive. Peter's prayer in Acts 4:24–31 may offer an analogy. The apostle interprets his arrest in light of David's prophetic word about the Lord's messiah in Ps 2:1–2 (Acts 4:26). Just as the nations gathered together "against your holy servant Jesus, whom you anointed" (Acts 4:27), declares an emboldened Peter, so now the same antagonism depicted in the opening verses of Psalm 2 is leveled against the messianic community (4:29).[49] As Sam Janse astutely notes,

> The words "their threats" [τὰς ἀπειλὰς αὐτῶν] have two referential points: the persons and groups mentioned in v. 27 (Herod, Pontius Pilate, the nations and the "people of Israel"), that is to say, they who have crucified Jesus, and the ἄρχοντες of vv. 5, 8, who according to v. 17 (ἀπειλησώμεθα) and v. 21 (προσαπειλησάμενοι), threaten the *ekklèsia*. In this way Luke constructs a subtle identification of the situation of Jesus' crucifixion with the persecution of his earliest followers.[50]

For Luke, as for the interpreter of 4Q174, Psalm 2 projects a symbolic world inhabited by an elect community living "in the last days" (cf. Acts 2:17). The primary difference is the writers' respective locations vis-à-vis their messiahs: whereas the interpreter of 4Q174 applies Ps 2:1–2 to his community prior to the advent of the messiah, the historiographer of the people of "the way" applies the same text to the messiah's community after his exaltation. Both writers attest to the fungibility of the referent of "his messiah" in Psalm 2.[51] Yet Luke-Acts equally provides clear evidence that individual

---

[49] This point is made clear by Luke's introduction of key lexemes from Ps 2 LXX (οἱ ἄρχοντες συνήχθησαν) at the beginning of the unit: Ἐγένετο δὲ ἐπὶ τὴν αὔριον συναχθῆναι αὐτῶν τοὺς ἄρχοντας καὶ τοὺς πρεσβυτέρους καὶ τοὺς γραμματεῖς ἐν Ἰερουσαλήμ (Acts 4:5; cf. 4:8).

[50] Janse, *"You Are My Son,"* 93.

[51] Depending on an author's interests, the role of the protagonist in Psalm 2 could be filled by either the community (cf. Sib. Or. 3:663–664) or an individual representative of the community (cf. Wis 1:1; 6:1, 21). While the sibyl envisages God's people receiving help from a Cyrus-esque "king from the sun" (Sib. Or. 3:652–656), the specific eschatological scenario to which Ps 2:1–2 applies comes later, beginning at 3:663, wherein the "sons of the great God" are defended by God alone (3:669–731). Pseudo-Solomon echoes the language of the anointed king's refrain addressed to "the kings and the rulers of the earth" (cf. Ps 2:10; Pss. Sol. 2:31–35) at the open and close of the "Book of Eschatology" (Wis 1:1; 6:1, 21). The writer also claims that the Lord "will laugh," ἐκγελάσεται, at those who have dishonored his righteous (Wis 4:18), just

and corporate accounts of Psalm 2 are neither at odds nor mutually exclusive.[52] Even if one grants Annette Steudel's extreme position, "[a]n messianischen Stellen in Qumran sucht man Ps 2-Bezüge vergeblich,"[53] there is still every reason to suspect that the sectarians would understand what the writers of Pss. Sol. 17, 1 En. 37–71, and 4 Ezra were doing when they applied this psalm to their messiahs. Indeed, it may be instructive that all three of the aforementioned writers weave together allusions to Psalm 2 with allusions to Isaiah's oracle about a future descendant of David, Isa 11:1–10 (cf. Pss. Sol. 17:22–25; 1 En. 48:10–49:4; 4 Ezra 13:5–13, 32–47).

Citations of and allusions to Psalm 2 in the first-century texts produced by Christ followers tend to cluster around three discrete sections of the psalm.[54] (1) Luke and the seer of Revelation each draws imagery from the battle depicted in the opening verses (e.g., Acts 4:25–26; Rev 11:15; 19:19).[55] (2) Paul (cf. Rom 1:3–4), the Synoptic evangelists (cf. Mark 1:11 pars.; cf. Acts 13:33), the writer of the Epistle to the Hebrews (cf. Heb 1:5; 5:5), and the author of 2 Peter (cf. 1:17) all take interest in the divine address to the enthroned son (cf. Ps 2:7–8). (3) The seer of Revelation evokes Ps 2:9 – "[he will] shepherd the nations with an iron rod" – to depict the heavenly messiah as the one who will subject the nations to God's rule (cf. Rev 2:27; 12:5; 19:15). Close attention to these texts suggests that these writers shared an assumption that the anointed king of the psalm would be a future son of David.

---

as "he will laugh," ἐκγελάσεται, from heaven at those who rise up against his anointed (Ps 2:4). The use of Ps 2 in Wisdom is, however, but one element of the author's larger project aimed at "democratizing" royal features to every "child of God," as cogently argued by Judith H. Newman, "The Democratization of Kingship in Wisdom of Solomon," *The Idea of Biblical Interpretation: Essays in Honor of James L. Kugel*, eds. Hindy Najman and Judith H. Newman, JSJSup 83 (Leiden: Brill, 2004). While these examples are markedly different than the messiah texts survey in this chapter, they disclose what appears to be a widely held assumption, namely, that Ps 2 functions as an eschatological narrative moving from persecution to vindication.

[52] There appears to be a similar logic at work in Rev 2:26–27. The exalted Christ, who has conquered and received authority from his father (cf. Ps 2:7–9), promises to share his authority with those who imitate him in enduring to the end, so that they too might "rule them with an iron rod, as when clay pots are shattered" (cf. Ps 2:9).

[53] Steudel, "Psalm 2," 192.

[54] Following Janse's chart (*"You Are My Son,"* 80; see also the helpful index in Steven Moyise and Maarten J. J. Menken, eds., *The Psalms in the New Testament* [London: T&T Clark, 2004], 247–248).

[55] One might also detect echoes of Ps 2:2 when Paul speaks in 1 Cor 2:8 of "rulers of this age" (so Marcus, *Way*, 63).

An obvious point of departure is the consensus that Paul used a protocreedal statement, reflecting the language of 2 Sam 7:12–14 and Ps 2:7, at the opening of his letter to the churches in Rome (Rom 1:3–4).[56] Christopher Whitsett cogently argues that this collocation of royal intertexts, far from being ancillary to the apostle's theology, is central to his understanding of how God's mercy comes to the gentiles – namely via the enthronement of a descendant of the Davidic line (cf. Rom 15:1–13).[57] Luke's portrayal of Paul's speech in Acts 13 runs in a similar direction:

> from this man's [David's] seed as promised, God has brought to Israel a Savior, Jesus (13:23). . . . And we announce to you the gospel: the promise which came to the ancestors that God has fulfilled for us, their children,[58] by raising Jesus, as also it is written in the second psalm, [citing Ps 2:7] "You are my son; today I have begotten you." As to his raising him from the dead, no more to return to corruption, he has spoken in this way, [citing Isa 55:3] "I will give you the holy promises made to David."   (13:32–34)

God's promise to "raise up" David's seed (cf. 2 Sam 7:12) finds its fulfillment, Luke contests, when God raised David's son from the dead and enthroned him at his right hand, as promised in Ps 2:7.[59] The author of Hebrews cites Ps 2:7 alongside 2 Sam 7:14 (cf. Heb 1:5), leaving little doubt as to why he thinks Jesus's Judahite descent is self-evident (cf. Heb 7:14). Finally, the seer of Revelation, like the writers of Psalms of Solomon 17, the Parables of Enoch, 4 Ezra,

---

[56] The connection between 2 Sam 7:12–14 and Ps 2 in Rom 1:3–4 is widely recognized (see, e.g., Donald Juel, *Messianic Exegesis: Christological Interpretation of the Old Testament in Early Christianity* [Minneapolis, MN: Fortress, 1988], 80–81; Janse, *"You Are My Son,"* 104–105; cf. Tertullian, *Carn. Chr.* 22.6; Eusebius, *Dem. ev.* 3.2.39; Athanasius, *Dion.* 7.2.4.; Peter Abelard, *Comm. Ep. Rom.*, on 1:3–4). Christopher G. Whitsett's analysis, in particular, suggests Paul reflected carefully on the language of Ps 2 ("Son of God, Seed of David: Paul's Messianic Exegesis in Romans 2:3–4 [sic]," *JBL* 119 [2000]: 661–681, esp. 677).

[57] Whitsett, "Son of God;" see also J. Ross Wagner, *Heralds of the Good News: Isaiah and Paul in Concert in the Letter to the Romans*, NovTSup (Leiden: Brill, 2002), 311–328.

[58] For the sake of convenience, I have followed the printed text in the NA[28]: τοῖς τέκνοις [αὐτῶν] ἡμῖν. There is, however, strong MS evidence for τοῖς τέκνοις ἡμῶν (e.g., P74 א A B C* D Ψ lat) – thus, "God has fulfilled this [i.e. the promise] *for our children.*" Neither reading is of particular significance for the discussion at hand.

[59] For a sound treatment of this passage, see Mark L. Strauss, *The Davidic Messiah in Luke-Acts: The Promise and Its Fulfillment in Lukan Christology*, JSNTSup 110 (Sheffield: Sheffield Academic Press, 1995), 148–178.

links the anointed king of Psalm 2 with Isaiah's shoot of Jesse (cf. Rev 19:11–16). If one can speak here of a messianic "grammar," perhaps one should say that these early Christ followers believed Psalm 2 was about Jesus precisely because they believed he is the son of David.[60]

The extant evidence allows for several observations. First, virtually every messiah text containing a citation of or allusion to Psalm 2 actualizes the son-of-David frame latent in the writers' encyclopedia. The Parables of Enoch offers a noteworthy exception to this trend,[61] but this is not particularly surprising given how the writer handled an oracle explicitly about a future descendant of the Davidic line, Isaiah 11 (cf. 1 En. 49:3–4; 62:2). Second, every text surveyed earlier (excepting 1Q28a) combines references to Psalm 2 with references to either Isa 11:1–10 (cf. 1 En. 48:10; 49:1–3; 4 Ezra 13; Rev 19:11–16), or 2 Sam 7:12–14 (cf. 4Q174; Heb 1:5; Acts 13:22–33), or both (cf. Pss. Sol 17:21–25; Rom 1:3–4; 15:12). Third, every instance where Psalm 2 is read without reference to the messiah son of David (excepting the Parables) may be attributed to either a lack of interest in messianism tout court (cf. Sib. Or. 3:663–664; Wis 1:1; 6:1, 21; Pss. Sol. 2:31–35) or the deferral of the royal role to a community still awaiting its messiah (4Q174). At the very least, then, we may say that those inclined to read that Psalm 2 messianically tended to assume that this anointed son of God would be the son of David.

In the following chapter, I will treat the Markan allusion to Ps 2:7 at some length. My interest here, however, is methodological: to what extent should Markan allusion to Ps 2:7 count as

---

[60] I should note that this is strictly an observation about how Ps 2 functions in early Christian texts, not a judgment about when and how the notion that Jesus is a descendant of David entered into the tradition. Duling ("Promises to David," 70–77) makes a compelling case that at an early point in the tradition a connection was made between YHWH's promise to "raise up" (קום/ἀνιστάναι) David's seed and God's act of "raising up" (ἀνιστάναι) Jesus from the dead. Whether this observation can explain the origin of the notion of Jesus's Davidic descent seems doubtful. For one thing, this hypothesis only works if early Christian traditions about Davidic descent can be traced to a singular point of origin, a point at which our historical knowledge simply fails us, despite the confidence of some that early Christians must have contrived the idea of Jesus's Davidic descent (e.g., David Friedrich Strauss, *The Life of Jesus Critically Examined*, trans. George Eliot [London: Sonnenschein, 1982 {German, 1835}], 117–118). For another, Duling's case depends on a hard-and-fast distinction between "seed of David" (metaphorical) and "son of David" (actual), a distinction which appears artificial when one considers how these interact in the tradition (cf. 1 Chr 17:11; Jer 33:21–22; etc.).

[61] 2 Baruch alludes to Ps 2 without indicating whether the messiah is a descendant of David. Yet the scribe stops short of suggesting the messiah is *not* a son of David.

counterevidence against a Wredean "plain sense" reading of the *Davidssohnfrage*? The ramifications of this question are potentially significant. If an allusion to Psalm 2 would activate a son-of-David frame for members of Mark's linguistic community, as the evidence suggests, then one needs to account for the evangelist's decision to evoke this particular psalm at points in the narrative designed to disclose vital information about the identity of Jesus (cf. Mark 1:11; 9:7; 12:6; 14:61).

2.4.3   Widening the Lens: Additional Features of Markan Messiah Language

The presence of Davidic traditions in Mark is not limited to popular messianic source texts. Most interpreters recognize, for instance, that the evangelist's parenthetic comment – unique to Mark's Gospel – that Jesus had compassion on the crowd "because they were like sheep without a shepherd" (Mark 6:34) evokes Ezekiel's oracle about the end of Israel's exile: "I will set up over them one shepherd, my servant David, and he shall feed them: he shall feed them and be their shepherd. And I, YHWH, will be their God, and my servant David shall be prince among them; I, YHWH, have spoken" (Ezek 34:23–24).[62] An additional point of intrigue is the evangelist's penchant for drawing on royal psalms at pivotal junctures in the narrative: baptism (Ps 2:7); the first passion prediction (Ps 118 [LXX 117]:22); transfiguration (Ps 2:7); triumphal entry (Ps 118 [LXX 117]:26); opening and closing of the controversy cycle in the temple (Ps 118 [LXX 117]:22; Ps 110 [LXX 109]:1); and the trial before the Sanhedrin (Pss 2:7; 110[109]:1).[63] Particularly note-worthy for our purposes is the allusion to Psalm 118 (LXX 117) in the first passion prediction (cf. Mark 8:31), since this pericope has frequently been interpreted as the evangelist's rejection of a "triumphalist," son-of-David Christology.[64] In addition to these,

---

[62] Other ancient writers characterize their messiahs with language drawn from Ezek 34:23–24 (cf. Pss. Sol. 17:40–42; John 10:1–18). Moreover, the title נשיא [כל] העדה, "prince of the (whole) congregation," likely derives from the use of נשיא in Ezek 34:24; 37:25 (cf. 1QM 5:1; CD 7:20; 1Q28b 5:20; 4Q161 2:15; 4Q285). I treat Mark's allusion to the oracle of restoration in Ezek 34 in Section 4.5.2.

[63] See Watts, "Lord's House."

[64] Although only one word, the likelihood that ἀποδοκιμασθῆναι marks an allusion to Ps 117:22 LXX is quite strong. The only other use of ἀποδοκιμάζειν in Mark occurs in a citation of Ps 117:22 LXX (cf. Mark 12:10–11), and every occurrence of ἀποδο-κιμάζειν in the New Testament (excepting Heb 12:17) sits within a citation of or

Mark's passion narrative is saturated with citations of and allusions to Davidic psalms of lament, which the evangelist appears to have read as prefiguring the suffering of Christ.[65] Does this suggest that Mark read Davidic superscriptions in the Psalter as an invitation to fuse the "past King David with the future Messiah," as Richard Hays suggests Paul did in Romans?[66] It seems to me that this possibility needs to be taken seriously and, as such, may provide further evidence relevant to our son-of-David debate.

allusion to the psalm (see J. Ross Wagner, "Psalm 118 in Luke-Acts: Tracing a Narrative Thread," in *Early Christian Interpretation of the Scriptures of Israel: Investigation and Proposals*, eds. Craig A. Evans and James A. Sanders, JSNTSup 148 [Sheffield: Sheffield Academic Press, 1997], 162). I treat Mark 8:31 at the end of Chapter 4 (Section 4.5).

[65] "Prefiguration" recognizes, on the one hand, that the authors and redactors of the Jewish scriptures were not consciously predicting the advent of the Christ and, on the other, that the authors of the New Testament, convinced that Christ was the hermeneutical key to their scriptures, embarked on a process of "reading backwards" (so Hays, *Echoes of Scripture in the Gospels*, 2–5). On the use of Davidic psalms in Mark, see esp. Adela Yarbro Collins, "The Appropriation of the Psalms of Individual Lament by Mark," in *The Scriptures in the Gospels*, ed. C. M. Tuckett, BETL 131 (Leuven: University Press, 1997), 223–241; Ahearne-Kroll, *Psalms of Lament*. On the association of Davidic authorship with the Psalms and the growth of Davidic superscriptions, see Brevard Childs, "The Psalm Titles and Midrashic Exegesis," *JSS* (1971): 137–149; Albert Pietersma, "Exegesis and Liturgy in the Superscriptions of the Greek Psalter," in *X Congress of International Organization for Septuagint and Cognate Studies*, ed. Bernard A. Taylor, SCS 51 (Atlanta, GA: Society of Biblical Literature, 2001), 99–138; Esther M. Menn, "Sweet Singer of Israel: David and the Psalms in Early Judaism," in *Psalms in Community: Jewish and Christian Textual, Liturgical, and Artistic Traditions*, eds. Harold W. Attridge and Margot E. Fassler, SymS 25 (Atlanta, GA: Society of Biblical Literature, 2003), 61–74. There remains significant debate about the implications of the Davidic superscriptions in the Greek Psalter; compare, e.g., Martin Rösel, "Die Psalmüberschriften des Septuaginta-Psalter," in *Der Septuaginta-Psalter: Sprachliche und theologische Aspekte*, ed. Erich Zenger, BibS(F) 32 (Freiburg: Herder, 2001), 125–148 to Albert Pietersma, "Septuagintal Exegesis and the Superscriptions of the Greek Psalter," in *The Book of Psalms: Composition and Reception*, eds. Peter W. Flint and Patrick D. Miller, VTSup 99 (Leiden: Brill, 2005), 443–475. Pietersma's contention has to do with how one should account for the intention of the Greek translators; he readily acknowledges that the Greek Psalter "as it now stands has the *potential*" for the eschatological interpretations proposed by Rösel (461, his emphasis).

[66] Hays, *Conversion*, 115. His recent work on the Gospels suggests that his answer to the question would be a resounding "yes!"; see also Harold W. Attridge, "Giving Voice to Jesus: Use of the Psalms in the New Testament," in *Psalms in Community: Jewish and Christian Textual, Liturgical, and Artistic Traditions*, eds. Harold W. Attridge and Margot E. Fassler, SymS 25 (Atlanta, GA: Society of Biblical Literature, 2003), 101–112. Attridge distinguishes between instances in which David "foretells what Jesus will say or do" and those in which "[t]he words of the psalms are the words of Jesus" (107).

2.4.4   Christological Titles as Examples of Messiah Language

2.4.4.1 Son of God

Related to how interpreters handle Markan allusions to Psalm 2 is the wider significance of the christological title (the) son of God (cf. Mark 1:1; 3:11; 5:7; 9:7; 12:6; 14:61; 15:39).[67] Two questions have dominated the landscape of early Christology in general and Markan Christology in particular. First, what "pre-Christian" evidence do we have to suggest that the epithet (the) son of God functioned as a messianic title? Second, if we grant that divine sonship language could have messianic connotations in early Judaism, must we then conclude that it retains these in Mark? Scholars have been divided on both questions for quite some time.

Horsley conveniently summarizes the argument for why son-of-God language is nonmessianic in Mark. He asserts,

> it is difficult to find Judean or other texts prior to the time of Jesus that suggest that "son of God" in Mark is a reference to or synonym for "the messiah." Christian interpreters often take "son of God" in Mark as a reference to or synonym for "the messiah." But that appears to be reading back into Mark an identification that was made only later, when various roles, images, and terms ("titles"?) used in connection with Jesus became synthesized into an emergent "christology."[68]

Horsely bolsters his case by way of appeal to the study of late Joseph Fitzmyer on the so-called Son of God Text (4Q246), in which Fitzmyer refrained from labeling the son-of-God figure a "messiah" on the grounds that the *terminus technicus* משיחא is absent in the text.[69] In responding to criticism from John Collins, Fitzmyer specified his position further,

---

[67] It is uncertain whether υἱοῦ θεοῦ is original to Mark 1:1; see my discussion in Section 3.1.

[68] Horsley, *Hearing*, 250. Curiously, Horsley (*Hearing*, 285 n. 15) cites Adela Yarbro Collins ("Mark and His Readers: The Son of God among Jews," *HTR* 92 [1999]: 393–408) in support of his claim that "Mark portrays Jesus as a prophet" without mentioning that she concludes, in the very same study, that Mark's Jesus is a *Davidic messiah.*

[69] Horsley, *Hearing*, 285 n. 16, citing Joseph A. Fitzmyer, "4Q246: The 'Son of God' Document from Qumran," *Bib* (1993): 153–174, at 170–173; see also Fitzmyer, *A Wandering Aramean: Collected Aramaic Essays*, Volume 2 of *The Semitic Background of the New Testament* (Missoula, MT: Scholars Press; repr, Grand Rapids, MI: Eerdmans, 1997).

> But Collins still has not given any evidence of the use of the title "Son of God," for a Davidic Messiah either in the Old Testament or in Qumran literature. His reference to 4Q174 rightly builds on 2 Sam 7:14, but that text is not yet "messianic," as used in Qumran literature. The double predication of "Son of God" and "Messiah" for one individual is still first attested in Christian usage ... It is not to be foisted on a pre-Christian Jewish writing.[70]

Fitzmyer's argument, if I understand him correctly, is twofold. First, since 2 Sam 7:14 was not originally written with a first-century messiah in mind, it cannot, by definition, denote such a figure. Second, since no "pre-Christian" text includes both titles, son of God and messiah, their appositional relationship in early Christian literature must be the consequence of Christian innovation (cf. Mark 14:61).

There are serious flaws with both of these points. That the first is a clear non sequitur is laid bare by Novenson's dictum, "there may not be any messiahs in the Hebrew Bible, but some Jewish authors of the Hellenistic and Roman periods evidently thought there were."[71] The veracity of Fitzmyer's claim about the "original" meaning of 2 Sam 7:12–14, in other words, has precisely no bearing on what first-century authors thought the text meant. The second aspect of his argument merely begs the question, since it demands acceptance of the dual premises that (1) only titular son-of-God language counts as legitimate "pre-Christian" evidence for the christological title (the) son of God, and (2) the titles son of God and messiah must occur in the same document in order for the former to be considered "messianic." But it is not obvious why these premises should be accepted, particularly since Fitzmyer agrees with Collins that "a future 'successor to the Davidic throne' in an apocalyptic or eschatological context is by definition a Davidic messiah."[72] If, therefore, Fitzmyer and Collins are correct that the titles son of God and son of the Most High in 4Q246 are scripturally derived

---

[70] Joseph A. Fitzmyer, *The One Who Is to Come* (Grand Rapids, MI: Eerdmans, 2007), 107.

[71] Novenson, *Christ among the Messiahs*, 52–53. Novenson has since challenged, convincingly to my mind, the supposition that the messiahs of the Hebrew Bible are fundamentally different than the messiahs of early Judaism: "But in the case of משיח or χριστός, there is no *geistesgeschichtlich* flip of a switch from an earlier, Israelite, mundane sense ('anointed one') to a later, *spätjüdisch*, eschatological sense ('messiah')" (*Grammar of Messianism*, 54).

[72] Fitzmyer, *One Who Is to Come*, 107; citing Collins, *Scepter*, 264 (p. 184 in 1st edn.).

epithets for a future Davidic king, then this Aramaic apocalypse would offer an important antecedent to first-century Christian use of the title (the) son of God.

The problem, of course, is that the identity of the son-of-God figure in 4Q246 is highly ambiguous. Scholars have identified this figure as the antichrist,[73] a pagan king in the mold of Antiochus IV Epiphanes,[74] an angelic redeemer (Michael/Melchizedek),[75] the Davidic messiah,[76] and a corporate cipher for the people of God.[77] The preserved text begins with a figure (presumably an interpreter modeled on Daniel) doing obeisance before the throne of a king (1:1). The interpreter goes on to describe an eschatological schema culminating in the arrival of a great king,[78] who will be called ברה די אל, "son of God," and בר עליון, "son of the Most High" (2:1) and whose advent will be followed by the uprising of the nations (2:2–3). Then a break at the beginning of line 4 signals a major shift:

> (*vacat*) Until the people of God arise and make everyone rest from the sword. Their kingdom [מלכותה] will be an

---

[73] David Flusser, "The Hubris of the Antichrist in a Fragment from Qumran," *Imm* 10 (1980): 31–37.

[74] E. M. Cook, "4Q246," *BBR* 5 (1995): 43–66; Annette Steudel, "The Eternal Reign of the People of God – Collective Expectations in Qumran Texts (4Q246 and 1QM)," *RevQ* 17 (1996): 507–525; Emile Puech, "Apocryphe de Daniel," in *Qumran Cave 4 XVII: Parabiblical Texts, Part 3*, eds. Brooke et al., DJD 22 (Oxford: Clarendon, 1996), 165–184, at 178–184, though he has since shifted his opinion and now intereprets the son-of-God figure as a messiah ("Le fils de Dieu, le fils du Très-Haut, messi roi en 4Q246," in *Le jugement dans l'un et l'autre testament: Mélanges offert à Raymond Kuntzmann*, ed. Oliver Artus, LD 197 [Paris: Cerf, 2004], 271–286); Geza Vermes, *The Complete Dead Sea Scrolls in English* (London: Penguin, 2004), 617.

[75] Florentino García Martínez, *Qumran and Apocalyptic: Studies on the Aramaic Texts from Qumran*, STDJ 9 (Leiden: Brill, 1992), 162–179. Recently, Michael Segal has proposed that the son-of-God figure is an angelic representative of the final kingdom in Dan 7 that does battle against the people of God ("Who Is the 'Son of God' in 4Q246? An Overlooked Example of Biblical Interpretation," *DSD* 21 [2014]: 289–312). He summarizes his interpretation as follows: "the heavenly beings who are condemned to die in Ps 82 correspond to the heavenly representatives of the four empires that emerged from the mythic waters of the Great Sea in Dan 7. In light of the correspondence proposed here between Ps 82 and 4Q246, the character identified as 'son of God/the Most High' should therefore be taken as a heavenly representative of one of these kingdoms, who was originally conceived as a divine being, but who will eventually fall due to his actions. He is neither a human sovereign over an earthly kingdom nor a divine messianic figure" (311).

[76] See Yarbro Collins and Collins, *King and Messiah*, 66 n. 87.

[77] Martin Hengel, *The Son of God: The Origin of Christology and the History of Jewish-Hellenistic Religion*, trans. John Bowden (Minneapolis, MN: Fortress, 1976 [German 1975]), 44–45.

[78] The text is fragmentary at the beginning of line 9; see Puech, "Apocryphe," 173.

eternal kingdom, and all their ways will be in truth. They-will jud[ge] [[וֹ]יְדִי] the earth in truth and all will make peace. The sword will cease in the earth, and all the provinces will render homage to them. The great God himself is their strength and he fights for them [לֹה]; he places the people in their hand and casts them away before them. Their rule [שׁלְטָנה] will be an eternal rule and all the abysses.   (2:4–9)[79]

The primary issue is the relationship between 1:4–2:3 and 2:4–9. Specifically, is everything that precedes the *vacat* in 2:4, including the son-of-God figure, cast in a negative light? Or does the document's genre allow for a more complex temporal structure?

Steudel is convinced that the *vacat* demarcates "a radical change" from the period of tribulation to the period of vindication.[80] She concludes, "The positive 'people of God' in ii, 4–9 corresponds to the negative 'Son of God' in I, 4–ii, 3. And the power of the king who will be great over the earth in I, 4–ii, 3 is contrasted with the power of the people whose force is the Great God Himself in ii, 4–9."[81] Collins, however, points out that apocalypses frequently replicate the same sequence of events, offering Daniel 7 as an analogue:

> There [Dan 7] the sequence of tribulation followed by deliv-erance is fully laid out in Daniel's vision. Then the interpret-ation gives a brief summary of the same sequence in other terms (vv. 17–18) and finally the tribulation and deliverance are reviewed again, with more emphasis on the fourth beast. The conferral of the kingdom is repeated three times: first it is given to the "one like a son of man," then to the holy ones of the Most High, finally to the people of the holy ones of the Most High.[82]

Based on this Danielic analogy, he concludes, "[t]he description of the conflict between the peoples in column 2 is redundant, but such redundancy is a feature of apocalyptic style," and, therefore, "[t]he fact that the 'Son of God' appears before the definitive rise

---

[79] Text in Puech, "Apocryphe," 173.   [80] Steudel, "Eternal Reign," 514.
[81] Ibid., 515–516.
[82] Collins, *Scepter*, 177. In addition, Tucker Ferda has recently argued that the dream-interpretation sequences in Dan 2 and 4 problematize the notion that 4Q246 advances in a linear temporal sequence ("Naming the Messiah: A Contribution to the 4Q246 'Son of God' Debate, *DSD* 21 [2014], 158–163).

of the people of God does not necessarily mean that he is a negative figure."[83]

The advantage of Collins's solution is that his analogy derives from the writer's primary source text, Daniel 7.[84] The lexical and thematic similarities between Daniel 7 and 4Q246 are remarkable: (1) "service" (שמש) rendered to God (אלף אלפים ישמשונה, Dan 7:10; וכלא ישמשין, 4Q246 1:8);[85] (2) the description of the fourth beast/kingdom "trampling" (דוש) the earth (ותדושנה ותאבל כל־ארעא; Dan 7:23; ימלכון על ארעא וכלא ידשין, 4Q246 2:2–3); (3) the phrases "their kingdom shall be an eternal kingdom" (מלכותה מלכות עלם; Dan 7:27; 4Q246 2:5) and "their rule shall be an eternal rule" (שלטנה שלטן עלם; Dan 7:14; 4Q246 2:9). Tucker Ferda has recently made an additional observation about these linguistic parallels hitherto unrecognized. He notes that in parallels 2 and 3 listed the situation in 4Q246 corresponds to the situation in Daniel 7 – thus "trample" occurs in the description of a negative period (cf. Dan 7:23), while "his/its kingdom is an eternal kingdom" (cf. Dan 7:27) and "his/its dominion is an eternal dominion" (cf. Dan 7:14) occur in the description of a positive period. Ferda thus postulates, "[i]t is most likely, then, that 'all will serve him' in i 8 is also positive, and thus part of the positive presentation of the named 'son' in the next line."[86]

While I am persuaded that Collins offers the best interpretation of the text as we have it, the fragmentary nature of 4Q246 suggests dogmatism of any sort would be unwise. Fortunately, the point I wish to make is at the linguistic level and is not contingent on our capacity to disambiguate the identity of the son-of-God figure. As is widely recognized, the Lukan infancy narrative offers the closest linguistic parallel to the text of 4Q246:[87]

---

[83] Collins, *Scepter*, 177.

[84] Extensive parallels to Daniel are noted by Puech ("Apocryphe," 170–184).

[85] ישמשונה, "they served," in Dan 7:10 is a scriptural *hapax legomenon*. Ferda notes that "[t]he term [שמש] also appears in 4Q530 ii 17, which quotes Dan 7:10" ("Naming the Messiah," 163 n. 55).

[86] Ferda, "Naming the Messiah," 163. The first verb in 2:1 יתאמר is a t-stem verb (cf. יתאמר and יתכנה in 1:9) and so may be translated passively, thus "he will be called 'son of God,'" or reflexively, thus "he will call himself 'son of God;'" cf. Takamitsu Muraoka, *A Grammar of Qumran Aramaic*, ANESSup 38 (Leuven: Peeters, 2011), 171. Most interpreters now agree that יתאמר should be rendered passively, in this instance.

[87] Fitzmyer, *A Wandering Aramean*, 105–106; Collins, *Scepter*, 173. Segal's argument against the majority view is unconvincing ("Who Is the 'Son of God,'" 305). What he shows is that there does not need to be a literary (or any other sort of direct) relationship between 4Q246 and Luke 1:32–33. But this hardly tells against the

4Q246 1:9–2:1, 9	Luke 1:32–35
he will be called great	he will be great
and they will call him son of the Most High	and will be called son of the Most High
he will be called son of God	he will be called son of God
its/their kingdom will be an eternal kingdom	and of his kingdom there will be no end

Given the strong possibility that Luke's text is dependent on some form of 2 Sam 7:12–14, it seems probable that the epithets son of God and son of the Most High in 4Q246 reflect similar language about the Davidic monarch.[88] Whether the writer of 4Q246 used this language to depict a positive or a negative figure will likely remain uncertain.[89] That he used it at all, however, is an important linguistic development in its own right, since it illustrates how natural it would be for an author of the late Second Temple period to transmit scriptural idioms about the Davidic king – i.e., "he shall be my son" (2 Sam 7:14); "you are my son" (Ps 2:7) – as titles befitting a monarch, whether upright or degenerate, human or angelic.

What is peculiar about early Christian literature is not the fact that these authors refer to Jesus as (the) son of God but the frequency with which and variety of ways in which they do so. Fitzmyer is undoubtedly correct that early Christian use of divine sonship language is idiosyncratic when compared to Jewish contemporaries. This in no way, though, negates the reality that *when* Jewish and Christian authors wanted to characterize their messiahs using divine sonship language, the pool of linguistic resources they had at their

likelihood that these striking linguistic similarities are the result of both writers reflecting on common scriptural traditions.

[88] I agree with Collins (*Scepter*, 236) that the language in 4Q246 "had a clear scriptural basis in 2 Samuel 7 and Psalm 2." On Luke's dependence on 2 Sam 7, see Raymond E. Brown, *The Birth of the Messiah: A Commentary on the Infancy Narratives in the Gospels of Matthew and Luke* (London: Chapman, 1993), 310.

[89] George Brooke thinks the dating of 4Q246 may provide a clue, since the text was "being copied at a time when several compositions are implying an increased interest in the expectation of an eschatological king, specifically a Davidic figure (4Q161; 4Q174; 4Q252; 4Q285)" ("Kingship and Messianism in the Dead Sea Scrolls," in *King and Messiah in Israel and the Ancient Near East: Proceedings from the Oxford Old Testament Seminar*, ed. John Day, LHBOTS 270 [Sheffield: Sheffield Academic Press, 1998], 447). That is, the preservation of this presectarian text may be due, in part, to an early tradent's perception that this so-called "son of God" was the coming branch of David.

disposal was quite small (i.e., 2 Sam 7:14; Pss 2, 89, 109:3 LXX). Thus, when we shift our point of inquiry from a *religionsgeschichtlich* question, can we trace the development of ideas from "Judaism" into early "Christianity?" to a sociolinguistic one, would competent language users understand what an author meant if he designated a messiah (the) son of God?, the answer seems clear: they would.

At this point, one runs head on into another objection, traditionally posed by conservative scholars still battling to exercise the demons of Reimarus – namely, what if Mark's son-of-God language means more than "mundane messiah"? The answer, it seems to me, is that it probably does but that this should not detract from its messianic connotations. Paul's letters offer a case in point. The apostle clearly espouses a "high" Christology, including the belief that Jesus was a preexistent being sent by God the father (cf. Rom 8:3; 1 Cor 8:6; Gal 4:4; Phil 2:6–8; Col 1:16).[90] And yet, as Larry Hurtado observes,

> if we make an inductive analysis of Paul's references to Jesus as God's Son, it becomes clear (1) that the background lies in biblical and Jewish traditions, and (2) that in Paul's usage Jesus' divine sonship does not function as a way of expressing his divinity or of justifying worship of him, but instead primarily expresses Jesus' unique standing and intimate favor with God, and God's direct involvement in Jesus' redemptive work. To be sure, in the beliefs and devotional practice reflected in Paul's letters the glorified Christ holds a status that connotes a participation in divinity. But, contra Bousset and Bultmann, in Paul the christological category of sonship was not the principal way of expressing this.[91]

---

[90] See Larry W. Hurtado, *Lord Jesus Christ: Devotion to Jesus in Earliest Christianity* (Grand Rapids, MI: Eerdmans, 2003), 118–126; Richard Bauckham, *Jesus and the God of Israel: God Crucified and Other Studies on the New Testament's Christology of Divine Identity* (Grand Rapids, MI: Eerdmans, 2008), 26–30, 41–45. As far as I can tell, James D. G. Dunn now stands virtually on an island in arguing that Paul did not have a concept of "real" or "personal" preexistence (*Christology in the Making: A New Testament Inquiry into the Origins of the Doctrine of the Incarnation*, 2nd edn. [Grand Rapids, MI: Eerdmans, 1989]).

[91] Hurtado, *Lord Jesus Christ*, 104; see also Yarbro Collins and Collins, *King and Messiah*, 101–122. Unfortunately, Hurtado's reading of Mark is far less nuanced than his reading of Paul. The following summary statement is especially problematic: "In the 'discourse world' of the canonical Gospels, this emphatic way of referring to Jesus as human functions along with the clear assertion of Jesus' transcendent significance, even his 'intrinsic divinity.' This latter emphasis is what seems to be included in the

To be sure, "the scope and basis of Jesus' sonship are distinguishable from that of the Davidic kings and Jewish messianic figures ... But in all these Pauline passages we have motifs, imagery, and terms from Jewish royal-messianic traditions adapted to express boldly beliefs about Jesus' exalted place in God's purposes."[92] I see no reason why Hurtado's comments about divine sonship in Paul could not mutatis mutandis apply to the language we encounter in Mark.

Even a cursory look at the Second Gospel suggests that the evangelist retains messianic nuance in the ways he uses "son of God." The most notable is the close relationship the narrative charts between the christological title son of God and the suggestion that Jesus of Nazareth is the anointed son of Psalm 2 (cf. 1:9–11).[93] The relationship between messiah and son of God also comes to the fore at Jesus's trial before the Sanhedrin, when the high priest's question casts ὁ χριστός and ὁ υἱὸς τοῦ εὐλογητοῦ in "restrictive apposition," whereby the epithet "son of the Blessed One" qualifies what the high priest intends by "messiah" (Mark 14:61).[94] The audience encounters a second appositional construction a chapter later, in the crucifixion account, when this same group of leaders taunts Jesus as "the messiah, the king of Israel [ὁ χριστὸς ὁ βασιλεὺς Ἰσραήλ]"

---

presentation of Jesus as God's 'Son,' which features prominently in all four canonical accounts. Surely, early readers of these accounts could not have avoided the pairing of these two related and contrasting ways of referring to Jesus in filial terms: as 'the son of man' and God's 'Son.' The one designates Jesus operating in the human/historical sphere, and the other discloses the higher significance of who this human figure really is. This dynamic relationship of these two filial categories seems to be operative in Mark and in all the other canonical Gospels as well" (306). This type of language flattens the various ways in which divine sonship language functions in the Synoptic Gospels and is rightly critiqued by Peppard (*Son of God*, 22).

[92] Hurtado, *Lord Jesus Christ*, 105.

[93] The demonic utterance σὺ εἶ ὁ υἱὸς τοῦ θεοῦ, "you are the son of God," in Mark 3:11, replicates the syntax of a typical messianic recognition formula: "X is the messiah." Note Luke's redaction of Mark: "Demons also came out of many, shouting, 'You are the son of God [σὺ εἶ ὁ υἱὸς τοῦ θεοῦ]!' But he rebuked them and would not allow them to speak, because they knew that he was the messiah [ὅτι ᾔδεισαν τὸν χριστὸν αὐτὸν εἶναι]" (Luke 4:41; cf. Acts 9:20, 22).

[94] Joel Marcus, "Mark 14:61: 'Are You the Messiah-Son-of-God?" *NovT* 31 (1989): 125–141. *Pace* Marcus, however, the high priest's reaction in Mark is not to Jesus's answer to the question – e.g., "Yes, I am, the messiah, the son of the Blessed One" – but to what he adds to his affirmation – "and 'you will see the son of man seated at the right hand of the Power' and 'coming with the clouds of heaven'." The high priest's verdict forms an inclusio with the charge of "blasphemy" at the opening of the first controversy cycle (Mark 2:7) when, again, Jesus made a claim about his authority qua son of man (Mark 2:5, 10).

(Mark 15:32).[95] In both instances, Jesus's opponents qualify "messiah," ὁ χριστός, with language suggestive of a Davidic king.

On balance, then, Horsley would appear to be doubly mistaken: not only is there solid evidence that early Jewish authors used scripturally derived divine sonship language to speak about their messiahs, but it also seems Mark gladly followed suit. Once this point is established, it becomes more difficult to drive a wedge between divine and Davidic sonship, as Markan interpreters are often wont to do. Rather, the evidence suggests that divine sonship language retains its scriptural rootedness throughout Mark's Gospel.

2.4.4.2 Son of David

Although most interpret the Markan epithet "son of David" as a straightforward messianic designation, a significant minority has pushed back, arguing instead that it points away from messianism toward the characterization of Jesus as a Solomonic exorcist.[96] Two reasons likely drive this decision. First, the most influential studies on son-of-David language begin with its emergence as a messianic title in the first century BCE (cf. Pss. Sol. 17), without considering its usage in the Jewish scriptures.[97] This approach shapes the data such that, as Dennis Duling observes, "if one gathers up the *non*-synoptic references to the Davidic descent, what one immediately has are metaphorical, non-titular references derived from the promise tradition. Thus, apart from the synoptic Son of David sayings, the

---

[95] ὁ βασιλεὺς Ἰσραήλ is a common expression in 1–4 Kgdms (e.g., 1 Kgdms 15:17, 26, 35; 24:15; 29:3; 2 Kgdms 5:3, 17; 12:7; 3 Kgdms 20:4, 7, 11; 21:21–22; 4 Kgdms 3:9–13; cf. Pss. Sol. 17:42).

[96] See esp. Dennis C. Duling, "Solomon, Exorcism, and the Son of David," *HTR* 68 (1975): 235–252; Bruce D. Chilton, "Jesus *ben David*: Reflection on the Davidssohnfrage," *JSNT* 14 (1982): 88–112; James H. Charlesworth, "The Son of David: Solomon and Jesus (Mark 10.47)," in *The New Testament and Hellenistic Judaism*, eds. Peder Borgen and Søren Giversen (Peabody, MA: Hendrickson, 1995), 72–87; Ahearne-Kroll, *Psalms of Lament*, 138–144.

[97] Foundational in this regard are Wrede, *Vorträge*; Burger, *Jesus als Davidssohn*; Duling, "Promises to David;" and Eduard Lohse, "υἱὸς Δαυίδ," in volume 8 of *Theological Dictionary of the New Testament*, eds. Gerhard Kittle and Gerhard Friedrich, trans. Geoffrey W. Bromiley (Grand Rapids, MI: Eerdmans, 1972), 478–488. Anthony Le Donne is exactly right when he notes that "The few studies that have devoted attention to the pre-messianic development of the phrase [son of David] have tended to bracket these results when the discussion shifts to messianic texts. This tendency has painted the title as a tradition-historical conundrum that emerged in the first century rootless and without precedent" (*The Historiographical Jesus: Memory, Typology, and the Son of David* [Waco, TX: Baylor University Press, 2009], 95).

phenomena of early Christianity look very much like the [Jewish] phenomena discussed so far."[98] Once one is convinced that the title son of David is sui generis, the decision to locate its background in non-messianic traditions seems but a short, logical step. This inference gains additional credence from a second observation: son-of-David language in the Synoptic Gospel tends to occur in the context of healings and exorcisms (cf. Mark 10:46–52 pars.; Matt 9:27–31; 12:22–32; 15:21–28), activities that do not align with what we might traditionally expect of a messiah but do show affinity with traditions about David and Solomon as exorcists endowed with the spirit of YHWH.[99]

There is a real danger, however, in treating the categories of "messiah" and "exorcist-healer" as mutually exclusive, since many of the exorcistic traditions about David and Solomon are inspired by sources that connect royal anointing and charismatic activity.[100] According to the Deuteronomistic historian, the very moment at which the young man was anointed king was also the point at which he received the spirit of YHWH, the source of his exorcistic power (cf. 1 Sam 16:14–23). In his magisterial account of Israel's history, Liber Antitquitatum Biblicarum (LAB), the first-century writer known as Pseudo-Philo preserves this link between royal office and charismatic power when he introduces the Lord's anointed as both an adroit exorcist and the progenitor of the royal line (cf. LAB 60).[101] In this instance, the writer traffics the exorcistic power of the Lord's messiah – from David to David's son, Solomon – using language reflective of the Davidic promise tradition (LAB 61:3; cf. 2 Sam 7:12).

Thus, it may be no accident that Psalms of Solomon 17, often identified as the lone first-century antecedent to son-of David language in the Synoptic Gospels, depicts a messiah whose prowess as a military warrior, curator of cultic purity, and instructor of heavenly

---

[98] Duling, "Promises to David," 68, his emphasis.

[99] See Klaus Berger, "Die königlichen Messiastraditionen des Neuen Testaments," *NTS* 20 (1974): 1–44; Duling, "Solomon."

[100] So rightly Le Donne, *Historiographical Jesus*, 145; see also William Horbury, *Jewish Messianism and the Cult of Christ* (London: SCM, 1998), 32; Yarbro Collins, *Mark*, 66–67; Marcus, *Mark 8–16*, 1119–1120, a correction to his earlier position in *Way*, 151–152; Novenson, *Grammar of Messianism*, 104–113.

[101] According to Josephus, the moment David received the "divine spirit" he began to prophesy (καὶ ὁ μὲν προφητεύειν ἤρξατο τοῦ θείου πνεύματος εἰς αὐτὸν μετοικισαμένου; *Ant.* 6.166 [LCL]) – a logical inference if one is familiar with 2 Sam 23:2 (cf. 11QPˢa 27:11 1 Sam 10:1–13).

wisdom is the result of his receiving the Lord's holy spirit. The psalmist appears to have derived the expression υἱὸς Δαυίδ from the prophet Jeremiah's iteration of the Davidic promise tradition: "See, Lord, and raise up for them their king, the son of David, to rule over your servant Israel" (cf. Jer 30:9 MT [LXX 37:9]).[102] It also seems probable that the appellation reflects the patronym בן־דויד, a popular locution of the Chronicler (cf. 1 Chr 29:22; 2 Chr 1:1; 11:18; 13:6; 30:26; 35:3).[103] Thus, while the occurrence of υἱὸς Δαυίδ in early messiah texts is unattested prior to Psalms of Solomon 17, the language itself is hardly sui generis. Rather, it always denotes a king from the line of David – from a historic perspective, Solomon (cf. 4Q389 frags. 11–13), from a future perspective, the messiah son of David.

Attendance to the function of son-of-David language in antiquity sheds significant light on the Gospel of Mark, a document that locates "son of David" within an intratextual network of spirit anointing, exorcisms, and healings. In Chapters 4 and 5, I take up the suggestion that the demon's identification of Jesus as "the holy one of God" (Mark 1:24) and Bartimaeus's identification of the famed teacher as "son of David" (10:47–48) are illuminated by the events that opened David's career in 1 Samuel 16–17.

2.5   Conclusion

Since at least the time of Wrede, scholars have assumed that Mark's position on the *Davidssohnfrage* can be assessed by isolating pericopae with the name (son of) David. Yet this assumption is only valid if the evangelist's linguistic community agreed that the only way to characterize a Davidic messiah is to use the name David, a position

---

[102] Atkinson, *Intertextual Study*, 330, 346. I cite here the English translation of Robert B. Wright, "Psalms of Solomon [First Century B.C.]," *OTP* 2: 639–670, here 667; the Greek text may be found in Robert B. Wright, *The Psalms of Solomon: A Critical Edition of the Greek Text*, Jewish and Christian Texts in Contexts and Related Studies 1 (London: T&T Clark, 2007), 187. Recently, however, Nathan Johnson has made a compelling case that παῖδά σου should be taken as modifying υἱὸν Δαυίδ, thus "so that the son of David might rule over Israel as a servant" ("Rendering David a Servant in *Psalm of Solomon* 17.21," *JSP* 26 [2017]: 235–250).

[103] In his reworking of the oracle in 2 Sam 7, the Chronicler renders זרעך, "your seed," with מבניך, "one of your sons" (1 Chr 17:11). Similar lexical connections between David's "son" and "seed" can be found elsewhere in the Jewish scriptures (e.g., Jer 33:21–22). Thus, messiah son of David becomes a stock phrase in rabbinic literature (cf. b. Meg. 17b; B. Ḥag. 16a; b. Yebam. 62a; b Ketub. 112b; b. Saḥn. 38a; Gen. Rab. 97; Exod. Rab. 25.12).

that no longer seems sustainable. Rather, we have seen that part and parcel of the idiolect of messiah language is its sustenance of *multiple* conventions for characterizing messiahs, because its users had recourse to the same linguistic pool and operate from the same encyclopedic framework. Mark's language about Jesus has its particular fit within this theater of discourse: the evangelist draws from a variety of resources, including Davidic scriptural traditions and titles, to articulate the significance of his Christ.

None of the observations I have made in this chapter about Mark's use of the Jewish scriptures is particularly novel, and indeed this is precisely the point. Any attempt at answering the question, is Mark's Christ David's son? and, by extension, how can Mark's Christ be David's son?, constructs its edifice on a foundation of sand if it ignores the cumulative weight of the evangelist's messiah language. At this point, someone may wish to object that I am merely confusing the presence of certain material in the narrative with the position of the implied author.[104] The value of this sort of an exercise, though, is that it brings to light the sheer volume of material the implied author must reject in order to maintain a negative assessment of the *Davidssohnfrage*. But, indeed, the proof is always in the exegesis, the degree to which an interpretation produces a satisfying reading of the text. Let us then turn to the Gospel of Mark.

---

[104] See, e.g., Malbon, *Mark's Jesus*, 119.

3

CHRISTENING JESUS OF NAZARETH

Semantic disclosures have a double role: they *blow up*
certain properties (making them textually relevant or pertinent) and *narcotize* some others
– Umberto Eco, *The Role of the Reader*, 22, his emphasis

Videte iunctiones significationesque verborum. Non dixit:
«Venit Christus»; non dixit: «Venit Filius Dei», sed: «*Venit
Iesus*». Dicat aliquis: «Quare non dixit: 'Christus'?» Secun-
dum carnem loquor: ceterum Deus semper sanctus est, nec
sanctificationem indigent, sed iam de carne Christi loquimur.
Nondum fuerat baptizatus et ab Spiritu sancto unctus fuerat
– Jerome, *Tractatus in Evangelium Marci*,
1C.2–8, original emphasis

In the previous chapter, I examined the ways in which ancient authors
drew upon their scriptural resources to construct their messiahs.
I observed, among other things, that claims about a messiah's ancestry
are pieces of larger game board, moving in accordance with its particular set of rules. The moment one sets the evangelist's language
about his Christ within this sociolinguistic field, it becomes apparent
why it is inappropriate to demand an answer to his *Davidssohnfrage* by
isolating pericopae with the name David. An alternative approach is
required, one that accounts for Mark's messiah language as a "creatively biblical linguistic acts" (Novenson), whereby the evangelist
selectively draws on frames in his encyclopedia, "blowing up" or
"actualizing" certain properties and "narcotizing" others (Eco).
   Accordingly, this chapter begins the process of discerning how
Mark constructs his Christ.[1] While scholars debate issues of

---

[1] For my discussion of how narratives construct identity, refer back to Section 1.2.3.

structure, grammar, and points of interpretation, all would agree that the prologue (1:1–13/15) equips the audience with the requisite spectacles for perceiving Jesus's identity.[2] Mark's prologue contructs a symbolic world in which God's promises to Israel are brought to fruition through the advent of Jesus of Nazareth, a spirit-anointed messiah come to liberate God's people from exilic bondage. Although the evangelist shows no interest, at least at this point in the narrative, in his messiah's ancestral lineage, an essential component of his rhetorical agenda is the suggestion that this Χριστός is a discernably Davidic figure.

3.1 Scripting the Advent of Jesus Christ: The Beginning of the Gospel According to Mark

The Gospel's incipit, "the beginning of the good news of Jesus Christ [son of God] [Ἀρχὴ τοῦ εὐαγγελίου Ἰησοῦ Χριστοῦ (υἱοῦ θεοῦ)]," dictates that the identity of Jesus of Nazareth cannot be properly apprehended apart from the honorific Χριστός, "Christ/messiah." Similar to the anarthrous Χριστός in the Pauline epistles, Χριστοῦ in Mark 1:1 fits the onomastic category of the honorific, as described by Novenson,

> An honorific was taken by or bestowed on its bearer, usually in connection with military exploits or accession to power, not given at birth. It was formally a common noun or adjective (e.g., hammer, star, savior, manifest, august, anointed), not a proper noun. In actual use, it could occur in combination with the bearer's proper name or stand in for the proper name. It was not a unique Semitic-language convention but one shared among ancient Mediterranean cultures and even translated from one language to another.[3]

---

[2] Scholars remain divided over whether the prologue ends at v. 13 (e.g., Frank J. Matera, "The Prologue as the Interpretative Key to Mark's Gospel," *JSNT* 34 [1988]: 3–20; Mary Ann Tolbert, *Sowing the Gospel: Mark's World in Literary-Historical Perspective* [Minneapolis, MN: Fortress, 1989], 108–113), or extends to v. 15 (e.g., Leander Keck, "The Introduction to Mark's Gospel," *NTS* 12 [1966]: 352–370; M. Eugene Boring, "Mark 1:1–15 and the Beginning of the gospel," *Semeia* 52 [1990]: 43–81). I tend to agree with Joanna Dewey (*Oral Ethos*, 68) that vv. 14–15 are best handled as "transitional verses."

[3] Novenson, *Christ among the Messiahs*, 95, full discussion at 64–97. Throughout the narrative Mark uses ὁ χριστός (8:29; 12:35; 13:21; 14:61; 15:32), except in 9:41: "For I tell you, whoever gives you a cup of water to drink in the name, that is, *because you belong to Christ* [ὅτι Χριστοῦ ἐστε], truly I tell you that that person will surely not lose his/her reward." The Markan Christ also speaks of ψευδόχριστοι, "false messiahs" (13:22), as those "who will come *in my name* [ἐπὶ τῷ ὀνόματί μου],

To label Jesus "Christ" suggests the bestowal of the honorific as the result of his being anointed, a symbolic gesture of one's accession to power. As we will soon see, the narrative progression of the prologue invites the inference that this man from Nazereth is Χριστός precisely because God christened him with the holy spirit at his baptism in the river Jordan (cf. Mark 1:9–11).

The titular son of God is more complex, due in large measure to the question of whether it is "original" to 1:1.[4] The criterion of transcriptional probability would seem to weigh heavily in favor of the shorter reading (lacking υἱοῦ θεοῦ), since one does not anticipate a scribe to omit the *nomina sacra* at the outset of the Gospel but could conceive of a scenario in which a scribe would be motivated to append it.[5] There are, however, numerous examples of scribal omission of *nomina sacra* at the outset of early Christian documents, including the omission of the *nomen sacrum* Χριστοῦ (χ̄ῡ) at Mark 1:1 (28*).[6] Moreover, there is no concrete evidence that ancient readers perceived the shorter reading of Mark 1:1 to be problematic,

claiming, 'I am he [ἐγώ εἰμι]'" (13:6) – likely, "I am (the) messiah" (see Yarbro Collins, *Mark*, 603–604).

[4] See Peter Head, "A Text-Critical Study of Mark 1.1: 'The Beginning of the Gospel of Jesus Christ,'" *NTS* 37 (1991): 621–629; Bart D. Ehrman, *The Orthodox Corruption of Scripture: The Effects of Early Christological Controversies on the Text of the New Testament* (Oxford: Oxford University Press, 1993); Adela Yarbro Collins, "Establishing the Text: Mark 1:1," in *Texts and Contexts: The Function of Biblical Texts in Their Textual and Situational Contexts*, eds. Tord Fornberg and David Hellholm (Oslo: Scandinavian University Press, 1995), 111–127; Tommy Wasserman, "'The Son of God' Was in the Beginning (Mark 1:1)," *JTS* 62 (2011): 20–50; Max Botner, "The Role of Transcriptional Probability in the Text-Critical Debate on Mark 1:1," *CBQ* 77 (2015): 467–480. J. K. Elliot ("Mark 1.1–3 – A Latter Addition to the Gospel?" NTS 46 [2000]: 584–588) and N. Clayton Croy (*The Mutilation of Mark's Gospel* [Nashville, TN: Abingdon, 2003], 115–124) argue that v. 1 is a later addition. The critical editions of Greek New Testament either place υἱοῦ θεοῦ in the text in brackets (NA[28] and UBS[5]), or excise it altogether (SBLGNT). The UBS[5] maintains the "C" rating of former editions. For a brief discussion of the committee's decision, see Bruce M. Metzger, *A Textual Commentary on the Greek New Testament*, 2nd edn. (Stuttgart: Deutsche Bibelsgesellschaft, 1994), 62.

[5] As summarized in Botner, "Role," 469–470.

[6] See Wasserman, "'The Son of God,'" 44–50. Elsewhere, Wasserman has shown that, contrary to what we might initially anticipate, the *pregenealogical coherence* of the longer reading is in fact significantly stronger than that of the shorter (Tommy Wasserman and Peter J. Gurry, *A New Approach to Textual Criticism: An Introduction to the Coherence-Based Genealogical Method*, RBS 80 [Atlanta: SBL, 2017], 43–50). He thus concludes, "Paradoxically, then, these witnesses to the shorter reading are in fact witnesses against it, considering transcriptional probability based on pregenealogical evidence" (50). That is to say, the pregenealogical coherence of the shorter reading attests to the likelihood of multiple scribal omissions of the *nomina sacra* in the transmission of Mark 1:1.

theologically or otherwise.[7] When one accounts for additional factors such as external evidence, the longer reading has just as much, if not more, a claim to the "original" text.[8] Given the distinct possibility that the longer reading is original and, perhaps more importantly, that most modern interpreters assume this to be the case, it seems expedient to offer here a brief interpretation. At bare minimum, the longer reading implies that this Χριστός is a royal figure. Perhaps the best analogue we have from antiquity is the collocation *Caesar Augustus Divi filius*/Καῖσαρ Σέβαστος Θεοῦ υἱός, in which the honorific *Augustus* is paired with the royal titulus *divi filius*, "son of God."[9] As we saw in the previous chapter, the evangelist's linguistic community had an established practice of using scripturally derived divine sonship language to talk about its royal messiahs. The probability that υἱὸς θεοῦ entails something similar in Mark 1:1 is supported by the presence of an allusion to Ps 2:7 at Jesus's baptism in 1:11, a text in which Israel's God addresses his messiah as υἱός μου, "my son."

This takes place in a story that is already in medias res. The ἀρχή τοῦ εὐαγγελίου – i.e., the "beginning" and "origin" of the gospel – (1:1) is prefigured in the Jewish scriptures – "as it is written in Isaiah the prophet" (1:2)[10] – an important indication of the kind of reading

---

[7] *Pace* Ehrman, *Orthodox Corruption*, 72–75; see Botner, "Role," 473–480.

[8] So rightly Wasserman, "'The Son of God.'"

[9] Mine is strictly a linguistic observation, though one may detect resonances with imperial Roman propaganda in Mark 1:1; see Craig A. Evans "The Beginning of the Good News and the Fulfillment of Scripture in the Gospel of Mark," in *Hearing the Old Testament in the New Testament*, ed. Stanley E. Porter (Grand Rapids, MI: Eerdmans, 2006), 83–103. As Peppard (*Son of God*) has shown, the titular *divi filius* certainly belongs to the broader theatre of discourse in which Mark would have been heard.

[10] Robert Guelich argues that v. 1 is grammatically attached to the following scripture citation in vv. 2–3, since the citation formula καθὼς γέγραπται never begins a new sentence in the NT or LXX ("'The beginning of the gospel': Mark 1:1–15," *BR* 27 [1982]: 5–15). Hatina (*In Search*, 141–142) points to 1 Cor 2:9 as a potential breach of Guelich's "rule," but I am not persuaded this warrants his conclusion that "Mark appears to assert that, just as the Scriptures foretold of a voice crying in the wilderness, so the Baptist came preaching." This is certainly part of what Mark asserts, but it seems to me that the driving revelation of the prologue is the disclosure of a conversation between God and his Christ (Max Botner, "Prophetic Script and Dramatic Enactment in Mark's Prologue," *BBR* 26 [2016]: 369–380). My proposal is that vv. 2–3 function as a prophetic "script" for the remainder of the prologue. Irenaeus's comment is instructive here: "Truly Mark, *by the prophetic spirit which descends upon people from above* [ἀπὸ τοῦ προφητικοῦ Πνεύματος, τοῦ ἐξ ὕψους ἐπιόντος τοῖς ἀνθρώποις], began by saying, 'The beginning of the Gospel, just as it has been written in Isaiah, the prophet ['Αρχὴ τοῦ εὐαγγελίου, ὡς γέγραπται ἐν Ἡσαΐᾳ τῷ προφήτῃ]'" (*Haer.* 3.11.8;

competence the Markan narrative encodes.[11] Indeed, how else is the audience supposed to grasp the central message of the prologue, that the eschatological turning point of Israel's story is the beginning of Jesus's?

3.2   Messianic Might: Presaging the Stronger One

The Baptist's declaration, "one who is greater (or stronger) than me comes after me [ἔρχεται ὁ ἰσχυρότερός μου ὀπίσω μου]," gestures, albeit subtly, to a Davidic frame. Whatever one concludes about what the historical John could have intended by this prophecy, Mark leaves little to the imagination: ὁ ἰσχυρότερος, "the stronger one," is Χριστός and so, by definition, John's prophecy *in Mark* is about a coming messiah.[12] This is reinforced at the syntactical level. The collocation of a verb of "coming" (ἔρχεται) plus a temporal marker (ὀπίσω μου)[13] in the Baptist's prophecy in 1:7, which in turn is mirrored by the collocation of a temporal marker (ἐν ἐκείναις ταῖς ἡμέραις) plus a verb of "coming" (ἦλθεν) at Jesus's entry in 1:9, is one of the most common ways to introduce a messiah (cf. 1QS 9:11; CD 19:10–11; 4Q252 5:3; 4 Ezra 12:32).[14] The Markan account of Jesus's "triumphal entry" (cf. 11:1–11) may suggest the evangelist

---

Adelin Rousseau and Louis Doutreleau, eds., *Irénée de Lyon Contre les Hérésies: Livre III*, 2 vols., SC 210 and 211 [Paris: Cerf, 1974], 2: 166).

[11] Cf. Eco, *Role*, 7. One might say here that Mark evinces an "intertextual disposition" towards the Jewish scriptures (Alkier, *Neues Testament*, 164–165).

[12] Early Christian traditions are emphatic that the Baptist acts as the messianic forerunner (cf. Mark 1:4–8; Matt 3:1–17; Luke 3:1–21; John 1:20–27; 1 Clem 17:1). Note, in particular, the Baptist's question in the tradition shared by Matthew and Luke: "Are you *the one who is to come* [ὁ ἐρχόμενος], or should we wait for another?" (Matt 11:3; Luke 7:19); see Robert L. Webb, *John the Baptizer and Prophet: A Socio-Historical Study*, JSNTSup 62 [Sheffield: JSOT Press, 1991], 286–288). Whether the notion of Elijah as forerunner to the messiah is "pre-Christian" is disputable, though hardly implausible (cf. Justin, *Dial.* 8.4; Pesiq. Rab. 43; Tg. Ps.-J. Deut 30:4); see the debate in M. M. Faierstein, "Why Do the Scribes Say That Elijah Must Come First?" *JBL* 100 (1981): 75–86; Dale C. Allison, "Elijah Must Come First," *JBL* 103 (1984): 256–258; Joseph Fitzmyer, "More about Elijah Coming First," *JBL* 104 (1985): 295–296; Marcus, *Way*, 94–110.

[13] ὀπίσω usually functions as a spatial term, "behind," but, in this instance, it is better taken as a temporal marker (BDAG, 716 2b).

[14] See Webb, *John the Baptizer*, 233 n. 58; Novenson, *Christ among the Messiahs*, 54–55. Simon Gathercole's objection that verbs of "coming" are not messianic *termini technici* is well taken (*The Pre-Existent Son: Recovering the Christologies of Matthew, Mark, and Luke* [Grand Rapids, MI: Eerdmans, 2006], 111–112). In this particular instance, however, the collocation ἐρχέσθαι + ὁ ἰσχυρότερος + temporal marker fits a syntactical pattern wherein "come" signifies the advent of a messiah.

read certain scriptures about a "coming" (בּוֹא/ἐρχέσθαι) king as anticipating the messiah's entrance into the holy city (cf. Gen 49:10; Zech 9:9; Ps 118 [117 LXX]:26). The language John the Baptist uses to describe Jesus may also be significant. As Adela Yarbro Collins notes, ὁ ἰσχυρότερος "could well have had connotations of the Davidic messiah as God's agent in the eschatological battle,"[15] since it evokes a strand of scriptural traditions that associate royal anointing, the receipt of YHWH's spirit, and military might (cf. 1 Sam 16:13; Pss 45:4, 7–8; 89:20–22; Isa 9:5; 11:1–2; Mic 5:4).[16] The function of the Markan epithet may be likened to what Eric Eve refers to as *traditional referentiality* – that is, the use of "a formula or theme to allude, not to another specific text, but to the way that formula or theme operates in the tradition as a whole."[17] So, for example, the description of Achilles as "swift-footed" in Homeric epic becomes a stock phrase, "because to those immersed in the tradition, the phrase 'swift-footed Achilles' evokes the character of the hero in all its fullness (through familiarity with the way in which the phrase is used throughout the tradition)."[18] Likewise, to those immersed in the Jewish scriptures, the description of an anointed figure as "strong" or "mighty in spirit" evokes stock features of the traditional agent through whom YHWH delivers his people. It is thus hardly surprising that divine strength becomes a desideratum both for future sons of David (cf. Pss. Sol. 17:37; Acts 10:38) and for non-Davidides who sought to legitimate their authority by displaying traits traditionally associated with the rulers of old (cf. 1 Macc 2:66).[19]

In Mark, Christ's role as ὁ ἰσχυρότερος is linked to his receipt of the holy spirit (1:9–11) for the purpose of liberating Israel from bondage

---

[15] Yarbro Collins, *Mark*, 64.

[16] The association between the Davidic line and YHWH's strength is well attested in early Jewish literature (cf. Sir 47:5; 1QM 11:1–6; 1Q28b 5:24, 28; 11QPs 28:13; Jub. 31:18; Pss. Sol. 17:22, 36–40; LAB 59–61).

[17] Eve, *Behind the Gospels*, 104.

[18] Ibid., 103; e.g., πόδας ὠκύς (*Il.* 1.58); ποδαρκής (*Il.* 1.121); ποδώκης (*Il.* 2.860); etc. (eds. Murray and Wyatt [LCL]).

[19] Jonathan A. Goldstein observes instances in which the author of 1 Maccabees re-routes Davidic promises to the Hasmonean line ("How the Authors of 1 and 2 Maccabees Treated the 'Messianic' Promises," in *Judaisms and Their Messiahs at the Turn of the Christian Era*, ed. Neusner et al. [Cambridge: Cambridge University Press, 1987]). Note also Josephus's description of a certain Athronges, a revolutionary shepherd-turned-mighty warrior (*J. W.* 2.60–65; *Ant.* 17.278–285).

to Satan (1:12–13).[20] This theme rises to a crescendo during the Beelzebul controversy (3:22–30), at which point Jesus claims to have the ability to deliver God's people from ὁ ἰσχυρός, "the strong man" (3:24–27).[21] While the metaphor of the strong man is playfully polyvalent,[22] one of the archetypal strong men of Jewish tradition is Goliath the Phillistine. The Tosefta Targum of 1 Sam 17:43, though later than our period, offers an enticing comparison to Mark's strong man imagery: "[Goliath says to David] Woe to you! because you are engaged in battle with *one who is stronger than you.*"[23] Like the Targum, David's defeat of Goliath is commemorated by early Jewish authors – not so much because YHWH (or the angel of YHWH) gave him the strength to overcome the giant, although this was certainly important, but because the young shepherd entrusted his life to YHWH. Thus, the author of the War Scroll petitions the God of Israel, "you delivered [Goliath] into the hands of David, your servant, for he trusted in your powerful name [כיא בטה בשמכה הגדול] and not in sword or spear" (1QM 11:2; cf. LAB 59–61). Perhaps there is a reason that the decisive moment at which the "strong man"

---

[20] Luke appears to have followed Mark on this point (cf. Luke 4:14; Acts 10:36–38). See Max Turner, *Power from on High: The Spirit in Israel's Restoration and Witness in Luke-Acts*, Journal of Pentecostal Theology Supplement Series 9 (Sheffield: Sheffield Academic Press, 1996), 207–211. See also Gene Davenport's astute observation about the son of David in Pss. Sol. 17: "The authority and power which rest in his descent are strictly the consequence of God's determination and promise, not the consequence of anything naturally inherent in David's family. From the standpoint of the things which the king is to achieve, therefore, there is only one basic characteristic – the empowering by God's Holy Spirit. The king's descent from David will be important as a sign of God's dependability, but the actual enactment of the significance of that dependability will lie in the actions made possible by the empowering" ("The 'Anointed of the Lord' in Psalms of Solomon 17," in *Ideal Figures in Ancient Judaism*, eds. George W. E. Nickelsburg and John J. Collins, SCS 12 [Chico, CA: Scholars Press, 1980], 82).

[21] On the intratextual and thematic connections between Mark 1:9–13 and 3:22–30, see Elizabeth E. Shively, *Apocalyptic Imagination in the Gospel of Mark: The Literary and Theological Role of Mark 3:22–30*, BZNW 189 (Berlin: De Gruyter, 2012), 47–48, 73–81.

[22] Watts (*Isaiah's New Exodus*, 147–148) may be correct that Mark's strong man metaphor evokes Isa 49:24–26 (cf. Pss. Sol. 5:3) and, perhaps, Isa 53:12 – both of which portray YHWH as the mighty one who plunders the strong man. Nonetheless, the point of the parable is that the *source* of Jesus's power is the *holy spirit* (cf. Mark 3:28–30), a connection that Mark's Christ shares with other messiahs from antiquity.

[23] I follow here the translation of C. T. R. Hayward, "The Aramaic Song of The Lamb (The Dialogue between David and Goliath: A New Translation and Introduction)," in *Old Testament Pseudepigrapha: More Noncanonical Scriptures*, volume 1, eds. Bauckham, Davila, and Panayotov [Grand Rapids, MI: Eerdmans, 2013]), 272–286, at 284, my emphasis.

is plundered in Mark is punctuated by Jesus's cry to his father in words once spoken by David (Mark 15:34, citing Ps 22:1; on which see 6.2).

3.3   Spirit, Power, Messiah: The Baptism of Jesus

If the first eight verses of the Gospel offer subtle hints and intimations about the identity of Mark's Christ, the evangelist's account of Jesus's baptism rends the curtain of mystery. The combination of the spirit's descent and the voice from heaven transforms this event into "a *disguised* royal anointing."[24] Like the kings of old, Mark's Jesus emerges from the waters as a messiah anointed with God's spirit to vanquish the enemy of God's people and to lead out the blind and the captives on the path of liberation, the way of the Lord.

3.3.1   Pneumatic Unction at the Eschaton

Mark presents Jesus "coming" (ἦλθεν) in direct response to John's claim that "the stronger one comes [ἔρχεται] after me." The geographical marker Ναζαρὲτ τῆς Γαλιλαίας whence he comes is significant. Throughout the Second Gospel, Jesus is identified with his *patris* to highlight the claim that the one whom God anointed and raised from the dead is none other than the man Jesus of Nazareth (cf. Mark 16:6).[25] Mark employs the Nazarene designation at pivotal

---

[24] Hays, *Echoes of Scripture in the Gospels*, 48, his emphasis.

[25] So rightly Kingsbury, *Christology*, 60–61. Contra Lührmann (*Markusevangelium*, 209) and Boring (*Mark*, 44, 256), Jesus's advent from Nazareth of Galilee does not necessarily militate against Davidic associations. As Meier ("From Elijah-Like Prophet," 54) correctly observes, "close connection between the Messiah of Davidic descent and birth in Bethlehem is not common in Jewish texts composed around the turn of the era." Moreover, Jesus's Nazarene identity appears to be an important aspect of a number of early traditions (cf. Acts 2:22; 3:6; 4:10; 6:14; 10:38; 22:8; 24:5; 26:9). Although Matthew's notorious (for some, ignominious) scripture citation, Ναζωραῖος κληθήσεται, "He will be called a Nazarene" (Matt 2:23), is obscure, Joseph Blenkinsopp argues convincingly that "the best candidate would appear to be Isa 11:1, which speaks of the 'shoot' (*nēṣer*) from Jesse's stock, in other words, the Davidic messiah" (*Opening the Sealed Book: Interpretations of the Book of Isaiah in Late Antiquity* [Grand Rapids, MI: Eerdmans, 2006], 156). This has now been argued in some detail by Nicholas G. Piotrowski (*Matthew's New David at the End of Exile: A Socio-Rhetorical Stud of Scriptural Quotations*, NovTSup 170 [Leiden: Brill, 2016], 150–172), though he probably overstates his case. That Jerome makes this connection (cf. *Comm. Isa.* 4.11.1–3) suggests, at the very least, that scripturally literate readers could recognize a wordplay between "Nazarene" and "shoot [נצר]" (of Jesse)."

junctures in the narrative to highlight important facets of Jesus's identity (cf. Mark 1:24; 10:47; 14:67; 16:6).[26] The tacit suggestion here is that Jesus has come to the Baptist to participate in the same baptism with which John baptized "all Israel" (cf. Mark 1:5).[27] As such, the narrative looks backward to the identification of the Christ with Israel in the opening scripture citation (Mark 1:2; cf. Exod 23:20) as well as forward to God's invasive act adumbrated by the prophet Isaiah, the rending of the heavens and the descent of the holy spirit (Isa 63:19 [LXX 64:1]).[28] According to this recitation of Israel's history, God's answer to the prophet's lament had long hung in abeyance: "The skies [had] not [opened], God [had] not come down or even [looked] down, and there [was] no answer to the complaint!"[29] Only when the spirit descended upon *this* man, Jesus of Nazareth, can one say that "[d]ie Zeit des Wartens auf den Geist ist zu Ende."[30] Mark thereby refracts God's promise to restore Israel through "the one man in whom that role of Israel's sonship is realized."[31]

---

[26] On the function of the Nazarene designation in the Markan narrative, see Edwin K. Broadhead, "Jesus the Nazarene: Narrative Strategy and Christological Imagery in the Gospel of Mark," *JSNT* 52 (1993): 3–18; Edwin K. Broadhead, *Naming Jesus: Titular Christology in the Gospel of Mark*, JSNTSup 175 (Sheffield: Sheffield Academic Press, 1999), 31–42.

[27] Along with other interpreters (e.g., Kingsbury, *Christology*, 59–60; Tolbert, *Sowing*, 113, 208, 246; Marcus, *Way*, 24; Hooker, *Gospel*, 37), I take the emphasis on "all" in 1:5 (πᾶσα ἡ Ἰουδαία χώρα καὶ οἱ Ἱεροσολυμῖται πάντες) as Mark's theological construct of repentant Israel awaiting its eschatological restoration.

[28] On the plausibility of an allusion to Isa 63:19 (64:1 LXX), see Robert H. Gundry, *The Use of the Old Testament in St. Matthew's Gospel, with Special Reference to the Messianic Hope*, NovTSup 18 (Leiden: Brill, 1967), 28–29; Marcus, *Way*, 49–50, 56–58; Watts, *Isaiah's New Exodus*, 102–108. Watts in particular redresses the objections to the allusion leveled by Lentzen-Deis (*Die Taufe Jesu*).

[29] Joseph A. Blenkinsopp, *Isaiah 56–66: A New Translation with Introduction and Commentary*, AB 19B (New York: Doubleday, 2003), 258.

[30] Joachim Gnilka, *Das Evangelium nach Markus*, 2 vols. in 1, EKKNT 2 (Neukirchen-Vluyn: Neukirchener, 1977–1978; repr., Neukirchen-Vluyn: Neukirchener, 2010), 1:52. There is long-standing debate over whether εἰς αὐτόν is best translated "upon him" (e.g., BDF 112, §207 [1]) or "into him" (e.g., Edward P. Dixon, "Descending Spirit and Descending Gods: A 'Greek' Interpretation of the Spirit's 'Descent As a Dove' in Mark 1:10," *JBL* 128 [2009]: 759–780). For a synopsis of the issues at stake, see Max Botner, "How Do the Seeds Land? A Note on ΕΙΣ ΑΥΤΟΝ in Mark 1:10," *JTS* 66 (2015): 547–552.

[31] Hooker, *Gospel*, 47. It may be significant that divine sonship is at the heart of Isa 63:7–64:12 (cf. Isa 63:16; 64:7[8]). Justin's *Dialogue* offers a potential hint as to how Isa 63:15–64:12 was received by early Christ followers. While engrossed in an argument with his interlocutor Trypho about the divine inheritance (*Dial.* 25.1–6), Justin cites Isa 63:15–64:12 in extenso, introducing his citation with the claim, "They who

The spirit's descent transforms Jesus's baptism into a messianic anointing.[32] As previously noted, there is a strong connection in the Jewish scriptures between royal anointing and endowment of YHWH's spirit; at least one tradition presents the spirit as the *medium* of anointing (cf. Isa 61:1–2).[33] Thus we should not be surprised when the author of Luke-Acts draws precisely this inference (cf. Luke 4:14; Acts 4:27; 10:37–38).[34] Nor should we find it curious if Mark's account of Jesus's baptism encourages a similar

attempt to justify themselves and claim that they are sons of Abraham hope to receive with us [Christians] a small part of the divine inheritance [Σὺν ἡμῖν καὶ κληρονομῆσαι βουλήσονται κἂν ὀλίγον τόπον]." He justifies this comment by insinuating that the words, "For you are *our father*, and Abraham has not known *us*, and Israel has been ignorant of *us*," are voiced by the prophet *on behalf of Christians* (*Dial.* 25.2; Edgar J. Goodspeed, ed., *Die ältesten Apologeten: Text emit kurzen Einleitungen* [Göttingen: Vandenhoeck & Ruprecht, 1914], 118; English translation follows Thomas B. Falls, *St. Justin Martyr: Dialogue with Trypho*, ed. Michael Slusser, Selections from the Fathers of the Church 3 [Washington, DC: Catholic University of America, 2003], here 39, my emphasis). Justin's polemic assumes that Isa 63:15–64:12 is about divine sonship and inheritance in the covenant community, an intriguing assumption in light of the fact that Mark introduces his Christ as the messianic son of Ps 2, a figure whom the psalm identifies as the divine heir (cf. Ps 2:8; Mark 12:1–12).

   [32] Mark likely also conceives of the unnamed woman's act at Bethany as a messianic anointing (14:3–9); precedent for multiple anointings is established in Deuteronomistic Historian's life of David (cf. 1 Sam 16:6–13; 2 Sam 5:1–5); see further my discussion in Section 6.1.

   [33] W. C. van Unnik noted this point long ago ("Jesus the Christ," *NTS* 8 [1962]: 101–116); cf. Isa 61:1–2: "The spirit of the Lord is upon me [πνεῦμα κυρίου ἐπ' ἐμέ], because he has anointed me [ἔχρισέν με]; he has sent me to proclaim good news [εὐαγγελίσασθαι] to the poor." The anointed figure mentioned in Third Isaiah was likely a prophetic leader of his community. Later readers, however, were convinced that Isaiah is speaking about the messiah (Luke 4:14; Matt 11:2–6; 4Q521). Mark's presentation of a spirit-anointed messiah proclaiming the gospel (cf. 1:14–15) certainly fits within this milieu (Yarbro Collins, *Mark*, 149).

   [34] Luke would hardly be alone in exploiting the link between divine *pneuma* and messianic unction. For example, John the evangelist appears to have adapted the Baptist's role to align better with Samuel's role in 1 Samuel 16 (cf. John 1:29–34; see David E. Aune, "Christian Prophecy and the Messianic Status of Jesus," in *The Messiah: Developments in Earliest Judaism and Christianity*, ed. James H. Charlesworth [Minneapolis, MN: Fortress, 1992], 404–422, esp. 414–415). I have proposed elsewhere that some early Christ followers would have noticed the parallel between the Davidic king's anointing with holy oil (cf. Ps 89:21; 11QPs[a] 28:11; Josephus, *Ant.* 6.157; Tg. Ps.-J. 2 Sam 23:8) and Christ's anointing with the holy spirit ("The Messiah Is 'the Holy One': ὁ ἅγιος τοῦ θεοῦ as a Messianic Title in Mark 1:24," *JBL* 136 [2017]: 419–435, at 428). Philo's allegorical interpretation of priestly anointing, though distinct in its own right, offers another illustration of the potential connection between anointing and inner (perhaps even pneumatic) transformation: "and because his [the priest's] head has been anointed with oil [τὴν κεφαλὴν κέχρισται ἐλαίῳ], by which I mean the principle part of him is illuminated with a light like the beams of the sun" (*Fug.* 1.110 [LCL]).

conclusion. Indeed, Jerome, one of our rare patristic commentators on Mark's Gospel, exhorts us,

> Videte iunctiones significationesque verborum. Non dixit: «Venit Christus»; non dixit: «Venit Filius Dei», sed: «*Venit Iesus*». Dicat aliquis: «Quare non dixit: 'Christus'?» Secundum carnem loquor: ceterum Deus semper sanctus est, nec sanctificationem indigent, sed iam de carne Christi loquimur. Nondum fuerat baptizatus et ab Spiritu sancto unctus fuerat. (*Tract.* 1C.2–8)[35]
>
> Observe the arrangement of the words and what they signify. *He did not say: "Christ came;" he did not say, "the son of God came;" but [he said]: "Jesus came."* [But] someone may ask: *"Why did he not say: 'Christ?'"* I am speaking according to the flesh: certainly God is always holy and does not need sanctification, but for the moment we are speaking about Christ's flesh. *He had not yet been baptized and he had not yet been anointed by the holy spirit.*
>
> (translation and italics are mine)

3.3.2   Rendering Jesus a Messiah Like David

Interpreters generally agree that Mark 1:11 constitutes a conflate allusion to two (Ps 2:7; Isa 42:1), or perhaps three (Ps 2:7; Gen 22:2, 12, 16; Isa 42:1), scriptural source texts.[36] The primary issue still up

---

[35] Latin text in Jean-Louis Gourdain, ed. *Jérôme Homélies sur Marc*, SC 494 (Paris: Cerf, 2005), editor's emphasis.

[36] See, e.g., Schweizer, *Good News*, 40–41; Gnilka, *Evangelium*, 1: 52–54; 60–64; Kingsbury, *Christology*, 60–68; Matera, *Kingship*, 77–78; Juel, "Origin;" Boring, *Mark*, 45; Watts, "Lord's House," 309–313; Yarbro Collins, *Mark*, 150; Malbon, *Mark's Jesus*, 75–77; O'Brien, *Use of Scripture*, 164–165; Hays, *Echoes of Scripture in the Gospels*, 48. There was a time when interpreters seemed more interested in a supposed earlier layer of the text than with the actual words of Mark 1:11 (e.g., Bousset, *Kyrios Christos*, 96–97; Jeremias, "παῖς θεοῦ," 700–702), but this move has since lost its currency. Marcus (*Way*, 54) shows that if the evangelist has modified an earlier tradition dependent on Isa 42:1, this would only further illustrate *Mark's* intent to bring Ps 2:7 into play. Early interpreters of the Synoptic Gospels were well aware of the psalmnic allusion (cf. Luke 3:22 D; Justin, *Dial.* 88; 103; Clement, *Paed.* 1.6.25; Gosp. Eb. frag. 4), and there are no good reasons for doubting their instincts. Contra Carl R. Kazmierski (*Jesus, the Son of God: A Study of the Markan Tradition and Its Redaction by the Evangelist*, FB 33 [Würzburg: Echter, 1979], 39–40) and Lührmann (*Markusevangelium*, 37), the evangelist's interest in other scriptural intertexts, whether Isa 42:1 or Gen 22:2, does not warrant the rejection of an allusion to Ps 2:7. Peppard's recent attempt at undermining the allusion appears (at least to me) to be driven more

for debate seems to be whether the label ὁ ἀγαπητός, "the beloved," represents a discrete allusion to Genesis 22 LXX or merely reflects the influence of Isa 42:1.[37] For the purposes of the discussion at hand, I restrict my attention to the allusions to Ps 2:7 and Isa 42:1, both of which I will argue contribute to the growing sense that Χριστός is a messiah like David.

3.3.2.1 "You Are My Son" (Psalm 2:7)

In the previous chapter, I examined the various and sundry ways in which ancient authors made use of Psalm 2 to characterize their messiahs (2.4.2). My analysis revealed, first, that the vast majority of messiah texts containing citations of or allusions to Psalm 2 also contain direct claims of Davidic ancestry (cf. Pss. Sol. 17; 4 Ezra; Rom; Matt; Luke-Acts; Heb; Rev). Second, I observed that these texts tend to combine allusions to Psalm 2 with allusions to oracles explicitly about a descendant of David, Isa 11:1–5 and/or 2 Sam 7:12–14. Based on these findings, I concluded that an author's decision to characterize a messiah with the language of Psalm 2 would implicitly communicate that the messiah under discussion is the

by his desire to read Mark 1:11 in light of Roman adoption practices than it does a sober assessment of the evidence (*Son of God*, 95). At any rate, it remains unclear why his proposal necessitates that Mark 1:11 does not evoke Ps 2.

As with the allusion to Ps 2:7, the allusion to Isa 42:1 is rarely questioned, though see Hooker, *Gospel*, 47; Peppard, *Son of God*, 96. The observation that the clause ἐν σοὶ εὐδόκησα lacks verbal correspondence with Isa 42:1 LXX – προσεδέξατο αὐτὸν ἡ ψυχή μου – is not as damaging as it seems when one considers: (1) thematic coherence between Mark 1:10–11 (pars.) and Isa 42:1, (2) textual pluriformity of Isa 42:1 (see W. D. Davies and Dale C. Allison, *A Critical and Exegetical Commentary on the Gospel According to Saint Matthew*, 3 vols., ICC [Edinburgh: T&T Clark, 1988–1997], 1: 337–343), and (3) Theodotion's and Symmachus's translations of their Hebrew *Vorlage(n)*; θ′ reads: ιδου ο παις μου αντιληψομαι αυτου ο εκλεκτος μου <u>ον ευδοκησεν η ψυχη μου</u>; σ′ reads: ιδου ο δουλος μου ανθεξομαι αυτου ο εκλεκτος μου <u>ον ευδοκησεν η ψυχη μου</u> (listed in Joseph Ziegler, ed., *Isaias*, 3rd edn., Septuaginta 14 [Göttingen: Vandenhoeck & Ruprecht, 1983], at 276).

[37] The different options are summarized in Marcus, *Way*, 51–52. For studies that give maximal weight to Gen 22, see Geza Vermes, *Scripture and Tradition in Judaism: Haggadic Studies*, Studia post-biblica 4 (Leiden: Brill, 1961), 193–227; Kazmierski, *Jesus*; Jon D. Levenson, *The Death and Resurrection of the Beloved Son: The Transformation of Child Sacrifice in Judaism and Christianity* (New Haven, CT: Yale University Press, 1993), 200–232. Donald Juel posits that the identification of Jesus as the "seed of David," and thus "seed of Abraham," helped facilitate the interpretive link between the Davidic promise tradition and Gen 22 (*Messianic Exegesis: Christological Interpretation of the Old Testament in Early Christianity* [Philadelphia: Fortress, 1988], 85–87). If such a connection is present in Mark, it lies well beneath the surface.

messiah son of David. To be sure, this supposition may be narcotized, even obliterated, as it is in the Parables of Enoch. Yet the evidence strongly suggests that, all things being equal, an appeal to Psalm 2 in messianic discourse would activate a son-of-David frame. Mark employs the language of the psalm to narrate the divine designation of Israel's messiah.[38] Oracular legitimation by a prophet was a common feature of dynastic ascent in ancient Mediterranean culture (e.g., Plutarch, *Alex.* 27.9; Josephus, *J.W.* 3.339–408; 6.313), including the rise of certain messianic figures (e.g., John 1:29–34; y. Ta'an. 4:8/27), whose liaisons no doubt took inspiration from traditions in which YHWH granted prophetic insight to those who were charged with anointing the messiah (cf. 1 Sam 10:1–2; 16:6–13).[39] In Josephus's rendition of David's anointing, for instance, Samuel is said to have whispered under his breath, "This is he ... whom it has pleased God to make king [οὗτός ἐστιν ... ὁ βασιλεύειν ἀρέσας τῷ θεῷ]." The prophet then proceeded to anoint the young man, again whispering, this time in David's ear, "that God had chosen him to be king [ὅτι βασιλεύειν αὐτὸν ὁ θεὸς ᾕρηται]" (*Ant.* 6.164–165). The Markan locution σὺ εἶ ὁ υἱός μου, "you are my son," appears to have a similar function, though the Markan mise-en-scène has no role for the prophet.[40] Rather, the evangelist

---

[38] See, e.g., James D. G. Dunn, *Baptism in the Holy Spirit: A Re-Examination of the New Testament Teaching on the Gift of the Spirit in Relation to Pentecostalism Today* (London: SCM, 1970), 28; Kingsbury, *Christology*, 60–68; Matera, *Kingship*, 77–78; Yarbro Collins, *Mark*, 150; Watts, "Mark," 127–129; O'Brien, *Use of Scripture*, 164–165. Marcus's study (*Way*, 59–79) also supports this interpretation, though he gets bogged down, unnecessarily in my view, by the question of whether Jesus "became" something new at his baptism (72–75).

[39] On oracular legitimation in the ancient world and its influence on the canonical Gospels, see Aune, "Christian Prophecy," 411–415. This phenomenon fits within what Gerd Theissen has referred to as "status contingency" ("From the Historical Jesus to the Kerygmatic Son of God: How Role Analysis Contributes to the Understanding of New Testament Christology," in *Jesus Research: New Methodologies and Perceptions, The Second Princeton-Prague Symposium on Jesus Research*, ed. James H. Charlesworth et al. [Grand Rapids, MI: Eerdmans, 2014], 235–260): "This is a basic axiom in antiquity that might be paraphrased as follows: No one can give status and role to him- or herself. No one can announce his or her own status. In antiquity we find an awareness of *status and role contingency*. Status is received, roles are assigned" (242, his emphasis).

[40] The use of the εὐδοκ-root in the next clause (ἐν σοὶ εὐδόκησα) supports the inference that this is an appointment to an office (Watts, "Mark," 129; Peppard, *Son of God*, 103–112). Note, e.g., the language of Ps 151 LXX: David recounts, "He sent his angel/messenger and took me from my father's flock, and anointed me [ἔχρισέν με] with his anointing oil. My brothers were handsome and tall, but the Lord was not

invites his audience to eavesdrop on private disclosure (cf. 1:2–3). Significantly, however, the rhetoric of God's speech to the one on whom he previously sent his spirit mimics the rhetoric of Psalm 2, in which the phrase "you are my son" functions as a performative utterance designed to instanciate the messiah's authority over the nations (cf. Ps 2:7–8).

There is ample evidence that other first-century Christians interpreted the psalm in this fashion. Both Luke-Acts and Hebrews apply the divine address in Ps 2:7 to the moment of Jesus's enthronement at the right hand of God (cf. Acts 13:33; Heb 1:5; 5:5).[41] Paul, likewise, affirms the protocreedal statement that Jesus was "set apart" (ὁρισθέντος) as "son of God in power through the spirit of holiness by resurrection from the dead" (Rom 1:4).[42] In all three instances, the language of Ps 2:7 signals the enthronement of a descendant of

pleased with them [οὐκ εὐδόκησεν ἐν αὐτοῖς κύριος]" (vv. 4–5). The implication is that the Lord was pleased to choose (εὐδόκειν) David as Israel's king.

[41] Neither of these writers thinks the divine utterance marks the point at which Jesus "becomes" God's son. The words of the psalm are used, rather, to mark the moment when David's greater son – vindicated from the grave – takes up his session at the right hand of his father in heaven. For more on the function of Ps 2:7 in Luke-Acts, see Strauss, Davidic Messiah, 62–67, 92–94, 202–208. C. Kavin Rowe's response to attempts at detecting fragments of an earlier Christology in Luke-Acts bears reiterating: "Loosing a statement from its narrative mooring as a means to determine specifically Lukan Christology immediately involves a methodological confusion. In the act of disengaging any statement or passage from the narrative, the means of identifying what is Lukan are actually lost, for the Lukan context itself is rendered irrelevant as meaning-determining discourse" (Early Narrative Christology: The Lord in the Gospel of Luke, BZNW 139 [Berlin: De Gruyter, 2006], 190–191). In the case of Hebrews, there is no doubt that the author thinks Jesus is the preexistent son. Indeed, it is precisely because he takes this point for granted that he can focus his attention on the significance of the son's heavenly enthronement (G. B. Caird, "Son by Appointment," in The New Testament Age: Essays in Honor of Bo Reicke, ed. William C. Weinrich, 2 vols. [Macon, GA: Mercer University Press, 1984], 1:73–81).

[42] For a judicious discussion of the evidence that Rom 1:3–4 is comprised of pre-Pauline material, see Robert Jewett, "The Redaction and Use of an Early Christian Confession in Romans 1:3–4," in The Living Test: Essays in Honor of Ernest W. Saunders, eds. Dennis E. Groh and Robert Jewett (Lanham, MD: University of America Press, 1985), 99–122, esp. 100–102. The notion that Paul's appropriation of this material evinces hostility towards Davidic descent is untenable (cf. Rom 9:5; 15:12). Moreover, since Paul thinks that Christ is the preexistent son (cf. Rom 8:3; Gal 4:4; 1 Cor 8:6; Phil 2:6–8; Col 1:16), it is equally inappropriate to classify the Christology of Rom 1:3–4 as "adoptionist;" see N. T. Wright, Paul and the Faithfulness of God, Volume 4 of Christian Origins and the Question of God (London: SPCK, 2013), 699–701. I part company with Wright, however, when he claims that this language "does not confer or create a new status or identity for Jesus" (700, his emphasis). It seems to me that this is precisely what it does: the preexistent son whom God sent and who was born of the Davidic line has now been raised from the dead and enthroned in his heavenly office by his father as "son of God in power" (so rightly

David. It seems plausible, therefore, that Mark, followed by Matthew and Luke (cf. Matt 3:17; Luke 3:22), developed the language of Psalm 2 along similar lines – that is, as an indication that his baptism was the moment at which God designated Jesus the messiah.[43]

The interpretive practice of reading Psalm 2 as an eschatological narrative may also help to illuminate Mark's narrative landscape.[44] Depending on an author's perspective, the messiah son of God in Psalm 2 could engage in the eschatological battle either on earth (e.g., Pss. Sol. 17:22–23) or in heaven (e.g., 1 En. 48:10; Rev 11:15; 19:19) during the turbulent period of "the end of days."[45] Mark enacts this eschatological conflict in the life of Jesus: (1) cosmic

Matthew W. Bates, "A Christology of Incarnation and Enthronement: Romans 1:3–4 as Unified, Nonadoptionist, and Nonconciliatory, *CBQ* 77 [2015]: 107–127, esp. 125–126). Mark may have something similar in mind when he introduces the transfiguration account with the logion, "there are some standing here who will not taste death until they see that the kingdom of God come *with power* [ἕως ἂν ἴδωσιν τὴν βασιλείαν τοῦ θεοῦ ἐληλυθυῖαν ἐν δυνάμει]" (Mark 9:1). Given that the transfiguration offers a proleptic glance at Jesus's resurrection glory, one wonders whether the coming of the kingdom ἐν δυνάμει refers to Jesus's post-resurrection session at the right hand of God (cf. Mark 12:35–37; 14:62).

[43] In fact, the longest-standing objection to this interpretation does not arise from those who conclude that Mark rejects all things Davidic, but from those who share the theological concern so poignantly articulated by Lagrange, "Est-ce à dire qu'il deviant ce qu'il n'était pas, Fils de Dieu ou Messie?" (*L'Évangile*, 11); cf. Taylor, *Gospel*, 162; C. E. B. Cranfield, *The Gospel according to St. Mark: An Introduction and Commentary*, CGTC (Cambridge: Cambridge University Press, 1959), 55; William Lane, *The Gospel according to St. Mark*, NICNT 2 (Grand Rapids, MI: Eerdmans, 1974), 57–58; Marcus, *Way*, 72–75; R. T. France, *The Gospel of Mark: A Commentary on the Greek Text*, NIGTC (Grand Rapids, WI: Eerdmans, 2002), 82. The issue with raising the question, does Jesus become something he was not?, is that it lacks specificity. An affirmative answer could imply either (1) that Jesus becomes a divine being at his baptism, a christological position often denoted as "adoptionism" under the influence of Adolf von Harnack (*History of Dogma*, trans. Neil Buchanan et al., 7 vols. [London: Williams & Norgate, 1894–1898], 1:183–204), or (2) that he "becomes," or perhaps better, is "designated," Israel's messiah via his spirit anointing. The latter suggests a shift in status – not-yet anointed to anointed – along the lines of what Jerome suggests in the passage cited above, while the former implies a shift in ontology – not-yet divine to divine – which is apparently how some early Christ followers interpreted Jesus's baptism, though it is uncertain which account of this event they had in mind (cf. Irenaeus, *Haer.* 3.11.7).

[44] Cf. Marcus, *Way*, 61; Steudel, "Psalm 2," 191–192.

[45] The concept of the "end of days," as a protracted period of trial and refining, is well attested in the Dead Sea Scrolls, in which the locution אחרית הימים occurs at least 33 times (Steudel, "אחרית הימים"). For Mark, this period is marked by the theme of being "handed over" (παραδιδόναι) – a fate that befalls the Baptist (1:14), Jesus (14:10, 21, 41; 15:1), and finally the disciples (and perhaps the auditors of the Gospel, too) (cf. 13:9).

and human hostility are directed toward God through Jesus (cf. Ps 2:1–2);[46] (2) Jesus manifests the power of the kingdom by binding Satan and demons by the power of the spirit (Mark 3:27; 5:1–13; cf. Ps 2:3); and (3) Jesus identifies himself as the rejected-but-vindicated cosmic heir, ὁ κληρονόμος (Mark 12:1–12; cf. Ps 2:8). These points of thematic coherence between the Christ of Mark and the anointed Davidide of Psalm 2 suggest that it is not simply the psalm's language of divine sonship that attracted the evangelist, but also its depiction of a messiah as the very locus of God's kingdom power. One might say that the icon of the anointed son furnished Mark with a scriptural messiah who is "[le] véritable lieutenant de Yahvé sur terre."[47]

3.3.2.2 *"Behold My Servant" (Isaiah 42:1)*

As with a number of his contemporaries, the evangelist characterizes his messiah as both the anointed king of Psalm 2 and an Isaianic figure upon whom YHWH's spirit would come to rest (cf. Isa 11:2; 42:1; 61:1). Rather than alluding to an oracle about the shoot from the stump of Jesse (cf. Isaiah 11), however, Mark casts his gaze to the first of Second Isaiah's servant poems: "Here is my servant [LXX adds: 'Jacob'], whom I uphold, my chosen [LXX adds: 'Israel'], in whom my soul delights; I have put my spirit upon him [ἔδωκα τὸ πνεῦμά μου ἐπ᾽ αὐτόν]; he will bring forth justice to the nations" (Isa 42:1). How should one account for this Isaianic intertext? The standard answer is that the evangelist had ready to hand a "servant" Christology, which he then fused with the "royal/messianic" Christology of Psalm 2.[48] Yarbro Collins's comments are representative of the field,

---

[46] Malbon (*Mark's Christ*, 44) observes that "the background conflict, the foundational conflict underlying the story, is God's: God struggles with Satan through the main character Jesus." Malbon's observation about the grounding conflict at the literary level coheres with the kingship model in Ps 2 (see esp. Marcus, *Way*, 66–69). Malbon also discusses a "middle-ground conflict" between Jesus and the Judean authorities (*Mark's Christ*, 46–48). This, too, coheres with the model of kingship portrayed in Ps 2. As Watts ("Mark," 128) notes, the writer of Pss. Sol. 17 agrees with Mark (and the other Synoptic evangelists) in casting certain Judean authorities in the role of the "nations" in Ps 2 (cf. Acts 4).

[47] To borrow an apposite turn of phrase from J.-B. Dumortier ("Un Rituel D'Intronisation: Le Ps. LXXXIX 2–38," *VT* 22 [1972]: 176–196, here 187).

[48] Sometimes Ps 2:7 and Isa 42:1 are set in opposition to one another (e.g., Lührmann, *Markusevangelium*, 37). Boring (*Mark*, 46) speaks of a "tension between royal power as God's anointed Son and human weakness as the Suffering Servant."

By combining Ps 2:7 and Isa 42:1, the text of Mark interprets Jesus as *both* the messiah *and* as the Servant of the
Lord. This close association of the two epithets has several
implications. One is that the author of Mark, or the tradents
upon whom he was dependent, read the poems about the
Servant of the Lord in Second Isaiah messianically, at least
in part. The striking similarities between the fate of the
Servant as described in Isaiah 53, on the one hand, and
the fate of Jesus as interpreted by his followers, on the other,
may have been the impetus for the messianic interpretation
of these poems. Another implication is that the messiahship
of Jesus is not presented in royal and military terms; instead
the idea of the messiah of Israel is *reinterpreted* in prophetic
terms.[49]

This line of reasoning is striking. For one thing, if one concedes that
Mark reads parts of Isaiah "messianically," then to posit that he
treats Isaiah's servant as a figure distinct from the messiah seems
unjustified. For another, it is unclear why an allusion to Isa 42:1
would necessitate that "the idea of the messiah of Israel is reinterpreted in prophetic terms." As Yarbro Collins herself has demonstrated, the categories of "prophet" and "king" are hardly antithetical
in early Jewish traditions; indeed, the observation that the kings of
old sometimes behaved like prophets explains why some royal messiahs manifest prophetic traits.[50] All this suggests that conventional
wisdom about a separate "servant" Christology is shaky, at best.
Rather than treat Second Isaiah's servant as constitutive of an early
christological idea, I propose to trace points of resonance between the

---

Most scholars are concerned to distinguish between "pre-Christian" readings of
Isaiah's servant poems and the Christian conception of a "suffering-servant" messiah.
While this concern is commendable to a point, it has clouded our judgment on two
fronts. First, we have solid evidence that some Second Temple Jews read parts of
Second Isaiah messianically. As VanderKam notes, "1 Enoch 37–71 is perhaps the
most ancient but hardly the only witness to the messianic interpretation to the servant"
("Righteous One," 190). Jews no doubt read Isaiah differently than their Christian
counterparts, but the fact that some did detect a messiah in oracles about YHWH's
servant is significant in its own right. Second, I continue to be persuaded by Juel's
argument (*Messianic Exegesis*, 131) that "[i]t is more likely that servant passages were
applied to Jesus by his followers because they believed him to be the Messiah," rather
than the alternative: Christians believed Jesus was the Christ and then subsequently
tacked on a "servant" Christology which was floating around somewhere in the ether
of early Christian ideas.
   [49] Yarbro Collins, *Mark*, 150–151, my emphasis.   [50] Ibid., 44–84.

first servant poem (Isa 42:1–7) and Davidic scriptural traditions, both internal and external to the Isaianic corpus.

Two features of Isaiah's first servant poem, in particular, facilitate messianic interpretations of this passage. First, although the identity of the servant is notoriously elusive, the language used to depict this individual (or coterie) is unequivocally royal.[51] The oracle unfolds with YHWH summoning the one whom he designates עבדי, "my servant,"[52] and בחירי, "my chosen one," appellations that show strong affinity within Davidic traditions, such as the psalmist's appeal to the oath YHWH swore to David long ago: "I have made a covenant with my chosen one [לבחירי], I have sworn to David, my servant [לדוד עבדי]" (Ps 89:4).[53] Second, a unified reading of the Isaianic corpus suggests that the servant in Isa 42:1 is summoned to take up the same vocation as the shoot of Jesse (cf. Isa 11:1–5, 10). Both the shoot and the servant receive YHWH's spirit: (1) to establish "justice," משפט, among the nations (cf. Isa 11:3–4, 10; 42:1, 3, 4),[54] (2) to bring about Israel's "new exodus" (cf. Isa 11:10–16; 42:6–7, 14–17; cf. Isa 40:1–11), and (3) to draw the gentiles into worship of the one true God – as the gentiles will inquire of the shoot of Jesse (אליו גוים ידרשו; Isa 11:10; LXX: ἐπ' αὐτῷ ἔθνη ἐλπιοῦσιν, "the gentiles will hope in him"), so the coastlands await the servant's torah (ולתורתו איים ייחילו; Isa 42:4; LXX: καὶ ἐπὶ τῷ ὀνόματι αὐτοῦ ἔθνη ἐλπιοῦσιν, "the gentiles will

---

[51] In its original context, Isa 42:1 may have referred to Cyrus the Persian, whom the prophet refers to as משיחו, "his [YHWH's] messiah" (Isa 45:1); see further in Joseph A. Blenkinsopp, *Isaiah 40–55: A New Translation with Introduction and Commentary*, AB 19A (New York: Doubleday, 2002), 210–212; Joseph A. Blenkinsopp, *David Remembered: Kingship and National Identity in Ancient Israel* (Grand Rapids, MI: Eerdmans, 2013), 64–70. The reception history of this text reveals how easily a passage about "Cyrus," Κῦρος, could be taken as a reference to Jesus the "lord," Κύριος (see apparatus in Ziegler, ed., *Isaias*, 290). Alternatively, the servant figure in Isa 42:1 may stand for the collective people of Israel (e.g., Isa 42:1 LXX; Justin, *Dial.* 123.8; cf. Isa 41:9–10); see further in Antti Laato, *Josiah and David Redivivus: The Historical Josiah and the Messianic Expectations of Exilic and Postexilic Times*, ConBOT 33 (Stockholm: Almqvist & Wiksell, 1992), 74–87.

[52] עבדי דוד or עבדי דוד דוד עבדי in 1 Chr 17:4; Ps 89:4, 21–22; Isa 37:35; Jer 33:21, 22, 26; Ezek 34:23, 24; 37:24; Hag 2:23; Zech 3:8, inter alia. As Bultmann noted, "the title [servant of God] clings especially to David of whom it became traditional" (*Theology*, 50).

[53] This same psalm later juxtaposes "my servant" and "my messiah": "But now you have spurned and rejected him; you are full of wrath against your messiah [משיחך; τὸν χριστόν σου]. You have renounced the covenant with your servant [עבדך; τοῦ δούλου σου]; you have defiled his crown to the dust" (Ps 89[88]:39–40; cf. 51–52).

[54] The declaration that YHWH will set his spirit upon his servant for the purpose of establishing משפט is suggestive of a vocation traditionally reserved for David's line (cf. Ps 72:1–4, 12–14; Isa 11:3–5; Jer 23:5).

hope in his name").[55] These points of thematic coherence do not demand a messianic reading of Second Isaiah's first servant poem, but they do explain why some scripturally literate authors concluded the prophet had the messiah in his purview.

Moreover, Jewish and Christian messiah texts hint at a common assumption: the servant of YHWH in Isa 42:1–7 is the *same* figure as the spirit-anointed descendant of David in Isa 11:1–10. This certainly seems to be the suggestion of the Parables of Enoch, whose writer characterizes his messiah with language drawn from both Isa 42:1 (cf. 1 En. 39:6; 40:5; 45:3–4) and Isa 11:1–10 (cf. 1 En. 46:3; 49:1–4; 62:2–3).[56] The Isaiah targumist is more overt, ascribing משיחא both to the shoot who "shall be exalted from the sons of his [Jesse's] sons" (Tg. Isa 11:1) and to "my servant [the messiah]" (Tg. Isa 42:1; cf. 52:13–53:12).[57] And Matthew follows the lone citation of Isa 42:1–4 in the New Testament with the pressing question, placed ironically on the lips of a perplexed crowd, "Can this be the son of David? [μήτι οὗτός ἐστιν ὁ υἱὸς Δαυίδ]" (Matt 12:23).[58] There can be little doubt

---

[55] For a discussion of the intratextual links between Isa 11, Isa 42:1–7, and Isa 61:1–3, see Rowe, *God's Kingdom*, 63–84. While I disagree with his interpretation of the "original" meaning of these oracles, his analysis illustrates how Second Isaiah's servant (and indeed Third Isaiah's "messiah") could be read as presaging the messiah, if a later reader was so inclined (so also Strauss, *Davidic Messiah*, 233–249).

[56] See VanderKam, "Chosen One," 189–190. The author of the Parables also reads language about the servant in Isa 49:1–6 as descriptive of the same figure (e.g., 1 En. 48:3–4; cf. Rev 19:15).

[57] I follow the English translation of Bruce D. Chilton, *The Isaiah Targum*, ArBib 11 (Edinburgh: T&T Clark, 1987). Although משיחא is secondary in Tg. Isa. 42:1, the figure in view is clearly the messiah (Chilton, *Isaiah Targum*, 80–81). For more on the messiah in Targum Isaiah, see Samson H. Levey, *The Messiah: An Aramaic Interpretation: The Messianic Exegesis of the Targum's*, HUCM 2 (Cincinnati, OH: Hebrew Union College-Jewish Institute of Religion, 1974), 43–67; Bruce D. Chilton, *The Glory of Israel: The Theology and Provenance of the Isaiah Targum*, JSOTSup 23 (Sheffield: JSOT Press, 1983), 86–96; and Jostein Ådna, "The Servant of Isaiah 52:13–53:12 in Targum Isaiah with Special Attention to the Concept of the Messiah," in *the Suffering Servant: Isaiah 53 in Jewish and Christian Sources*, eds. Bernd Janowski and Peter Stuhlmacher, trans. Daniel P. Bailey (Grand Rapids, MI: Eerdmans, 2004), 189–224. While the dating of Tg. Ps.-J. is late (c. third to fifth century CE), Chilton (*Glory*, 109–110; *Targum*, xx–xxv) argues that some material in the Targum, including its messianism, dates back to the early Tannaitic period (c. 70–135 CE).

[58] For an overview of the issue surrounding the Matthean text-form of Isa 42:1–4, see Richard Beaton, *Isaiah's Christ in Matthew's Gospel*, SNTSMS 123 (Cambridge: Cambridge University Press, 2002), 123–132. There are a number of factors that may have influenced the evangelist's conclusion that ὁ παῖς μου in Isa 42:1 is ὁ υἱὸς Δαυίδ, including: (1) the Markan link between υἱὸς Δαυίδ and healing of the blind (Mark 10:46–52; cf. Matt 9:27–31; 20:29–34); (2) Ezekiel's prophecy that YHWH would heal his people by installing "my servant David" (Ezek 34:24; so Young S. Chae, *Jesus As the Eschatological Shepherd: Studies in the Old Testament, Second Temple Judaism,*

that the evangelist reads Isa 42:1–7 as an oracle about the messiah son of David, likely in concert with Isa 11:1–10 and Isa 61:1–2 (cf. Matt 11:2–6).

Luke's use of the lexeme παῖς, "servant" or "child," throughout his two-volume work allows us to make plausible deductions about how he interpreted the term in Isa 42:1.[59] Aside from the lone ascription of παῖς to Israel in 1:54, every occurrence of the word in Luke-Acts falls into one of two categories: a designation for either (1) a child/household servant (cf. Luke 2:43; 7:7; 8:51; 8:54; 9:42; 12:45; 15:26; Acts 20:12) or (2) David/Jesus (cf. Luke 1:69; Acts 3:13, 26; 4:25, 27, 30). The logic driving the second category is straightforward: the God of Israel fulfills his promises to his παῖς, David, through the life, death, and resurrection of his παῖς, Jesus (cf. Luke 1:30–35; Acts 13:22–33). The evangelist foregrounds this motif in the Benedictus (cf. Luke 1:68–79) and then returns to it in Peter's prayer, in which the apostle declares that "your servant David" prophesied in the spirit about the sufferings of God's messiah (citing Ps 2:1–2), that is, "your holy servant Jesus" (Acts 4:27).[60] The prayer thus brings to light a latent Lukan hermeneutical assumption. The one whom

and in the Gospel of Matthew, WUNT 2/216 [Tübingen: Mohr Siebeck, 2006], 292–302); and (3) Solomonic-exorcist traditions (so Duling, "Solomon"). In my judgment, Le Donne (_Historiographical Jesus_, 145–146) comes closest to the mark: "We cannot say with any confidence that therapeutic activity was a prominent feature among the messianic expectations of the first century. But we can say that any messianic ideology that took seriously the promises of Isaiah would have been open to the concept of messianic therapy."

[59] Probable Lukan allusions to Isa 42:1 include the evangelist's use of the Markan allusion at Jesus's baptism (Luke 3:22) and the voice from heaven at the transfiguration (Luke 9:35); note also allusions to Isa 42:6 (cf. Isa 49:6) in Luke 2:32 and Acts 13:47. Luke's programmatic citation of Isa 61:1–2 (4:18–19) is often handled as an example of a "prophet" Christology, but this is misleading. As Strauss (_Davidic Messiah_, 245) notes, "It must be kept in mind that it is _Luke_ who narrates his story by first introducing Jesus as the expected Davidic messiah in his birth narrative and then presenting his role as that of the prophet-herald of Isa. 61.1–2 ... The Davidic messiah functions as servant and prophet-herald. On the other hand, it is not correct to say that Luke intentionally merges previously separate messianic figures. Rather for Luke, Isaiah gives various descriptions of the one messiah. All the Scriptures speak of Christ" (his emphasis).

[60] Cf. Did. 9:2: "We give you thanks, our Father, for the holy vine of David your servant [Δαυεὶδ τοῦ παιδός σου], which you have made known to us through Jesus your servant ['Ιησοῦ τοῦ παιδός σου]" (Ehrman, LCL) (cf. 1 Clem 59:2–4). The phrase "my servant (the messiah)" is used in 4 Ezra (cf. 7:29; 13:32, 37, 52, 14:9) as well as in 2 Bar. 70:9 (ܡܫܝܚܐ ܕܝܠܝ; Daniel M. Gurtner, ed., _Second Baruch: A Critical Edition of the Syriac Text with Greek and Latin Fragments, English Translation, Introduction, and Concordances_, Jewish and Christian Texts in Contexts and Related Studies 5 [London: T&T Clark, 2009], 114). I am in agreement with Stone (_Fourth Ezra_, 207–208) that the

YHWH calls "my servant" in the book of Isaiah (Isa 42:1 in Luke 3:22; Isa 52:13 in Acts 3:13, 26) is the same figure as the servant king about whom David prophesied in the Psalms.[61]

Finally, although Paul and the author of 1 Peter neither cited nor alluded to Isa 42:1, each took for granted that Christ is both the shoot of Jesse (Isa 11:1–10) and the servant in Second Isaiah's final servant poem (Isa 52:13–53:12). For Paul, the discovery that the Isaianic servant (cf. Rom 4:25; 15:21) is the shoot of Jesse (cf. Rom 15:12) serves to confirm the promises Israel's God made to the patriarchs and to open the way for gentiles to worship the one true God (Rom 15:8–9).[62] One suspects that the linguistic similitude between the final clause in Isa 11:10 LXX (ἐπ᾽ αὐτῷ ἔθνη ἐλπιοῦσιν) and the final clause in Isa 42:4 LXX (ἐπὶ τῷ ὀνόματι αὐτοῦ ἔθνη ἐλπιοῦσιν; cf. Matt 12:21) would incline the apostle to equate these figures. For the author of 1 Peter, any Χριστιανός reviled ἐν ὀνόματι Χριστοῦ, "on account of the name of Christ," should count herself blessed, since such opprobrium attests that the same spirit which rested on Χριστός has come to rest upon her as well (τὸ τοῦ θεοῦ πνεῦμα ἐφ᾽ ὑμᾶς ἀναπαύεται; 1 Pet 4:14) – an extension of the oracle about the shoot of Jesse to the people of Christ (ἀναπαύσεται ἐπ᾽ αὐτὸν πνεῦμα τοῦ θεοῦ; Isa 11:2).[63] This peculiar manner of reasoning is preceded by an exposition of the social implications of identifying Christ as the servant in Isa 52:13–53:12 (cf. 1 Pet 2:18–25).

The notion that an appeal to Isa 42:1 recasts a "messianic" Christ-ology "in prophetic terms"[64] is, in the end, little more than a myth of modern scholarship, one that has been perpetuated and regurgitated

---

Greek *Vorlage* on which the various recensions of 4 Ezra are dependent read παῖς (likely rendering עבד) in each instance.

[61] See Peter Doble, "Luke 24.26, 44 – Songs of God's Servant: David and His Psalms in Luke-Acts," *JSNT* 28 (2006): 267–283; and Joshua W. Jipp, "Luke's Scriptural Suffering Messiah: A Search for Precedent, a Search for Identity," *CBQ* 72 (2010): 255–274. Each argues persuasively that Jesus's role as the messianic servant in Luke-Acts is influenced by the words of David in the Psalms. Overlapping language in the Psalms and Isaiah may have encouraged some to read these texts in tandem (Blenkinsopp, *Opening the Sealed Book*, 200).

[62] See Wagner, *Heralds*, 318–329.

[63] On the allusion to Isa 11:2 in 1 Pet 4:14, see Juel, *Messianic Exegesis*, 108; Steven Moyise, "Isaiah in 1 Peter," in *Isaiah in the New Testament*, eds. Steven Moyise and Maarten J. J. Menken (London: T&T Clark, 2005), 175–188, at 185. If one insists on following Juel's language about the "democratization" of messianic texts to the Christian community, then it at least needs to be said that the democratic move had been made in certain strands of Israel's sacred traditions well in advance to the early Christian movement (cf. Jer 31:9 MT [38:9 LXX]; Jub. 1:24–25).

[64] Yarbro Collins, *Mark*, 151.

ad nauseum in the commentary literature. In contrast, every ancient author who concluded that עבדי/ὁ παῖς μου in Isa 42:1 signified a messiah also concluded that this was the messiah son of David (cf. Matt 1:1; 12:15–32; Luke 1:32, 69), or the same figure described in Isa 11:1–10 (cf. 1 En. 37–71), or both (Tg. Isa). Other early Christians who were convinced that their messiah was the servant in Isa 52:13–53:12 were equally convinced that he was the shoot of Jesse (cf. Rom 15:12; 1 Pet 4:14). Thus, it seems that *if* an ancient author was inclined to take the referent of "my servant," עבדי/ὁ παῖς μου, as the messiah, he would likely conclude, no doubt aided by the language in Isa 11:1–10, that this is the messiah son of David.

There is reason to speculate that Mark read Isa 42:1 in a similar fashion. First, it seems plausible, given the number of references to Isaiah in the Gospel, that the evangelist was aware of Isaiah 11, one of the quintessential fonts of Jewish messianism in antiquity.[65] Second, if, as some have argued,[66] the evangelist fashions his so-called way section (8:22–10:52) after Second Isaiah's holy war march to Zion, specifically focusing on the motif of the servant opening the eyes of the blind (8:22–26; 10:46–52; cf. Isa 42:7, 10–16), it seems significant that this section concludes with the healing of a blind man who addressed Jesus as υἱὸς Δαυίδ, "son of David" (Mark 10:46–52).[67] The line Mark's narrative traces between the Isaianic servant and the son of David is more subtle than Matthew's (cf. Matt 12:18–23), to be sure, but it raises the possibility that the evangelist agreed with one of his earliest tradents; or, to put it the other way around, that Matthew got Mark right. Third, the primary way Mark articulates the significance of Christ's suffering is through scriptural allusions, not only to the final servant poem of Second Isaiah (cf. Isa 52:13–53:12),[68] but also and especially to the petitionary cries of David in the Psalter.[69] That is, Mark appears to

---

[65] On Mark's use of Isaiah, see Watts, *Isaiah's New Exodus*. Messianic interpretations of Isaiah 11:1–10 include the following: Pss. Sol. 17:24, 37; 4Q161 3:11–25; 4Q285 frag. 5; 1 En. 48:10–49:4; 2 Thess 2:8; Rom 15:8–12; 1 Pet 4:14; Rev 5:5; 19:11–13; 22:16; 4 Ezra 12:32; 13:11, 27, 37–38; 2 Bar. 40:2.

[66] See Marcus, *Way*, 34–37; Watts, *Isaiah's New Exodus*, 236–257.

[67] See Watts, *Isaiah's New Exodus*, 289.

[68] For Mark's use of Isa 52:13–53:12, see Marcus, *Way*, 186–196, esp. 189.

[69] Yarbro Collins ("Appropriation of the Psalms," 277 n. 21) lists 6 or 7 (depending on whether Pss 41 and 42 LXX are counted separately) Davidic psalms of lament in Mark. I have rendered her list in accordance with the numbers in the Greek Psalter: Ps 21:2 at 15:34; Ps 21:7 at 9:12; Ps 21:8 at 15:29 (cf. Ps 108:25); Ps 21:19 at 15:24; Ps 41:10 at 14:18; Ps 41:6, 12 at 14:34 (cf. Ps 42:5); Ps 50:14 at 14:38; Ps 64:8 at 4:39; Ps

operate under the assumption that the fate of the Isaianic servant and the fate of Davidic king are one and the same: faithfulness in the face of persecution and suffering, followed by vindication and exaltation.

3.3.3   Summary

Jesus's baptism provides the audience with an interpretive key to unlock the identity of the one whom the evangelist calls "Christ" (cf. 1:1). The descent of the holy spirit upon the man from Nazareth, followed immediately by a performative scripturally derived speech from the heavens, would communicate to first-century auditors precisely what Jerome concluded several centuries later: the baptism of Jesus is an *anointing*. The audience must follow along to see how Mark develops his portrait of Christ, but there can be little doubt at this point that the messiah son of God in Psalm 2 and the messianic servant in Isaiah 42 are foundational brushstrokes he draws across his canvas.

3.4   Battle Royale: The Wilderness Temptation of Jesus

Immediately following his anointing in the spirit, Mark tells us, Jesus is ejected by the spirit into the wilderness to be tempted by the Satan for 40 days. The immediacy of this scene, coupled with the spirit's dynamic agency, implies some correlation between the baptism and wilderness temptation.[70] Beyond this point, there is very little on which modern interpreters can agree.[71] Recognizing the polyvalence of Mark's terse temptation account, I propose to explore an aspect of

---

68:9 at 3:21; Ps 68:22 at 15:23 and 15:36. She challenges Lothar Ruppert's claim that Mark identifies the speaker in these psalms as a generic "righteous sufferer" (*Jesus als der leidende Gerechte? Der Weg Jesu im Licht eines alt- und zwischentestamentlichen Motivs* [Stuttgart: KBW, 1972], 50–52), since it is precisely Jesus's suffering *as the messiah* to which these psalms give voice (231). The most plausible explanation for Mark's interpretation of these psalms written τῷ Δαυίδ is that the evangelist believed David spoke prophetically in the spirit (cf. Mark 12:36) about or, indeed, in the voice of, his future descendant, the messiah (so Attridge, "Giving Voice"). On the widespread Christian use of psalms of David, see Juel, *Messianic Exegesis*, 89–117.

[70]   Jeffrey B. Gibson, "Jesus' Wilderness Temptation According to Mark," *JSNT* 5 (1994): 3–34, here 8.

[71]   There are an array of proposals for the role/identity Mark's Jesus assumes in the temptation account: (1) a new Adam (Joel Marcus, "Son of Man as Son of Adam," *RB* 110 (2003), 38–61, esp. 55, 370–386, esp. 373–374), (2) the anointed king in Ps 2 (Marcus, *Way*, 66–69), (3) the shoot of Jesse in Isa 11 (Richard Bauckham, "Jesus and

this scene that remains largely underdeveloped in the secondary literature. Namely, I wish to suggest that the wilderness temptation advances the trajectory of the baptism by evoking traditions about the opening of David's messianic career. That is, like the young David, Mark's Jesus entrusts himself to the God of Israel while suspended between angels and beasts, thus registering an initial victory that forecasts the moment when he will deliver God's people from the hand of their enemy.

3.4.1 YHWH's Promise to the King (Psalm 91)

As a number of interpreters recognize, Psalm 91 (90 LXX):10–13 offers the closest linguistic parallel to Mark 1:13.[72] The pertinent section of the psalm reads as follows:

> No evil shall come before you, and no scourge shall come near your dwelling, because he will command his angels concerning you to guard you in all your ways [ὅτι τοῖς

---

the Wild Animals (Mark 1:13): A Christological Image for an Ecological Age," in *Jesus of Nazareth: Lord and Christ: Essays on the Historical Jesus and New Testament Christology*, eds. Joel B. Green and Max Turner [Grand Rapids, MI: Eerdmans, 1994], 3–21), (4) the corporate representative of Israel (Ulrich Mauser, *Christ in the Wilderness: The Wilderness Theme in the Second Gospel and Its Basis in the Biblical Tradition*, SBT 39 [Bloomsbury: SCM, 1963]), (5) the paradigmatic "righteous suffer" (Susan R. Garrett, *The Temptation of Jesus in Mark's Gospel* [Grand Rapids, MI: Eerdmans, 1998], 55–68), and (6) YHWH in Isa 43 (C. A. Gieschen, "Why Was Jesus with the Wild Beasts (Mark 1:13)?" *CTQ* 73 [2009]: 77–80). Of these, the latter two seem to me to be the weakest. Garrett's proposal depends almost entirely on reading Mark in light of Wis 2:12–20. Yet the resonances she detects between Mark and Wisdom are probably the result of each drawing on the same scriptural resources (e.g., Pss 2; 22[21]; Isa 52:13–53:12), rather than Mark's borrowing of Wisdom or an established Jewish tradition in which the "righteous sufferer" is stereotypically called God's "son." Gieschen's proposal, on the other hand, requires we interpret the phrase ἦν μετὰ τῶν θηρίων, "he was with the beasts," as a marked allusion to Isa 43:20: "The wild animals of the field will praise me [εὐλογήσει με τὰ θηρία τοῦ ἀγροῦ], sirens and the daughters of ostriches, because I gave water in the wilderness." I find this proposal highly unlikely for at least two reasons. First, it is not clear why Mark's language marks an allusion to this particular Isaianic text, since the collocation ὁδός (of the Lord) ἐν τῇ ἐρήμῳ + τὰ θηρία occurs in other places in Isaiah, which are equally, if not more, illuminating for the context of Mark 1:13 (cf. Isa 35:5–9; note also the negative connotations of τὰ θηρία in Isa LXX: 5:29; 13:21; 18:6 35:9; 56:9). Second, the context and syntax of Mark 1:12–13 make it more likely that the beasts are antagonists rather than worshipers (Gibson, "Jesus' Wilderness Temptation," 20).

[72] See Gibson, "Jesus' Wilderness Temptation," 21–22; Hooker, *Gospel*, 51; Ardel B. Caneday, "Mark's Provocative Use of Scripture in Narration: 'He Was with the Wild Animals and Angels Ministered to Him," *BBR* 9 (1999): 19–36, at 34–36; Boring, *Mark*, 48; Yarbro Collins, *Mark*, 151–153.

ἀγγέλοις αὐτοῦ ἐντελεῖται περὶ σοῦ τοῦ διαφυλάξαι σε ἐν πάσαις ταῖς ὁδοῖς σου]; upon their hands they will bear you up, so that you will not dash your foot against a stone. On the asp and the cobra you will tread, and you will trample lion and dragon under foot.   (Ps 90:10–13 LXX)

The psalmist's portrayal of an individual who stands between angels and beasts is unique among the Jewish scriptures, cohering closely with the language and imagery in Mark 1:13. Moreover, there is strong thematic coherence between the promises in Ps 91:10–13 and the Markan development of an Isaianic "new exodus." The rhetorical thrust of this section of the psalm highlights, as John Goldingay observes, that "the king will continue to have Israel's experience."[73] YHWH's promise to the monarch that he will command his angels τοῦ διαφυλάξαι σε ἐν πάσαις ταῖς ὁδοῖς σου, "to guard you in all your ways" (Ps 90:11 LXX), is the same promise he makes to Israel in Exod 23:20 (ἵνα φυλάξῃ σε ἐν τῇ ὁδῷ, "in order that he [the angel of YHWH] might guard you in the way") and through Israel to Christ at the opening of Mark's Gospel (cf. Mark 1:2, citing Exod 23:20).[74] For these reasons, it is hard to ignore that the only extant citations of Psalm 91 (90 LXX) in early messiah texts (cf. Matt 4:5–7; Luke 4:10–11) occur during Jesus's wilderness temptation, as a recapitulation of Israel's wilderness experience, under the guise that the addressee of the psalm is the messiah son of God (cf. Matt 4:6; Luke 4:9).[75]

The identification of Mark's Christ as the addressee of Psalm 91 carries with it implicit hermeneutical consequences. In particular, there is evidence to suggest that first-century readers of psalm assumed that the addressee was a Davidide. The Targum on Psalm 91 offers one highly illuminating example of how ancient readers might negotiate the dialogical movements of the psalm. The targumist grants that David is the speaker (Tg. Ps. 91:2) and so seeks to answer the question, With *whom* is David speaking? He supplies the answer:

---

[73] John Goldingay, *Psalms*, 3 vols., BCOTWP (Grand Rapids, MI: Baker Academic, 2008), 2: 47.

[74] Botner, "Prophetic Script," 371–375.

[75] Whether one adheres to the traditional two-source theory or adopts an alternative *Benutzungshypothese*, we are probably dealing here with a singular tradition. Nonetheless, this tradition offers insight into how some early Christ followers made sense of oral and written accounts of Jesus's wilderness temptation.

[David speaking] For he will deliver you, *Solomon my son,*
from the trap *and the snare,* from *death and tumult* ... You
[Solomon] will not be afraid of the terror of *the demons that
go about in* the night, nor of the arrow *of the angel of death
that he shoots* in the daytime, nor of the *death* that goes
about in the darkness, nor of *the company of demons that
destroy* at noon ... You [Solomon] will only look with your
eyes, and you will see *how the wicked are being
destroyed.* (Tg. Ps. 91:3–8)[76]

Solomon responds by addressing God directly and, in turn, receives
a word of promise: "No evil shall befall you, and no plague *or
demons* shall come near your tent. For he will give his angels charge
over you, to guard you in all your ways. In *their strength* they will lift
you up, lest *your foot stumbles through your evil inclination, which
may be compared to* a stone. You will tread upon the lion *cub* and the
adder; you will trample the lion and the basilisk" (Tg. Ps. 91:10–13).
According to this interpreter, Ps 91:10–13 constitutes a divine promise of protection against demonic beasts addressed to a descendant
of David.

Despite the Targum's late date (c. fourth to sixth century CE), the
interpreter draws inferences about the identities of the speaker and
addressee that can be traced back to the first century CE.[77] The
combined evidence of Psalm 90 LXX and the Hebrew version of
the psalm discovered in Cave 11 (11QApPs 6:2–15)[78] make it probable that most early interpreters assumed David was the speaker.
Further, the placement of Psalm 91 at the close of a collection of
psalms used for performing exorcisms (11QApPs) suggests that the
connection between "beasts" and demons in the Targum is part of an
interpretive tradition dating back to the late Second Temple period.
This collection also evinces a close association between the names
"David" (לדויד; 11QApPs 5:4) and "Solomon" (שלומה; 11QApPs 2:2),
which leads Émile Puech to speculate, "Dans la mesure où il été
possible d'en restaurer le début et la fin, le deuxième Psaume de

---

[76] I follow the translation of David M. Stec, *The Targum of Psalms: Translated with
a Critical Introduction, Apparatus, and Notes,* ArBib 16 (London: T&T Clark, 2004),
174–175, his emphasis.

[77] On the dating of the Targum, see Stec, *Targum of Psalms,* 1–2.

[78] In the previous column, directly following a *vacat,* לדויד indicates the beginning of
a Davidic psalm (11QApPs[a] 5:4; Florentino García Martínez, Eibert J. C. Tigchelaar,
and Adam S. van der Woude, eds., *Qumran Cave 11 II: 11Q2–18, 11Q20–31,* DJD 23
[Oxford: Clarendon, 1998], 198, 202–203).

11Q11 appartiendrait à un Psaume davidique et non salomonien, invitant l'exorciste à practiquer l'incantation de David comme le fit Salomon, son fils, qui devint l'exorciste par excellance, ainsi qu'il est bien connu de la tradition ancienne."[79] If Puech is correct, the targumist's inference that Solomon is the addressee in Ps 91:10–13 appears to reflect a first-century tradition.

Pseudo-Philo's recitation of the opening of David's career provides another important piece of evidence. Immediately after his anointing, the messiah of the Lord bursts into psalmic praise, "When Abel first shepherded flocks, his sacrifice was more acceptable than that of his brother, and his brother was jealous of him and killed him. But for me it is not the same, because God has protected me and because he has delivered me to his angels and to his guardians that they should guard me" (LAB 59:4). Although the point has yet to be recognized, David's claim to angelic protection likely stems from the language in Ps 91:11.[80] The following chart illustrates the shared lexical features between LAB and the psalm.

LAB 59:4	Ps 90:11 Vulg.	Ps 90:11 LXX	Ps 91:11 MT
et quoniam angelis suis tradidit me et custodibus suis ut custodiant me	*quoniam angelis suis mandabit de te ut custodiant te in omnibus viis tuis*	ὅτι τοῖς ἀγγέλοις αὐτοῦ ἐντελεῖται περὶ σοῦ τοῦ διαφυλάξαι σε ἐν πάσαις ταῖς ὁδοῖς σου	כי מלאכיו יצוה־לך לשמרך בכל־דרכיך

---

[79] Émile Puech, "Les Psaumes Davidiques du Rituel d'Exorcisme (11Q11)," in *Sapiential, Liturgical and Poetical Texts from Qumran: Proceedings of the Third Meeting of the International Organization for Qumran Studies (Oslo 1998)*, eds. Daniel K. Falk, Florentino García Martínez, and Eileen M. Schuller, STDJ 35 (Leiden: Brill, 2000), 160–181, here 180. His suggestion finds support in LAB's rendition of 1 Sam 16:14–23, in which David soothes Saul's torment by singing of a time when his offspring will rule over demons (LAB 60:3); cf. the use of the epithet "son of David" in T. Sol. Dennis Duling posits that "[t]he address 'Son of David' could be a link between the magical tradition about Solomon and the activity of Jesus as exorcist and healer" ("Testament of Solomon [First to Third Century A.D.]," *OTP* 1: 935–987, here 960 n. d). This tradition takes a strange twist in Testim. Truth 70.3–11, when the writer accuses David and Solomon of dwelling with demons (Craig A. Evans, "David in the Dead Sea Scrolls, in *The Scrolls and the Scriptures: Qumran Fifty Years After*, eds. Stanley E. Porter and Craig A. Evans, JSPSup 26 [Sheffield: Sheffield Academic Press, 1997], 183–197, at 196).

[80] See now my article, "'Then David Began to Sing This Song': Composition and Hermeneutics in Pseudo-Philo's Psalm of David (LAB 59.4)," *JSP* 28 (2018): 69–87.

Two observations enhance the likelihood that Pseudo-Philo is drawing on Psalm 91. First, LAB 59:4 incorporates multiple Davidic psalms, whereby Pseudo-Philo correlates the psalmist's plea that YHWH would preserve the life of his anointed (cf. Ps 61:1–2) and his statement of faith, "If my father and mother forsake me, YHWH will take me up" (cf. Ps 27:10), with the events surrounding David's anointing (LAB 59; cf. 1 Sam 16:6–13). This makes it less likely that distinct lexical features shared between LAB 59:4 and Ps 91:11 are the products of chance. Second, an erudite interpreter like Pseudo-Philo would have had scriptural recourse to correlate Ps 91:11 to this point in David's life, since it was around this time that the Lord is said to have delivered his elect one from "the paw of the lion" (cf. 1 Sam 17:37). As it happens, Pseudo-Philo subverts the narrative order of the Deuteronomistic History so that the attack of the lion occurs while David is still singing, which may suggest he interprets the legend of David's victory over the lion and the bear (cf. 1 Sam 17:34–37) as the immediate consequence of the promise God makes to the Davidic king in Ps 91:11.

Whether we can speak here of a common interpretive tradition of Psalm 91 must remain an open question. The above examples, however, attest to the possibility that an appeal to the psalm, and to verses 10–13 in particular, would activate a Davidic frame for ancient readers, perhaps calling to mind memories of the great king himself (LAB), or the quintessential Davidide of Israel's golden age, Solomon (Tg. Ps 91), or even a first-century claimant to the Davidic throne, Jesus of Nazareth (Matt; Luke).

3.4.2   Among Angels and Beasts (LAB 59–61;
          Psalms 152 and 153)

The collocation of beasts and angels in Mark 1:13 also resonates with a number of first-century recitations of the schema at the opening of David's career in 1 Samuel 16–17. As previously mentioned, Pseudo-Philo's rendition of these events links royal anointing (cf. 1 Sam 16:13), angelic protection, and deliverance from beasts (cf. Ps 91:10–13; 1 Sam 17:34–37).[81] Before the Lord's messiah can finish his song, he is assaulted by *ferae*, "wild beasts," and

---

[81] Daniel J. Harrington dates LAB to the mid-first century CE and argues that the Latin text, which is based on a Greek *Vorlage*, ultimately derives from a Semitic *Vorlage* (*OTP* 2: 298–299). I follow Harrington's translation throughout, including his

subsequently delivered by the hand of the Lord, presumably through angelic mediation (LAB 59:5; cf. LAB 61:8–9), in a scene that anticipates his triumph over Goliath (LAB 59:5).

Two Syriac psalms, Psalms 152 and 153, agree with LAB on two points of detail that go beyond 1 Sam 17:34–37.[82] First, both psalms refer to the "lion" and the "wolf,"[83] as "beasts" (Pss 152:5; 153:4); second, both specify that David was delivered from these beasts by means of angelic assistance (cf. Pss 152:6; 153:4). The reason for such agreement is not apparent. On the one hand, there is a clear literary relationship between Psalms 152 and 153, including indications that both psalms, at least in their final forms, contain multiple allusions to the Peshitta Psalter.[84] On the other hand, there is no evidence that the motif of angelic deliverance from beasts derives from a literary relationship with LAB or any Syriac version of 1 Sam 17:34–37. Thus it may be the case, though one can hardly be certain, that these points of agreement between LAB and the Syriac Psalms 152 and 153 attest to a broader tradition.

Mark 1:13 and its immediate context share a number of distinct lexical and thematic features with traditions dependent on 1 Samuel 16–17 (or parts thereof), as the following chart illustrates.

While these traditions agree that the lion and the bear/wolf are "beasts" from which, according to three of the four traditions,

---

italics, which are intended to signal, "[w]here the text agrees with a recognizable ancient biblical text (the MT, LXX, Samaritan Pentateuch, etc.)" (2: 303).

[82] For Pss 152 and 153, see W. Baars, ed., "Apocryphal Psalms," in *Canticles or Odes, Prayer of Manasseh, Apocryphal Psalms, Psalms of Solomon, Tobit, and 1 (3) Esdras, The Old Testament in Syriac according to the Peshitta Version*, Part IV, fascicle 6 (Leiden: Brill, 1972), 5–6. The original language and provenance of these psalms is uncertain. Martin Noth argued Ps 152 reworks an earlier lament psalm written in Hebrew and that Ps 153 introduces additional Davidic allusions into an earlier thanksgiving psalm ("Die fünf überlieferten apokryphen Psalms," *ZAW* 48 [1930]:1–23). Charlesworth surmises, on the basis of its style and inclusion in a collection with other Syriac psalms whose Hebrew *Vorlagen* have been discovered at Qumran, that Ps 152 "was probably composed by a Palestinian Jew during the Hellenistic period" ("More Psalms of David [Third Century B.C.–First Century A.D.]," *OTP* 2:609–624, here 615). He suggests a similar possibility in the case of Ps 153 (616). Patrick Shekan, however, argues that "[t]he simplest explanation would seem to be that they are the product of the peculiar piety of a Syrian Christian who saw in the lion and the wolf types of death, and in the David figure a type of Christ and of redemption from death" ("Again the Syriac Apocryphal Psalms," *CBQ* 38 [1976]: 143–158, here 155).

[83] The substitution of "wolf" for "bear" (cf. 1 Sam 17:36 Pesh) suggests a confusion of *debbā* and *dêbā* (Shekan, "Again," 149).

[84] On these points, see Shekan, "Again," 147–155.

1 Sam 16–17	1. Anointing (16:6–13)	2. Exorcistic power (16:14–23)	3. Attack from Beasts (17:34–37)
LAB 59–60	• David is called "the holy one, the anointed of the Lord" (LAB 59:2). • God's angels will guard David (59:4; cf. Ps 91).	• David the exorcist prophesies that his offspring will rule over evils spirits (LAB 60:1–3).	• David is attacked by the lion and the bear immediately after being anointed (LAB 59:4). • Animals are called *ferae*, "beasts," whose defeat foreshadows David's triumph over Goliath (LAB 59:5).
Josephus, *Ant.*	• "[Samuel] took the oil and anointed him and spoke low into his ear, explaining that God has chosen to make him king" (Ant. 6.164–165).	• Saul is plagued by δαιμόνια, "demons" (6.166) and David is said to be the μόνος ἰατρός, "only physician," for the "distress caused by the demons" (Ant. 6.168).	• David saved his flock from the jaws of the beast. • David reckons Goliath as "one of those wild beasts" (Ant. 6.181–183).
Ps 152	X	X	• The lion and the wolf are called "beasts." • David recieves angelic assistance.
Ps 153	X	X	• The lion and the wolf are called "beasts." • David recieves angelic assistance.

angels protected David, they diverge in how they account for the sequence of events. Josephus maintains the Deuteronomistic Historian's solution (or lack thereof) that the attack happened at some point in the past (cf. 1 Sam 17:34–37). The Syriac Psalms are vague on the timing, too, though they may assume that it took place after David had been anointed. Pseudo-Philo, by contrast, locates the attack immediately after David's anointing, a decision that brings the opening of David's career in LAB into proximity with the sequence of events at the opening of Jesus's career in Mark: (1) messianic anointing (Mark 1:9–11; LAB 59:3), (2) antagonism from "beasts" accompanied by angelic oversight (Mark 1:13; LAB 59:4–5), (3) deliverance of God's messiah forecasts his triumph over Israel's enemy (Mark 1:13; LAB 59:5),[85] and (4) the messiah is "the holy one" and an adroit exorcist (Mark 1:24; LAB 59:2; 60; on which see Section 4.2).

These observations lend credence to the not infrequent suggestion that the opening of David's career in the Deuteronomistic History belongs to the treasury of intertextuality on which early Christ followers drew to articulate the significance of Jesus's life.[86] While one would be hard-pressed to demonstrate definitively that the evangelist consciously culled material from 1 Samuel 16–17, one can make a case that the Markan presentation of the opening of Jesus's career – (1) baptism/anointing (cf. 1 Sam 16:13), (2) confrontation with the enemy (cf. 1 Sam 17), and (3) exorcistic therapy (cf. 1 Sam 16:14–23) – evokes iconic moments from the opening of David's. If, therefore, we answer yes to any of other intertextual proposals on offer, a new Adam, a sapiential righteous sufferer, an anointed prophet, and the like – and these are by no means mutually exclusive – then we should affirm that the temptation scene also casts Jesus as a messiah like David.

---

[85] Commentators differ as to whether Jesus's victory in the wilderness represents the decisive undoing of Satan's power, such that his exorcisms in the remainder of the narrative amount to a mere "mop-up" operation (so Ernest Best, *The Temptation and the Passion: The Markan Soteriology*, SNTSMS 2 [Cambridge: Cambridge University Press, 1965], 13–15), or whether it represents the beginning of an ongoing, protracted conflict (so James M. Robinson, *The Problem of History in Mark*, SBT 21 [London: SCM, 1957], 33–42). A convincing case for latter position has recently been made by Elizabeth E. Shively ("Characterizing the Non-Human: Satan in the Gospel of Mark," in Christopher Skinner and Matthew Hauge, eds, *Character Studies and the Gospel of Mark*, LNTS 483 [London: T&T Clark, 2014], 127–151).

[86] See, e.g., N. T. Wright, *The New Testament and the People of God*, volume 1 of *Christian Origins and the Question of God* [London: SPCK, 1992], 378–381; Daly-Denton, *David*, 289–315. A number of interpreters detect allusions to the life of David in Mark's passion narrative (e.g., John R. Donahue, "Temple, Trial and Royal Christology [Mark 14:53–65]," in *The Passion in Mark: Studies on Mark 14–16*, ed. Werner H. Kelber [Philadelphia: Fortress, 1976], 61–79, csp. 76; Raymond E. Brown, *The Death of the Messiah: From Gethsemane to the Grave: A Commentary on the Passion Narrative in the Four Gospels*, 2 vols. [New York: Doubleday, 1994], 1: 125; Yarbro Collins, *Mark*, 83–84).

3.5   Conclusion

Unlike the evangelists Matthew and Luke, Mark does not introduce his audience to the messiah son of David. Rather, much as the Deuteronomistic Historian introduced his David, and other first-century writers their messiahs, the evangelist introduces Jesus of Nazareth as a spirit-anointed messiah come to do battle with the one who holds Israel in bondage (cf. Mark 1:9–13). The cosmic struggle of the messiah son of God in Psalm 2 and the messianic servant in the latter parts of Isaiah are played out in the life of Mark's Jesus, a messiah who, it seems, will overcome the powers of darkness by entrusting his life to Israel's God.

Mark's construction of Christ is not participant to some predetermined formula; nor still is it an arbitrary creation built on the wiles of artistic fiat; rather, it is a "creatively biblical linguistic act," whereby, in this instance, an author has chosen to characterize his messiah with traits drawn from traditions that his linguistic community associated with David and his line. In the following chapters, I will trace the ways in which Mark continues to refine his portrait of Christ, including his answer to the pertinent question, must a legitimate messiah be a *descendant* of David? But on this point the prologue leaves little doubt: the man christened by the spirit in the waters of the Jordan is a messiah *like* David.

4

HOW A GALILEAN PROPHET BECOMES A MESSIAH LIKE DAVID

What do you want with us, Jesus of Nazareth? ... I know who you are, the holy one of God!

– Mark 1:24

He asked them, "But who do you say I am?" Peter answered, "You are the messiah."

– Mark 8:29

Since David and Solomon were associated with exorcism in the time of Jesus, it is not strange that the Gospel of Mark could present him both as the Davidic messiah and as a powerful exorcist.

– Adela Yarbro Collins, *Mark: A Commentary,* 68

In the previous chapter, I made the case that Mark provides his audience with the requisite cues to interpret the arrival of Jesus. In this chapter, I turn my attention to the remainder of the first half of the Gospel. The vast majority of interpreters have concluded that this section divulges little to no interest in Davidic messiahship, only then to climax in Peter's misguided – perhaps even erroneous – "confession" that Jesus is ὁ χριστός (cf. Mark 8:29). I fill out this putative messianic vacuum by demonstrating that there are, in fact, a number of points in the first half of Mark's Gospel that, to varying degrees, cast the prophet from Nazareth in a Davidic light. Four texts in particular will occupy our attention: (1) the opening of Jesus's public ministry at the Capernaum synagogue (1:21–28); (2) the controversy between Jesus and the Pharisees over plucking grain on the Sabbath (2:23–28); (3) the rift between Jesus and his family over the significance of his ministry (3:20–21, 31–35); and (4) Jesus's feeding of the 5,000 (6:30–44). This material enables the audience to evaluate the ensuing dispute between Peter and Jesus over the meaning of the term "messiah."

4.1 The Messiah Is the Holy One of God

It has become almost obligatory to being a discussion of the rare christological title ὁ ἅγιος τοῦ θεοῦ, "the holy one of God," by conceding that it "was not a messianic title in Judaism."[1] The title never occurs outside the New Testament and, outside of Mark 1:24, only in two other places (Luke 4:34; John 6:69).[2] In light of such paltry attestation, some reach the conclusion of Edwin Broadhead, that ὁ ἅγιος τοῦ θεοῦ is a "largely inconsequential description."[3] Such pessimism is perhaps further warranted by the fact that, despite the efforts of a number of interpreters, no compelling explanation for the derivation of this title has been offered.[4] Rather, it would appear

---

[1] Hooker, *Gospel*, 64. This section represents and develops material from my article, "The Messiah Is 'the Holy One': ὁ ἅγιος τοῦ θεοῦ as a Messianic Title in Mark 1:24," *JBL* 136 (2017): 419–435. I use this material with the journal's permission.

[2] Joseph Fitzmyer, *The Gospel According to Luke (I–IX): Introduction, Translation, and Notes*, AB 28 (Garden City, NY: Doubleday, 1981), 546. Luke 4:34 is dependent on Mark 1:24; John 6:69 appears to be an alternative version of Peter's christological confession in Mark 8:29; see Craig Keener, *The Gospel of John: A Commentary*, 2 vols. (Peabody, MA: Hendrickson, 2003), 1:697.

[3] Broadhead, *Naming Jesus*, 100; see also, France, *Gospel of Mark*, 104; Kingsbury, *Christology*, 86–88; Räisänen, *'Messianic Secret'*, 173.

[4] The most influential proposal at one time was Otto Bauernfeind's suggestion that Mark had reworked 3 Kgdms 17:18 (*Die Worte der Dämonen im Markusevangelium*, BWA(N)T 3/8 [Stuttgart: Kohlhammer, 1927], 3–18). The collocation of the phrase τί ἐμοὶ καὶ σοί and the vocative ἄνθρωπε τοῦ θεοῦ convinced Bauernfeind that he had located Mark's source. He posited that ὁ ἅγιος τοῦ θεοῦ was a Markan alteration of ἄνθρωπε τοῦ θεοῦ and, by comparing the demon's οἶδα-saying in Mark 1:24 to similar expressions in the Greek Magical Papyri, concluded that ὁ ἅγιος τοῦ θεοῦ signified a θεῖος ἀνήρ. The influence of Bauernfeind's proposal is apparent, to varying degrees, in Erich Klostermann, *Das Markusevangelium* HNT 3 (Tübingen: Paul Siebeck, 1950); 17; Robinson, *Problem*, 36; Johannes Schreiber, *Theologie des Vertrauens: Eine redaktionsgeschichtliche Untersuchung des Markusevangelium* (Hamburg: Furche-Verlag, 1967), 221; Karl Kertelge, *Die Wunder Jesu im Markusevangelium: Eine redaktionsgeschichtliche Untersuchung* (München: Kösel-Verlag, 1970), 53; Kee, *Community*, 120; Lührmann, *Markusevangelium*, 51; Räisänen, *'Messianic Secret'*, 172–173. Gerhard Friedrich, on the other hand, argued that ὁ ἅγιος τοῦ θεοῦ pointed to Jesus's role as the eschatological high priest who would bind and destroy demons (cf. T. Levi 18:12) ("Beobachtungen zur messianischen Hohepriestererwartung in den Synoptikern," *ZTK* 53 [1956]: 265–311). This proposal was subsequently attacked by Ferdinand Hahn (*Titles*, 229–235), and has never gained much currency, though see Walter Grundmann, *Das Evangelium nach Markus*, 2 vols., THKNT 2 (Berlin: Evangelische Verlags-Anstalt, 1965), 1:43, and to some extent, Marcus, *Mark 1–8*, 188. Another proposal, popular mostly in the 1960s and 1970s, is that ἅγιος is the result of *Wortspiel*, "wordplay," on Ναζαρηνός (Franz Mussner, "Ein Wortspiel in Mk

the best one can do is to offer a range of possible connotations that the title might evoke.

Four scriptural categories provide potential points of resonance with the Markan title. First, many hear echoes of traditions about two of Israel's most renowned charismatic prophets: (1) a widow of Zarephath addresses Elijah, "What have you against me, O man of God? [τί ἐμοὶ καὶ σοί ἄνθρωπε τοῦ θεοῦ]" (3 Kgdms 17:18) and (2) a Shunammite woman describes Elisha as "this man of God [who is] holy [ἄνθρωπος τοῦ θεοῦ ἅγιος οὗτος]" (4 Kgdms 4:9).[5] Second, a number of interpreters plausibly detect resonances with (high) priestly traditions (cf. Ps 106:16 LXX; Sira 45:6).[6] Third, some point to texts that describe the corporate people of Israel (cf. Deut 7:6; 14:2), or a subset thereof (cf. 1 En. 38:4), as holy.[7] And finally, several interpreters note that "holy one (of Israel)" is a common designation for the God of Israel (see esp. Isaiah).[8]

Markedly absent from this list, however, is any indication that ὁ ἅγιος τοῦ θεοῦ may be suggestive of traditions about anointed kings, a curious coincidence in light of the consensus that it functions as a

---

1,24?" *BZ* 4 [1960]: 285–286; Eduard Schweizer, "'Er wird Nazoräer heissen' [zu Mc 1.24; Mt 2.23]," in *Judentum, Urchristentum, Kirche*, W. Eltester, ed. [Berlin: Töpelmann, 1964]; Pesch, *Markusevangelium*, 1:122 n. 20). If, however, there was an early wordplay on "Nazareth/Nazarene," the most likely candidate would appear to be the Davidic appellation shoot [*nēṣer*] of Jesse (so Blenkinsopp, *Opening the Sealed Book*, 155–156; and Piotrowski, *Matthew's New David at the End of Exile*, 150–172).

[5] Hooker, *St Mark*, 64; Gnilka, *Evangelium*, 1:81; and n. 4 of this chapter. Other notable individuals called ἅγιος in the Jewish scriptures are Moses (Wis 11:1); Samson (Judg 16:17 LXX B), and Jacob/Israel (Dan 3:35 LXX and θ').

[6] E.g., Marcus, *Mark 1–8*, 188. For a more developed argument that the title signifies a priestly figure, see Crispin H. T. Fletcher-Louis, "Jesus as the High Priestly Messiah: Part 2," *JSHJ* 5 (2007): 57–79, at 63–64. I suspect Fletcher-Louis is partially correct, though, as we will see, he is mistaken when he claims that "the acclamation does not suit a king" (63).

[7] Lagrange, *Saint Marc*, 22. Kee points to the language in 1 Enoch in particular (*Community*, 120); 1QS and CD use אנשי הקודש (1QS 5:13, 18; 8:17, 24; CD 4:6), עצת הקודש (1QS 2:9; 8:21), and עדת הקודש (1QS 1:12–13; 2:16). John Collins notes that, by far, the most common referent(s) for holy one(s) in early Jewish literature is (are) angel(s), though he does list some exceptions (*Daniel: A Commentary on the Book of Daniel*, Hermeneia [Minneapolis, MN: Fortress, 1993], 313–318). New Testament interpreters rarely suggest that the christological title ὁ ἅγιος τοῦ θεοῦ has angelic connotations, though see Gathercole, *Pre-Existent Son*, 152.

[8] E.g., M. Eugene Boring points out that YHWH is called "Holy One (of Israel)" 39 times in Isaiah (*Mark: A Commentary*, NTL [Louisville, KY: Westminster John Knox, 2006], 64). On the wider significance of Isaiah in Mark, see Marcus, *Way*, 12–45; Watts, *Isaiah's New Exodus*.

messianic title *in* Mark (cf. Mark 1:24; 3:11; 5:7).[9] The textual traditions I examine in the following sections establish that there is an inherent link between royal anointing and the appellation "the holy one" within the body of linguistic resources from which ancient authors derived their messiah language. My proposal is that this link is, in part, responsible for the ascription of this appellation to one particular messiah, Mark's Jesus.

4.1.1   Psalm 88:19 LXX

Psalm 89 (88 LXX) evinces an integral link between royal anointing and YHWH's holiness: "I [YHWH] have anointed him [David] with my holy oil" (89:21 בשמן קדשי משחתיו MT; ἐν ἐλαίῳ ἁγίῳ μου ἔχρισα αὐτόν 88:21 LXX).[10] While the Jewish scriptures are replete with references to the Davidic king as YHWH's anointed (e.g., 1 Sam 16:13; Pss 2:2, 18:50, 132:10), this verse is the lone instance in which the oil used to anoint David is specifically classified as "holy."[11] In fact, the construction "with holy oil" (instrumental ב or ἐν + dative) only occurs in two other places in the Jewish scriptures (Num 35:25; Sir 45:15), both with reference to the means of high priestly consecration.[12]

More importantly, the MT and LXX differ with respect to the referent of "holy one of Israel" (v. 19). On the one hand, the MT reads, "for our shield belongs to YHWH [כי ליהוה מגננו], and our king belongs to the holy one of Israel [ולקדוש ישראל מלכנו]." Both clauses have the subject in final position (מלכנו; מגננו) and use a possessive *lamed* to indicate a belonging to YHWH. On the other hand, the LXX reads, "for help comes from the Lord [ὅτι τοῦ κυρίου ἡ ἀντίλημψις], and from the holy one of Israel, our king [καὶ τοῦ ἁγίου Ἰσραὴλ βασιλέως ἡμῶν]."[13] The syntax of the Greek dictates that τοῦ

---

[9] Wrede, *Messiasgeheimnis*, 22–23; Kingsbury, *Christology*, 86–88; Räisänen, '*Messianic Secret*', 172; Marcus, *Mark 1–8*, 192–193; Malbon, *Mark's Jesus*, 82.

[10] מן שמן קדשי 4QPs^x 1:3; listed in Ulrich, ed., *Biblical Scrolls*, 3: 652–653.

[11] I discuss additional references to David's anointing by holy oil later in this chapter.

[12] Holy anointing oil is used, of course, to consecrate the *sancta* (e.g., Exod 30:25, 31; 37:29; 38:25) and (high) priests (e.g., Lev 21:10); but the specific expression in Ps 89 (88):21 is quite rare.

[13] Even if one assumes a *Vorlage* equivalent to the MT, there is not enough evidence to discern any recognizable pattern in how the translator renders possessive *lameds*: (1) לך שמים אף־לך ארץ is rendered σοί [possessive dative] εἰσιν οἱ οὐρανοὶ καὶ σή [predicate adjective] ἐστιν ἡ γῆ (v. 12); (2) לך זרוע עם־גבורה is rendered σὸς [predicate

ἁγίου Ἰσραήλ is in apposition with βασιλέως ἡμῶν, implying that David is designated the holy one of Israel. Some recensions add a copula to clarify this very point – thus, *sanctus Israel est rex noster*.[14] This reading is coherent with the wider context of the psalm, in which (1) YHWH anoints David with "my holy oil" (ἐν ἐλαίῳ ἁγίῳ μου ἔχρισα αὐτόν; v. 21), (2) YHWH's hand will help David (συναντιλήμψεται αὐτῷ), and (3) David will cry out to YHWH, "You are my father, my God, and the helper of my salvation" (ἀντιλήμπτωρ τῆς σωτηρίας μου; v. 27).[15] Thus, while the underlining message of the LXX remains the same as the MT – Israel's help comes from YHWH via his messiah – the Greek psalm suggests that David is the holy one of Israel because he is YHWH's messiah.

This shift in referent, while inconsequential to the meaning of Psalm 88 LXX, has the potential to be significant for how we understand the development of the christological title ὁ ἅγιος τοῦ θεοῦ. Although none of the earliest Christian writers cite Psalm 88 LXX, there is evidence to suggest that the psalm functioned as important linguistic resource from which they drew their messiah language.[16] There are, in fact, a number of places in Mark's Gospel where the language the evangelist uses to describe his Christ, as Daniel Kirk and Steven Young note, "trades on a set of descriptions . . . similar to those found in the psalm."[17] These are as follows: (1) David's anointing is correlated with his receipt of YHWH's strength (Ps 88:20–21 LXX); God's spirit comes upon Jesus to empower him as "the stronger one" (Mark 1:7–11;

adjective] ὁ βραχίων μετὰ δυναστείας (v. 14). The decision to render the possessive *lamed* with a genitive is unique to v. 19 and, whatever the intent, opens the Greek text to a different reading than the MT's.

[14] Bo and Sa are listed in Alfred Rahlfs, ed., *Psalmi cum Odis*, 2nd edn., Septuaginta 10 (Göttingen: Vandenhoeck & Ruprecht, 1979), 234.

[15] The final clause is missing in 4QPs[x].

[16] By my count, the NA[28] lists 26 possible allusions to Ps 89 (88 LXX). On the use of the psalm in early Christian literature, see Juel, *Messianic Exegesis*, 104–110; Knut M. Heim, "The (God-)Forsaken King of Psalm 89: A Historical and Intertextual Enquiry," in *King and Messiah in Israel and the Ancient Near East: Proceedings of the Oxford Old Testament Seminar*, ed. John Day, LHBOTS 270 (Sheffield: Sheffield Academic Press, 1998), 296–322; Daly-Denton, *David*, 245–253; Hays *Conversion*, 110–111; Doble, "Luke 24.26, 44," 277–278. Although allusions to Ps 89 (88 LXX) are less frequent in Jewish messiah texts, there is at least one plausible allusion in Pss. Sol. 17:4 (Atkinson, *Intertextual Study*, 337). Note also the clear allusion to Ps 89 (88):1–4, 34–37 in T. Jud. 22:3.

[17] J. R. Daniel Kirk and Stephen L. Young, "'I Will Set His Hand to the Sea': Psalm 88:26 LXX and Christology in Mark," *JBL* 133 (2014): 333–340, at 338.

3:23–28); (2) YHWH delegates his cosmic power over the sea) – the same power he displayed when he slew Yam and Rahab at the *Chaoskampf* (88:10–11 LXX) – to David (88:26 LXX);[18] Jesus exercises the cosmic authority he received from God to rebuke the wind and the sea (Mark 4:35–41; 6:45–52); (3) David is described as YHWH's "servant" (δοῦλος, Ps 88:4, 21, 40, 51 LXX); Jesus embodies the position of a "servant" in his self-giving death (δοῦλος, Mark 10:45); (4) David cries out to YHWH, "You are my father [πατήρ μου εἶ σύ], my God, and the helper of my salvation!" (Ps 88:27 LXX); at his most vulnerable moment, Jesus cries out "abba, father [ἀββὰ ὁ πατήρ]" (Mark 14:36);[19] and (5) Psalm 88 LXX closes with the mockery (ὀνειδίζειν) of YHWH's messiah by his enemies and his plea to YHWH for deliverance (Ps 88:52); while hanging on the cross, Jesus is mocked (ὀνειδίζειν) by his adversaries and cries out to God (15:32–34).[20] Although these points of resonance do not demonstrate that the evangelist had access to a text-form of the psalm in agreement with LXX manuscripts at verse 19, they open up the distinct possibility that he had engaged with the psalm and, therefore, that he may have encountered a text describing the Davidic messiah as the holy one of Israel.

---

[18] Dumortier observes that the Davidic king in Ps 89 is "le roi, véritable lieu-tenant de Yahvé sur terre, possède une puissance directement proportionnelle à la puissance divine" ("Un Rituel," 187). The language he uses to describe this figure is remarkably similar to the language Joel Marcus uses to describe the Markan Jesus when he exercises his power over the watery chaos (*Mark 1–8*, 338).

[19] Jesus's *abba*-prayer is unique to Mark's Gospel (cf. Gal 4:5; Rom 8:15; perhaps Heb 5:7). Joachim Jeremias famously attributed the expression ἀββὰ ὁ πατήρ to Jesus's practice of addressing God as "my father" (*Abba: Studien zur neutestamentlichen Theologie und Zeitgeschichte* [Göttingen: Vandenhoeck & Ruprecht, 1966], 1–67). And, although James Barr largely dismantled Jeremias's case, he did acknowledge that the ambiguity of *abba* "in its common vocative function" allowed it to signify "my father" ("'Abbā Isn't 'Daddy,'" *JTS* 39 (1988): 28–47; repr., in *Bible and Interpretation: The Collected Essays of James Barr*, 3 vols., ed. John Barton (Oxford: Oxford University Press, 2013), 3: 262–280, at 273). While we now know that the address "my father" was not as unique in Palestinian Judaism as Jeremias once thought (see, e.g., Eileen M. Schuller, "The Psalm of 4Q372 1 with the Context of Second Temple Prayer," *CBQ* 54 [1992]: 67–79), this does not detract from the possibility that scripturally literate Christians would notice the similarities between Jesus's *abba*-prayer and the Davidic king's invocation in Ps 88:27 LXX.

[20] To be sure, Jesus's words from the cross mark a citation of the opening of Ps 22. Nevertheless, Juel (*Messianic Exegesis*, 110) is likely correct that some early Christ followers read Ps 89 (88 LXX) alongside other psalms depicting the Christ's suffering (esp. Pss 22, 31, 69).

4.1.2   Liber Antiquitatum Biblicarum 59:2

In Pseudo-Philo's account of 1 Sam 16:6–13, the prophet sets his eye on Eliab, Jesse's firstborn, and inquires, "Behold now is this the holy one, *the anointed of the Lord* [sanctus *christus Domini*]?" (LAB 59:2).[21] Specialists in LAB have proposed a number of possible source texts for the expression *sanctus christus Domini*.[22] It may be the case that the young king is called *sanctus* on the understanding that he had been anointed with holy oil (cf. Ps 89:21; 11QPs[a] XXVIII, 11; Josephus, *Ant.* 6.157), but this is speculative. Germane for our purposes is simply that the writer assumed a logical relationship between *christus* and *sanctus*: David is holy because he is the Lord's messiah.

Pseudo-Philo implies that it is precisely as *sanctus christus Domini* that David possesses knowledge of the origin of evil (unclean) spirits and predicts a time when, "one born from my loins will rule over you [nascetur ... de lateribus meis qui vos domabit]" (LAB 60:1–3).[23] While the figure he has in mind is likely Solomon rather than a future descendant of David, the language of the prophecy is noteworthy because it suggests that the exorcistic power David received from YHWH's spirit was – and perhaps would be – passed on to the Davidic line. That is, Pseudo-Philo seems to have inferred that David's exorcistic power is indicative of the kind of the power his son would exercise because of the promise the Lord made to David, "When your days are fulfilled and you lie down with your ancestors, I will raise up your offspring after you, who shall come forth from your body" (2 Sam 7:12; Chr 17:11).[24] One wonders what

---

[21] I follow Harrington's translation throughout, including his italics, which are intended to signal, "[w]here the text agrees with a recognizable ancient biblical text (the MT, LXX, Samaritan Pentateuch, etc.)" (*OTP* 2:303). The Latin text, including italics, follows Pseudo-Philo, *Les Antiquités Bibliques*, ed. Daniel J. Harrington, trans. Jacques Cazeaux, commentary by Charles Perrot and Pierre-Maurice Bogaert, 2 vols., SC 229, 230 (Paris: Cerf, 1976).

[22] See Howard Jacobson, *A Commentary on Pseudo-Philo's Liber Antiquitatum Biblicarum: With Latin Text and English Translations*, 2 vols., AGJU 31 (Leiden: Brill, 1996), 2:1166. In the commentary volume, Perrot and Bogaert list Mark 1:24, Luke 4:34, and John 6:69 as the closest linguistic parallel (*Les Antiquités Bibliques*, 2:230).

[23] LAB is one of many traditions that portrays David as an exorcist (cf. 11QApPs[a] 5:4; 6:3–14; 11QPs[a] 27:9–10; Josephus, *Ant.* 6.166–169; y. Šabb. 6:8b; y. 'Erub. 10:26c; b. Šebu. 15b). Commentators on LAB are divided as to whether David's prophecy refers to Solomon or to a future messiah (see Jacobson, *Commentary*, 2:1180). I agree with Harrington that the former is more plausible (*OTP* 2:373 n. e).

[24] Le Donne, *Historiographical Jesus*, 152–153.

Pseudo-Philo would make of Mark's Christ, a spirit-anointed messiah who launched his public ministry with an exorcism as "the holy one of God."

4.1.3 Additional Evidence

As noted in the previous chapter, two Syriac psalms, Psalms 152 and 153, agree with LAB 59:4–5 that David received angelic protection from the attack of "beasts" (cf. 1 Sam 17:34–37).[25] Significantly, both psalms also refer to the king as the "holy one" of God: (1) "Spare, O Lord, your elect one [ܡܝ,ܒܟ], and deliver your holy one [ܡܝ,ܩܘܝ] from destruction" (Ps 152:4); (2) "For he delivered the physical life of his elect one [ܡ,ܒܟ] from the hands of death; and he redeemed his holy one [ܡ,ܩܘܝ] from destruction" (Ps 153:2).[26] While neither psalm provides a linguistic parallel to the Markan title ὁ ἅγιος τοῦ θεοῦ (one would instead expect ܙܝܕ), the root ,ܩܘ does connotes "holiness" along the lines of the Greek word ὅσιος used in Ps 16:10 LXX (cf. Acts 2:27; 13:35).[27] This then opens the possibility that the psalmist(s) would recognize the title ὁ ἅγιος τοῦ θεοῦ as an appropriate way of designating a Davidic king.

---

[25] For the Syriac text, see Baars, ed., "Apocryphal Psalms," 5 6. On the basis of its style and its inclusion in a collection with other Syriac psalms whose Hebrew *Vorlagen* have been discovered at Qumran, James H. Charlesworth concludes that "[Ps 152] was probably composed by a Palestinian Jew during the Hellenistic period" ("More Psalms of David [Third Century B.C. – First Century A.D.]." *OTP* 2: 609–625, here 615). The issues with dating Ps 153 are mutatis mutandis the same as with Ps 152. Shekan ("Again," 154–155) maintains that the author of Ps 152 was a Nestorian Christian writing in Syriac. If correct, then Ps 152 (and 153) indicates that a Syrian Christian recognized the Davidic "holy one" as a type of the Christ.
[26] Trans. Charlesworth (*OTP* 2: 616–617, my emphasis).
[27] See Michael Sokoloff, *A Syriac Lexicon: A Translation from the Latin, Correction, Expansion, and Update of C. Brockelmann's Lexicon Syriacum* (Winona Lake, IN: Eisenbrauns, 2009), 475. If the author(s) of Pss 152 and 153 is (are) drawing on Ps 16:10, then it is likely the case that ,ܩܘ renders חסיד. Curiously, the translators of the Peshitta Psalter render חסיד ("pious/faithful one") in a number of different ways: (1) "holy one" (,ܩܘ) in Pss 16:10; 18:26 (cf. Deut 33:8; 1 Sam 2:9; Prov 2:8; Mic 7:2); (2) "chosen/elect one" (,ܒܟ) in Pss 4:4; 30:5; 32:6; 50:5; (3) "good one" (ܟܐ) in Pss 12:2; 86:2 (cf. 2 Sam 22:26; Jer 3:12); (4) "righteous one" (ܩ,ܙ) Pss 31:24; 37:28; 52:11; 79:2; 85:9; 89:20; 97:10; 116:15; 132:9; 145:10; 148:14; 149:1; 149:5; 149:9 (cf. 2 Chr 6:41); (5) "merciful (one)" (ܡܪܚܡ) in Pss 43:1; 145:17; and (6) "watchman" (ܢ,ܕ) in Ps 132:16 (text in D. M. Walter, ed., *The Book of Psalms*, The Old Testament in Syriac according to the Peshitta Version, Part II, fasc. 3 [Leiden: Brill, 1980]). I am grateful to Kai Akagi for alerting me to the diversity of terms used to render חסיד in the Peshitta Psalter.

The author of Luke-Acts – indeed, perhaps more than any other ancient author – shows a strong penchant for a holy messiah. He cites Ps 16:10 LXX, on two separate occasions (Acts 2:27; 13:35), to argue that the referent of "your holy one," τὸν ὅσιόν σου, is not David but the son of David, Jesus Christ.[28] He also consistently refers to his Christ as ἅγιος, often in the context of messianic discourse (cf. Luke 1:35; 4:34; Acts 3:14; 4:27, 30). Particularly revealing is Peter's designation of Jesus as "your holy servant," τὸν ἅγιον παῖδά σου, in Acts 4:27, a title that recalls the apostle's description of David as God's παῖς in 4:25, a clear indication that παῖς is functioning here as a Davidic designation (cf. Luke 1:69). The prayer interprets the referent of "his messiah" in Ps 2:2 with the Lukan designation "you holy servant" because this Jesus, the apostle confesses, is the one whom God anointed (Acts 4:27). This strongly implies that the modifier ἅγιος is the corollary of messianic anointing: Christ is God's holy servant because he has been anointed with the holy spirit (cf. Luke 3:22; 4:18; Acts 10:38).[29]

Finally, the seer of Revelation offers one of the clearest examples of an early association between the Davidic line and the christological title the holy one. The angel informs the apocalypticist, "These are the words of the holy one [ὁ ἅγιος], the true one, who has the key of David [ὁ ἔχων τὴν κλεῖν Δαυίδ], who opens and no one will shut, who shuts and no one will opens" (Rev 3:7). "The key of David" is an unambiguous allusion to Isa 22:20–22:

> On that day I will call my servant Eliakim son of Hilkiah, and will clothe him with your robe and bind your sash on him. I will commit your authority to his hand, and he shall be a father to the inhabitants of Jerusalem and to the house of Judah. I will place on his shoulder the key of the house of David; he shall open, and no one shall shut; he shall shut, and no one shall open.[30]

---

[28] ὁ ὅσιος is simply a faithful rendering of חסיד, "devout one," and is never used in the Greek scriptures to render קדש. Its semantic range, however, does impinge upon that of ἅγιος/קדש (cf. Deut 32:4; Ps 144:17; Heb 7:26; Rev 15:4).

[29] It is also worth noting that Luke alludes to Ps 88:21 LXX in Acts 13:22–23 (cf. Luke 23:35), and thus may have encountered a psalmic text describing the Davidic king as the holy one of Israel (Ps 88:19 LXX).

[30] See David E. Aune, *Revelation*, 3 vols., WBC 52 (Dallas, TX: Word, 1997–1998), 1:235; Craig R. Koester, *Revelation: A New Translation with Introduction and Commentary*, AB 38A (New Haven, CT: Yale University Press, 2014), 323–324.

The prophet goes on to relate that YHWH's servant Eliakim will soon fall, creating an interregnum with no clear end in sight (cf. Isa 22:25). The seer of Revelation thus capitalizes on this indeterminacy, suggesting that the risen Christ qua holy one and offspring of David (cf. Rev 5:5; cf. 22:16) is the future servant about whom the prophet spoke, the one destined to receive the keys to the kingdom.

4.1.4 Summary

The investigation yields a number of results that could prove fruitful for interpretation of the christological designation ὁ ἅγιος τοῦ θεοῦ.[31] First, four texts identify an anointed Davidide (χριστός/ christus) as God's "holy one" (ὁ ἅγιος/sanctus), as illustrated in the chart below.

Text	Subject	Title	Relationship to Anointing
Ps 88:19 LXX	David	ὁ ἅγιος Ἰσραήλ	• "I have found my servant David; with my holy oil I have anointed him [ἔχρισα αὐτόν]" (88:21)
LAB 59:2	David	sanctus christus Domini	• "Samuel anointed him [unxit eum] in the midst of his brothers" (LAB 59:3)
Acts 4:27	Jesus Christ	ὁ ἅγιος παῖς	• "his messiah [τοῦ χριστοῦ αὐτοῦ]" (Ps 2:2; Acts 4:26) • "Jesus whom you anointed [ὃν ἔχρισας]" (4:27)
Rev 3:7	Jesus Christ	ὁ ἅγιος	• "his messiah [τοῦ χριστοῦ αὐτοῦ]" (Ps 2:2; Rev 11:15)

---

[31] Two additional pieces of evidence suggest ὁ ἅγιος τοῦ θεοῦ may have carried Davidic connotations for Mark and his early auditors. First, the blessing over the cup in the Didache constructs a David-Jesus comparison similar that of Acts 4: "First, concerning the cup: 'We give thanks, our Father, for the holy vine of David, your servant [ὑπὲρ τῆς ἁγίας ἀμπέλου Δαυὶδ τοῦ παιδός], which you have made know to us *through Jesus, your servant* [διὰ Ἰησοῦ τοῦ παιδός σου]; to you be the glory forever'" (Did. 9:2 [Ehrman, LCL]). Second, although he is not designated the "the holy one," the messiah son of David in Pss. Sol. 17 is describe as being "pure from sin" (καθαρὸς ἀπὸ ἁμαρτίας; 17:36) and appears as YHWH's principal agent of purgation and purity maintenance. The designation ὁ ἅγιος τοῦ θεοῦ would not be ill suited for such a figure.

Second, three texts identify an anointed Davidide as God's "holy one" using a term other than ἅγιος (ܩܕܝܫ in Pss 152 and 153; ὅσιος in Acts 2:27; 13:35). Third, a number of the traditions in which David is referred to as the holy one share points of resonance with Mark – for example, LAB presents *sanctus christus Domini* as an exorcist par excellence. I turn now to consider how this material might enhance our reading of Mark 1:21–28.

4.1.5 Demonic Disclosure: "Jesus of Nazareth ... I Know Who You Are!"

Many interpreters have observed intratextual links both between the baptism-temptation account (Mark 1:9–13) and the inauguration of Jesus's public ministry at the Capernaum synagogue (1:21–28), and between the demon's recognition of Jesus as the holy one of God and subsequent demonic recognition that he is God's son (cf. 3:11; 5:7).[32] If, therefore, Mark identifies the baptism as an anointing and uses son of God as a messianic title at points throughout his narrative, then one has reason to suspect that ὁ ἅγιος τοῦ θεοῦ designates the messiah. Yet, it is precisely here that scholars often balk on account of a lack of evidence that ὁ ἅγιος τοῦ θεοῦ was a "messianic title" in early Judaism. As a result, many have concluded that the title is either the remnant of an older prophetic-exorcistic tradition[33] or a curious anomaly in an otherwise stable messiah tradition.[34]

The evidence I have examined in this section suggests an alternative explanation: the title ὁ ἅγιος τοῦ θεοῦ references traditions in which the Davidic king is identified as the holy one as a result of his being anointed with YHWH's holy spirit/oil. If my solution is persuasive, this suggests that the function of ὁ ἅγιος τοῦ θεοῦ in Mark 1:24 is not only to contrast a holy Jesus with an "unclean" (ἀκάθαρτος) spirit but also to drive home the point that Jesus of Nazareth, like king David of old, is a messiah who has been anointed with God's spirit to liberate his people from the forces that hold them captive. The demon's exigent question, "Have you come to destroy us (pl.)?" emphasizes the point. It knows full well that this Jesus is the

[32] See esp. Robinson, *Problem*, 35–38; Marcus, *Mark 1–8*, 190–195; Shively, *Apocalyptic Imagination*, 154–166.
[33] E.g., Räisänen, '*Messianic Secret*', 173.
[34] E.g., Kingsbury, *Christology*, 86–88; France, *Gospel*, 104.

spirit-anointed holy one of God and is able to deduce that his "coming" is the ultimate demise of its kind. The implicit rhetoric of the Markan pericope could thus be summarized as follows: the holy spirit is the power of God at work in a messiah like David, who has inaugurated "eschatological holy war"[35] against the powers that hold Israel in bondage.

Mark's decision to open Jesus's public ministry with an exorcism strengthens the comparison I drew in the previous chapter between the events launching the careers of two messiahs. That is, like the youngest son of Jesse, Jesus publically demonstrates that he has been anointed with God's spirit by performing an exorcism (cf. 1 Sam 16:14–23; LAB 60). What may have been apparent to Mark and his early auditors has rarely occurred to modern scholars operating with the assumption that Davidic messiahs are, ipso facto, not exorcists. But once we acknowledge that there is no stable messianic idea, and that every messiah is the result of an author's negotiating present circumstances in light of his scriptural traditions, then it becomes plausible that some would conclude – again, based on what they inherited in their scriptures – that the messiah would be a Davidic exorcist.

Mark brackets Jesus's public ministry outside of Jerusalem with two pericopae, 1:21–28 and 10:46–52, in which Jesus (1) performs an exorcism/healing, (2) is identified with his home town of Nazareth, and (3) is addressed as ὁ ἅγιος τοῦ θεοῦ and υἱὸς Δαυίδ, respectively. The more one recognizes the charismatic activity of the Nazarene as *messianic* ministry, the less the healing of Bartimaeus appears to be a bolt from the Davidic blue. (I explore this point further in the following chapter; see Section 5.1.1).

4.2   "Have You Not Read What David Did?"

The controversy over Jesus's disciples plucking grain on the Sabbath has been a point of substantial inquiry (Mark 2:23–28).[36] My interest

---

[35] Marcus, *Mark 1–8*, 195.

[36] See the list of studies in John P. Meier, "The Historical Jesus and the Plucking of the Grain on the Sabbath," *CBQ* 66 (2004): 561–581, 562 n. 3; see also Frans Neirynck, "Jesus and the Sabbath: Some Observations on Mark II,27," in *Jésus aux Origins de la Christologie*, ed. J. Dupont, 2nd edn., BETL 40 (Leuven: Peeters, 1989), 227–270. This section uses material from my article, "Has Jesus Read What David Did? Probing Problems in Mark 2:25–26," *JTS* 69 (2018): 484–499. I use this material with the journal's permission.

here lies with the logic of the final form of this pericope and with its fit within Mark's literary landscape.[37] More specifically, I am concerned with how an appeal to "what David did" contributes, if at all, to the Markan portrait of Christ. Interpreters have been bifurcated in their opinions on this issue for quite some time. On the one hand, many would agree with Burger's sentiment that "[d]iese Rechtfertigung operiert jedoch nicht damit, dass Jesus ja Davids Sohn sei, sondern beruft sich auf das Vorgehen Davids als generellen Präzedenzfall."[38] On the other hand, there are those who detect an implicit messianic logic operative in this pericope.[39] Thus, for example, Hays claims that "[t]he implicit Davidic typology supports Jesus' claim in the halakhic controversy because Jesus' status parallels that of David in I Samuel 21: like David, he is the anointed king (cf. 1 Sam 16:1–13) whose authority has not yet been recognized within Israel, save by his fugitive band of followers."[40] While I suspect Hays is

[37] For an overview of the various perspectives on how this pericope was composed, see Arland J. Hultgren, "The Formation of the Sabbath Pericope in Mark 2:23–28," *JBL* 91 (1972): 38–43; and Robert Guelich, *Mark 1–8:26*, WBC 34A (Dallas, TX: Word, 1989), 119–120.

[38] Burger, *Jesus als Davidssohn*, 58; so also Maurice Casey, "Culture and Historicity: The Plucking of the Grain (Mark 2.23–28)," *NTS* 34 (1988), 1–24, esp. 8–13; Lührmann, *Markusevangelium*, 64–65; Étienne Trocmé, *L'Évangile selon Saint Marc*, CNT 2 (Genève: Labor et Fides, 2000), 81–82; Horsley, *Hearing*, 164–166; Boring, *Mark*, 90–91; Malbon, *Mark's Jesus*, 153.

[39] Pesch, *Markusevangelium*, 1:182; Burton L. Mack and Vernon K. Robbins, *Patterns of Persuasion in the Gospels* (Sonoma, CA: Polebridge, 1989), 126–127; Marcus, *Mark 1–8*, 245–246; Yarbro Collins, *Mark*, 204–205. J. D. M. Derrett goes beyond most in articulating an intriguing yet highly intricate and, to my mind, overly tortuous account of the grain-plucking incident ("Judaica in St. Mark," in *Studies in the New Testament, Volume 1: Glimpses of the Legal and Social Presuppositions of the Authors* [Leiden: Brill, 1977], 85–100). He proposes, among other things, that the construction ἤρξαντο ὁδὸν ποιεῖν (lit. "they began to make a way") indicates that the disciples were acting in accordance with m. Sanh. 2.4, which states that the king "may break through [the private domain of any man] to make himself a road and no one may protest against him: the king's road has no prescribed measure" (trans. Herbert Danby, *The Mishnah: Translated from the Hebrew with Introduction and Brief Explanatory Notes* [Oxford: Oxford University Press, 1933], 384).

[40] Hays, *Echoes of Scripture in the Gospels*, 49. Hays neglects to mention, however, that many interpreters find the argument incoherent, including Jesus's appropriation of haggadic material in halakhic debate (see, e.g., David Daube, *The New Testament and Rabbinic Judaism* [London: Athlone, 1956], 67–71; David Daube, "Responsibilities of Master and Disciples in the Gospels," *NTS* 19 [1972] 1–15, at 5–8; D. M. Cohn-Sherbok, "An Analysis of Jesus' Arguments Concerning the Plucking of Grain on the Sabbath," *JSNT* 2 [1979], 31–41). I address this issue in my article ("Has Jesus Read What David Did?"). Alex Jassen's recent study, in particular, demonstrates that the Qumran sectarians had no problem with using non-Pentateuchal (i.e., "haggadic") material to develop their halakhot (*Scripture and Law in the Dead Sea Scrolls*

right, it would be advantageous to move the conversation beyond generic appeals to a "Davidic typology." Two features of Mark's account of the grain-plucking incident suggest that such a move is possible – namely, (1) Jesus's suggestion that David's men were "with him" when he traveled to Nob and (2) his peculiar claim that David ate the bread "in the time of Abiathar, the high priest."[41]

4.2.1 The Messiah's Men

Mark's Jesus anchors his defense of his disciples' illicit Sabbath activity in the premise that David's cohort participated in the king's (permissible) breach of the Torah.[42] The overall cogency of the argument is thus contingent on what Jesus meant by describing David's warriors as "those [who were] with him" (οἱ μετ᾽ αὐτοῦ in 2:25; τοῖς σὺν αὐτῷ οὖσιν in 2:26).[43] The near ubiquitous interpretation of this phrase is that he has flouted the context of 1 Samuel 21,

[Cambridge: Cambridge University Press, 2014], 216–246). And Yigael Yadin has documented a number of instances in which the writer of the "statutes of the king" (11QT[a] 56:12–59:21) used Davidic traditions to develop his halakha (*The Temple Scroll*, rev. English edn.; 3 vols. + suppl. [Israel Exploration Society, The Institute of Archaeology of the Hebrew University of Jerusalem, The Shrine of the Book; Jerusalem: Ben-Zvi, 1983], 1:347, 361–362, 2:255–256, 260–264; Casey D. Elledge, *The Temple Scroll: The Hidden Law of the Dead Sea Sect* [London: Weidenfeld & Nicolson, 1985], 115–117, 194). Thus, it would seem that the argument of Mark's Jesus "may contain an argument that would not have been out of line" with at least some Second Temple Jews (so George J. Brooke, *The Dead Sea Scrolls and the New Testament* [Minneapolis, MN: Fortress, 2005], 104).

[41] To address all the issues involved with this pericope would take us well afield of our present line of inquire; for a complete list, see Robert H. Gundry, *Mark: A Commentary on His Apology for the Cross* (Grand Rapids, MI: Eerdmans, 1993), 141.

[42] On the structure of the argument, see Joanna Dewey, *Markan Public Debate: Literary Technique, Concentric Structure and Theology in Mark 2:1–3:6* (SBLDS 48; Chico, CA: Scholars Press, 1980), 95–96. My use of the word "illicit" here articulates the perspective of Jesus's interlocutors. To adjudicate whether the disciples' behavior is licit would require answers to the questions: what time is it? And who is Jesus of Nazareth?

[43] Some interpreters (e.g., Derrett, "Judaica," 91; Casey, "Culture," 9–10) are convinced that rabbinic traditions that place David's arrival at Nob on the Sabbath were widely known in the first century CE (e.g., b. Menaḥ. 95b; Yal. 2.130). If some form of these traditions goes back to the first century, then this might suggest that the timing of David's arrival at Nob is what attracted Mark (and possibly the historical Jesus) to 1 Sam 21. Yet, it is striking, as Marcus notes (*Mark 1–8*, 244), that Mark shows no interest in *when* David's arrival took place. Of potential significance, though beyond the purview of the present study, are traditions in which the Davidic king is remembered to have exercised priestly perogatives (cf. 2 Sam 6:14–17; 8:18). If such traditions are in view, the tacit argument may be that David had the right to partake of

either on account of his ignorance of what the text says or as part of his rhetorical strategy.[44] That is, in direct contradiction to the Deuteronomistic Historian, Jesus insists that David was *not* alone when he appeared before the priest at Nob.

The suggestion that Mark's Jesus, for one reason or another, botched his account of 1 Samuel 21 is undoubtedly a viable interpretation. Yet there are grounds for questioning that it offers the most compelling account of Mark's language. Consider, for instance, the ways in which the writer of the so-called statues of the king (11QT[a] 56:12–59:21)[45] deploys the similar expression עמו, "with him," about a group of warriors traveling with Israel's king:

> *At the king's appointment*: "And he shall select for himself a thousand of them … to be with him [עמו]: twelve thousand men of war who shall not leave him alone, lest he be seized by the hands of nations … and they shall continuously be with him day and night [והיו עמו תמיד יומם ולילה], and they shall guard him from every act of sin" (11QT[a] 57:5–11).
>
> *In the rules for defensive warfare*: "and they shall send with him [עמו] the tenth part of the people to go out [to war] with him [עמו] against their enemies. And they shall go out with him [עמו]. And if a larger host enters the land of Israel, they shall send with him [עמו] a fifth part of the men of war.

---

the sacred bread – in contradiction to Lev 24:9 – because he was a priest of a different order (cf. Ps 110:4; Josephus, *J.W.* 6.438; *Ant.* 20.226).

[44] See, e.g., Mack and Robbins, *Patterns of Persuasion*, 115. Judgments about this issue are complicated by what Jonathan Klawans describes as "contra-scriptural *halakhot*," that is, "Jewish legal rulings that fly in the face of what the Pentateuch seems to say" ("The Prohibition of Oaths and Contra-Scriptural Halakhot: A Response to John P. Meier," *JSHJ* 6 [2008]: 33–48, at 37). He notes that this phenomenon "poses some real problems for determining in any given case whether a specific ruling violates the written Torah in such an obvious way that it would be *inherently* recognized as such by ancient Jews" (42–43, his emphasis). One might likewise question whether Second Temple Jews would find anything inherently wrong with a recitation of 1 Sam 21:2–9 that contradicted some of the details of the version now contained in our MT.

[45] I use "statutes of the king" here solely as a literary designation for 11QT[a] LVI, 12–LIX, 21. The dominant hypothesis has been that this text is one of a number of separate documents that were later incorporated by the final author/redactor of the *Temple Scroll* (e.g., Andrew Wilson and Lawrence M. Wills, "The Literary Sources in the Temple Scroll," *HTR* 75 [1982]: 275–288). This postulate has now been challenged by Casey D. Elledge, *The Statutes of the King: The Temple Scroll's Legislation of Kingship* (11Q19 LVI 12–LIX 21), CahRB 56 (Paris: Gabalda, 2004), 32–36; and Molly M. Zahn, "4QReworked Pentateuch C and the Literary Sources of the *Temple Scroll*: A New (Old) Perspective," *DSD* 19 (2012): 133–158.

And if it is a king with chariots and horses and many men, then they shall send with him [עמו] a third part of the men of war."   (11QTa 58:5–8)

In the rules for offensive warfare: "And if he goes out to war against his enemies, a fifth part of the people shall go out with him [עמו]."   (11QTa 58:15–16)

The writer's insistence that the king be accompanied at all times is clearly motivated by a robust fear of the wiles of uncurtailed monarchy. This does not give the impression, however, that those who are "with" the king remain perpetually in his presence. Rather, the writer uses the phrase "with him" as a stereotyped expression to designate a group of warriors who are on campaign with Israel's monarch.

Jesus's description of the Davidic cohort might be taken in a similar fashion. That is, he may have inferred from the Samuel narrative that, upon his return to the war camp, David shared the bread with the group of warriors on campaign with him, οἱ μετ᾽ αὐτοῦ.[46] 1 Samuel 21 is clear that the reason Ahimelech gave the bread to David is so that he might share it with his warriors (21:4–6).[47] And so it seems

---

[46] One might still want to object that, in 1 Sam 21:2–9, David acts as a fugitive on the run rather than Israel's king. But this is not how the Deuteronomistic Historian recalls the matter, at least not when he views the course of David's life retrospectively: when the leaders of the tribes of Israel anointed David at Hebron, they address the Lord's anointed, "For some time, while Saul was king over us, it was you who lead out Israel and brought it in. YHWH said to you, 'It is you who shall be shepherd of my people Israel, you shall be ruler over Israel'" (2 Sam 5:2; par. 1 Chr 11:2). In other words, David had acted as king prior to his anointing in 2 Sam 5.

Some Second Temple Jews seemed to have viewed David's fugitive years as exemplary. Albert Pietersma shows, for example, that the superscription of Ps 26 LXX – τοῦ Δαυιδ πρὸ τοῦ χρισθῆναι, "[a psalm] of David *before* he was anointed" – evokes the *period* of David's life between "David's stop-over at the tabernacle at Nob (1 Sam 21)" and "his being anointed king in 2 Sam 2:4 (over Judah) and 2 Sam 5:3 (over Israel)" ("Exegesis," 104). This suggests that the translator perceived the events at Nob not as an instance of self-serving prevarication, but as an example of divine protection of the Lord's anointed (cf. Ps 26:4–5 LXX). In addition, Horsley and Hanson have made a plausible case that some of the so-called messianic pretenders mentioned by Josephus took inspiration from this period of David's life (*Bandits, Prophets & Messiahs*, 88–134; cf. Novenson, *Grammar of Messianism*, 104–113). David's career offered something of a blue-print for how someone without the right pedigree might nonetheless justifiably make a claim to the throne; in fact, Herod the Great may have been one such figure (see Tal Ilan, "King David, King Herod, and Nicolaus of Damascus," *JSQ* 3 [1998]: 195–240).

[47] The apodosis "you/they may eat [of it]" is implied by the syntax in the MT (as also in the Peshitta and Vulgate); ואכלתם ממנו, "then you [pl.] may eat of it" (4Q52 frags. 6–7, 17); καὶ φάγεται, "then it will be eaten [by you/them]" (B and hexaplaric recension of Origen); καὶ φαγόνται, "then they will eat [of it]" (Lucianic recension); καὶ φάγετε,

plausible that some ancient readers would conclude that the rendez-vous between David and his men took place, even though the Deuter-onomistic Historian never narrates its occurrence.[48]

Given the disciples' active role in the grain-plucking controversy (note the Pharisee's question, "Why are *they* doing what is unlawful on the Sabbath?"), it may be significant that the Deuteronomistic Historian recounts a time when David authorized his warriors to do what he did at Nob. While sojourning in the wilderness of Paran, the Lord's anointed and his band are once again in need of food. David responds by charging his men,

> [G]o to Nabal, and greet him in my name. Thus you shall greet him: "Peace be to you, and peace be to your house, and peace be to all that you have ... Therefore let my young men find favor in your sight; for we have come on a feast day. Please give whatever your hand can find [תנה־נה את אשר תמצא ידך; δὸς δὴ ὃ ἐὰν εὕρῃ ἡ χείρ σου] to your servants and to your son David." (1 Sam 25:6, 8)

These instructions replicate David's earlier request to Ahimelech: "Now then, what have you at hand? Give me five loaves of bread, or whatever you find [הנמצא]" (1 Sam 21:4 MT); "And now if there are under your hand five loaves, give into my hand whatever you find [δὸς εἰς χεῖρά μου τὸ εὑρεθέν]" (1 Sam 21:4 LXX). Thus a mere four chapters after he exercised his authority to procure the holy bread at Nob, the messiah-in-waiting commissions his warriors to participate in the authority of their king. David's is not a call for his followers to breach the Torah, to be sure, yet the observation that he commis-sioned his men to do what he did at Nob connects these two, otherwise disparate, events.

"then you [pl.] will eat [of it]" (Syro-Hexapla); listed in Eugene Ulrich, ed., *The Biblical Scrolls: Transcriptions and Variants, Volume 1: Genesis–Kings* (Leiden: Brill, 2013), 281.

[48] Aside from Casey ("Culture and Historicity," 9), this option has received almost no consideration. Daube's brief deliberation and dismissal of a possible meeting between David and his men is typical of the secondary literature: "It may be asked whether perhaps the Rabbis of the New Testament period, or some of them, detect in I Samuel a hint at a sharing of the meal by David with a retinue: the reply by Jesus might then proceed from his understanding of the narrative. I know of no such exegesis in the sources" ("Responsibilities," 5). On what grounds, though, does the silence of these sources, the earliest of which is the Bavli, obviate the possibility that a first-century reader could conclude that David shared the meal with his men?

Whether Mark made this connection cannot be discerned. There are, however, a number of points in his Gospel to suggest that the portrait of David and his men informs the movement of Jesus and his disciples. Jesus's appointment of the Twelve (cf. Mark 3:13–19), in particular, invites the audience to ponder more deeply the comparison between David's warriors and Christ's disciples. The expressed purpose of the appointment – "in order that they might be with him [Jesus] [ἵνα ὦσιν μετ' αὐτοῦ]" – echoes his earlier description of David's warriors, οἱ μετ' αὐτου (Mark 2:25).[49] In light of Mark's penchant for narrating exorcisms in terms of military conflict (cf. Mark 3:24–27; 5:1–13), the specific kind of authority Jesus gives his disciples – i.e., ἐξουσίαν ἐκβάλλειν τὰ δαιμόνια, "authority to cast our demons" – strengthens the comparison with David's warriors.[50] Although the battle is distinctly different in Mark, the messiah and his men appear to be engaged in a form of "holy war." The appointment of the Twelve also resonates with the mandate in the "statutes of the king" that the king's first task is to appoint for himself 12,000 men of war (1,000 from each tribe) to be "with him" (11QT[a] 57:2–8).[51] As with the monarch of Israel, Jesus's appointment to rule (cf. 1:10–11) seems to be intertwined with his right to appoint the Twelve to be "with him," a process that, when viewed retrospectively, began at the very outset of the Gospel (cf. 1:16–20).

4.2.2   Abiathar the High Priest and Life as the Messiah-Designate

Jesus's claim that David entered the tabernacle and ate the sacred bread ἐπὶ Ἀβιαθὰρ ἀρχιερέως, "when Abiathar was high priest," flies in the face of every extant version of the story (the priest's name is "Ahimelech" [MT] or "Abimelech" [LXX]).[52] Scholars offer a range of explanations for this curious Markan detail, and it would be

---

[49] When the restored Garasene demoniac later requests to join this exclusive group (ἵνα μετ' αὐτοῦ ᾖ; Mark 5:18) Jesus declines, sending him instead as an envoy to the cities of the Decapolis (5:19–20).

[50] For a discussion of Markan "holy war" imagery in exorcism pericopae, see Watts, *Isaiah's New Exodus*, 137–169.

[51] Yarbro Collins, *Mark*, 215–216. The timing of the census in the "statues of the king" – בים (lit. "on the day") – has to do with the perceived need for the monarch to appoint warriors soon after his installation (Jacob Milgrom, "Further Studies in the Temple Scroll," *JQR* 71 [1980]: 89–106, at 100).

[52] C. Shannon Morgan ("When Abiathar Was High Priest," *JBL* 98 [1979]: 409–410) lists a small number of Greek MSS that read Ἀχιμέλεχ, "Ahimelech," (in

superfluous to rehash them here.[53] Rather than focus on why this odd comment makes its way into the tradition, I propose instead to consider how its presence in the Markan narrative affects the Gospel's intertextual relationship to 1 Samuel 21.[54]

Particularly for auditors familiar with the wider context of 1 Samuel and ancillary Davidic traditions, the phrase ἐπὶ Ἀβιαθὰρ ἀρχιερέως may, I suggest, functions along the lines of what Michael Riffaterre describes as a textual "signpost." Signposts are, for Riffaterre,

> words and phrases indicating, on the one hand, a difficulty – an obscure or incomplete utterance in the text – that only an intertext can remedy; and, on the other hand, pointing the way to where the solution must be sought. Such features, lexical or phrasal, are distinguished from their context by their dual nature. They are both the problem, when seen from the text, and the solution to that problem when their other, intertextual side is revealed.[55]

The problematic construction ἐπὶ Ἀβιαθὰρ ἀρχιερέως finds a potentially satisfactory solution when read in light of the wider context of

---

agreement with MT) rather than Ἀβιμέλεχ, "Abimelech." Matthew and Luke each excised ἐπὶ Ἀβιαθὰρ ἀρχιερέως from their accounts (cf. Matt 12:4; Luke 6:4). And Patristic interpreters also wrestled with Mark 2:26, to various theological ends (see Craig A. Evans, "Patristic Interpretation of Mark 2:26: 'When Abiathar Was High Priest,'" *VC* 40 [1986]: 183–186).

[53] The most common explanation is that the prepositional phrase ἐπὶ Ἀβιαθὰρ ἀρχιερέως represents an error (e.g., Meier, "Historical Jesus," 577–578). John Wenham ("Mark 2,26," *JTS* 1 [1950] 156) argues that it means "in the section of Scripture having to do with Abiathar" (cf. Luke 20:37). Derrett ("Judaica," 92), on the other hand, suggests one should translate the phrase "in the presence of Abiathar the High Priest," reasoning that "[i]t was not Ahimelech's actually giving of bread which was significant; it was Abiathar's warranting, by his own adherence, the propriety of David's behaviour at that critical period." Marcus (*Mark 1–8*, p. 241) concludes, I think correctly, that ἐπὶ Ἀβιαθὰρ ἀρχιερέως invites a look ahead in the narrative of 1 Samuel, though he avoids speculating about the underlying motivation for this curious detail. Gundry (*Mark*, pp. 141–142) is confident, however, that the historical Jesus substituted "Abiathar" for "Ahimelech" to forge a connection with the Jerusalem temple. Meier has described this hypothesis, not unjustly, as "perhaps the most contorted explanation" (*A Marginal Jew: Rethinking the Historical Jesus, Volume 4: Law and Love* [New Haven, CT: Yale University Press, 2009] 329, n. 135).

[54] I discuss our extant witnesses to the Hebrew and Greek text-forms of 1 Sam 21 in my article ("Has Jesus Read?").

[55] Michael Riffaterre, "The Compulsory Reader Response: The Intertextual drive," in *Intertextuality: Theories and Practice*, eds. M. Worton and J. Still (Manchester: Manchester University Press, 1990), 58.

1 Samuel. That is, whether conscious or not, Jesus's claim that David ate of the bread of Presence ἐπὶ Ἀβιαθὰρ ἀρχιερέως impels those familiar with the story to look ahead to Abiathar's flight to David after Saul slaughtered all the priests at Nob (cf. 1 Sam 22:20–23), a connection encouraged by the Deuteronomistic Historian, who binds together the events in 1 Sam 22:20–23 and 1 Sam 21:8 via mention of "Doeg the Edomite."

For the attuned auditor of Mark, Abiathar's presence with David, evoked by the construction ἐπὶ Ἀβιαθὰρ ἀρχιερέως, serves to highlight the paradox of Jesus's life as God's messiah-designate. The reason Abiathar traveled with David from place to place is because the Lord's anointed had yet to be enthroned as king and, indeed, because his claim to the throne was a direct affront to the current regime. Likewise, Mark's Jesus has been anointed by God's spirit (Mark 1:10–11), moves around from place to place with a small band of men, and, as the audience learns in the very next passage (cf. Mark 3:6), faces the impending threat of death from those in power.[56] The curious phrase ἐπὶ Ἀβιαθὰρ ἀρχιερέως encourages Mark's audience to engage the events of 1 Samuel 21:2–10 within their wider narrative context and thus to grapple with the impending conflict between those currently in power and a new king like David.

4.2.3   Conclusion: Son of David and Son of Man

The points of thematic coherence between the lives of two messiah-designates, David and Jesus, strengthened at the intratextual level by the Markan description of David's men and the Twelve as "those with him," suggest that Jesus's appeal to "what David did" goes beyond circumstantial expedience. When the Pharisees questioned him, "Why are they [i.e., *your* disciples] doing what is unlawful on the Sabbath?" (2:24) Jesus could appeal to another scriptural messiah who not only exploited his authority to transcend the law, but also extended it to those who were "with him" during his period of

---

[56] Chilton ("Jesus *ben David*, 104) astutely notes that "in Mark 3.6 the resolve of the Herodians is mentioned after, albeit not immediately after, Jesus' appeal to the precedent of David for permitting his disciples to pluck grain on the Sabbath (2.25–26)." In fact, an allusion to Jesus's death and resurrection/ascension marks the center of the first controversy cycle (so Dewey, *Oral Ethos*, 58): "The days will come when the bridegroom is taken away [ἀπαρθῇ] from them, then they will fast on that day" (Mark 2:20).

itineracy. These observations add plausibility to Hays's suggestion that Mark operates here with an "implicit Davidic typology."[57]

Of course, the legal issue under dispute in Mark is not consecrated bread but time. Mark's Jesus argues, accordingly, that the protological intent of the Sabbath finds its eschatological realization in the lordship of the son of man: the Sabbath has always been God's gift to humanity (τὸν ἄνθρωπον), therefore, the son of man (ὁ υἱὸς τοῦ ἀνθρώπου) is lord (κύριος) even over the Sabbath. As in Mark 2:10, Jesus exercises an authority qua son of man that far surpasses any authority previously exercised by other human beings, including the great kings of old. Davidic messiahship is thus neither the point of the controversy nor the telos of the argument. Rather, it appears to be a presuppositional node on which "the agenda modulates from Halakha to Christology."[58] The first time Mark's Jesus defends his authority vis-à-vis the Jewish scriptures is also the first time the audience encounters the name David. In the next chapter, we will see that the last time the audience encounters the name David also occurs in a scriptural debate culminating in an exalted christological claim (cf. Mark 12:25–27).

4.3   The Messianic Family: Natural versus Fictive Kinship

Structural analysis of Mark 3:20–35 indicates that verses 22–30 are intercalated within verses 20–21 and 31–35 so that the Beelzebul controversy is framed by the subject of natural versus fictive kinship.[59] In so doing, Mark highlights, first, that the holy spirit is the power source by which "the stronger one" (1:7) plunders the kingdom/household of "the strong one" and, second, that the redeemed captives are called to participate in a new family oriented toward not natural but fictive kinship.[60] My concern is with this latter motif and, in particular, with the common claim that it offers evidence of an attempt to distance Jesus from David. By disparaging his own flesh and blood, so the argument runs, Mark the evangelist attempts to sever his Christ from early traditions that connected Jesus's parents

---

[57] Hays, *Echoes of Scripture in the Gospels*, 49.   [58] Boring, *Mark*, 90.
[59] See Shively, *Apocalyptic Imagination*, 51–54.
[60] On the subordination of natural to fictive kinship in Jewish and Greco-Roman literature, see Stephen C. Barton, *Discipleship and Family Ties in Mark and Matthew*, *SNTSMS* 80 (Cambridge: Cambridge University Press, 1994), 23–56.

(note the absence of Joseph in Mark!) to the Davidic line.[61] I wish to propose, by contrast, that the opprobrium Mark's Jesus faces from his family brings him into close intertextual relationship with the voice of David in Psalm 69 (68 LXX), one of the most popular psalms of the early church.

4.3.1 "I Became a Stranger to the Sons of My Mother" (Psalm 68:9 LXX)

Yarbro Collins shows that the intertext most likely to have informed the tension between Jesus and his family is a psalm "of David" (τῷ Δαυίδ), Psalm 68 LXX.[62] The relevant part of the psalm reads as follows:

[61] John Dominic Crossan, for example, avers that "the animosity of Mark to the relatives of Jesus points likewise against the Jerusalem church because it is there that James, the brother of the Lord, becomes important. ... The polemic against the disciples and the polemic against the relatives intersect as a polemic against the doctrinal and jurisdictional hegemony of the Jerusalem mother-church although, of course, this was most likely all provoked by heretics within the Markan community" ("Mark and the Relatives of Jesus," *NovT* 15 [1973]: 81–113, here 112). Others point to the absence of Joseph in Mark 3:31 (cf. Mark 6:3) as evidence of the evangelist's distancing Jesus from a Davidic ancestry (e.g., Boring, *Mark*, 256; Peppard, *Son of God*, 125–126). There are serious issues, however, with this proposal. First, as Tal Ilan's extensive study shows ("'Man Born of Woman ...' (Job 14:1): The Phenomenon of Men Bearing Metronymes at the Time of Jesus," *NovT* 34 [1992]: 23–45), there is nothing inherently polemical about the matronymic designation "the carpenter, *the son of Mary*" (Mark 6:3). (Josephus, for one, traces his Hasmonean ancestry through a maternal ancestor [cf. *Life* 2], on which, see Steve Mason, *Flavius Josephus: Translation and Commentary*, vol. 9: *Life of Josephus* [Leiden: Brill, 2001], 6–7 nn. 14–17). Second, Markus Bockmuehl ("The Son of David and His Mother," *JTS* 62 [2011]: 476–493) shows that Jesus's matrilineal genealogy quickly became the primary means of connecting him to the line of David (cf. Justin, *Dial.* 43, 45, 100; Ignatius, *Eph.* 18.2; Asc. Isa. 11:2; Irenaeus, *Haer.* 3.21.9; Tertullian, *Adv. Jud.* 9; *Marc.* 3.20; *Prot. Jas.* 10.1). He (491–492) floats the idea that Luke 1:27 served as something of an *Ausgangspunkt* for this emerging view, based on the observation that ἐξ οἴκου Δαυίδ can be interpreted as modifying παρθένον rather than ἀνδρί ᾧ ὄνομα Ἰωσήφ (cf. Origen, *Hom. Luke* frg. 20a; Chrysostom, *Hom. Matt* 2.7–8). Whatever one makes of this more speculative proposal, the thrust of Bockmuehl's study advises that it would be unwise to assume Joseph's absence in the Markan narrative derives from a strategy to distance Jesus from a Davidic ancestry.
[62] Yarbro Collins, "Appropriation of the Psalms," 235–236; the allusion is also proposed by the editors of the NA[28]. Mark seems to assume Davidic authorship of the Psalms (cf. Mark 12:36), and most ancient readers would take the superscription τῷ Δαυίδ and the epithet "your servant" (τοῦ παιδός σου; 68:18) as clear indicators that David was the speaker. (On the widespread assumption of Davidic authorship of the Psalms in early Judaism, see Daly-Denton, *David*, 59–113). Further, while a faithful translation of the Hebrew למנצח (Pietersma, "Septuagintal Exegesis," 468–471), the phrase εἰς τὸ τέλος could support an eschatological reading of the psalm, strengthened

May those who wait for you not be put to shame because of
me, O Lord, Lord of hosts; may those who seek you not be
embarrassed because of me, O God of Israel, because for
your sake I bore reproach [ὀνειδισμόν]; embarrassment
covered my face. I became estranged from my brothers
[ἀπηλλοτριωμένος ἐγενήθην τοῖς ἀδελφοῖς μου], and a stranger
to the sons of my mother [ξένος τοῖς υἱοῖς τῆς μητρός μου],
because the zeal for your house consumed me, and the
reproaches of those who reproach you fell on me [οἱ ὀνειδισ-
μοὶ τῶν ὀνειδιζόντων σε ἐπέπεσαν ἐπ᾿ ἐμέ].   (Ps 68:7–10 LXX)

Four observations suggest an allusion to this part of psalm. First,
Mark 3:31 clarifies that the nebulous group mentioned in Mark
3:21 – οἱ παρ᾿ αὐτοῦ – consists of ἡ μήτηρ αὐτοῦ καὶ οἱ ἀδελφοὶ αὐτοῦ,
"his mother and his brothers," the same distinct group mentioned in
the psalm. Second, the evangelist alluded to Ps 68:22 LXX during his
account of Jesus's crucifixion (cf. 15:23, 36), enhancing the likelihood that he was aware of other parts of the psalm. Third, Psalm
68 LXX was widely cited or alluded to in other early Christian
literature, suggesting that at least some of Mark's early auditors
would have detected resonances with the psalm.[63] Fourth, one
detects strong thematic coherence between this Davidic psalm and
Markan pericope: as David's fidelity to God results in alienation
from his family and in shame, so Jesus's results in his family's
concern that he has gone mad (3:21); as David bears reproach for
God's sake, so Jesus bears reproach because he acts by the power of
the holy spirit (Mark 3:30). What the audience encounters in Mark
3:20–35 is thus not an attempt to reject Davidic ancestry but, rather,
an invitation to conceive of the contempt the Christ faces on account
of his charismatic office in terms of the contempt David faced on
account of his.

perhaps by the phrase ὑπὲρ τῶν ἀλλοιωθησομένων, "over the things/people that will be
changed."
    [63] C. H. Dodd wrote long ago that "[i]t can scarcely be accidental that five separate
authors have turned to this particular psalm for *testimonia*, although they have
selected different sentences for quotation" (*According to the Scriptures: The Sub-
Structure of New Testament Theology* [New York: Scribner's Sons, 1953], 57–58);
see also Lindars, *New Testament Apologetic*, 106; Juel, *Messianic Exegesis*, 110.
Citations of Ps 69(68) in the New Testament include John 2:17 (Ps 68:10); 15:25 (Ps
68:5); Acts 1:20 (Ps 68:26); Rom 11:9 (citing Ps 68:23); and Rom 15:3 (Ps 68:10). The
clearest allusions to the psalm are in the crucifixion accounts (Matt 27:34, 48 pars.;
alluding to Ps 68:22 LXX).

My proposal has an important analogue in another first-century text, LAB 59:4. According to Pseudo-Philo, David responds to his anointing in song, the pertinent section of which reads as follows: "For my brothers were jealous of me [Quoniam fratres mei zelaverunt me], and my father and my mother neglected me [et pater meus et mater mea neglexerunt me]. And when the prophet came, they did not call to me. And when the anointed of the LORD was to be designated, they forgot me."[64] These lines are the product of creative exegetical reflection.[65] Inspired by the scriptural analogue of the brothers' jealousy in the Joseph novella (cf. Gen 37:11),[66] and aided by his reading Ps 69:9 – "I have become a stranger to *my brothers*, an alien to *my mother's sons*" – as Davidic autobiography,[67] Pseudo-Philo determined that the moment Samuel anointed David in the presence of his brothers (cf. 1 Sam 16:13) also happened to be the moment fratricidal hostility sprung to life. He also read Ps 27:10 – "If my father and mother forsake me, YHWH will take me up" – autobiographically,[68] concluding that the Lord's choice of David overturned the parents' conviction that their youngest was unfit to stand among his brothers when Samuel arrived to anoint the messiah. Pseudo-Philo thus inferred, on the basis of what the king himself says in multiple psalms, that messianic anointing had set David in conflict with his own flesh and blood.

Pseudo-Philo's historicizing strategy markedly differs from Mark's. Nonetheless, it suggests that anyone well versed in the

---

[64] Pseudo-Philo, *Les Antiquités Bibliques*, 1:364; trans. Harrington, *OTP* 2:372.

[65] See my article, "'Then David Began to Sing,'" esp. 79–81.

[66] *Quoniam fratres mei zelaverunt me* reflects Gen 37:11 (so rightly Jacobson, *Commentary*, 2:1170); Vulg. reads: *zelaverunt autem eum fratres sui*, agreeing with MT's וקנאו־בו אחיו, and LXX's ἐζήλωσαν δὲ αὐτὸν οἱ ἀδελφοὶ αὐτοῦ. Ambrose's exposition of Ps 119 (118 LXX):141 links Joseph and David as two "of the many saints, who were cast off from the beginning of their adolescence" (*Expos. Ps. 118* 18.23; Michael Petschenig and Michaela Zelzer, eds., *Sancti Ambrosi Opera Pars V: Exposition Psalmi CXVIII*, CSEL 62 [Vienna: Österreichische Akademie der Wissenschaften,1999], 408).

[67] Jacobson, *Commentary*, 2:1171.

[68] The allusion to Ps 27 is noted both by Harrington (*OTP* 2:372) and by Jacobson (*Commentary*, 2:1171). The speaker in the *Hodayot* also appears to take up Ps 27:10 when he confesses, "For my father did not acknowledge me, and my mother abandoned me to you [כיא אבי לא ידעני ואמי עליכה עזבתני], but you are father to all the children of your truth" (1QHᵃ XVII, 34–35; Hartmut Stegemann, Eileen Schuller, and Carol Newsom, eds., *1QHodayotᵃ with Incorporation of 1QHodayotᵇ and 4QHodayotᵃ⁻ᶠ*, DJD 40 [Oxford: Clarendon, 2009], 227, 233). In this instance, the supplicant makes explicit what appears to be implicit in LAB, namely, that the psalmist's identity is now conceived of primarily in terms of divine sonship.

Psalms is unlikely to perceive of familial hostility as anti-Davidic, since the royal supplicant laments of this reality on multiple occasions. Although Pseudo-Philo depicts hostility from both David's parents, apparently drawing on the language of Ps 27:10, his awareness of Ps 69:9 suggests he could recognize the absence of a father figure in Mark as enhancing an allusion to the psalm. In any event, he is part of a group of first-century writers, including Paul (cf. Rom 15:3 citing Ps 68:10b LXX) and John the evangelist (cf. John 2:17 citing Ps 68:10a LXX), that we can plausibly infer were aware of the language in Ps 69 (68 LXX):9. If, as is highly likely, Mark assumed David was the author of the psalm, then one might rightly inquire why the evangelist concluded, in contrast to Pseudo-Philo but in agreement with Paul and John, that the speaker in Ps 68:7–10 LXX is King Jesus rather than King David. The most plausible explanation for this hermeneutical move is the supposition that the Christ's voice is heard in and through "the persona of his purported ancestor."[69] Davidic messiahship would appear, then, to be the unspoken assumption attracting the evangelist to the Psalter.

Mark's attraction to psalms "of David" becomes particularly acute in the passion narrative (chs. 14–16), to such an extent that interpreters have tended to overlook potential manifestations of this phenomenon at other points in the narrative.[70] Yet if Hays is correct that the crucifixion account trains the audience "to see *the Psalms as particularly important intertexts for interpreting the shape of Jesus' life and death*,"[71] then perhaps we should not be surprised to find reverberations of a Davidic psalm at precisely the moment when rejection of Christ's vocation reaches a new narrative crest. For those who have ears to hear, subjection to opprobrium – including, and perhaps particularly, rejection from one's own kin (Ps 68:9 LXX) – seems to be part and parcel of what it means to be the "Davidic" messiah in the Gospel according to Mark.

---

[69] Attridge, "Giving Voice," 102.

[70] So, for example, the title of Juel's chapter is "The Role of the Psalms *in the Passion Tradition*" (*Messianic Exegesis*, 89–117, my emphasis); see also Ahearne-Kroll, *Psalms of Lament*; Carey, *Jesus' Cry from the Cross*; O'Brien, *Use of Scripture*.

[71] Hays, *Echoes of Scripture in the Gospels*, 83, his emphasis. As Yarbro Collins ("Appropriation of the Psalms," 236) notes, "The reproach and shame borne by the speaker are not connected primarily with the physical suffering and death of Jesus, but with the misunderstanding of his charismatic activity. This misunderstanding is tantamount to a rejection of his divine mission, and thus, in the context of Mark as a whole, of his messianic role".

4.3.2 "Whoever Does the Will of God"

The claim that Mark 3:20–35 provides evidence that Mark's Jesus is not a descendant of David rests on several tenuous assumptions. There is, for instance, no way to test the conjecture that Joseph's absence in Mark is part of an intentional ploy to distance Jesus from Davidic heritage. Nor is there a way to verify that Jesus's response to his family in 3:33–35 results from a similar motivation. My approach, on the other hand, poses a set of questions that can be tested against the evidence – namely, is there evidence that the evangelist presents the conflict between Jesus and his family in light of the conflict between David and his family in Psalm 68 LXX? And is there evidence that other members of Mark's linguistic community could detect the allusion? As we have seen, there is good reason to answer both of these in the affirmative.

The thrust of Mark 3:31–35 is not, of course, about Davidic messiahship. The point, rather, is that the messiah is gathering a people marked out by a singular distinctive feature – doing the will of God – and that identity in this particular group is conceived of in terms of fictive kinship: doing the will of God makes one a "brother" or "sister" of God's son and thus a "son" or "daughter" of his father.[72] Nonetheless, the motif of a *rejected* messiah like David, not just in death but also in life, is integral to the Markan construction of Christ and his new family.

4.4   The Davidic Shepherd

Mark's comment that Jesus had compassion on the crowd because they were "like sheep without a shepherd [ὡς πρόβατα μὴ ἔχοντα ποιμένα]" (Mark 6:34) is unique to the Second Gospel, opening the possibility that the evangelist has intentionally highlighted the metaphor.[73] Interpreters agree that the pastoral metaphor is drawn from

---

[72] Whether Mark thinks one becomes a descendant of Abraham through pneumatic regeneration is unclear (cf. Rom 8:17; 9:8; Gal 3:29). At the very least, he probably assumes spirit baptism renders one a son or daughter of God (cf. Mark 1:8; 13:11).

[73] Mark's is the only account that includes the pastoral metaphor (pars. Matt 14:13–21; Luke 9:12–17; John 6:1–15). Marcus (*Mark 1–8*, 414–16) and Henderson (*Christology and Discipleship*, 177–179) argue that the Gospel's emphasis on the wilderness and the disciples' participatory role is due to Markan redaction. Their analysis lends support to the conclusion that the metaphor is important to the evangelist, a proposal Boring (*Mark*, 182) makes on narrative-critical grounds: "The omniscient narrator lets the reader know that Jesus, who, so it seems, had attempted to

or at least significantly informed by two scriptural source texts, Num 27:17 and Ezek 34:5, 7. The immediate context of the feeding of the 5,000 (Mark 6:30–44), including the wilderness locale, strongly evokes Num 27:17.[74] When, however, the feeding is read as a critique of Herod Antipas's banquet (6:14–29), as Mark apparently intended it, there are equally strong resonances with the broader context of Ezekiel 34.[75] Both intertexts contribute to the Markan portrait of a Davidesque messiah.

4.4.1   Summoning Ἰησοῦς (Numbers 27:17)

I do not wish to challenge the notion that an allusion to Num 27:17 casts Jesus's feeding of the 5,000 in a Mosaic register,[76] but to supplement this model with an essential observation: the role to which that YHWH appoints Joshua (LXX: Ἰησοῦς) in Numbers 27 has distinctively royal connotations.[77] Moses implores YHWH to appoint his heir, someone "who will go out before them and come in

get away from the crowd, actually views them with eyes of divine compassion. 'Like sheep without a shepherd' is not an ad hoc casual comment of the Markan Jesus as narrator, but echoes the phrase found explicitly in Num 27:17".

[74] Mauser, *Christ in the Wilderness*, 135; Henderson, *Christology and Discipleship*, 183–185.

[75] Robert M. Fowler, *Loaves and Fishes: The Function of the Feeding Stories in the Gospel of Mark*, SBLDS 54 (Chico, CA: Scholars Press, 1981), 120.

[76] Henderson, *Christology and Discipleship*, 186–188; Marcus, *Mark 1–8*, 406, 417–421. It is worth noting that a Mosaic register is not ipso facto antimonarchical (cf. Deut 33:5; Philo, *Mos.* 1.60–61; *Agr.* 39–66; Ezek. Trag. 70–82). Note the comparison between Moses and David near the opening of Midrash Tehillim: "*For this is the law of man*: Scripture does not say here 'for this is the law of Abraham, of Isaac, or of Jacob,' but '*for this is the law of man*.' But what man? He who is foremost among the prophets; he who is foremost among kings. The foremost among prophets – he is Moses, of whom it is said *And Moses went up unto God* (Ex. 19:3); the foremost among kings – he is David. You find that whatever Moses did, David did. As Moses led Israel out of Egypt, so David led Israel out of servitude to Goliath. As Moses fought the battles of the Lord against Sihon and Og, so David fought the battles of the Lord in all the regions around him, as Abigail said: *My lord fighteth the battles of the Lord* (1 Sam. 25:28). As Moses became king in Israel and in Judah, for it is said *And he became king in Jeshurun, when the heads of the people ... were gathered together* (Deut. 33:5), so David became king in Israel and in Judah. As Moses divided the Red Sea for Israel, so David divided the rivers of Aram for Israel, as it is said *David ... divided the rivers of Aram* (Ps. 60:1, 2) ..." (Midr. Ps. 1:1); the English translation follows that of William G. Braude, *The Midrash on Psalms*, 2 vols., YJS 13 (New Haven, CT: Yale University Press, 1959), 1:4–5, his emphasis; cf. Tg. Ps.-J. Exod. 12:24; Sifre Deut. 348.

[77] See Baruch A. Levine, *Numbers 21–36: A New Translation with Introduction and Commentary*, AB 4A (New York: Doubleday, 2000), 42–43.

before them, who will lead them out and bring them in [ואשר יוציאם
ואשר יביאם], so that the congregation of YHWH may not be like sheep
without a shepherd" (Num 27:17). This distinct idiom, "to lead out
and bring in" (hiphil forms of יצא and בוא), is shared by only one
other scriptural text. When the leaders of the tribes of Israel anointed
David at Hebron, they addressed him, "For some time, while
Saul was king over us, it was you who led out Israel and brought it
in [אתה היית מוציא והמבי את־ישראל]. YHWH said to you, 'It is you who
shall be shepherd of my people Israel, you who shall be ruler over
Israel" (2 Sam 5:2; par. 1 Chr 11:2).[78] The tribal leaders make clear,
in other words, that David was already the de facto king of Israel
because he had enacted a particular role – the same role Moses gave
to Joshua.[79]

The Temple Scroll's "statutes of the king" (11QT^a 56:12–59:21)
offers demonstrable evidence that some Second Temple Jews read
Num 27:21 as descriptive of the vocation of Israel's king. The writer
mandates, in the section on "offensive warfare," "on his [the high
priest's] orders he [the king] shall go out and on his orders he shall
return, he [the king] and all the sons of Israel who are with him [הוא
וכול בני ישראל אשר אתו]" (11QT^a 58:19–20); an expression he borrows
from Num 27:21: "at his [Eleazar, the priest's] word they shall go
out, and at his word they shall come in, both he [Joshua] and all the
sons of Israel with him [הוא וכל־בני־ישראל אתו], the whole
congregation." That is to say, the referent of הוא in the final clause
of Num 27:21 no longer applies to Joshua but to the perpetual office
of the monarch.[80]

Mark may have concluded that the Ἰησοῦς in Num 27 LXX offered
a Pentateuchal prototype of Ἰησοῦς Χριστός. Jesus's instructions to
the Twelve to divide the crowd into hundreds and fifties (cf. Mark
6:40) evokes the topos of the 12 tribes encamped in the wilderness
(cf. Exod 18:21; Deut 15:1; CD 13:1–2; 1QS 2:21–23; 1QM 4:1–5),
perhaps a hint that the community gathered around Jesus is the
eschatological realization of the wilderness community in the
Pentateuch.[81] For someone without knowledge of Mark's narrative,

[78] Cf. Pss 2:9 LXX; 78 (77 LXX):70–72; Mic 2:12–13. For a discussion of David's
role as Israel's shepherd, see Blenkinsopp, David Remembered, 149–160.

[79] Cf. Jacob Milgrom, Numbers, JPSTC 4 (Philadelphia: JPS, 1989), 235.

[80] Later interpreters agree that the referent of הוא in Num 27:21 is the king of Israel
(Yadin, Temple Scroll, 2:264).

[81] John says the crowd reacted to the sign of the 12 baskets with the desire ἁρπάζειν
αὐτὸν ἵνα ποιήσωσιν βασιλέα, "to conscript him [Jesus] to be their king" (6:15).

it might be possible to conclude that this symbolic act was the work of a charismatic prophet of renewal. Based on the portrait the evangelist has developed thus far, however, it seems more likely that the role Jesus takes up is that of Israel's king, particularly when we consider the import of Ezekiel 34.

4.4.2   Rest under the Davidic Shepherd (Ezekiel 34)

Mark employs a negative foil to accentuate Jesus's role as Ezekiel's Davidic servant. As Robert Fowler notes,

> Although Jesus is not specifically referred to as king in Mark 6, it is no small matter that his actions are deliberately set over against those of King Herod. Mark 6:14–29 is the only place in the gospel where the deeds of a publicly recognized king are set forth. By juxtaposing the deeds of Herod with the deeds of Jesus, Mark adroitly demonstrates the ways in which King Herod and Jesus are similar while simultaneously contrasting their kingly behavior.[82]

The evangelist's depiction of "King" Herod's (6:14) opulent and ruthless behavior evokes the frame of Ezekiel 34 (cf. Jer 23:1–5), in which the prophet rails against the shepherds of Israel who, like Herod Antipas, feed themselves instead of the sheep (Ezek 34:3, 8). According to the prophet, these shepherds are the very reason Israel went into exile: "my sheep were scattered [διεσπάρη τὰ πρόβατά μου], because there were no shepherds [τὸ μὴ εἶναι ποιμένας]" (Ezek 34:5 LXX). Yet YHWH promises the end of exile will come in due course: "I will bring them out from the peoples and gather them from the countries, and will bring them into their own land; and I will feed them on the mountains of Israel ... I will feed them with good pasture, and the mountain heights of Israel shall be their pasture" (Ezek 34:13–14). The oracle culminates in YHWH's promise, "I will raise up over them one shepherd, and he will shepherd them; my servant David, and he will be their shepherd [καὶ ἀναστήσω ἐπ᾽ αὐτοὺς ποιμένα ἕνα καὶ ποιμανεῖ αὐτοὺς τὸν δοῦλόν μου Δαυιδ καὶ ἔσται αὐτῶν ποιμήν]" (Ezek 34:23 LXX). Whereas Ezekiel's oracle says YHWH himself will feed the flock, Mark's narrative implies

---

[82] Fowler, *Loaves*, 121; see also Henderson, *Christology and Discipleship*, 172–174; Yarbro Collins, *Mark*, 324.

that it is in and through Jesus of Nazareth – a shepherd like David – that Israel's God sustains his people.

And yet, one wonders: if Mark draws on Ezekiel's oracle of postexilic restoration, why does he present the action διδάσκειν, "to teach," a feature absent from Ezekiel's text, as an essential element of the shepherd's office? Here, it is worth noting that sapiential instruction features in multiple early Jewish texts at precisely the point at which their authors turned to Ezekiel 34. Consider the role of המבקר למחנה, "the examiner of the camp," in the Damascus Document:

> And this is the rule for the Examiner of the camp: Let him instruct the Many [ישכיל את הרבים] about the works of God, and allow them to discern the wonder of his mighty deeds, and relate to them the happenings of eternity together with their interpretations. Let him pity them [וירחם עליהם] like a father does his children and watch over them in all their distress as a shepherd his flock [כרועה עדרו]. Let him loosen all chains that bind them so that there shall be none deprived and crushed in his congregation.   (CD 13:7–10)[83]

The writer of the Damascus Document apparently conceives of instruction as an integral component of the ways in which YHWH would work through the examiner, in accordance with Ezekiel 34, to "feed" and "shepherd" his flock.[84]

The writer of the Psalms of Solomon 17, likewise, waxes eloquent about another Ezekielian shepherd,

> Then who will be stronger than he? He will be mighty in his actions and strong in the fear of God, faithfully and

---

[83] For the Damascus Document, I follow the critical text and English in Charlesworth et al., eds., *The Dead Sea Scrolls Hebrew, Aramaic, and Greek Texts with English Translations, Volume 2: Damascus Document, War Scroll, and Related Documents*, The Princeton Theological Seminary Dead Sea Scrolls Project (Tübingen: Mohr Siebeck, 1995), 54–55. Others (Yarbro Collins, *Mark*, 325; Bruce Chilton et al., eds., *A Comparative Handbook to the Gospel of Mark: Comparisons with Pseudepigrapha, the Qumran Scrolls, and Rabbinic Literature*, New Testament Gospels in Their Judaic Contexts 1 [Leiden: Brill, 2010], 219) note parallels between Mark 6:30–43 and CD 13:7–10 .

[84] George Brooke has examined the influence of Ezek 34:11–12, 16 on CD 13:9–10 ("Ezekiel in Some Qumran and New Testament Texts," in *The Madrid Qumran Congress: Proceedings of the International Congress on the Dead Sea Scrolls, Madrid 18–21 March 1991*, eds. Julio Trebolle Barrera and Luis Vegas Montaner, 2 vols., STDJ 11 [Leiden: Brill, 1992], 317–337, at 332).

righteously shepherding the Lord's sheep [ποιμαίνων τὸ ποίμ-νιον κυρίου], he will not let any of them stumble in their pasture. He will lead them all impartially, And there will be no arrogance among them, that any should be oppressed. This is the magnificence of the king of Israel that God acknowledged, to raise him [ἀναστῆσαι αὐτόν] over the House of Israel to discipline it. In the assemblies he will judge the tribes of a sanctified people. His words will be as the words of the holy ones [οἱ λόγοι αὐτοῦ ὡς λόγοι ἁγίων], among sanctified people.   (Pss. Sol. 17:40b–43)[85]

As with the writer of CD, the psalmist is convinced that instruction is central to the program of Ezekiel 34. Yet, in contrast to the writer of CD, but closer to the vision of leadership in oracle of Ezekiel, he envisages the messiah son of David as the one through whom Israel would be instructed in the way of the Lord.

Mark's intimation that Ezekiel's vision is enacted through the teaching ministry of Jesus does not appear to be particularly innovative when set within the early reception history of this oracle. In fact, the evangelist seems quite close to the writer of Psalms of Solomon 17: what the prophet promised long ago about a future descendant of David is now coming to fruition in the ministry of the messiah. We may defer judgment about whether Mark's Christ is an actual descendant of David. But there is no doubt that this pericope actualizes a Davidic frame latent in the encyclopedia of the users of messiah language.

4.4.3   Summary: A Meal for the Messiah's People

Mark's description of the crowd as those "like sheep without a shepherd," as many interpreters have recognized, opens up "a field of whispered or unstated correspondences"[86] about the identity of his Christ. I have argued that the Markan Jesus does indeed take up the role of a Ἰησοῦς in Numbers 27 but that this role has been refracted through a monarchical lens (cf. 2 Sam 5; 11QT[a]

---

[85] For the Psalms of Solomon I follow the Greek text and English translation in Robert B. Wright, *The Psalms of Solomon: A Critical Edition of the Greek Text*, Jewish and Christian Texts in Contexts and Related Studies 1 (London: T&T Clark, 2007), 198–201. For a summary of Ezek 34's influence on Pss. Sol. 17:40b–42, see Chae, *Jesus as the Eschatological Shepherd*, 118–119.

[86] Hays, *Echoes of Scripture in the Letters of Paul*, 20.

58:19–20). This, in turn, coheres with the likelihood that Jesus's feeding and teaching of the shepherdless crowd evokes Ezekiel 34, an oracle that climaxes in the installation of the Davidic servant. The gathering of the 12 baskets, taken up by the Twelve, signals to the audience that God is, at last, gathering his scattered people back under their rightful king (cf. Ezek 34:23–24). A meal for the messiah's people.

4.5   Conclusion: "You Are the Christ!"

Peter's messianic "confession" (8:29) has long been a point of debate within Markan scholarship. At the height of *redaktionsgeschichtlich* work on the Second Gospel in the 1960s and 1970s it became de rigueur to claim that the evangelist rejected the title ὁ χριστός to distance his community from the apostolic community and/or to subvert a "Jewish" or "Jewish-Hellenistic" *christologia gloriae*.[87] Currently, the leading diagnosis of Peter's malady is the sense that brash disciple longed for a "Davidic-warrior."[88] If, however, one sticks to the Markan narrative, the issue at stake is clearly whether a rejection-death-resurrection schema is in accordance with the divine will (cf. Mark 8:31).

Frame of reference matters.[89] For those who have heard the first half of Mark's Gospel, Peter's confession and Jesus's ensuing passion prediction advance an established motif: the audience already knows that the Christ has been rejected (cf. 3:20–35) and will eventually be killed (cf. 2:20; 3:6), a point the evangelist adumbrates through echoes of and allusions to traditional Davidic resources. The raison

---

[87] E.g., Tyson, "Blindness;" Grundmann, *Evangelium*, 167–69; Weeden, "Heresy;" Kelber, *Kingdom*, 82–83; Perrin, "Christology of Mark."

[88] Collins's (*Scepter*, 78) summary of Davidic messianism encapsulates what many interpreters assume Peter meant by ὁ χριστός: "This concept of the Davidic messiah as the warrior king who would destroy the enemies of Israel and institute an era of unending peace constitutes the common core of Jewish messianism around the turn of the era."

[89] Nothing in the narrative suggests Peter has the ability to deduce Jesus's identity. Indeed, just prior to his confession Jesus rebukes the Twelve: "Do you *not yet* understand?" (8:21). Thus, the natural conclusion is that Peter's insight into Jesus's identity must be the result of divine revelation (cf. Matt 16:17). From the audience's perspective, however, Peter's confession caps a crescendo of rhetorical questions concerning Jesus's identity: (1) "*What is this*? A new teaching with authority!" (1:27); (2) "*Who then is this*? For even the wind and sea obey him!" (4:41); (3) "Where does *this man* get these things from?" (6:2) (Marcus, *Mark 1–8*, 611).

d'être of the first passion prediction, then, is to bring Mark's "breach of the canonical,"[90] the notion that the messiah must die in accordance with the scriptures, into sharper focus, lest the audience mistake people for trees. Not only must the messiah be rejected by the Jewish leaders (ἀποδοκιμασθῆναι),[91] suffer, die, and be raised after three days, argues Mark's Jesus, but the scriptures in general and a royal psalm in particular bear witness to the *necessity* (δεῖ)[92] of this event: "The stone that the builders rejected [ἀπεδοκίμασαν] has become the chief cornerstone" (Ps 117:22 LXX; cited in Mark 12:10).[93] Peter's problem with this revelation is not alleviated by the substitution of one messianic idea for another, such that all is set right so long as the apostle puts to death his hope for the Davidic-warrior messiah, but resides in his need to reorient his disposition from τὰ τῶν ἀνθρώπων to τὰ τοῦ θεοῦ (cf. Mark 8:33). Psalm 117:22 LXX, even if Peter cannot bring himself to accept its message within the confines of the narrative, provides the scriptural frame for such a tectonic epistemological shift. The more the trees come into focus, the more, it seems, rejection and crucifixion make up the very center of Mark's peculiar brand of Davidic messianism.

---

[90] Recall Bruner's point that "breaches of the canonical" (i.e., departures from the norm) are typically mediated through accepted tradition ("Narrative Construction," 12). Mark intimates that certain scriptures about the Davidic king, when read through fresh eyes, offer an interpretive key for processing messianic suffering.

[91] The verb ἀποδοκιμάζιεν marks an allusion to Ps 117:22 LXX (cf. Chapter 2 n. 69).

[92] δεῖν appears to be part of the early Christian lexicon for expressing the *necessity* of the Christ's suffering in accordance to the scriptures (cf. Matt 26:54; Luke 17:25; 22:37; 24:7, 26, 44; John 3:14; 12:34; 20:9; Acts 1:16; 17:3).

[93] Most commentators conclude that the main speaker in Ps 118 (117 LXX) is the Davidic king (see Jamie Grant, *King as Exemplar: The Function of Deuteronomy's Kingship Law in the Shaping of the Book of Psalms*, AcBib 17 [Atlanta: SBL, 2004], 127 n. 13), though see Hans-Joachim Kraus, *Psalms*, trans. Hilton C. Oswald, 2 vols., CC (Minneapolis, MN: Fortress, 1993), 1:396–401. A Davidic superscription is not an essential feature of royal psalms and, as Gerald Wilson notes ("Shaping the Psalter: A Consideration of Editorial Linkage In the Books of the Psalms," in *The Shape and Shaping of the Psalter*, ed. J. C. McCann, JSOTSup 159 [Sheffield: JSOT Press, 1993], 73), such designations are largely lacking in Books 4 and 5 of the Psalter. While a Davidic interpretation of the psalm would not necessarily be self-evident to all first-century Jews, there is good reason to think that Mark read the psalm in this way (see Section 5.2.3).

5

THE SON OF DAVID AND THE JERUSALEM TEMPLE

Die spärliche Überlieferung zum Davidssohn ist nicht über das Evangelium verstreut, sondern auf drei zusammenhangende Kapitel konzentriert, die eine geographische und wohl auch theologische Einheit bilden.

– Christoph Burger, *Jesus als Davidssohn*, 59

[T]exts were received in a linear way, the overall thrust becoming evident as the structure unfolded in succession. Exordium, narrative, and peroration provided a recapitulative framework which carried the listener to conviction by reminder and variation. Reference back depended upon memory, reference forward upon expectation, or known classic outcome. As the roll gradually unwound, so a narrative or argument moved toward its climax or ending.

– Frances M. Young, *Biblical Exegesis and the Formation of Christian Culture*, 11–12

In the previous two chapters, I have assessed how Mark developed his portrait of Jesus Christ through the first half of the Gospel, paying particular attention to how he resourced Davidic traditions. Attention to the ways in which the evangelist used his Davidic material leads one to suspect that other competent language users – other adherents to the "grammar of messianism" – would arrive at the conclusion that Jesus of Nazareth is a messiah *like* David. Mark actualizes Davidic identity in terms of cosmic and human opposition to God's kingdom and God's son, on the one hand, and in terms of messianic rejection and suffering, on the other. Indeed, well in advance of the passion narrative (chs. 14–16), one detects hints that Davidic psalms offer a traditional frame whereby the evangelist articulates the significance of the suffering and death of his Christ.

In the present chapter, I argue that the previously given portrait provides the requisite backdrop for interpreting Jesus's activity in the Jerusalem temple (10:46–12:44). As such, my approach prescinds from two common assumptions – first, that Markan interest in Davidic messiahship can be relegated to a single section of the Gospel (so Wrede, Burger, et al.) and, therefore, second, that the healing of blind Bartimaeus (10:46–52), read as an isolated pericope, offers the *crux interpretum* for Mark's *Davidssohnfrage*. What the audience encounters in 10:46–12:44 is not, I argue, the story of how a charismatic Galilean prophet suddenly became interested in rejecting or affirming scriptural promises God made to David, but the story of how a charismatic messiah came to claim those promises, after having been rejected by the temple hierarchs – as David said he would be (cf. Mark 8:31; 12:10–11) – and yet boldly claimed – again, based on what David said – that he would be enthroned as "lord" (12:35–37). When the *Davidssohnfrage* is adjudicated on the basis of *this* narrative, there can be little doubt that the riddle aims to elicit a not-only-but-also resolution – that is, the Christ is not only David's son but also David's Lord, the one whom has been summoned by his father to reign from a throne in heaven.

5.1   A Messianic Key: Mark 10:46–52 *als Schlüsseltext*

As the title of Hans-Joachim Eckstein's article suggests, Mark 10:46–52 has long been recognized as an interpretive key in the narrative progression of the Gospel.[1] While there are a number of ways in which this pericope functions *als Schlüsseltext*, the most relevant for my purposes is the longstanding assumption that it has the potential to resolve the *Davidssohnfrage*. That is, if, on the one hand, one can demonstrate that the evangelist offers a positive, even if tempered, appraisal of the title son of David, then this pericope functions as a deterrent against the conclusion that Mark's *Davidssohnfrage* negates the premise that the messiah would be the son of David.[2] If, on the other hand, one can detect evidence of an incipient

---

[1] Hans-Joachim Eckstein, "Markus 10,46–52 als Schlusseltext des Markusevangeliums," *ZNW* 87 (1996): 33–50.

[2] E.g., Burger, *Jesus als Davidssohn*, 58–63; Robbins, "Healing of Bartimaeus," 236–243; Chilton, "Jesus *ben David*," 101–105; Kingsbury, *Christology*, 102–114; Marcus, *Way*, 140–141; Smith, "Function," 527–528; Eckstein, "Markus 10,46–52," 38–45; Ahearne-Kroll, *Psalms of Lament*, 138–144.

rejection of the title, then this passage launches a trajectory climaxing in the Gospel's definitive disposal of all things Davidic.[3]
The turn toward narrative criticism, as we saw in Chapter 1, has only exacerbated the problem. Whereas, for example, Kingsbury is convinced that the Markan Jesus's decision to heal Bartimaeus constitutes an unambiguous affirmation of the title son of David,[4] Malbon is persuaded – by the very same data – that the Markan Jesus decides to heal Bartimaeus despite his use of the title.[5] Both are well aware that the history of interpretation of this pericope involves widespread division on this point, and yet each remains resolute that a sober and straightforward reading of Mark 10:46–52 should be able to settle the debate.[6] It seems to me, however, that the recent history of interpretation should lead to precisely the opposite conclusion: when Mark 10:46–52 is treated as an isolated pericope, there is no way to adjudicate whether Mark's Jesus (and the implied author) accepts or rejects the title son of David.

Yet where disputes over minute and ambiguous data may fail to provide exegetical consensus, setting this pericope within its narrative framework could provide the way forward. The reason such an approach is largely unattested in modern Gospels scholarship is the widespread assumption that "die spärliche Überlieferung zum Davidssohn"[7] constitutes the only material of relevance to Mark's *Davidssohnfrage*. As I demonstrated in Chapter 2, however, an explicit claim of Davidic ancestry is just one of a number of ways in which ancient authors chose to characterize their messiahs as Davidic. It seems arbitrary, therefore, to assume that one can get at Mark's view on Davidic messiahship by isolating passages containing the name David. When we treat the Gospel of Mark like any other messiah text, that is, as the literary product of a competent language user of a particular linguistic community, we discover a number of passages prior to the healing of Bartimaeus that color Mark's Christ in Davidic hues. It seems reasonable to assume that this material should inform our interpretation of 10:46–52.

---

[3] E.g., Schreiber, "Christologie," 164; Kelber, *Kingdom*, 95; Achtemeier, "'And He Followed,'" 115, 131; Telford, *Theology*, 51; Boring, *Mark*, 305; Malbon, *Mark's Jesus*, 88–92.

[4] Kingsbury, *Christology*, 105 n. 164.   [5] Malbon, *Mark's Jesus*, 88.

[6] Kingsbury, *Christology*, 105 n. 161; Malbon, "Jesus of Mark," 180–184.

[7] Burger, *Jesus als Davidssohn*, 59.

At this point, it may be instructive to compare my approach to that of Malbon. First, while we agree that Mark 1:11 evokes Ps 2:7, this intertext does not feature in her assessment of 10:46–52 (or 12:35–37). I have argued, by contrast, that an allusion to Psalm 2 is relevant to an assessment of Mark's *Davidssohnfrage*, since it evokes a frame that the evangelist's linguistic community associated with David and his descendants. Second, the only material in Mark 1:1–10:45 she finds even tangentially related to Mark's *Davidssohnfrage* is the grain-plucking controversy (2:23–28), a passage that she argues serves merely "as a legitimization for questioning cultic regulations on the basis of God's care for hungry persons."[8] Yet it seems more likely, as I argued earlier, that the argument in 2:25–26 relies on an implicit logic that invites the audience to draw correlations between two messiah-designates, David and Jesus. Third, Malbon never broaches points of intertextual contact between the first half of the Gospel and ancillary Davidic traditions, including royal/Davidic psalms (e.g., Pss 69 [68 LXX]:9 and 118 [117 LXX]:22) and Ezekiel 34. In so doing, she misses the manifold ways in which Mark's language shapes Christ as a messiah in the mold of an ideal Davidide.

Certainly the evangelist would be free to repurpose his traditions to suit his ideological aims, including, if he so desired, the decision to downplay Davidic ancestry (e.g., 2 Bar.; John), or to do away with it altogether (e.g., 1 En. 37–71). What seems highly implausible, though, particularly when one considers the ways in which Mark uses this material prior to the healing of Bartimaeus, is that he expected his audience to reject the title son of David without any explicit instruction to do so. In other words, while nothing in 1:1–10:45 demands that Jesus of Nazareth be declared the son of David, quite a bit of material conditions the audience to accept new information indicating that such is the case. The following discussion examines how Mark 10:46–52 functions *als Schlüsseltext* both by recapitulating Jesus's ministry outside of Jerusalem (1:1–10:45) and by preparing the way for his entry into the holy city (11:1–11).

5.1.1   Recapitulating Jesus's Ministry outside of Jerusalem

Prior to any consideration of how Mark 10:46–52 frames Jesus's public ministry outside of Jerusalem, three general observations are

---

[8] Malbon, *Mark's Jesus*, 167.

in order. First, this pericope concludes the so-called way section (8:22–10:52), a section that is bracketed by both the only two healings of blind men in the Gospel (8:22–26; 10:46–52) and the introduction of two christological titles, ὁ χριστός in 8:29 and υἱὸς Δαυίδ in 10:47–48.[9] If one concludes, as the vast majority of interpreters do, that Peter's confession of Jesus as ὁ χριστός provides an accurate, though clearly misguided, understanding of Jesus's identity, then one should assume, unless given clear evidence to the contrary, that Bartimaeus's identification of Jesus as υἱὸς Δαυίδ functions similarly.[10] Just as Peter's metaphorical blindness does not prevent him from recognizing that Jesus is ὁ χριστός, so too Bartimaeus's physical blindness does not hinder him from seeing that υἱὸς Δαυίδ is approaching. As is often the case in Mark, the intentions of the characters (human or demonic) have no bearing on the validity of the christological titles they utter (cf. 1:24; 3:11; 5:7; 8:29; 10:47–48; 14:61; 15:25, 32, 39).

Second, the crowd's attempt to silence Bartimaeus in 10:48 provides evidence for a positive evaluation of the title son of David. The verb ἐπιτιμᾶν, "to silence/rebuke," occurs a total of nine times in the Gospel (cf. 1:25; 3:12; 4:39; 8:30, 32, 33; 9:25; 10:13, 48).[11] On four of these occasions, ἐπιτιμᾶν is used specifically to silence christological titles: (1) ὁ ἅγιος τοῦ θεοῦ (1:24–25), (2) ὁ υἱὸς τοῦ θεοῦ (3:11–12); (3) ὁ χριστός (8:29–30); and (4) υἱὸς Δαυίδ (bis 10:47–48). To be sure, the last instance slightly deviates from the pattern in that the crowd, rather than Jesus, is the subject of the verb. Nonetheless, it seems plausible that the pattern – accurate christological title followed by ἐπιτιμᾶν – holds true in the case of Bartimaeus.

Third, a survey of the Nazarene designation in Mark suggests that whenever Jesus is identified with his *patris* the accompanying information is always central to his christological identity.[12] Following

---

[9] While the evangelist identifies Jesus as Χριστός in the opening line of the Gospel (1:1), 8:29 marks the first instance in which a character in the narrative recognizes ὁ χριστός.

[10] Although Malbon (*Mark's Jesus*, 88) appropriately draws the comparison between Peter and Bartimaeus, she fails to consider properly its implications. For more plausible accounts, see Watts, *Isaiah's New Exodus*, 288; Yarbro Collins, *Mark*, 510.

[11] Whenever Jesus is the subject of the verb ἐπιτιμᾶν, he rebukes either the demons or the watery chaos (cf. Mark 1:25; 3:12; 4:39; 8:30, 33; 9:25). When others fill this role (cf. 8:32; 10:13; 10:48), they invariably display the mindset that remains under the auspices of Satan (cf. 8:33).

[12] Cf. Broadhead, *Naming Jesus*, 36, "The value of the Nazarene imagery is created through the vital position it occupies in the plot line of the Gospel of Mark."

his introduction in 1:9, Mark's Jesus is identified with his *patris* at only four other points in the narrative: (1) at the inauguration of his public ministry (1:24), (2) upon his approach to Jerusalem (10:47), (3) at Peter's "trial" in the high priest's courtyard (Mark 14:66–72),[13] and (4) at the empty tomb (Mark 16:6).[14] The accompanying christological information in these scenes may be summarized as follows: Jesus *of Nazareth* is the holy one of God, the son of David, the messiah son of God and son of man, and the crucified one who has been raised by God. Again, while it is possible that the title son of David represents an anomaly, it seems far more likely that it is intended to convey accurate information about the identity of Mark's Christ.

Beyond these observations, we should note the remarkable similarity between the two scenes framing Jesus's public ministry outside of Jerusalem (cf. 1:21–28; 10:46–52). In both instances, a character cries out ([ἀνα]κράζειν, 1:23; 10:47) a christological title based on its transcendent insight into the identity of the man from Nazareth (cf. 1:24; 10:47–48). As such, these scenes form an inclusio around Jesus's activities outside of Jerusalem, drawing together his public profile as an exorcist, healer, and authoritative teacher (1:21–22, 27; 10:51).[15] Moreover, if the christological designation the holy one of God evokes traditions about an anointed Davidide, as argued in the previous chapter, then it would appear that the narrative frames Jesus's public ministry outside of Jerusalem as that of a charismatic *Davidic* figure. This, in turn, could lend support to the suggestion that the address "son of David" in 10:47–48 connotes an exorcist-healer,[16] though, as I argued previously (see Section 2.3.4.2), portraits of David and Solomon as exorcists should not be treated as an isolated idea in competition with a putative messianic idea.

---

[13] Juel (*Messiah and Temple*, 67) notes the juxtaposition of Jesus's trial scene (14:55–65) with the scene of Peter's "trial" by the light of the fire (cf. 14:66–72). Whereas Jesus stays true to his identity (14:62), Peter thrice denies the claim, "You were with *the Nazarene, Jesus* [σὺ μετὰ τοῦ Ναζαρηνοῦ ἦσθα τοῦ Ἰησοῦ]!" (16:67).

[14] The final time the audience hears the Nazarene designation is the angel's declaration to the women at the empty tomb: "Do not be alarmed. You are looking for Jesus of Nazareth who was crucified. He has been raised; he is not here" (16:6).

[15] The address ῥαββουνί, "my teacher" (10:51); is sometimes suggested to offer evidence that Bartimaeus lacks sufficient insight (e.g., Boring, *Mark*, 306; Malbon, *Mark's Jesus*, 91). If, however, Mark 10:46–52 gestures back to 1:21–10:45, then a close connection between healing/exorcistic power and teaching is to be expected. Also note the Markan Jesus's positive use of ὁ διδάσκαλος, "the teacher," in 14:14.

[16] Duling, "Solomon," 250–252; see also Chilton, "Jesus *ben David*;" Ahearne-Kroll, *Psalms of Lament*, 141–144.

Ancient authors could find intelligible the portrait of a son of David who is both an exorcist-healer and the claimant to David's throne because they inherited this connection within their sacred traditions (cf. 1 Sam 16:14–23; LAB 59–60).

5.1.2 The Son of David Approaches the City of David

Mark 10:46–52 not only glances back at the Gospel's profile of the messiah from Nazareth; it also looks forward to his entry into the city of David and into the temple that some of his contemporaries hoped a future descendant of David would restore (11:1–11).[17] Several traditions state explicitly that this restorative act would be the means by which the God of Israel would dispatch his mercy upon Zion and the nations. The writer of Psalms of Solomon 17, for instance, envisages a scenario in which the messiah son of David would purify Jerusalem (and implicitly the temple) of its defilement on account of the Romans and the current temple regime, thus unlocking the promise of Isa 55:5 (cf. Pss. Sol. 17:30–31). Only then would the nations of the earth stream to Zion to receive God's mercy through the son of David (ἐλεήσει πάντα τὰ ἔθνη ἐνώπιον αὐτοῦ ἐν φόβῳ; Pss. Sol. 17:34). The writer of Psalm of Solomon 18 prays similarly, "May God cleanse Israel for the day of mercy [εἰς ἡμέραν

---

[17] Jostein Ådna notes, "Obwohl die meisten alttestamentlichen und (früh)jüdischen Texte, die von Tempelkritik und –erneuerung handeln, vom Messias entweder ganz schweigen oder jedenfalls keine active Rolle für ihn in Verbindung mit der Beseitigung der gerügten Zustände und der Erneuerung vorsehen, ist dieses Bild eines abwesenden oder passive Messias keineswegs alleinherrschend in der alttestamentlich-(früh) jüdischen Tradition" (*Jesu Stellung zum Tempel: Die Tempelaktion und das Tempelwort als Ausdruck seiner messianischen Sendung*, WUNT 2/119 [Tübingen: Mohr Siebeck, 2000], 88). The clearest example in support of Ådna's claim is Pss. Sol. 17, in which the poet depicts David's son as one who will restore and purify Jerusalem and its temple. In addition, Herod the Great's expansion of the Jerusalem temple may have been inspired by traditions that depict the king as temple builder (cf. 2 Sam 7; 1 Chr 17; Zech 6:12). Herod may have concluded that, although he was not a veritable son of David, at least he could accomplish, perhaps even surpass, what the scriptures foretold about a future Davidide (Ilan, "King David;" Adam Kolman Marshak, *The Many Faces of Herod the Great* [Grand Rapids, MI: Eerdmans, 2015], 278–284; William Horbury, *Messianism among Jews and Christians: Biblical and Historical Studies*, 2nd edn. [London: T&T Clark, 2016], 115–132). Broadly speaking, however, scriptural traditions of the Davidide as temple-builder are not reactivated until after the destruction of the Second Temple, for obvious reasons (cf. Tg. Isa. 52:13–53:12; Tg. Zech. 6:12–13; Juel, *Messiah and Temple*, 199; Ådna, *Jesu Stellung*, 89).

ἐλέους] in blessing, for the appointed day when [he] raises up his messiah [ἐν ἀνάξει χριστοῦ αὐτοῦ]" (Pss. Sol. 18:5).[18]

The lone occurrence of the verb ἐλεεῖν, "to have mercy," in Mark's Gospel is situated just prior to a son of David's entry into the Jerusalem temple. Whether the evangelist has a similar prophetic frame in mind to that of the psalmists mentioned earlier cannot be determined. But the language of Bartimaeus's plea, υἱὲ Δαυὶδ Ἰησοῦ, ἐλέησόν με, "son of David, have mercy on me" (10:47), in conjunction with Jesus's proximity to the temple, evokes traditions that tie David and his line to the Jerusalem temple. Mark 10:46–52 works *als Schlüsseltext* both by recapitulating Jesus's ministry outside of Jerusalem and by preparing the way for his entry into the city of David – the place where, according to the Markan account of the Jewish scriptures, the messiah must go to be rejected and killed.

5.2   The One Who Comes in the Name of the Lord

Mark's account of the triumphal entry begins with the freshly heralded son of David positioned atop the Mount of Olives (11:1). While overlooking the holy city, Jesus commissions two of his disciples to make the necessary preparations for his entry: "Go into the village ahead of you, and immediately as you enter it, you will find tied there a colt that has never been ridden; untie it and bring it. If anyone says to you, 'Why are you doing this?' just say this, 'The Lord needs it and will send it back here immediately'" (11:2–3). These instructions, as Burton Mack and Vernon Robbins observe, share a "constellation of references" with Jesus's earlier appeal to "what David did" in 1 Samuel 21 (cf. 2:25–26).[19] Once again the messiah extends his authority qua κύριος to his companions on account of situational need (ὁ κύριος αὐτοῦ χρείαν ἔχει; 11:3). Moreover, and of particular significance for my argument, the words and actions of Mark's Jesus in this scene place him in conversation with a strand of scriptural traditions about a "coming" king from the line of David (Gen 49:10–11; Zech 9:9).

---

[18] One encounters similar language in Jer 33:26 MT and the 14th benediction of the Palestinian recension of the Amidah.

[19] Mack and Robbins, *Patterns of Persuasion*, 127. For my treatment of Mark 2:25–26, see Section 4.2.

5.2.1 The "Coming" Descendant of Judah (Genesis 49:10–11)

According to Heinz Kuhn and Joseph Blenkinsopp, respectively, Jesus's preparation for his entry alludes to an ancient oracle about the Judahite dynasty in Gen 49:9–11.[20] Their case rests on five observations: (1) the repetition of the lexeme πῶλος, "colt," always modified by the perfect passive particle "tied" (11:2, 4) or "untied" (11:2, 4, 5); (2) the presence of syntactic double entendre, "the Lord/ it's master has need of it [ὁ κύριος αὐτοῦ χρείαν ἔχει]," perhaps subtly raising the question of the colt's true owner;[21] (3) the concentric structure of the pericope, placing emphasis on the action of untying the colt; (4) the widespread assumption that Gen 49:9–11 is about a future son of David (cf. 4Q252 5:3–4; 4 Ezra 12:32; Heb 7:14; Rev 5:5);[22] and (5) the narrative location of Jesus's instructions to his disciples, just after he has been heralded "son of David" (10:47–48)

[20] Heinz W. Kuhn, "Das Reittier Jesu in der Einzugsgeschichte des Markusevangelium," *ZNW* 50 (1959): 82–91; Joseph Blenkinsopp, "The Oracle of Judah and the Messianic Entry," *JBL* 80 (1961): 55–64; and more recently, Deborah Krause, "The One Who Comes Unbinding the Blessing of Judah: Mark 11.1–10 as Midrash on Gen 49.11, Zechariah 9.9, and Psalm 118.25–26," in *Early Christian Interpretation of the Scriptures of Israel: Investigation and Proposals*, eds. Craig A. Evans and James A. Sanders, JSNTSup 148 (Sheffield: Sheffield Academic Press, 1997), 141–153. In fact, many interpreters take it for granted that 11:2–6 should be interpreted with reference to Gen 49:10–11: e.g., Klostermann, *Markusevangelium*, 113; Lane, *Gospel*, 395–396; Gnilka, *Evangelium*, 2:116; Watts, *Isaiah's New Exodus*, 306; Hatina, *In Search*, 313; Boring, *Mark*, 315; Yarbro Collins, *Mark*, 517–518; Marcus, *Mark 8–16*, 778.
It is unclear how שילה in 49:10 MT should be translated. The *qere* seems to agree with LXX's τὰ ἀποκείμενα αὐτῷ (cf. John William Wevers, ed., *Genesis*, Septuaginta 1 [Göttingen: Vandenhoeck & Ruprecht, 1974], 460). For other proposals on the textual tradition attested in the Masoretic Text, see Claus Westermann, *Genesis 17–50*, trans. John J. Scullion, CC (Minneapolis, MN: Augsburg, 1986), 231. There are also points of uncertainty about the Greek textual tradition. For example, while the referent of αὐτῷ in Gen 49:10 LXX appears to be a Davidic ruler, it is not entirely clear what the translator intended by the expression τὰ ἀποκείμενα (see Wevers, *Notes on the Greek Text of Genesis*, SCS 35 [Atlanta: Scholars Press, 1993], 826).
[21] Blenkinsopp, "Oracle," 55–56. Luke in particular draws a clear distinction between the colt's owners, οἱ κύριοι αὐτοῦ, and its real master, ὁ κύριος αὐτοῦ, Jesus (19:33).
[22] 4 Ezra's explication of the lion of Judah as the one "who will arise from the posterity of David" is lacking in the Latin textual tradition (see Robert L. Bensly, ed., *The Fourth Book of Ezra: the Latin Version Edited from the MSS*, Texts and Studies 3.2 [Cambridge: Cambridge University Press, 1895]), but present in the Syriac: cf. R. J. Bidawid, ed., "4 Esdras," in *Apocalypse of Baruch, 4 Esdras*, The Old Testament in Syriac according to the Peshitta Version, Part IV, fasc. 3 [Leiden: Brill, 1973], 39) and other recensions. The phrase is generally taken to be integral to the work (cf. Jacob M. Myers, *I and II Esdras: Introduction, Translation and Commentary*, AB 42 [Garden City, NY: Doubleday, 1974], 286; Bruce M. Metzger, "The Fourth Book

and just before the festal shout, "Blessed is the coming kingdom of our ancestor David" (11:10). Against these observations, however, one might object that the presence of the lexeme πῶλος can be explain by the Zecharian allusion alone (on which, see Section 5.5.2), and that when one removes πῶλος from consideration Mark's account of the triumphal entry lacks verbal correspondence to Gen 49:9–11.[23]

Regardless of whether one can "prove" that the evangelist intentionally alluded to the Genesis oracle, there is good reason to consider its interpretive significance for Mark 11:1–11, since it forms part of the encyclopedia early readers brought with them to the Second Gospel. Thus, it should come as no surprise when a scripturally literate writer such as Justin concludes,

[And the prophecy] "binding His foal to the vine, washing His robe in the blood of the grape" [Gen 49:10–11] was a significant symbol of the things that were to happen to Christ, and of what He was to do. For the foal of an ass stood bound to a vine at the entrance of a village, which He then ordered His companion to bring to Him; and when it

of Ezra [Late First Century A.D.]," *OTP* 1:517–559, here 550; Stone, *Fourth Ezra*, 360).

The prince of the congregation in 1Q28b also seems to have been characterized in terms of Gen 49:9: "[. . . all na]tions will serve you, and he will make you strong by his holy Name, so that you will be *like a li[on* [כאר]יה) . . .] your prey, with no-one to give it [back] (1Q28b V, 28; Dominique Barthélemy and J. T. Milik, eds., *Qumran Cave 1: I*, DJD 1 [Oxford: Clarendon, 1955], 128–129). Further, Nils Dahl (*Studies in Paul: Theology for the Early Christian Mission* [Minneapolis, MN: Augsburg, 1977], 131), followed by Donald Juel (*Messianic Exegesis*, 85–86), has proposed that Paul alludes to Gen 49:10 in Gal 3:19: "until the time when the seed [i.e., Christ] comes to whom the promise was made [ἄχρις οὗ ἔλθη τὸ σπέρμα ᾧ ἐπήγγελται]." Antique Jewish and Christian writers widely assumed that Gen 49:9–11 is about a coming descendant of David (cf. Tg. Onq. Gen 49:10; Tg. Ps.-J. 49:10; Frg. Tg. Gen 49:10; b. Sanh. 98b; Gen. Rab. 98:8; Yal. Shim. 160; Justin, *Apol.* 1.32, 54; *Dial.* 53; Ps.-Clem., *Recog.* 1.49–50; *Hom.* 49; Irenaeus, *Haer.* 4.10.2; Cyprian, *Test.* 1.21).

[23] The principle of Ockham's razor is generally a sound one, but in this instance there is reason to exercise caution. The Zecharian oracle may represent an exegetical reworking of Gen 49:10–11 (Fishbane, *Biblical Exegesis*, 501–502), and, in any case, its shared elements would allow later interpreters to bring these texts together (cf. Gen. Rab. 98.9). Mark has an affinity for weaving together source texts with similar lexical and thematic features, such as he does at the beginning of his Gospel when he conflates Exod 23:20 and Mal 3:1, the latter of which reworks the former (Beth Glazier-McDonald, *Malachi: The Divine Messenger*, SBLDS 98 [Atlanta: Scholars Press, 1987], 130–131); further instances of conflate allusions in Mark are noted by Marcus (*Way*, 200 n. 4).

was brought, He mounted and sat upon it, and entered
Jerusalem.   (*Apol.* 1.32; cf.Dial. 53.2–4)[24]

What was clear to Justin in the mid-second century CE would have
been equally lucid for those in the first century CE who were aware
of Gen 49:9–11: by sending his disciples to untie the colt, Jesus
thereby implies that he is the coming descendant from the line of
Judah.

The implications of this point are not always appreciated. After
sustained argument that "'Son of David' is a misunderstanding of
Jesus' true identity."[25] Boring comments en passant and without
qualification, "Mark ... does not cite Zech 9:9 or Gen 49:11 specifically, though both are in the background, and both had already
been interpreted messianically in first-century Judaism."[26] But one
ought to be more specific. It is not simply that Gen 49:10–11 "had
already been interpreted messianically in first-century Judaism," but
that the evangelist's linguistic community assumed that the figure in
question would be a descendant of Judah. If one concludes, therefore, that Mark's aim is to distance Jesus from the title son of David,
it is difficult to explain why he follows the healing of Bartimaeus with
a scene in which Jesus himself takes actions that would suggest to
other scripturally informed observers that he is the figure presaged in
Gen 49:9–11. One need not be persuaded that Mark intentionally
alluded to Gen 49:11 to recognize the conundrum caused by Boring's
position.

5.2.2   The "Coming" Davidic King (Zechariah 9:9)

Beyond a potential allusion to Gen 49:10–11, there is widespread
consensus among interpreters that Jesus's entry evokes another
oracle about a "coming" Davidic king: "Rejoice greatly,
O daughter Zion! Shout aloud, O daughter Jerusalem! Lo, your king
comes [ἰδοὺ ὁ βασιλεύς σου ἔρχεταί] to you; triumphant [δίκαιος; lit.
'righteous']27 and victorious is he, humble and riding on a donkey

---

[24] I follow the English translation of Leslie William Barnard, *St. Justin Martyr the
First and Second Apologies: Translated with Introduction and Notes*, ACW 56 (New
York: Paulist, 1997), 45; the Greek text may be found in Goodspeed, ed., *Die ältesten
Apologeten*, 47–48.

[25] Boring, *Mark*, 305.   [26] Boring, *Mark*, 315.

[27] Most translators render צדיק/δίκαιος as "triumphant." Laato (*Josiah and David
Redivivus*, 269) may be correct, however, that צדיק should be read in terms of "the
traditional royal ideology in which it was the king's duty to rule the people in

and on a new colt [ἐπιβεβηκὼς ἐπὶ ὑποζύγιον καὶ πῶλον νέον]"
(Zech 9:9 LXX).[28] The degree of thematic coherence between the
Zecharian oracle and Jesus's entry would not go unnoticed by first-
century auditors of the Gospel. Indeed, the fact that Matthew (Matt
21:4–5) and John (John 12:14–15) cite Zech 9:9 offers demonstrable
evidence that at least some of Mark's early auditors were attuned to
the allusion.[29] Just as Zechariah's "coming" (בוא/ἐρχέσθαι) king
enters Jerusalem on a young colt amidst the cheers of daughter Zion
(Zech 9:9), so Jesus enters Jerusalem mounted on an unridden colt
amidst the cheers of a crowd (Mark 11:9).[30] Mark did not need to
cite Zechariah in order for the point to be clear. Rather, as he elected
to do on numerous other occasions, he characterized his Christ by
way of an allusion to a discrete scriptural tradition about the arrival
of a Davidic king.

5.2.3   Summary: Actions Speak

Not infrequently, it is suggested that Mark's Jesus is mute with
respect to Davidic sonship prior to the *Davidssohnfrage* (12:35–37).
But if my assessment is anywhere near the mark, this simply cannot
be right. Moreover, and in contrast to 10:46–52, Jesus is not reacting
here to the cry, "son of David, have mercy on me." Rather, it is the

---

righteousness" (e.g., Ps 72:1–3; Jer 23:5–6). We find a renaissance of this hope
expressed in the messianic designations משיח הצדק (4Q252 5:3) and βασιλεὺς δίκαιος
(Pss. Sol. 17:32), respectively.

[28] Contra Horsley (*Hearing*, 251), the donkey does not have "peasant" connotations; they were a common choice of mount for kings in the ancient Near East (Carol
L. Meyers and Eric M. Meyers, *Zechariah 9–14: A New Translation with Introduction
and Commentary*, AB 25C [Garden City, NY: Doubleday, 1993], 129; Blenkinsopp,
David Remembered, 146–147). On the other hand, the reference to the donkey may
signal a rejection of riding in chariots and on horses (cf. Jer 17:24–25; Pss. Sol. 17:33),
a motif that aligns with Deuteronomy's "law of the king" (cf. Deut 17:14–20). Note,
for example, the contrast between David's donkey in 2 Sam 16:1 and Absalom's
chariot and horses in 2 Sam 15:1.

[29] All extant interpretations of Zech 9:9 take the rider as the messiah son of David,
on which see Mark C. Black, "The Rejected and Slain Messiah Who Is Coming with
the Angels: The Messianic Exegesis of Zechariah 9–14 in the Passion Narratives,"
PhD diss., Emory University, 1990, 95–111.

[30] Since Mark's Jesus is twice heralded "son of David" (10:47–48) just prior to his
entrance into Jerusalem, it seems worth noting that another son of David, Solomon,
was said to have mounted his father's mule when he was anointed king by the priest
Zadok (cf. 1 Kgs 1:38–40). This overt political act spelled out doom for the current
king and his supporters (cf. 1 Kgs 1:49), just as, according to the writer of Pss. Sol. 17,
God's raising up of a future son of David would spell doom for the current Judean
establishment (cf. Pss. Sol. 17:21–25).

other way around. This time a crowd, perhaps even the same crowd that heard Bartimaeus call Jesus son of David, responds to the Nazarene's symbolic act (cf. 11:9–10). As Heikki Räisänen notes, "Jesus does not get hold of the donkey only when the cries of jubilation are ringing out ... Rather, it is precisely the messianic king riding on the colt which evokes the cries of Hosanna. The obvious conclusion is that the crowd [sic] understand the meaning of Jesus's symbolic action."[31] Any attempt to distance Mark's Jesus from a Davidic ancestry must grapple not only with the totality of the Gospel's messiah language prior to the healing of Bartimaeus but also with the actions of Jesus himself immediately following the twice-repeated claim that he is the son of David. If the evangelist aims to narcotize Davidic sonship from the semantic range of "messiah," he has chosen an odd strategy indeed. If, on the other hand, he wants his audience to actualize the potential of "messiah" to connote "descendant of David," then the actions of his Jesus make a great deal of sense.

5.2.4   The Crowd Responds to the "Coming" King (Psalm 118 [117 LXX]:26)

Once we grasp that 11:1–6 constitutes the Markan Jesus's claim to be the messiah from the line of David, negative interpretations of the crowd's response become highly implausible (11:7–10).[32] In fact, the crowd's response to Jesus's symbolic gesture picks up the same psalm to which he alluded in the first passion predication (Mark 8:31, alluding to Ps 117:26 LXX) and to which he will return in the end of the parable of the wicked tenants (cf. 12:10). The crowd's enhancement of the festal shout, "Hosanna! Blessed is the one who comes in the name of the Lord [εὐλογημένος ὁ ἐρχόμενος ἐν ὀνόματι κυρίου]!" (11:9), with the benedictory refrain, "Blessed is the coming kingdom of our father David [εὐλογημένη ἡ ἐρχομένη βασιλεία τοῦ πατρὸς ἡμῶν Δαυίδ]!" (11:10), implies that ὁ ἐρχόμενος brings ἡ ἐρχομένη βασιλεία.[33] That is to say, the Markan crowd interprets the

---

[31] Räisänen, 'Messianic Secret', 234; see also N. T. Wright, Jesus and the Victory of God, vol. 2 of Christian Origins and the Question of God (London: SPCK, 1996), 490.
[32] Contra Kelber, Kingdom, 96; Lührmann, Markusevangelium, 189; Meyers, Binding, 296; Boring, Mark, 316; Malbon, Mark's Jesus, 100; Rhoads, Dewey, and Michie, Mark as Story, 110.
[33] Aloysius Ambrozic, The Hidden Kingdom: A Redaction-Critical Study of the References to the Kingdom of God in Mark's Gospel, CBQMS 2 (Washington, DC:

identity of the royal figure in Psalm 118 (117 LXX) as the future
descendant of David anticipated in a strand of scriptural traditions
(cf. 2 Sam 7:12–14; 1 Chr 17:11–14).[34]

All indications are that this interpretation represents the position
of the evangelist himself. Based on the observation that Gen
49:10–11, Zech 9:9, and Ps 118 (117 LXX):26 share distinct lexical
features, one might speculate about the presence of underlying midrashic strategy.[35] All three texts envisage a "coming" (בוא/ἔρχεσθαι)
king, while both Zechariah 9 and Psalm 118 (117 LXX) depict
his victorious return from battle (cf. Zech 9:1–8; Ps 118 [117
LXX]:5–18) – more still, Zechariah's "righteous" (צדיק/δίκαιος) king
possesses the singular quality necessary for entrance into the temple
according to Ps 118 (117 LXX):20.[36] Less speculative is our

Catholic Biblical Association of America, 1972), 39; Matera, *Kingship*, 72; Marcus,
Way, 115; Ahearne-Kroll, *Psalms of Lament*, 147; Watts, "Mark," 206–208; Hays,
Echoes of Scripture in the Gospels, 52. The other canonical Gospels accentuate the
crowd's interpretation of Ps 118 (117 LXX). Matthew adds: "Hosanna to the son of
David [ὡσαννὰ τῷ υἱῷ Δαυίδ]" (Matt 21:9); Luke adds: "the king [ὁ βασιλεύς] who
comes in the name of the Lord" (Luke 19:38); and John adds: "[even] the king of
Israel" [(καὶ) ὁ βασιλεὺς τοῦ Ἰσραήλ]" (John 12:13).

[34] Kelber (*Kingdom*, 96) thinks that the phrase "the coming kingdom of our father
David" has been redactionally inserted to shock the audience into questioning its
validity. But this is no less speculative than Ambrozic's (*Hidden Kingdom*, 39) suggestion that the phrase represents an early Christian gloss on Ps 117:26 LXX, based on
the community's belief that Jesus is the son of David. Malbon (*Mark's Jesus*, 100)
argues that "the crowd's call ... is problematic since Jesus continually speaks of the
coming and arrival of the kingdom not of David but of God" (so too Lührmann,
Markusevangelium, 189; Meyers, *Binding*, 296; Boring, *Mark*, 316). It is highly tenuous, however, to suppose that the evangelist and his early auditors would conceive of
Davidic kingship as antithetical to the actualization of God's reign on earth (cf. Pss 2,
89); see J. J. M. Roberts, "The Enthronement of Yhwh and David: The Abiding
Theological Significance of Kingship Language in the Psalms," *CBQ* 64 (1992):
675–686. The Chronicler illustrates how natural it would be to align the two: "I
[YHWH] will set him [David's son] over my house *and over my kingdom* [ובמלכותי]"
1) Chr 17:14); see William M. Schniedewind, *Society and the Promise to David*
(Oxford: Oxford University Press, 1999), 131.

[35] So Krause, "One Who Comes," 145.

[36] Grant (*King as Exemplar*, 132) notes that, according to Ps 118, "The only
grounds for the king's admission into the Temple is righteousness (צדקה; v 20)." Cf.
Midr. Ps. 118: *"Open to me the gates of righteousness* (Ps. 118:19). When a man is
asked in the world-to-come: 'What was thy work?' and he answers: 'I fed the hungry,'
it will be said to him: *'This is the gate of the Lord* (Ps. 118:20). Enter into it, O thou that
didst feed the hungry.' When a man answers: 'I gave drink to the thirsty,' it will be said
to him: *'This is the gate of the Lord.* Enter into it, O thou that didst give drink to the
thirsty.' When a man answers: 'I clothed the naked,' it will be said to him: *'This is the
gate of the Lord.* Enter into it, O thou that didst clothe the naked.' This will be said
also to him that brought up the fatherless, and to them that gave alms or performed
deeds of loving-kindness. And David said: I have done all these things. Therefore

observation that the crowd seems to react appropriately to Jesus's symbolic act.[37] Although these bystanders likely had no recourse to the information that Israel's liberation has been reconfigured around the rejection, suffering, and death of the king in Psalm 118 (cf. Mark 8:31; 12:10–11), their words nonetheless conform to the divine will, albeit ironically. In order for this son of David to be enthroned at God's right hand, he must first be rejected by the temple authorities and crucified by Roman temple guards.

5.2.5 Silence from the Temple

Mark 11:11 resounds in ominous silence: the son of David enters the temple, looks around, and then departs to Bethany with the Twelve. Notably absent at this point in the narrative is any mention of the temple priests, an arresting feature given what we know about royal entries in ancient Mediterranean cultures.[38] The absence of temple priests is all the more striking when one considers the language of Ps 117:26 LXX, cited by the evangelist in the previous verse.[39] In its original context, verse 26 of the psalm functioned as a word of

---

let all the gates be opened for me. Hence it is said *Open to me the gates of righteousness; I will enter into them, I will give thanks unto the Lord* (Ps 118:19)" (Midr. Ps. 118.17; trans. Braude, *Midrash on the Psalms*, 2:243, his emphasis).

[37] Cf. Hatina, *In Search*, 305–324.

[38] Royal entries typically climaxed in greetings from the temple priests and in sacrifice; see D. R. Catchpole, "The 'Triumphal' Entry," in *Jesus and the Politics of His Day*, eds. Ernst Bammel and C. F. D. Moule (Cambridge: Cambridge University Press, 1984), 319–334, esp. 319–321; Paul Brooks Duff, "The March of the Divine Warrior and the Advent of the Greco-Roman King: Mark's Account of Jesus' Entry into Jerusalem," *JBL* 111 (1992): 55–71, esp. 58–64; cf. 1 Macc 5:45–54; 13:49–52; Josephus, *Ant.* 11.325–339; 12.348–49; 13.304–306; 16.12–15; 17.194–239.

[39] In the Matthean account, the chief priests and the scribes are present but remain silent until they hear children echoing the cries of the crowd, "Hosanna to the son of David" (Matt 21:15). When they confront Jesus, "Do you hear what these are saying?" he responds, "Yes; have you never read, 'Out of the mouths of infants and nursing babes you have prepared praise for yourself?'" (Matt 21:16; citing Ps 8:5). In the Lukan account, the messianic interpretation of Ps 117:26 LXX (Luke 19:38) generates immediate rebuke from some of the Pharisees in the crowd. "Teacher," they say, "order your disciples to stop;" to which Jesus responds, "I tell you, if these were silent, the stones would shout out" (19:39). Although the Pharisees are not "the builders" in a strict sense (cf. Luke 20:1, 18), it is not accidental that both Matthew and Luke depict groups refuting the association of Jesus with the figure describe in Ps 118. Mark, by contrast, uses the priests' silence as a "prolegomenon to the ensuing conflict" (Hatina, *In Search*, 316).

blessing spoken by the temple priests to the king as he led the congregants into the temple.[40] Although we can only speculate as to how the psalm functioned in the first century CE, its connection with the festivals of Passover (cf. m. Pesaḥ. 5.5; 10.6; b. Pesaḥ. 117a; 118a; 119a) and Tabernacles (cf. b. Sukk. 45a and b) may go back to our period, enhancing the likelihood that ancient auditors would be attuned to the psalm's liturgical and antiphonal qualities. Since, moreover, the evangelist cites Ps 117:22–23 LXX in the next chapter (cf. 12:10–11), explicitly equating the temple leaders with "the builders" who have rejected the elect "stone," it seems plausible that the citation of Ps 117:26 LXX in 11:9 is intended to be ironic. That is, the crowd, rather than the temple leaders, takes up the first half of verse 26, "Blessed is the one who comes in the name of the Lord;" the latter half of the blessing, "We bless you *from the house of the Lord*," has been left out entirely.[41]

For the moment, triumph ends in rejection. And yet, for the attuned auditor of Mark's narrative and, indeed, for those who have learned from the evangelist to read Psalm 118 (117 LXX), rejection of the messiah is not the last word but a necessary stage of his enthronement. Jesus returns to this point when, for the first time after his entrance into Jerusalem, he is confronted by the chief priest, the scribes, and the elders – the very group that must reject him according to Mark's interpretation of the Jewish scriptures (cf. 8:31).

5.3   The Rejected-but-Vindicated Stone

In contrast to the healing of blind Bartimaeus (10:46–52) and the triumphal entry (11:1–11), the parable of the wicked tenants (12:1–12) appears, prima facie, to be uninterested in Davidic descent.[42] Cilliers Breytenbach's essay, "Das Markusevangelium, Psalm 110,1 und 118,22f.: Folgetext und Prätext," illustrates what

---

[40] See James A. Sanders, "A New Testament Hermeneutic Fabric: Psalm 118 in the Entrance Narrative," in *Early Jewish and Christian Exegesis: Studies in Memory of William Hugh Brownlee*, eds. Craig A. Evans and William F. Stinespring (Atlanta, GA: Scholars Press, 1987), 177–190, at 183–184.

[41] My interpretation runs along the lines of Matera, *Kingship*, 82–84; Evans, *Mark 8:27–16:20*, 146; Hatina, *In Search*, 315–322, Yarbro Collins, *Mark*, 520; and Watts, "Mark," 208.

[42] This may explain Burger's decision not to treat this passage in his study (*Jesus als Davidssohn*, 42–71).

is potentially at stake.[43] Although he recognizes that "[b]eide Psalm-zitate [i.e., Pss 109:1 LXX; 117:22 LXX] sind ... in den breiteren narrative Kontext des Evangeliums eingebunden,"[44] Breytenbach concludes that only Ps 109:1 LXX is of any relevance to the *Davidssohnfrage*, a question he believes must be answered negatively, if Mark's Jesus is to be upheld as the messiah.[45] In contrast to Breytenbach, I find it likely that the Markan citation of Ps 117:22–23 LXX is suspended by a Davidic substructure and thus provides yet another piece of the son-of-David puzzle.

I need not engage every detail of the parable and its surrounding context to make my case.[46] Rather, I limit my focus to three points that, when taken together, appear to divulge an underlying assumption that the person identified as the "son" in the parable and the "stone" in the psalm is a descendant of David. I argue, first, that a proper account of the citation of Ps 117:22 LXX in Mark 12:10–11 must account for the citation of the same psalm at the triumphal entry (cf. 11:9–10); second, that the parable conflates the messiah son of God in Psalm 2 with the vindicated messianic stone in Psalm 118 (117 LXX); and third, that Mark's allusion to the Joseph novella (Gen 37:20) may have been facilitated by way of comparison to traditions about David.

5.3.1   Tying up Loose Ends: Reading Mark 11:27–12:12 in Light of 11:1–11

Breytenbach's analysis of Ps 117:22–23 LXX in Mark, though help-ful in many ways, overlooks that the triumphal entry (11:1–11) is meant to inform the parable of the wicked tenants and its immediate context (11:27–12:12).[47] The group that confronts Jesus in Mark

---

[43] Cilliers Breytenbach, "Das Markusevangelium, Psalm 110,1 und 118,22f.: Folgetext und Prätext, in *The Scriptures in the Gospels*, ed. C. M. Tuckett, BETL 131 (Leuven: Leuven University Press, 1997), 197–222.

[44] Ibid., 221.   [45] Ibid., 205.

[46] For a detailed study of the parable of the wicked tenants, see Klyne Snodgrass, *The Parable of the Wicked Tenants: An Inquiry into Parable Interpretation*, WUNT 27 (Tübingen: Mohr Siebeck, 1983). On the use of Isaiah 5 in 4Q500 and its relevance to Mark 12:1–12 and pars., see Brooke, *Dead Sea Scrolls*, 235–260. For the most thorough commentary on Mark 12:1–12, see Evans, *Mark 8:27–16:20*, 210–240. A truncated version of the parable is found in Gospel of Thomas 65–66, which lacks the climactic citation of Ps 118 (cf. Marvin Meyer, "The Gospel of Thomas with the Greek Gospel of Thomas," in *The Nag Hammadi Scriptures: The Revised and Updated Translation of Gnostic Texts*, ed. Marvin Meyer [New York: HarperCollins, 2007], 133–156, at 148).

[47] Breytenbach, "Das Markusevangelium," 216–221.

11:28, "the chief priests, the scribes, and the elders," is the same group that was conspicuously absent at his entrance into the city. Although the chief priests and scribes were present when Jesus invoked the words of the prophets against the temple (cf. 11:18), 11:28 marks the first time that this group speaks to Jesus. By breaking their silence, they remove any lingering doubt that they are "the builders" about whom the royal psalmist spoke (Ps 117:22 LXX).[48]

It seems unlikely, then, that crowd's appeal to Psalm 117 LXX in 11:9 is nugatory for our assessment of Jesus's appeal to the same psalm in 12:10–11. Rather, these characters attest to *a unified christological interpretation of the psalm*. And since the audience already knows that "the one who comes [ὁ ἐρχόμενος] in the name of the Lord" (Ps 117:26 LXX) is the messiah son of David (cf. 10:46–11:10), there can be little doubt that "the stone [λίθον] that the builders rejected" (Ps 117:22 LXX) is, too. Yet what the narrative takes for granted, while sufficient in and of itself for our interpretation of the parable, is likely only the surface of Mark's scriptural *imaginaire*.

5.3.2   The Beloved Son and the Messiah Son of God

Mark's interpretation of Ps 118 (117 LXX) dovetails with his interpretation of Psalm 2.[49] To the set of questions, "By what authority [ἐν ποίᾳ ἐξουσίᾳ] are you doing these things? Who gave you this authority [τὴν ἐξουσίαν ταύτην] to do them?"[50] (11:28), Jesus poses

[48] In some Second Temple traditions, the term "builders" clearly designates a group of religious leaders (cf. CD 4:19–20; 8:12, 18; 19:31). As E. P. Sanders (*Jewish Law from Jesus to the Mishnah: Five Studies* [London: SCM, 1990], 105) notes, "the view that only priests could enter the *area* of the Court of the Priests was understood by Herod (that is, by his advisers) to mean that priests had to be trained as masons (*Antiq.* 15.390). According to Ezra 3.10, builders worked on the temple and the priests blew trumpets, but by Herod's time a different purity law was accepted, and the priests built the most sacred areas themselves" (his emphasis). Certainly, the sense in Mark is that οἱ οἰκοδομοῦντες refers to those who have been charged with stewarding the temple (cf. Acts 4:11; 1 Cor 3:10).

[49] The link between Psalms 2 and 118 (117 LXX) is attested in other early Christian literature; see, in particular, Acts 4:11, 25–27, in which the author aligns the raging of nations against the Lord's messiah (Ps 2:1–2) with the builders rejection of the "stone" (Ps 117:22 LXX). The link between these two texts may have been facilitated by wordplay on "son" (בן) in Ps 2 and "stone" (אבן) in Ps 118 (see Snodgrass, *Parable of the Wicked Tenants*, 113–118).

[50] While ταῦτα, "these things," point directly to Jesus's demonstration against the temple (11:15–17), they also likely refer to his entry into the city (11:1). Indeed, from the audience's perspective, ταῦτα echoes the launching of Jesus's messianic ministry at

a counter-question, "Did the baptism of John come from heaven [ἐξ οὐρανοῦ], or was it of human origin [ἐξ ἀνθρώπων]?" Regardless of what the temple leaders know about John's baptism – the narrative is silent on this point – there is no question that, from the audience's perspective, John's baptism was the moment when the heavens were torn open and a voice declared, "You are *my son, the beloved*, in whom I am well pleased" (Mark 1:11). Since the baptism is the narratival moment at which Mark's Jesus is identified from heaven as the son of God (see 3.4.2.1), it seems significant that he chooses to raise this issue just prior to telling a story about a υἱὸς ἀγαπητός, "beloved son," whom a vineyard owner sent ἔσχατον, "last of all" (cf. 1:14–15).

Resistance to hearing echoes of the psalm in the parable is largely the result of a methodological decision to prioritize one intertext, Genensis 22, over and against another, Psalm 2.[51] Yet this decision appears to be based almost entirely on whether one treats the expression υἱὸς ἀγαπητός in isolation from other instances of divine sonship language in the Markan narrative. Prior to 12:6, the distinct collocation ὁ υἱός μου ὁ ἀγαπητός occurs at two critical junctures in the narrative: Jesus's baptism (1:11) and transfiguration (9:7). In each of these instances, ὁ υἱός μου ὁ ἀγαπητός reflects a fusion of the language in Ps 2:7 and Isa 42:1, such that subsequent son-of-God language "reinforces the application of this royal title to Jesus."[52]

The parable's description of a υἱὸς ἀγαπητός who is ὁ κληρονόμος, "the heir," to his father's κληρονομία, "inheritance," is remarkably similar to the language in Psalm 2: "The Lord said to me, 'You are my son [υἱός μου εἶ σύ]; today I have begotten you. Ask of me, and I will give you the nations as your inheritance [δώσω σοι ἔθνη τὴν κληρονομίαν σου]" (Ps 2:7–8 LXX).[53] According to the parable and ensuing psalm citation, after the beloved son has been rejected and killed by the land tenants qua builders, he will be vindicated and his

---

the Capernaum synagogue, when the crowd marveled because he teaches "as one having authority [ὡς ἐξουσίαν ἔχων], and not as the scribes" (1:22). This, in turn, leads back to the source of Jesus's authority and, thus, to his spirit-baptism.

[51] See, e.g., Kazmierski, *Jesus*, 53–56; Evans, *Mark 8:27–16:20*, 234–235; Marcus, *Mark 8–16*, 803. In my view, one should not have to choose between Gen 22 and Ps 2. Levenson (*Death and Resurrection*, 206) is helpful in this regard: "the two vocabularies of sonship, that of the beloved son and that of the Davidic king as the son of God, reinforce each other powerfully."

[52] Hays, *Echoes of Scripture in the Gospels*, 48.

[53] So also Lövestam, *Son and Saviour*, 97; Matera, *Kingship*, 78; Watts, "Mark," 316; O'Brien, *Use of Scripture*, 165.

father will give the vineyard, the son's inheritance, ἄλλοις, "to others." If, as is likely, the referent of ἄλλοις in 12:9 is the Twelve and, by extension, anyone who becomes a disciple of Jesus, then it is conceivable that the rejection–vindication scheme in Ps 117:22 LXX has been reimagined as the means by which the messianic son receives the nations as his inheritance, à la Psalm 2.[54]

This proposal is speculative, to be sure, but there are hints in Mark to suggest it is speculation worth entertaining. Note, in particular, the language of Jesus's final parable, at the conclusion of the Olivet discourse:

> But about that day or hour no one knows, neither the angels in heaven, nor the son [ὁ υἱός], but only the father [ὁ πατήρ]. Beware; keep alert; for you do not know when the time will come. It is like a man going on a journey [ἀπόδημος], when he leaves his house [τὴν οἰκίαν αὐτου] and puts his slaves in charge [δοὺς τοῖς δούλοις αὐτοῦ τὴν ἐξουσίαν], each with his work, and commands the doorkeeper to be on the watch. Therefore, keep awake – for you do not know when the lord of the house will come [ὁ κύριος τῆς οἰκίας ἔρχεται] ... And what I say to you [ὑμῖν], I say to all [πᾶσιν]: Keep awake!

The story Jesus tells here mimics the scenario of the parable of the wicked tenants with one important difference. This time, the ἄνθρωπος who goes away on a journey (ἀπόδημος) is *Jesus* rather than God. Instead of a vineyard with tenants, a lord resides over a household of slaves to whom he has delegated his authority and whom he will hold accountable when he returns. Not only are these the only instances of ἀποδήμειν or its cognate ἀπόδημος in Mark, but they also just so

---

[54] The language of the first "Song of David" discovered in the Cairo Genizah may be instructive: "From the beginning You swore to David Your servant and You anointed Jesse's root with Your mercy. You sustained his arm with Your holiness, for he established Your praise up to the ends of the earth. You established his name as a pillar of the world, and as a repair of a breach and as a re-builder of ruins. The rejected cornerstone, which the builders rejected, rose to be the head of nations. You made him inherit turban and crown with joy and You called out his name to be praised among all the nations ... You made his greatness (as) the great number of all angels and You appointed him king of all nations for ever" (CŠD 1.15–23; trans. Lorein and Staalduine-Sulman, in *Old Testament Pseudepigrapha: More Noncanonical Scriptures*, 265). Although dating this text is "a rather hypothetical enterprise" (259), Lorein and Staalduine-Sulman conclude that "an origin during the latter period of the Qumran Community seems a valid option" (262). In any case, the connection between the rejected cornerstone of Ps 118 and David's rule over the nations is a logical, albeit striking, interpretive move.

happen to occur in parables that speak about the "coming" (ἐρχέσθαι) of ὁ κύριος.[55] This implies that the referent of τοῖς δούλοις, "the servants," in 13:34 is the same as that of ἄλλοις, "others," in 12:9, and thus that Jesus's repeated call to vigilance (cf. 13:33, 34, 35, 37) against which the disciples will serve as a foil in the passion narrative (cf. 14:34, 37, 38, 40, 41), speaks directly to household communities – πᾶσιν, "to all" – living under the lordship of the resurrected son.

Mark's Jesus, of course, never says that the beloved son in the parable is the son of God in Psalm 2, and not a few commentators have happily breezed over this point. But the narrative context in which the parable is embedded invites such an inference. The parable suggests that God sent his beloved son at just the appropriate time to face those hostile to the reign of God (cf. Ps 2:1–3); the subsequent citation of Ps 117:22–23 LXX reinterprets the son's death in terms of the rejected-but-vindicated stone. And all this, for the attentive listener, harkens back to the Markan introduction of Ps 117:22 LXX at the first passion prediction, in 8:31, and to the insistence of the divine voice that rejection and death are indeed the path to his son's glorification, in 9:7.

5.3.3 From Joseph to the Beloved Son: A Possible Davidic Link

When the tenants recognize the beloved son, they exhort one another, "This is the heir; *come, let us kill him* [δεῦτε ἀποκτείνωμεν αὐτόν], and the inheritance will be ours" (12:7), marking an allusion to words of the brothers in the Joseph novella:

> Now they saw him beforehand from a distance before he came near to them, and they intended to act wickedly to kill him. They said, each to his brother, "Here comes that dreamer. *So come now, let us kill him* [νῦν οὖν δεῦτε ἀποκτείνωμεν αὐτόν] and throw him into one of the pits; and we shall say, 'an evil animal has devoured him,' and we shall see what will become of his dreams." (Gen 37:20)[56]

---

[55] Daniel Johansson, "*Kyrios* in the Gospel of Mark," *JSNT* 33 (2010): 101–124, at 110.

[56] Matthew and Luke amplify the allusion by adding that tenants began to conspire when they *saw* (ἰδόντες) the son coming from a distance (Matt 21:24; Luke 20:14).

The customary explanation for the presence of this allusion is that the evangelist perceived a typological relationship between two beloved sons, Joseph and Jesus.[57] As Jon Levenson observes, "[w]hat the Joseph story more than any other tales of the beloved son contributes to the Gospels is the theme of disbelief, resentment, and murderous hostility of the family of the one mysteriously chosen to rule."[58] Levenson is right to draw attention to the impact of the Joseph novella on early christological reflection, but he may have overlooked a link in the exegetical chain.

I return, once again, to a portion of David's psalm in LAB 59:4:

> When Abel first shepherded flocks, his sacrifice was more acceptable than that of his brother, and his brother was jealous of him and killed him [et zelans eum frater eius occidit eum]. But for me it is not the same, because God has protected me and because he has delivered me to his angels and to his guardians that they should guard me. For my brothers were jealous of me [Quoniam fratres mei zelaverunt me], and my father and my mother neglected me. And when the prophet came, they did not call to me. And when the anointed of the LORD was to be designated, they forgot me.[59]

Pseudo-Philo's *Tendenz* for detecting analogues in the divine economy leads him to three scriptural shepherds, each of whom was persecuted by his older brother(s): Abel (cf. Gen 4:8–9), Joseph (cf. Gen 37:18–24), and David (cf. 1 Sam 16:6–13; interpreted with reference to Pss 27:10; 69:9–10).[60] This enables the adroit interpreter of Israel's history to attribute a near citation of Gen 37:11, "For my brothers were jealous of me [Quoniam fratres mei zelaverunt me],"[61]

---

[57] E.g., Marcus, *Mark 8–16*, 803, 813. He notes that "[s]everal of the references to the Joseph story in the *Testament of the Twelve Patriarchs* emphasize Jacob/Israel's love for his son Joseph as the motivation for the other sons' attempt to kill him (*T. Sim.* 2:6–7; *T. Dan* 1:5–7; *T. Jos.* 1:2–3; cf. *T. Gad* 1:5), and Joseph calls himself 'the beloved of Israel' in *T. Jos.* 1:2–4, creating links with the 'beloved son' of Mark;" he also points to Acts 7:9–16 and 1 Clem 4:9 (803).

[58] Levenson, *Death and Resurrection*, 202.

[59] Pseudo-Philo, *Les Antiquités Bibliques*, 1:364; trans. Harrington, *OTP* 2:372.

[60] What links these three figures together is that (a) they are all first encountered in their respective narratives in the act of "shepherding" (רעה; Gen 4:2; 37:2; 1 Sam 16:11); (b) they are all the younger/youngest brother; (c) they are each favored by God before doing anything, either good or bad; and, as a result, (d) they incur the ire of their older brother(s) (Botner, "Then David Began to Sing," 75–77).

[61] See Jacobson, *Commentary*, 1170.

to the moment of David's anointing (1 Sam 16:13), a move facilitated by David's words in Ps 69:9, "I have become a stranger to my brothers, an alien to my mother's children."

The line Pseudo-Philo traces between Joseph and David could illuminate the logic of the Markan parable.[62] As with LAB 59:4, the parable both is directly informed by the Psalms, overtly in the case of Psalm 117 LXX (11:28; 12:10–11) and implicitly in the case of Psalm 2 (12:6), and appropriates a line from the opening of the Joseph novella to describe the persecution of another beloved son, an anointed king (1:11; 9:7). Later interpreters even applied Ps 118:22 to the moment when David was rejected by his family in the presence of the prophet (cf. Tg. Ps. 118:22; Ambrose, *Expos. Ps. 118* 18.23).[63] Awareness of a tradition linking the stone in Ps 118 (117 LXX):22 with "the theme of disbelief, resentment, and murderous hostility of the family"[64] in the story of David may have attracted some early Christ followers to the Joseph novella. In other words, the exegetical line from Joseph to Jesus may run through David.

5.3.4   Summary: A Davidic Reading of Psalm 118 (117 LXX)

All agree that Mark reads Psalm 118 (or parts thereof) as a narrative of the persecution and vindication of the Christ. Yet very little has been made of the possibility – in my view, likelihood – that the pericope presupposes Jesus's Davidic descent, and is thus, *pace* Breytenbach, of relevance to Mark's *Davidssohnfrage*. The parable sits at a pivotal juncture in Mark's narrative. On the one hand, it looks back to the motif of messianic rejection, a theme that has been

---

[62] The writer of 1 Clement also connects Joseph and David, albeit in a slightly different manner: "*Jealousy* [ζῆλος] caused Joseph to be persecuted nearly to death, and to be sold into slavery... *Because of jealousy* [διὰ ζῆλος] David not only was envied by the Philistines but also was persecuted by Saul, king of Israel" (1 Clem 4:9, 13).

[63] Tg. Ps. 118 renders אבן, "stone," as טלי, "child": "*The architects forsook the youth* [טליא] *among the sons of Jesse, but and he was worthy to be appointed king and ruler.* 'This has been from *before* the LORD,' said *the architects*; 'it is wonderful in our presence,' said the sons of Jesse [בנוי דישי]" (Ps 118:23; Stec, *Targum of Psalms*, 210, his emphasis). The midrash on Ps. 118.21 interprets the "stone" as Jacob/Israel, but the writer then goes on to claim: "*This is the Lord's doing* alludes to king David, king of Israel, who at one moment was keeping his father's sheep, and in the very next moment was made king, so that everyone exclaimed: One moment David keeps sheep, and the next he is king. And he replied: You wonder at me! Verily, I wonder at myself more than you do. But the Holy Spirit replied: *This is the Lord's doing*" (Braude, *Midrash on Psalms*, 2:244, his emphasis).

[64] Levenson, *Death and Resurrection*, 202.

building since the first passion prediction (8:31; cf. Ps 117:26 LXX) and that was amplified by the temple authorities' absence at the son of David's entrance into Jerusalem (11:9–11; cf. Ps 117:26 LXX). On the other hand, as the first pericope in the temple controversy cycle (11:27–12:44), the parable looks ahead to the *Davidssohnfrage* (12:35–37), in which the royal psalmist identifies the enthroned Christ as "my lord." If "Mark's use of LXX Psalm 117 aligns Jesus with David, in general, and with the aspect of the persecuted and saved David, in particular,"[65] then it would appear the evangelist's strategy follows a progression moving from rejection and death toward resurrection and enthronement.

5.4   The *Davidssohnfrage*: How Then Can the Christ Be David's Son?

Throughout this study, I have advance an approach to Mark's *Davidssohnfrage* that has less to do with our interpretation of those select few passages that include the name David, though these too are important, and more to do with our assessment of the manifold ways in which the evangelist constructs his Christ through the telling of a coherent narrative. If what I have argued thus far is persuasive, it should be obvious why every negative appraisal of the *Davidssohnfrage* has been outflanked. Nonetheless, it seems prudent to revisit the reasons why many interpreters are convinced that Mark's Christ cannot be David's son before moving on to my own interpretation of the passage.

5.4.1   An Unsatisfactory Solution: Denying Davidic Descent

In Chapter 1, we saw that there are three primary reasons why interpreters conclude that the Markan Christ is not the son of David. The first is the argument, dressed up in various guises, that Markan Christology is incompatible with the populist strand of Jewish messianism (e.g., Pss. Sol. 17).[66] In this instance, we would do well to heed the now century-old warning of Wrede:

---

[65] So rightly Ahearne-Kroll, *Psalms of Lament*, 159–160.

[66] Kelber, *Kingdom*; Meyers, *Binding*; Telford, *Theology*, 35–38; Horsley, *Hearing*, 251; Boring, *Mark*, 348–349; Malbon, *Mark's Jesus*, 159–169; Rhoads, Dewey and Michie, *Mark as Story*, 110, 149.

Der Gegensatz zwischen Sohn und Herr ist völlig schief, wenn eine politische und eine geistig sittliche Auffassung der Messianität gegenüber gestellt werden sollen. Diese weitverbreitete Auffassung, als ob der Begriff Davidssohn eine politische Farbe habe, ruht überhaupt auf sehr mangelhafter Ueberlegung. Zu Grunde liegt der Schluß: weil der jüdische Messias als wirklicher König aus Davids Geschlecht erwartet wird, so muß der christliche Titel dem entsprechen. Aber dann schließe man auch: weil der Begriff Christus, d.h. der gesalbte König im Judentum, einen politischen Sinn hat, so deutet er auch im Christentum einen politischen Charakter des Messias an. Auch nicht eine christliche Stelle, die vom Davidssohn redet, weist auf eine besondere politische Wendung des Messiasbegriffes.[67]

My own assumption, at any rate, is that every messiah is the product of an author's negotiation of the Jewish scriptures in light of the ideological commitments of his community.[68] There are no scriptural traditions about David and his descendants that Mark reads apart from the life, death, and resurrection of Jesus Christ.[69] The scriptures about Israel's ancient kings serve this end, not the other way around.

Second, those who answer the *Davidssohnfrage* negatively argue that this pericope provides the only "plain" statement about Davidic sonship in the Gospel.[70] Yet, as the scholarly project of locating the *Sitz* of the "plain meaning" of this tradition advanced, it became clear that things were not so clear, so that Alfred Suhl could write, in 1965, "Trotz vieler Versuche, den ursrpünglichen Sinn dieser Perikope vor ihrer Eingliederung in den Mk-Zusammenhang zu erheben, ist es nicht gelungen, über blosse Behauptungen hinaus den mutmasslichen Sinn stringent zu erweisen;"[71] and, therefore, "Wir sind

---

[67] Wrede, *Vorträge*, 169–170.

[68] Following Novenson, *Christ among the Messiahs*, 53; Novenson, *Grammar of Messianism*.

[69] See now Hays's notion of "reading backwards" (*Echoes of Scripture in the Gospels*, 4–5), and especially Novenson's point: "Jewish messianism – of which Christian messianism can be thought of as just an extraordinary well-documented example – always and everywhere involves the interplay of biblical tradition and empirical circumstance" (*Grammar of Messianism*, 196).

[70] Wrede, "Jesus als Davidssohn," in *Vorträge und Studien*, 168.

[71] Alfred Suhl, *Die Funktion der alttestamentlichen Zitate und Anspielungen im Markusevangelium* (Gütersloh: Gütersloher, 1965), 89.

darum genötigt, die Perikope zunächst nur im Zusammenhang der Evangelien zu interpretieren."[72] If our access to the meaning of *Davidssohnfrage* comes primarily, if not entirely, by way of the Markan narrative, then it is highly implausible that the "plain meaning" of this pericope is a straightforward denial of Davidic sonship. This much, at least, was clear to Matthew and Luke, both of whom took over the *Davidssohnfrage* from Mark without the slightest hint of discomfort (cf. Matt 22:41–45; Luke 20:41–44).

Third, interpreters who answer the *Davidssohnfrage* negatively contend that, on the rare occasions when Mark does address the issue of Davidic descent, he appears circumspect, at best.[73] This, too, goes back to Wrede's influential essay.[74] Yet we have seen that Wrede was methodologically mistaken and thus interpretively infelicitous in his decision to limit Markan interest in Davidic messiahship to pericopae containing the name David. Thus, the same logic interpreters apply to the *Davidssohnfrage* in Matthew and Luke ought to be applied to Mark: the totality of the material prior to the *Davidssohnfrage* makes it such that "internal textual coherence"[75] cannot be maintained if one interprets 12:35–37 as a rejection of the premise that the messiah would be David's son. Mark may lack the genealogical material we find in Matthew and Luke, but so does, for that matter, every authentic and disputed letter of Paul, Hebrews, Psalms of Solomon 17 and 18, all of the Dead Sea Scrolls, and 4 Ezra. Mark's Christ has just as much a claim to the label "son of "David" as any of these messiahs.

The issue, then, is not an alternative between either overwhelming Mark with our "Christian" presuppositions or allowing the text to speak for itself.[76] The issue, rather, is whether we should allow one possible interpretation of 12:35–37 to overwhelm what the rest of the Gospel communicates. Should we choose the former, we are opting for an interpretation that no scripturally literature first-century auditor of the Gospel would recognize.[77] Mark's *Davidssohnfrage* requires a more satisfactory solution.

[72] Ibid., 91.   [73] E.g., Malbon, *Mark's Jesus.*
[74] Wrede, *Vorträge*, 176; see further in Section 1.2.1.
[75] Eco et al., *Interpretation*, 65.   [76] So Malbon, *Mark's Jesus*, 160–161.
[77] There is a clear analogue here to the ways in which modern interpreters have handled Rom 1:3–4, on which, see Joshua Jipp, "Ancient, Modern, and Future Interpretations of Romans 1:3–4: Reception History and Biblical Interpretation," *JTI* 3 (2009): 241–259, esp. 254; Nathan C. Johnson, Romans 1:3–4: Beyond Antithetical Parallelism, *JBL* 136 (2017): 467–490.

5.4.2   Resolving, Not Dissolving, the Puzzle

If the (plain) meaning of the *Davidssohnfrage* is not to encourage the
audience to reject the premise that the Christ is David's son, what is
its purpose? While there are a number of ways in which interpreters
have answered this question, every attempt involves some form of a
not-only-but-also resolution. Perhaps the most popular of these goes
back to the view Schweitzer ascribed to the historical Jesus, namely
that the Christ is David's lord "by reason of the metamorphosis and
Parousia in which natural relationships are abolished and the scion
of David's line who is the predestined Son of Man shall take posses-
sion of his future glory."[78] Since, however, the vast majority of
critical scholars followed Wrede in situating the *Davidssohnfrage* in
the early history of Christian dogma, Schweitzer's solution morphed
into the *Zweistufenchristologie* of the "Jewish-Hellenistic" sphere,
the view that David's messianic offspring only became his lord at
the ascension.[79] Although scholars today are less inclined to appeal
to an alleged *Zweistufenchristologie*, this kind of an approach
remains the dominant way of resolving the *Davidssohnfrage*.[80]

While this solution boasts a long and venerable interpretive tradition, I find it to be inadequate for the following reasons:

(1) *A Zweistufenchristologie misdiagnoses the problem posed by the
question.* One of the primary reasons this solution garnered widespread appeal is that, in effect, it expurgates Christology of those
elements of messianism modern scholarship finds distasteful. The
vast majority of scholars who have opted for a not-only-but-also
solution to *Davidssohnfrage* basically agree with those who answer

---

[78] Schweitzer, *Quest*, 393; cf. Albert Schweitzer, *The Mysticism of the Apostle Paul*,
trans. William Montgomery (Baltimore, MD: Johns Hopkins University Press, 1998),
82–83, 87.

[79] See, e.g., Hahn, *Titles*, 251–258; Fuller, *Foundations*, 188–197; Burger, *Jesus als
Davidssohn*, 64–68. Daube's proposal (*New Testament*, 163) that the *Davidssohnfrage*
is an haggadic argument designed to reconcile two apparently competing points,
though unique, still depends on either Schweitzer's or a *zweistufenchristologisch* resolution: "the Messiah is David's son up to a certain moment in history, but his Lord
from then, or – this would mean that we have before us an adumbration of
Rom. 1,3f. – he is David's son according to the flesh, but his Lord according to the
spirit."

[80] See, e.g., Dodd, *According to the Scriptures*, 120; Lindars, *New Testament
Apologetic*, 48–51; Evald Lövestam, "Die Davidssohn," *SEÅ* 27 (1962): 72–82; Pesch,
Markusevangelium, 2:254–256; Matera, *Kingship*, 88; Juel, *Messianic Exegesis*, 144;
Hay, *Glory at the Right Hand*, 67; Yarbro Collins, *Mark*, 582; Ahearne-Kroll, *Psalms
of Lament*, 164–165.

the question negatively that the "problem" of messianism is the prime impetus of the question.[81] One camp gets rid of the problem by denying the Christ's Davidic ancestry; the other sweeps it aside by locating the Christ's throne in heaven, whence he may reign over a kingdom unconcerned with earthly "politics." The language may have changed over the years, but the root assumption that the *Davidssohnfrage* is about the "problem" of messianism persists.

Yet, whereas one might posit that militant forms of messianism initially motivated the historical Jesus to pose the *Davidssohnfrage* (although, even here, I think there are better solutions),[82] the latter finds no basis in Mark. To conclude, as Ahearne-Kroll does, that the narrative function of 12:35–37 is to distance "Jesus from the earthly, militaristic aspects of a Davidic messiah" is to beg the question.[83] Mark's narrative suggests that the *Davidssohnfrage* is not about conflicting messianic "ideas" but about who wields the authority of Israel's God. This is, after all, the question that launches the controversy cycle in the temple (11:27–12:44).

The structure of the second controversy cycle is significant. It begins with an account of the temple hierarchy challenging Jesus's authority (11:27–33) and ends with an account of Jesus hinting that the temple has been defiled by the economic malpractice of his challengers (12:38–44).[84] In close proximity to each of these episodes is a psalm citation (Ps 117:22–23 LXX in 12:10; Ps 109:1 LXX in 12:36) that has been interpreted christologically. Framed between these citations are three questions posed to Jesus, each of which subtly raises the issue of the nature and scope of his reign. The question about paying taxes to Caesar (12:13–17), though cryptic and multivalent in nature, suggest that the cosmos, including Caesar's empire, belongs to the lord God and to whomever he delegates to rule. The question about resurrection reveals that the creator God has the power to raise the dead and thus the power to

---

[81] See, e.g., Cullmann, *Christology*, 132; Georges Minette de Tillesse, *Le secret messianique dans l'Évangile de Marc*, LD 47 (Paris: Cerf, 1968), 79; Kingsbury, *Christology*, 113; Hay, *Glory at the Right Hand*, 111; Evans, "David," 195; Ahearne-Kroll, *Psalms of Lament*, 165–166.

[82] See, e.g., Wright, *Jesus and the Victory of God*, 509.

[83] Ahearne-Kroll, *Psalms of Lament*, 166.

[84] On the issue of economic malpractice defiling the temple, see Jonathan Klawans, *Purity, Sacrifice, and the Temple: Symbolism and Supercessionism in the Study of Ancient Judaism* (Oxford: Oxford University Press, 2006), 235–241; cf. Mark 7:10–13.

vindicate his Christ by raising him from the dead (12:18–27). And the question about the greatest commandment raises the issue of what it means to honor the one God as king (12:28–34). Jesus's response, "You are not far from the kingdom of God" (12:34), tantalizingly suggests that what the scribe still lacks is the appropriate christological framework within which to carry out Israel's covenant vocation.

This brings us to the *Davidssohnfrage* (12:35–37). Jesus's issue with the scribes here is not, as I have argued, that they assumed that the messiah would be the son of David. Nor is there any hint that they anticipated a militaristic messiah. The issue at hand, rather, is that the scribes have failed to take into account what Psalm 110 (109 LXX) says about the Christ.[85] Three observations support this inference. First, the person David describes as "my lord" is the only scriptural figure outside of Melchizedek in Gen 14:18 explicitly designated as a priest-king (110 [109 LXX]:4).[86] There is ample evidence to suggest that some Jews, perhaps even Jewish-Christians, took exception to the notion that the son of David could legitimately serve as a priest.[87] Second, the throne to which Israel's God summons David's lord is the heavenly throne from which he is called

---

[85] Mark's citation of Ps 110(109):1 reads ὑποκάτω τῶν ποδῶν σου instead of LXX's ὑποπόδιον τῶν ποδῶν σου, which may suggest the influence of Ps 8:7 LXX: "And you set him [the son of man] over the works of your hands; you subjected all things under his feet [ὑποκάτω τῶν ποδῶν αὐτοῦ]." Matthew 22:24 follows Mark 12:36, but Luke 20:42 changes ὑποκάτω to ὑποπόδιον to match Ps 109:1 LXX. Psalm 8 and Dan 7:13–14 coalesced early on in Christian interpretation of the Jewish scriptures (cf. 1 Cor 15:24–28; Heb 2:5–9), and seemingly also for Mark (cf. 14:62). The superscription of Ps 8 LXX, εἰς τὸ τέλος ὑπὲρ τῶν ληνῶν ψαλμὸς τῷ Δαυιδ, may have encouraged the inference that υἱὸς ἀνθρώπου in v. 5 is the messiah son of David.

[86] For a helpful survey of Melchizedek traditions, see Eric F Mason. 2008. *"You Are a Priest Forever": Second Temple Jewish Messianism and the Priestly Christology of the Epistle to the Hebrews*, STDJ 74 (Leiden: Brill, 2008; repr., Atlanta, GA: Society of Biblical Literature), 164–190.

[87] The diarchic model of governance espoused by the Qumran sectarians, for instance, suggests they would be suspicious of attempts to conflate the offices of king and priest (Collins, *Scepter*, 79–109). This may explain, in part, why they understood "Melchizedek" to be an angelic priest of an order not in competition with the Zadokite priesthood (cf. 11Q13 2:13–16; 4Q401 frag. 11:1–3). The author of Hebrews argues that the Melchizedekian priesthood provided a superior alternative to the Levitical priesthood, because it offered a legitimate means by which the resurrected Christ, that is, a descendant of Judah, could serve as a high priest in the heavenly sanctuary (cf. Heb 7:11–19); on which, see David M. Moffitt, *Atonement and the Logic of Resurrection in the Epistle to the Hebrews*, NovTSup 141 (Leiden: Brill, 2011), 200–208. Josephus, too, makes a number of intriguing observations about the figure of Melchizedek: "Its [Jerusalem's] original founder was a Canaanite chief, called in the native tongue 'Righteous King' [βασιλεὺς δίκαιος]; for such indeed he was. In virtue thereof he

to participate in God's reign over the cosmos. Some Jews would likely find this an affront to monotheism (cf. Mark 2:7; 14:63).[88] Third, if one follows the narrative sequence, it is clear that the temple authorities – the chief priests, the scribes, and the elders – have already rejected the messiah (cf. 12:1–12) and are thus among those whom God promises to put under Christ's feet (12:36). If, therefore, the function of the *Davidssohnfrage* is to expunge the Gospel of the "triumphalist spirit" of messianism, Jesus has chosen a poor piece of scripture to make the point. If, on the other hand, he wanted to assert that the Christ whom the temple leaders rejected does indeed wield God's authority, even his authority over the temple, then it seems he has chosen the ideal text to make his point.

(2) *A Zweistufenchristologie superimposes a religionsgeschichtlich hypothesis about the development of early Christology onto the Christology of Mark.* The interpreter begins with the hypothesis of an exaltation Christology, the notion that Jesus's divine status is the result of the resurrection, and then infers that the Christology of Mark 12:35–37 reflects this position. This seems unlikely, though, not least because Mark opens by encouraging the audience to view

was the first to officiate as priest of God and, being the first to build the temple, gave the city, previously called Solyma, the name of Jerusalem. The Canaanite population was expelled by David, the king of the Jews, who established his own people there" (*J.W.* 6.438 [Thackeray, LCL], my emphasis). Not only does Josephus link Melchizedek to the temple and to David, he also suggests that what qualified Melchizedek to minister as a priest of Israel's God was the observation that he was a "righteous king," an etymological play on his name (cf. Philo, *Leg.* 3.79). Further, Josephus is well aware that the model of the priest-king which made its way into Israel's royal theology (cf. 2 Sam 6:14, 18; Ps 110:4) is *Canaanite* in origin, in contrast to the Aaronic priesthood (cf. *Ant.* 20.226). Finally, the writer of Aramaic Levi may have attempted to link Levi to the Melchizedekian priesthood when he when he refers to the patriarch as "priest of God Most High" (Mt. Athos Greek frag. 2; cf. *Jub.* 32:1). Greenfield, Stone, and Eshel inquire, "Is the attribution to Levi of a title used of Melchizedek intentional, just as the Judah language was deliberately used of Levi?" (*Aramaic Levi Document*, 155). The question is intriguing, since it may suggest the writer felt compelled to connect Levi's ancestral line with a model of priesthood that antedates it in the Pentateuch.

[88] Marcus, *Way*, 145–146; Bauckham, *Jesus and the God of Israel*, 172–181. To be sure, this would not be a problem for all Jews (cf. 1 En. 37–71). In fact, the so-called David Apocalypse, a mystical text of unknown provenance that was later inserted into Hekhalot Rabbati, attempts to solve the problem posed by Jesus's heavenly session not by denying the possibility of such a session, but by transferring it from Jesus to David (so Peter Schäfer, *The Jewish Jesus: How Judaism and Christianity Shaped Each Other* [Princeton, NJ: Princeton University Press, 2012], 85–94; and his translation in Peter Schäfer et al., ed., *Übersetzung der Hekhalot-Literatur§§ II 81–334*, 2 vols., TSAJ 17 [Tübingen: Mohr Siebeck, 1987]: 2:56–59).

the advent of Jesus Christ as the eschatological arrival of Israel's God (cf. 1:2–3).[89] There are, moreover, a number of hints in the narrative that when the characters encounter Jesus, they are in fact encountering the divine presence of Israel's God.[90]

There is also the question, convoluted though it may be, of the potential frames associated with a citation of Psalm 110 (109 LXX).[91] In particular, the psalm offers some of the strongest scriptural warrant for the notion of a preexistent messiah.[92] On the day of his enthronement, God addresses the figure at his right hand, "With you is rule on a day of your power among the splendor of the holy ones. From the womb, before the morning star, I begot you [ἐκ γαστρὸς πρὸ ἑωσφόρου ἐξεγέννησά σε]" (Ps 109:3 LXX). Such language implies, or at least could be read to imply, that prior to the enthronement scene, which, incidentally, one could interpret as a heavenly enthronement among the "holy ones" (i.e., angels), the lord God begot David's lord.[93] Thus it may be the case, though one can

---

[89] Watts, *Isaiah's New Exodus*, 53–90; Johansson, *"Kyrios,"* 103–105; Botner, "Prophetic Script," 61–65.

[90] Marcus, *Way*, 144–145; Watts, *Isaiah's New Exodus*; Hurtado, *Lord Jesus Christ*, 286–316; Bauckham, *Jesus and the God of Israel*, 254–268; Gathercole, *Pre-Existent Son*; Daniel Johansson, "Jesus and God in the Gospel of Mark: Unity and Distinction," PhD diss., University of Edinburgh, 2011; Hays, *Echoes of Scriptures in the Gospels*, 61–78. While I disagree with these on number of substantive issues, many of which have now been addressed head-on by J. R. Daniel Kirk (*A Man Attested by God: The Human Jesus of the Synoptic Gospels* [Grand Rapids, MI: Eerdmans, 2016]), they still make, to my mind, a strong cumulative argument that Mark's Christ is a divine being who is both united to and distinct from the one he calls "father" (cf. Mark 13:32).

[91] Hay's conclusion (*Glory*, 85) that the writer of Hebrews was the only early Christian interested in the wider context of Ps 110 seems overly cautious. Crispin Fletcher-Louis goes too far, however, when he contends, "It is absurd to imagine that Jesus' audience (and implied readers of the Gospels) did not have in mind the rest of the Psalm that Jesus cites" ("Jesus and the High Priestly Messiah: Part 1, *JSHJ* 4 [2006]: 155–175, at 174). Perhaps the best we can do is to follow Bauckham in observing that "It is very clear that Psalm 110:1 was not only cited, but also interpreted with care, both very early and very widely in the early Christian movement" (*Jesus and the God of Israel*, 173). Such careful interpretation would seem to suggest that at least some early Christians were aware of and possibly cared about the wider context of the psalm.

[92] Yarbro Collins and Collins, *King and Messiah*, 57–58.

[93] See now Matthew W. Bates, *The Birth of the Trinity: Jesus, God, and the Spirit in New Testament & Early Christian Interpretation of the Old Testament* (Oxford: Oxford University Press, 2015), 47–62. How one construes the identity of David's "lord" in v. 1 depends on how one reads the second half of verse, since אתה כהן לעולם עד־דברתי מלכי־צדק can be rendered either, "You are a priest forever, after the line of Melchizedek," or, "You are a priest forever by my order, O Melchizedek." The latter may explain why some concluded that YHWH's principal angel was named

hardly be certain, that when Mark's Jesus asks his audience to puzzle out the meaning of Ps 109:1 LXX, his aim is to elicit the response that before the Christ became the son of David, he was *already* the son of God, begotten before the dawn of time. This interpretation has the advantage of locating the solution to the riddle about human and divine filiation in the scriptural source text to which the Markan Jesus appeals.

(3) *A Zweistufenchristologie tends to deemphasize the significance of Davidic messiahship.*[94] Thus, for example, Marcus claims,

> The relatively high Christology associated with divine sonship in passages like Mark 12:35–37 and 14:61–62 goes beyond what is normally associated with the "Son of David" in Judaism, and it is probably the openness of "Son of God" to such higher interpretations that drives a

"Melchizedek" (so James Kugel, *Traditions of the Bible: A Guide to the Bible as It Was at the Start of the Common Era* [Cambridge, MA: Harvard University Press, 1998], 279–280). The identification of Melchizedek in 11Q13 as an angel goes back to Adam S. van der Woude ("Melchisedek als himmlishe Erlösergestalt in den neugefundenen eschatologischen Midraschim aus Qumran Höhle XI," *OtSt* 14 [1965]: 354–373), and receives potential support from the fragmentary evidence in the Songs of the Sabbath Sacrifice: [מלכי[צדק כוהן בעד]ה אל] (4Q401 frag. 11:3),]כי צדק[(4Q401 frag. 22:3); see the critical text in Eshel et al., eds., *Qumran Cave VI: Poetical and Liturgical Texts*, Part 1, DJD 11 [Oxford: Clarendon, 1998], 205, 213). The general notion that YHWH's principal angel is a warrior and a heavenly priest, however, may not be relegated to the Dead Sea Scrolls. In Testament of Moses, for instance, God's *nuntius*, "angel/messenger," is ordained as the heavenly priest who also comes to avenge Israel of its enemies: "Then, the hands of the messenger, when he will be in heaven, will be filled [*Tunc implebuntur manus nuntii qui est in summo constitutes*], and he will avenge them against their enemies" (T. Mos. 10:2; text and translation in Johannes Tromp, *The Assumption of Moses: A Critical Edition with Commentary*, STVP 10 [Leiden: Brill, 1993], 18–19). While it is possible that the *nuntius* is a human, Moses (cf. T. Mos. 11:17) or Taxo (so Tromp, *Assumption*, 299–331), the writer's dependence on traditional material also found in Dan 12:1–3 suggests that he is YHWH's principle angel (Nickelsburg, *Resurrection*, 43–45).

[94] In my estimation, the de-emphasis on Davidic messiahship in modern scholarship is largely the byproduct of a *zweistufenchristologisch* approach to Paul's theology, which postulates that what mattered to the apostle was not that the messiah was descended from the seed of David according to the flesh – in fact, he may be rather ambivalent about the idea – but that he was son of God according to the spirit (see, e.g., Wilhelm Heitmüller, "Zum Problem Jesus und Paulus," *ZNW* 13 [1912]: 320–337).

wedge between it as "Son of David" and causes it not to develop as a significant messianic title in Jewish tradition.[95]

Like Wrede, Marcus seems to assume that "high" Christology is, by nature, at odds with what the scriptures say about David and his descendants. Indeed, he concedes on the previous page that if the "chief background" of the title son of God "lies in the Old Testament and postbiblical Jewish picture of the Davidic king ... this interpretation would militate against our suggested exegesis of Mark 12:35–37, in which Jesus is not just the 'Son of David' because he is the 'Son of God.'"[96] I fail to see why this is the case, particularly since some of those first-century authors who most clearly depict the son in preexistent relationship with the father, most notably Paul and the author of Hebrews, also maintain that he is the anointed Davidide of the Psalter. Michael Stone's comments about the messiah in 4 Ezra highlight the affinity of modern critics for constructing dichotomies where the ancients apparently saw none:

> It has been suggested that certain editorial adjustments have been made within this vision, in the verses touching the Messiah. ... The basis for these suggestions is supposed 'contradictions' in the book's ideas about the Messiah. Preexistence supposedly contradicts Davidic descent ... These supposed anomalies are, in fact, far less serious than might be thought. They arise, basically, because modern critics apply to the book categories of logic and consistency that are too rigid.[97]

In order to do justice to the complex identity of Mark's Christ, it seems to me that one has to acknowledge the multivalence of divine sonship as encompassing both Christ status as an anointed ruler and the sense in which he participates in "God's very power and being" (so Marcus), or, if one prefers, in what Richard Bauckham describes as the "divine identity."[98]

---

[95] Marcus, *Way*, 143.

[96] Marcus, *Way*, 142. I would much prefer what Marcus writes several chapters earlier: "In Markan Christology, therefore, there can be no dichotomy between a royal interpretation of Jesus' divine sonship and a concept of that sonship that sees Jesus as participating in some way in God's very power and begin" (*Way*, 72).

[97] Stone, *Fourth Ezra*, 210.

[98] Bauckham (*Jesus and the God of Israel*, 6–59) develops the category of "divine identity" as a third way beyond "functional" and "ontic" Christology. While aspects

With these caveats in place, I am in full agreement with the *zweistufenchristologisch* judgement that the design of the *Davidssohnfrage* is to direct the audience's gaze toward the one currently enthroned in the heavens. Those who are ignorant of or misinterpret Psalm 110 (109 LXX), Mark suggests, miss David's prophetic claim that the messiah, his lord, was destined to rule at the right hand of God (perhaps they also miss the point that God begot his messiah in heaven before the dawn of time [cf. Ps 109:3 LXX]). Wrede was right that such a christological interpretation of Ps 109:1 LXX invites the inference that David's lord is *God's* son (cf. Mark 1:1; 9:7), but he was wrong to conclude that Davidic and divine sonship are diametric poles in a zero-sum game. Others may have been content to accept such terms; not so the evangelist Mark.

5.5   Conclusion

In this chapter, I have sought to bring together the methodological and interpretive consequences of the previous three. Rather than isolating passages with the name David, and thereby transforming 10:46–52 into the *crux interpretum* of Mark's *Davidssohnfrage*, I have interpreted Markan messiah language in light of the conventions of his linguistic community (Chapter 2) through the diachronic progression of the narrative (Chapters 3 and 4). This approach has informed my account of the much contested "spärliche Überlieferung zum Davidssohn" in 10:46–12:44. First, I have argued that the key to evaluating the title son of David in 10:46–52 resides neither in Bartimaeus's condition nor in Jesus's reaction to the blind man, but in how the evangelist has presented Jesus in 1:1–10:45. When assessed from this vantage point, it is almost certain that "son of David" represents an appropriate designation for the Markan Jesus. Second, contrary to the sensibilities of many modern interpreters, the function of 10:46–52 is not solely anticipatory. Rather, the revelation that Jesus is the son of David also sheds explanatory light back on his baptism, authoritative claims, gathering of the Twelve, and so forth. Third, I have contended that 1:1–12:34 should curtail "the

of his model have rightly been criticized (e.g., Crispin C. T. Fletcher-Louis, *Jesus Monotheism*, volume 1: *Christological Origins: The Emerging Consensus and Beyond* [Eugene, OR: Cascade, 2015], 88–101), the term itself may still offer a useful shorthand for expressing the reality to which some of the more remarkable claims early Christians made about Jesus point.

otherwise uncontrollable drives"[99] of modern interpreters of the *Davidssohnfrage*. Although Mark does not follow the same path as his Synoptic successors, he too obviates a negative appraisal of the question, how then can the Christ be David's son?

Mark 12:35–37 does not represent an abstract piece of Christology but sits at the climax of progression in which the identification of Jesus as the rightful heir of the ancient promises Israel's God made to David, on the one hand, and Jesus's insistence that the divine will is for the Christ to be rejected, suffer, and die, on the other, shape the audiences' perspective of Davidic messiahship. Mark constructs a symbolic world in which the only possibility for David's son to receive the throne and inheritance promised him is for the creator God to raise his Christ from the dead. The *Davidssohnfrage* thus presses the audience to embrace the evangelist's understanding of the relationship between David and his greater son: Jesus is David's lord because he is God's son in a way that Israel's ancient kings never were; or, as another early Christ follower once put it, "For David did not ascend into the heavens, but he himself says, "The Lord said to my Lord, 'Sit at my right hand, until I make your enemies your footstool'" (Acts 2:34–35).

---

[99] Eco et al., *Interpretation*, 65.

6

CRUCIFIXION AND RESURRECTION AS A MARKAN HERMENEUTIC

The irony in the passion story works because the reader possesses information not available to the characters in the story. The privileged information includes knowledge that 'the Son of man goes as it is written of him' (Mark 14:21). A script is provided for the story, which provides the author both with a way of testifying that the events occurred in accord with the will of God and with a way of making sense of raw data that require interpretation. ... In the account of Jesus' crucifixion, it is the words and phrases from the psalms that perform this function.

> – Donald Juel, *Messianic Exegesis*, 94–95

[T]his citation of Psalm 22 intensifies the clues already scattered through Mark's story that lead us to see the Psalms as particularly important intertexts for interpreting the shape of Jesus' life and death.

> – Richard B. Hays, *Echoes of Scripture in the Gospels*, 83

Throughout the previous chapters, I have built a cumulative argument that a narrative assessment of Mark's messiah language provides the best means of answering the question, how can Mark's Christ be David's son? We have seen that the Markan portrait of Christ pressures the audience to integrate "son of David" and "son of God" in light of what David prophesied about the messiah in Psalm 110 (109 LXX). I now turn, in the penultimate chapter of this study, to the passion narrative to explore further the hermeneutic undergirding Mark's account of the Jewish scriptures. It appears that the magnitude of the Christ-event – the immense significance of the Christ's crucifixion, resurrection, and exaltation – fundamentally shapes how the evangelist reads scriptural traditions about David and his descendants.

My approach here is twofold. First, I trace the general contours of messiah language in the Markan passion narrative, in dialogue with Malbon's proposal that the Gospel is "antimonarchical" in outlook.[1] The aim here is not so much to redress Malbon's proposal as it is to outline which traditional Davidic frames the narrative encourages us to actualize. Second, I assess Mark's use of Psalm 22 (21 LXX) in the crucifixion account, paying particular attention to his practice of hearing the voice of Christ in the words of his ancestor David. This psalm offers a window through which we may glimpse, even if only in part, the evangelist's scriptural imagination at work.

6.1   Off with the King!

It has long been assumed that if one wants to find a royal or Davidic messiah in Mark, one should begin with the passion narrative and then, if possible, work backwards.[2] Yet it is just here, Malbon contends, that a great many have run afoul. Although these interpreters are correct that "such [royal] imagery is present in the narrative," they make the mistake of interpreting this imagery "as evidence of the implied author's affirmation of the Markan Jesus, as, ironically, 'king.'"[3] So she offers an alternative: Mark's narrative implies that "the kingship model is rejected in Jesus' story."[4] While I suspect that many will not find such an extreme proposal compelling, it nonetheless provides fresh stimulus for an assessment of Davidic material in Mark's passion. *Pace* Malbon, it seems to me that such material, as in the rest of the Markan narrative, has been refracted through the base narrative of Christ's death, resurrection, and exaltation. At least five points support this conclusion.

(1) The opening unit of the passion narrative links kingship with messianic death and resurrection through an unnamed woman's anointing Jesus for burial (14:3–9). As Morna Hooker observes, "[s]ince Mark's story shows us that it is through death that Jesus is revealed as 'Messiah' or 'anointed', it seems likely that he interpreted this anointing for burial as the symbol of Jesus' messianic anointing also."[5] Yarbro Collins demurs, noting that "in the classic

---

[1] Malbon, *Mark's Jesus*, 121.
[2] See esp. Donahue, *Are You the Christ?*; Juel, *Messiah and Temple*; Matera, *Kingship*.
[3] Malbon, *Mark's Jesus*, 119.   [4] Ibid., 121.
[5] Hooker, *Gospel*, 328; see also, Cranfield, *Gospel*, 415; Evans, *Mark 8:27–16:20*, 359–362. A messianic interpretation of the woman's act plays a prominent role in

scriptural passages of royal anointing, what is poured on the king's head is 'olive oil' (ἔλαιον), not 'aromatic oil' (μύρον) as here [in Mark]."[6] But the lexical disparity is not as damaging to Hooker's interpretation as one might think. μύρον is a better lexical fit for the stated purpose of anointing for burial (14:8),[7] and so it may be the case, as Hooker suggests, that Mark expects his audience to make the connection that preparation for burial is preparation for messianic enthronement. We also have evidence to suggest that ancient auditors could recognize μύρον as a suitable term for ritual unction (cf. Exod 30:25 LXX; Ps 132:2 LXX), as well as the act of pouring ointment on the head (κατέχεεν αὐτοῦ τῆς κεφαλῆς; Mark 14:3) as evocative of royal anointing (cf. 1 Kgdms 10:1: ἐπέχεεν ἐπὶ τὴν κεφαλὴν αὐτοῦ; 4 Kgdms 9:6: ἐπέχεεν τὸ ἔλαιον ἐπὶ τὴν κεφαλὴν αὐτοῦ).[8] When we weigh these lexical observations in light of the immediate context, Jesus's declaration that this woman's act will be a central component of the gospel message (14:9; cf. 1:1), it seems likely that one facet of this pericope is its function as a veiled messianic anointing.

This anonymous woman's act brings Mark's life of Jesus into closer intertextual relationship with the Deuteronomistic Historian's life of David. We have already seen that both figures launch their respective careers with anointing and reception of God's spirit (cf. 1 Sam 16:13; Mark 1:10–11). Here then we find a second point of convergence: just as David was anointed a second time prior to his capture of Jerusalem (cf. 2 Sam 5:3), so too the Markan Jesus is anointed a second time, just outside of the city limits of Jerusalem at Bethany. The first anointing marks both figures as messiah designates, while the second paves the way for their enthronements (cf. 2 Sam 7; Mark 14:61–62). But, of course, there is one rather significant difference. In David's story, the leaders of Israel are the ones who anoint the king (cf. 2 Sam 5:3); in Jesus's, they plot to destroy God's messiah in order to prevent him from receiving the throne (cf. Mark 14:1–2, 10–11). For Mark, the chief priests and the scribes are "the builders" of Psalm 118 (117 LXX), who have rejected the Lord's anointed both when he approached the city of Jerusalem (cf. 11:10–11) and when he claimed authority over its temple (12:10).

    [6] Yarbro Collins, *Mark*, 642.
    [7] E.g., the burial of the Davidic king Asa (2 Chr 16:14 LXX).
    [8] So too Evans, *Mark 8:27–16:20*, 360.

It is probably not coincidental that the passion narrative opens with
an anointing scene at Bethany, the place to which Jesus retreated
after he was snubbed by the temple hierarchs during his initial entry
(cf. 11:11), sandwiched between an account of the chief priests and
the scribes – i.e., "the builders" – plotting to destroy the messiah.[9]
The builders may do their worst, Mark implies, but Jesus knows, and
somehow, mysteriously, this unnamed woman anticipates, that
Israel's king must be anointed for ritual burial because God will
vindicate his Christ from the grave.

(2) Jesus's ascent up the Mount of Olives and his ensuing prayer in
the Garden of Gethsemane (14:26–50) markedly echo what Raymond Brown has appositely described as "the most desperate
moment of David's life."[10] There are numerous points of resonance
between these scenes:

(a)   Jesus is betrayed by his close associate, Judas (Mark 14:17–21) //
       David is betrayed by his close associate, Ahithophel
       (2 Sam 15:31; 16:23)
(b)   Judas arranges for the arrest of Jesus at night (Mark 14:30) //
       Ahithophel plots to pursue David at night (2 Sam 17:1)
(c)   Jesus solemnly journeys with the disciples to the Mount of
       Olives (Mark 14:26) // David solemnly journeys with his
       loyal supporters to the Mount of Olives (2 Sam 15:30)
(d)   Jesus supplicates God in sorrow and distress (Mark 14:32–42) //
       David supplicates God in sorrow and distress (2 Sam
       15:30–31)
(e)   Jesus predicts that after the shepherd is stricken (πατάξω τὸν
       ποιμένα in Mark 14:27, citing Zech 13:7) all his disciples will
       flee (ἔφυγον πάντες; 14:50) //
       Ahithophel boldy declares, "I will come upon him
       [David] while he is weary and discouraged, and throw him

---

[9] The plot to arrest Jesus ἐν δόλῳ in Mark 14:1 evokes the voice of David in Ps 41: "My
enemies spoke evil against me; against me they would devise evil" (Ps 41:7 [40:8 LXX]).
The plan to enlist Judas, one of the Twelve, to betray (παραδιδόναι) Jesus (14:10) ties this
event to the last supper, at which time Jesus declares, "Truly I tell you, one of you will
betray me [εἷς ἐξ ὑμῶν παραδώσει με], one who is eating with me [ὁ ἐσθίων μετ' ἐμοῦ];" "it is
one of the twelve, one who is dipping bread into the bowl with me" (14:18, 20), marking
an allusion to Ps 41: "For even the man of my peace, in whom I trusted, who ate of my
bread [ὁ ἐσθίων ἄρτους μου], has lifted up his heel against me" (Ps 40:10 LXX).
[10] Brown, *Death of the Messiah*, 2:1448; see also Donahue, "Temple," 76; Marcus,
Way, 162 n. 29; Daly-Denton, *David*, 291. The scene also evokes David's prayer in Pss
41–42 LXX (Ahearne-Kroll, *Psalms of Lament*, 179–186).

into a panic; and all the people who are with him will flee [φεύξεται πᾶς ὁ λαὸς ὁ μετ' αὐτοῦ]. I will strike down the king all alone [πατάξω τὸν βασιλέα μονώτατον]" (2 Kgdms 17:2).

These points of resonance offer yet another instance in which the Markan narrative encourages the audience to actualize Davidic frames that associate the ancient monarch with painful endurance in the face of suffering. Once again, then, it seems the evangelist employs a Davidic register to make sense of the rejection and betrayal of his Christ.

(3) The Markan passion narrative inundates the audience with implicit claims that the Christ suffers in accordance with the scriptures. The most conspicuous example of this phenomenon is the ubiquity of Davidic psalms of lament, including Jesus's last words on the cross (on which, see Section 6.2).[11] But there are other significant examples, too, such as when the Markan Jesus identifies himself as the stricken shepherd of Zech 13:7. The identity of this figure in the Zecharian oracle is ambiguous.[12] Yet, given what we can discern about the evangelist's engagement with Zechariah 9–14 in general[13] and his association of Jesus with the "coming" king in Zech 9:9 in particular (cf. Mark 11:7), it seems likely that he interprets the Zech 13:7 as presaging a Davidic king.[14]

The stricken David shepherd he encountered in Zechariah 13 was an ideal fit to articulate the fate of the Christ and his followers. As Marcus notes, "In Zechariah 9–14 itself, all the references to the

---

[11] Ahearne-Kroll (*Psalms of Lament*, 168–214) looks at Pss 22 (21 LXX), 41 (40 LXX), 42–43 (41–42 LXX), and 69 (68 LXX). He makes a compelling case that Jesus's statement at the last supper, "for the son of man goes as it is written of him [καθὼς γέγραπται περὶ αὐτοῦ]" (14:21), refers to, among other things, these psalms of David. Unfortunately, he does not tie this observation back to the first passion prediction in 8:31 (alluding to Ps 118 [117 LXX]:22), which introduces the audience to the *necessity* of messianic rejection and suffering.

[12] See Laato, *Josiah and David Redivivus*, 286–293; Meyers and Meyers, *Zechariah 9–14*, 384–389. The Greek translator seems to equate τοὺς ποιμένας μου, (pl.) "my shepherds," in Zech 13:7 LXX with the bad shepherds mentioned earlier in 10:3 and in 11:4. We find an eschatological interpretation of Zech 13:7 in the Damascus Document, in which רועי, (sg.) "my shepherd," appears as a wicked leader who will be among those "delivered up to the sword when there comes the messiah of Aaron and Israel" (CD 19:5–10). Mark's iteration of the Zecharian oracle agrees with MT and CD in that the one stricken is a singular shepherd, but shifts the divine command "strike" to the future indicative πατάξω, "I will strike." It is difficult to say whether this reflects an intentional editorial decision on the part of the evangelist.

[13] See Marcus, *Way*, 154–164.

[14] Douglas J. Moo, *The Old Testament in the Gospel Passion Narratives* (Sheffield: Almond, 1983), 182–187.

shepherd and his sheep (Zech. 9:16; 10:3; 11:4–17; 13:7) appear in contexts that speak of battle . . . Mark 14:27–28, therefore, draws on Old Testament images that suggest the injury of a leader who is also the commander in chief of an army, a consequent scattering of his army, and its later regroupment under the revived leader."[15] Thus, "Mark does not efface the military lineaments of the 'shepherd' described by Zechariah, but he emphasizes the paradox that this shepherd's victory involves an element of divinely willed suffering – a suffering in which the 'sheep' are also involved."[16] This is well said. I would only want to add that, in Mark, both the narrative introduction to the motif of the divinely willed suffering (8:31) and its narrative instantiation (15:34) are mediated through royal/Davidic psalms, Psalms 118 (117 LXX) and 22 (21 LXX), respectively. Whenever Mark looked for a "suffering" messiah in his scriptures, he seems invariably to have turned to traditions about David and his descendants.

(4) At his trial before the Sanhedrin, Jesus not only affirms that he is the messiah son of God but also indicates that he will reign at the right hand of God in heaven. The high priest's question, "Are you the messiah, the son of the Blessed One? [σὺ εἶ ὁ χριστὸς ὁ υἱὸς τοῦ εὐλογητοῦ]" capitalizes on the juxtaposition of "messiah" and "my son" in Psalm 2 (14:61).[17] The Markan Jesus, however, is not satisfied simply to answer in the affirmative, but goes on to align this figure with both the Danielic son of man (Dan 7:13) and the enthroned lord in Ps 110:1 (14:62). This move explicates the tacit logic of the *Davidssohnfrage*: following Jesus's resurrection, "after three days" (14:58), the son of David ascended to the heavens, was presented before the divine throne (cf. Dan 7:13) and heard the address of his father, "Sit at my right hand, until I put your enemies under your feet" (Ps 109:1 LXX). Enthronement thus remains an important aspect of this son of David's story, but it must occur in its rightful place – namely, at the ascension. Indeed, Jesus's bold declaration to the high priest and his cohort, "'you [pl.] will see [ὄψεσθε]

[15] Marcus, *Way*, 161.   [16] Ibid., 164.
[17] See esp. O'Brien, *Use of Scripture*, 155–166. I follow Marcus's suggestion that the relationship between ὁ χριστός and ὁ υἱὸς τοῦ εὐλογητοῦ is one of "restrictive apposition" ("Mark 14:61"). I disagree with Marcus, however, that the point of the title ὁ υἱὸς τοῦ εὐλογητοῦ is to imply that ὁ χριστός is not a mundane messiah, but a "quasi-divine" being. Rather, it seems that the high priest asks the Markan Jesus if he is the messiah of the sort mentioned in Ps 2, and that Jesus's interpretation of what it means to be messiah son of God is what the high priest finds blasphemous.

the son of man seated at the right hand of the Power' and 'coming with the clouds of heaven'" (14:62), encourages the audience to perceive the crucifixion account in light of his resurrection (cf. 16:6). Suffering and humiliation cannot be the end of this messiah's story, because the God of Jesus Christ has power over death (cf. 12:27).

(5) Mark is emphatic, almost obnoxiously so, that Jesus was mocked and crucified as a king. For the Romans, he is ὁ βασιλεὺς τῶν Ἰουδαίων, "the king of the Judeans" (15:2, 9, 12, 18, 26); for Israel's leaders, he is an imposter, someone who simply cannot be ὁ χριστὸς ὁ βασιλεὺς Ἰσραήλ, "the messiah, the king of Israel" (15:32).[18] And yet, Mark informs us, when a Roman centurion saw how this pretender died, he confessed ἀληθῶς οὗτος ὁ ἄνθρωπος υἱὸς θεοῦ ἦν, "Truly, this man was God's son!" (15:39). The most plausible account of these events is that the Roman centurion saw, on the other side of the cross, as it were, what the other characters in the Markan narrative could not: the *crucified* Jesus is the "king of the Jews," the long-awaited "king of Israel," and indeed the son of God.[19]

This hardly appears to be a demolition job of Malbon's "kingship model." But, of course, her argument is that the majority of interpreters have failed to sift the Markan wheat from its monarchical chaff:

> Perhaps there is a deeper irony to this imagery, not that the Markan Jesus is a "king" of a different sort but that the concept of human "kinship" has, in Mark's good news of Jesus Christ, Son of God, and in Jesus' good news of the in-breaking *king*dom of God, been subverted entirely. Perhaps the Markan Gospel is as antikingship in its orientation as the antimonarchical strand of tradition in the David stories in the Hebrew Bible![20]

---

[18] Matera, *Kingship*, 136.

[19] Earl Johnson's critique of the standard interpretation that the centurion gets Jesus right is more an exercise in hypothesizing what a Roman centurion could have meant by the words "truly this man was God's son" than it is a careful analysis of what *Mark* suggests the words mean ("Is Mark 15.39 the Key to Mark's Christology," *JSNT* 31 [1987]: 3–22). Whether one wants to call Mark 15:39 the "key" to Markan Christology – and I certainly would not go that far – it clearly plays an essential role in transforming the cross into the symbol of the messianic enthronement. For more on the link between crucifixion and enthronement, see Joel Marcus, "Crucifixion as Parodic Exaltation," *JBL* 125 (2006): 73–87.

[20] Malbon, *Mark's Jesus*, 120–121, her emphasis.

How, though, does Malbon know that Mark is "antikingship in its orientation"? Her answer, it seems, is that the implied author is antimonarchical because the characters that use the title ὁ βασιλεύς are unreliable.[21]

This move is dubious for at least two reasons. First, Malbon's method assumes that we can get at the implied author's position on a title, say, "king," by isolating it from everything else Mark says and indicates about Jesus – not unlike her treatment of the title son of David. When one takes the totality of Markan messiah language into account, however, it seems highly likely that the audience is supposed to approach the crucifixion account with the assumption that Jesus is a king. Second, Malbon's method cannot deliver what she claims. Even if one grants, for the sake of argument, that Mark rejects one particular royal title, king, this does not justify the conclusion that he also rejects the *concept* of kingship (or lordship). The book of Daniel, for example, never designates the one like a son of man a "king," but it does say that when this figure approaches the ancient of days he will receive "dominion and glory and *kingship* [מלכו], that all peoples, nations, and languages should serve him" (Dan 7:14).[22] It may be telling that a mere two pages after Malbon concludes that "the kingship model is rejected in Jesus' story,"[23] she asserts that "the centurion, a responsible, if low-ranking, member of the Roman imperium, endangers his station by his statement: if the dying Jesus is 'Son of God,' the Roman emperor is not."[24] Has Mark substituted "the kingship model" for an "imperial model"?[25] Are we free to conceive of Jesus as *divi filius* as long as we do not elide this title with *rex*? No matter how we parse christological titles, sooner or later we must all come to terms with the indelible conclusion: for Mark, Jesus Christ is God's appointed ruler over the cosmos.[26]

Rather than servicing an antimonarchical agenda, it seems that the surfeit of Davidic traditions in the Markan passion narrative

---

[21] Ibid., 115–121.

[22] What the one like a son of man is said to receive varies slightly in LXX and θ' recensions, but the basic point remains the same.

[23] Malbon, *Mark's Christ*, 119.   [24] Ibid., 123.

[25] As Peppard (*Son of God*, 95) points out, the title *divi filius*, son of God, designates "the most powerful man in the world." Later, when discussing the Markan crucifixion account, he writes, "the Son of God was about to inherit the Empire of his Father" (131).

[26] So rightly Tat-siong Benny Liew, though, on his account, the lordship of Christ is an inherently "imperial" (i.e., negative) feature of the Second Gospel (*Politics of Parousia*).

have been pressed to a specific ideological end, to inculcate *God's* orientation toward kingship (cf. 8:31–33; 10:45). Mark, as I have argued, interprets the scriptural promises YHWH made to David about his future descendant in a particular way, so that the central feature of the Christ's Davidic status becomes his willingness to entrust his life to the God of Israel in the hope that this God will vindicate him from the dead and exalt him on high. This is not an obvious deduction from the Jewish scriptures but involves an act of "reading backwards,"[27] as Hays has suggests, a double movement of recognizing retrospectively that words once spoke about and by David and his line find their *telos* in the life, death, and resurrection of Jesus Christ. There is perhaps no greater witness to this hermeneutical conviction than the Markan crucifixion account.

6.2   The Crucified Son of David: Psalm 22 in Markan Scriptural Imagination

Numerous studies have been devoted to the scriptural allusions in Mark's crucifixion narrative, so we need not retrace old ground.[28] I will focus instead on what can be discerned about the scriptural hermeneutic informing Markan allusions to psalms of David in this visceral-yet-calculated section of the Gospel, taking up Stephen Ahearn-Kroll's proposal that when Mark encounters the voice of the lamenting David in the Psalter, he hears the voice of the suffering Christ.

6.2.1   The Voice of the Lamenting David, the Voice of the Suffering Christ

Among the studies that treat Mark's use of the Psalms in the passion narrative, Ahearne-Kroll's *The Psalms of Lament in Mark's Passion: Jesus' Davidic Suffering* is exemplary. First, against the notion that psalms of individual lament align the Markan Christ with a generic "righteous sufferer," a supposed construct of early Judaism, Ahearne-Kroll contends that "David must be reckoned with when

---

[27] So Richard B. Hays, *Reading Backwards: Figural Christology and the Fourfold Gospel Witness* (Waco, TX: Baylor University Press, 2014).

[28] See, e.g., Donahue, *Are You the Christ?*; Donahue, "Temple;" Juel, *Messiah and Temple*; Matera, *Kingship*; Marcus, *Way*, 153–198; Yarbro Collins, "Appropriation of the Psalms;" Ahearne Kroll, *Psalms of Lament*; Watts, "Lord's House;" O'Brien, *Use of Scripture*; Hays, *Echoes of Scripture in the Gospels*, 78–87.

considering how the PssLam are appropriated by these later authors and communities."[29] Second, he treats the voice of David in the Psalms as a flexible linguistic resource rather than a prepackaged article of faith, whether about the messiah or a particular messianic ideology. Third, he recognizes that psalms of David – and to a lesser extent, Isa 52:13–53:12 – furnished the evangelist with a traditional framework for processing the significance of Jesus's suffering.[30] How then does the evangelist deploy his Davidic resources?

On this point, Ahearne-Kroll offers something of a revisionist interpretation. For him, the primary import of the Davidic psalms in Mark's passion narrative is to question and protest the divine will that the messiah must suffer and die.[31] He concludes his monograph with this poignant remark: "Mark's attempt at understanding Jesus' suffering and death is just as much about Mark's appreciation of the horror of human suffering as it is about the hope that belief in Jesus' resurrection can generate for Mark's readers."[32] As attractive – even theologically productive – as it maybe to explore the pathos of Mark's Gospel as it relates to questions of theodicy and human suffering, this does not offer a plausible historical explanation for what we encounter in the Gospel, if only for the reason that we would not have a "Gospel according to Mark" apart from "the hope that belief in Jesus' resurrection" generated for the evangelist and his community.[33] Close attention to context of the cry of dereliction suggests an alternative account to that of Ahearne-Kroll.

---

[29] Ahearne-Kroll, *Psalms of Lament*, 56; see also Yarbro Collins, "Appropriation of the Psalms;" Daly-Denton, *David*. The motif of the so-called righteous sufferer owes much to Lothar Ruppert's synthesis of a vast amount of early Jewish literature and has been taken up by Marcus (*Way*, 172–194) and by Carey (*Jesus' Cry from the Cross*, 95–138), among others (see Ahearne-Kroll, *Psalms of Lament*, 15 n. 38). Whatever one makes of Ruppert's study, his argument that Mark's use of psalms in the passion narrative is not messianically motivated cannot be sustained (so rightly Yarbro Collins, "Appropriation of the Psalms," 231).

[30] Ahearne-Kroll, *Psalms of Lament*, 205: "By aligning Jesus' suffering with that of David in Psalm 21, Mark also shows that the suffering David of the PssLam proves to be an excellent model to which the reader can turn for understanding Jesus' suffering, perhaps even better than the Suffering Servant from Isaiah 53." Even to put it like this, though, creates an unnecessary dichotomy between the Psalms and Isaiah. Studies that attempt to rehabilitate the significance of the Psalter in Luke-Acts also seem to do so at the expense of Isaiah (e.g., Doble, "Luke 24.26, 44;" Jipp, "Luke's Scriptural Suffering Messiah").

[31] Ahearne-Kroll, *Psalms of Lament*, 196–197, 213–226.   [32] Ibid., 226.

[33] Contrary to much modern scholarship, we should not conceive of Mark as a "film noir" (so, rightly, Holly J. Carey, "'Is It as Bad as All That?' The Misconception of Mark as a *Film Noir*," in *Mark, Manuscripts, and Monotheism*: Essays in Honor of

6.2.2   Psalm 22 (21 LXX) and the Cry of Dereliction

At the ninth hour, Jesus cried out in a loud voice, "Eloi, Eloi, lema sabachthani?" which Mark tells his audience means, "My God, my God, why have you forsaken me? [ὁ θεός μου ὁ θεός μου, εἰς τί ἐγκατέλιπές με]" (15:34). The evangelist's rendering of the Aramaic is a citation of Ps 21:1 LXX: ὁ θεὸς ὁ θεός μου πρόσχες μοι ἵνα τί ἐγκατέλιπές με, "O God, my God, why have you forsaken me?" Following the likes of C. H. Dodd and Joel Marcus (and, ultimately, Augustine, *Ex. Ps.*, on Ps 37:6), Ahearne-Kroll claims, "it is highly unlikely that a biblically literate member of Mark's community would not have thought of the whole the psalm when hearing this verse."[34] This may be a step too far. I would prefer to say that the numerous points of resonance between Psalm 22 and Mark's crucifixion account would invite "a biblically literate member of Mark's community" to take the metaleptic leap into the wider context of the psalm. The following chart (p. 185) traces points of intertextual contact between Psalm 21 LXX and the Markan crucifixion account.[35]

Given the remarkable degree of lexical and thematic coherence between Psalm 21 LXX and our earliest extant account of Jesus's death and resurrection, it is hardly surprising that Augustine would conclude centuries later,

> *Quid quod ipse dominus in cruce pendens, primum uersum psalmi ipsius ore suo protulit, et dixit: deus meus, deus meus, utquid me dereliquisti? Quid uoluit intellegi, nisi illum psalmum totum ad se pertinere, quia caput ipsius ipse pronuntiauit?* (*Ps.* 37.6)[36]

Why did the Lord himself, hanging atop the cross, pronounce the first verse of this psalm with his own mouth and say: "My God, my God, why have you abandoned me?" What did he wish to make us understand except that the entire psalm pertains to him, since he himself pronounced its beginning?   (My translation and emphasis)

Larry W. Hurtado, eds. Chris Keith and Dieter T. Roth, LNTS 528 [London: Bloomsbury T&T Clark, 2014], 3–21).

[34] Ahearne-Kroll, *Psalms of Lament*, 209, following Dodd, *According to the Scriptures*, 96–98; Marcus, *Way*, 180–182; see also Watts, "Lord's House;" Carey, *Jesus' Cry*, 139–188; Hays, *Echoes of Scripture in the Gospels*, 85.

[35] My chart is adapted from Marcus's (*Way*, 182; cf. Carey, *Jesus' Cry*, 187).

[36] Augustine, *Enarrationes in psalmos I-L*, eds. Eligius Dekkers and Jean Fraipont, CCL 38 (Turnhout: Brepols, 1956).

Mark 15	Psalm 21 LXX
[Narrator] And they crucified him, and *divided his clothes among them* [διαμερίζονται τὰ ἱμάτια αὐτοῦ], *casting lots* to decide what each should take [βάλλοντες κλῆρον ἐπ' αὐτὰ τίς τί ἄρῃ] (v. 24).	[David] *They divided my clothes among themselves* [διεμερίσαντο τὰ ἱμάτιά μου ἑαυτοῖς], and for my clothing *they cast lots* [ἐπὶ τὸν ἱματισμόν μου ἔβαλον κλῆρον] (v. 19).
[Narrator] Those who passed by derided him, *shaking their heads* [κινοῦντες τὰς κεφαλὰς αὐτῶν] (v. 29). In the same way the chief priests, along with the scribes, were also mocking him among themselves (v. 31).	[David] All who saw me mocked me; they talked with [their] lips; *they shook [their] heads* [ἐκίνησαν κεφαλήν] (v. 8).
[Bystanders] "*Save yourself* [σῶσον σεαυτόν], and come down from the cross!" (v. 30).	[Adversaries] "He hoped in the Lord; let him rescue him; *let him save him* [σωσάτω αὐτόν], because he wanted him'" (v. 9).
[Scribes and chief priests] "*He saved others; he cannot save himself* [ἄλλους ἔσωσεν, ἑαυτὸν οὐ δύναται σῶσαι]. Let the messiah, the king of Israel, come down from the cross now, so that we may see and believe" (v. 32).	[David] "In you our fathers hoped … To you they cried and *were saved* [ἐσώθησαν]; in you they hoped and were not put to shame" (vv. 4–5).
[Narrator] those who were crucified with him also reproached him [ὠνείδιζον αὐτόν] (v. 32)	[David] "But as for me, I am a worm and not human, *a reproach of humankind* [ὄνειδος ἀνθρώπου] and despised by people" (v. 7).

Cry of Dereliction: "My God, my God, why have you forsaken me?"
(Mark 15:34; Ps 21:1 LXX)

[Narrator] Then Jesus gave a loud cry and breathed his last (v. 37).	[David] "… to death's dust you brought me down (v. 16)
[Narrator] Now when the centurion, who stood facing him, saw that in this way he breathed his last, he [a *gentile* centurion] said, "Truly this man was God's son!" (v. 39).	[David] "All the ends of the earth shall remember and turn to the Lord, and *all the paternal families of the gentiles shall do obeisance before him*" (v. 28).
[Narrator] Joseph of Arimathea, a respected member of the council, who was also himself waiting expectantly for *the kingdom of God* [τὴν βασιλείαν τοῦ θεου], went boldly to Pilate and asked for the body of Jesus (v. 43).	[David] "*because kingship is the Lord's* [ὅτι τοῦ κυρίου ἡ βασιλεία], and it is he who is master over the gentiles" (v. 29)
[Angel] "Do not be alarmed; you are looking for Jesus of Nazareth, the crucified one. He has been raised; he is not here" (16:6). [...] But go, tell his disciples and Peter that he is going ahead of you to Galilee; there you will see him, just as he told you" (16:7).	[David] "[A]nd my offspring will serve him; the coming generation will be announced to the Lord, and they shall announce his righteousness to a people to be born, because the Lord has acted" (vv. 31–32).

Some may wish to counter that Augustine is merely using Psalm 22 to smuggle in a theological agenda the evangelist never intended. This is certainly possible. The bishop of Hippo clearly has a theological axe to grind, and he needs the wider context of the psalm as grist for the mill. Yet one wonders if proponents of the minimalist view – that Mark cited the first verse of Psalm 22 without ever imagining his auditors would impose its wider context onto the crucifixion account – have any greater claim to theological neutrality.[37] At a time when we are acutely aware of mass genocide, political atrocities, ecclesial abuses, and the like, the raw and unbridled cry of Mark's Jesus from the cross profoundly addresses the human experience of suffering and injustice in a way few words have or ever could. To admit the wider context of the psalm might attenuate the extent to which Jesus empathizes with our experience of doubt in the face of suffering – the messiah hangs on the cross with an escape hatch, as it were. In any case, it seems to me that all interpreters of the cry of dereliction are ideologically motivated, so that any attempt to dismiss an opposing position on the grounds of theological expediency should be ruled out of bounds.[38]

If, on the other hand, one concedes, as Ahearne-Kroll does, that Mark has the whole psalm in mind, then it becomes highly implausible that the primary function of the cry of dereliction is to elicit issues of theodicy. Rather, Jesus's cry, even as it "evoke[s] overtones of outrage, abandonment, and incomprehension, similar to David's in the psalm,"[39] demonstrates his utter fidelity to the God of Israel ("*my* God, *my* God"), the God not of the dead but of the living (cf. Mark 12:27). The cross cannot be the end of Christ's story, for, as Mark goes on to narrate it, perhaps reading Ps 21:23–32 LXX in light of Jesus's resurrection, God hears the cry of his messiah and vindicates him from the grave. Jesus of Nazareth is forever ὁ ἐσταυρωμένος, "the crucified one," who has been raised (ἠγέρθη) by

---

[37] For example, John Goldingay is quick to say that interpretation of the crucifixion account in light of the wider context of Ps 22 "may imply an attempt to make premodern interpretation work on a basis that modern interpretation can accept" (*Psalms*, 1:342). Yet, two pages earlier he writes, "It would be a shame if 'Psalm 22 cannot be the prayer of just any afflicted Israelite.' It offers a most suggestive concrete expression of a mature spirituality" (340). Every interpreter of Ps 22 has theological skin in the game.

[38] For a helpful treatment of the theological issues involved in the cry of dereliction, see Gérard Rossé, *The Cry of Jesus on the Cross: A Biblical and Theological Study* (New York: Paulis, 1987).

[39] Ahearne-Kroll, *Psalms of Lament*, 209.

God (16:6). The evangelist does not minimize the shock and horror of the cross; he inscribes it into the identity of the one he believes now reigns in glory at the right hand of God.

Mark narrates the mockery of Jesus so as to echo his trial before the Sanhedrin. Both passages share the same two-part structure:

(1)   *An accusation concerning the temple from an anonymous group*:

"I will destroy this temple that is made with hands, and in three days, I will build another, not made with hands"   (14:58).

"Aha! You who would destroy the temple and build it in three days, save yourself, and come down from the cross"   (15:29).

(2)   *An ironic confession of Jesus's identity from the chief priest and/or his cohort*:

"Are you the messiah, the son of the Blessed One?"   (14:61).

"Let the messiah, the king of Israel, come down from the cross now, so that we may see and believe"   (15:32).

The bystanders, scribes, and chief priests all assume the cross is the quintessential obstacle to messianic enthronement (cf. 8:31–33). Quite the contrary, says Mark. The very moment when Jesus breathed his last breath, the God of Israel rent the curtain dividing the sanctuary in two and, at last, a human character – a Roman centurion, no less – gives voice to the mystery of the divine will.

The entire scene presupposes Jesus's resurrection. The rending of the temple curtain is proleptic of his heavenly enthronement (cf. Dan 7:13; Ps 110), the place from which he pours out the holy spirit on communities of his followers (cf. Mark 1:8). The centurion's declaration, "truly *this* man was God's son," stands over and against the taunts of priestly aristocracy. He "sees" (ὁρᾶν) what they could not: the cross is the means of messianic enthronement, such that if Jesus were to come down he would be rejecting the vocation of ὁ χριστός. God will raise this crucified man from the dead and, in so doing, vindicate his claim before the Sanhedrin: "'you will see [ὄψεσθε] the son of man seated at the right hand of the Power,' and 'coming with the clouds of heaven'" (14:62). And because God has not abandoned David's son to the grave, *whoever* takes up his cross and follows the crucified messiah, *whoever* loses her life for the sake of Christ and the gospel, will be vindicated "when he [the son of man] comes in the glory of his father with the holy angels" (Mark 8:34–38).

6.3   Conclusion

Mark is undoubtedly a theologian of the cross. His Christ has come to suffer and die in accordance with the divine will. This fundamental conviction casts its shadow over the entirety of the Jewish scriptures, not least traditions about David and his descendants. But the pressure points of the Markan trial and crucifixion accounts reveal that shame and death are not the end of the story. Rather, resurrection becomes the prerequisite to hearing the Markan narrative aright. *Faithful endurance in the face of suffering*, on the one hand, and *vindication and enthronement*, on the other, function as the twin axioms guiding the evangelist's selection and interpretation of Davidic traditions. A *Markan* hermeneutic accepts, rejects, augments, and attenuates features of this traditional reservoir based on principle convictions about the significance of the life, death, and resurrection of the man Jesus of Nazareth.

7

CONCLUSION

Second Temple Jewish theology, including early Christian theology, was primarily a tradition of exegesis, not a tradition of ideas passed on independently of exegesis … Teachers and writers of the period did not work primarily by transferring models from one heavenly or eschatological figure to another, but by asking to which figure particular texts applied or which texts applied to a particular figure, and what such texts said about the figure in question. The extent to which early Christology is novel in its Jewish context is the extent to which, in view of the unique features of Jesus' history, it applied to Jesus a particular selection and configuration of key texts, some already well used for certain heavenly or messianic figures, some not previously so used, but *as a particular selection and configuration novel.*
– Richard Bauckham, *Jesus and the God of Israel*,
174–175, his emphasis

7.1 Summary of the Argument

I began this study with the question of why many – perhaps even most – modern scholars are convinced that Mark the evangelist is ambivalent about Davidic filiation. The answer I proposed in Chapter 1 is that these interpreters have assumed the viability of the *traditionsgeschichtlich* approach set forth by Wrede: the only material that counts as evidence of interest in Davidic sonship is the *spärlich*, "sparse," set of pericopae with the name David. This assumption resulted, rather inevitably, in the longstanding exegetical impasse over whether Bartimaeus's cry, "son of David, have mercy on me" (10:47–48), secures or undermines the "Jewish" *theologoumenon* that the messiah would be the son of David. If the interpreter can "prove" that the evangelist approves of the title son of David in 10:47–48, then the Davidic sonship of Mark's Christ may be delivered from the refinery of the *Davidssohnfrage*, even if only barely escaping through the fire. If, on the other hand, the interpreter can "prove" that the evangelist is ambivalent about the title, this then gives ground to a trajectory climaxing in the definitive rejection of all things Davidic. The impetus for the present study was the observation that this impasse has arisen from faulty assumptions about the encyclopedia informing ancient discourse about messiahs or, in Novenson's terms, from a general failure to attend to the "grammar of messianism."

In Chapter 2, therefore, I attempted to situate son-of-David language within its appropriate sociolinguistic framework. I posed the heuristic question: how did the users of ancient messiah language, in various and sundry ways, draw upon scriptural resources about David and his descendants? At least four observations emerged from this line of inquiry. First, some ancient writers who were interested in characterizing their messiahs with Davidic traditions appear to have been indifferent with respect to Davidic ancestry (e.g., 2 Baruch; John); in fact, some elected to do away with it altogether (e.g., Aramaic Levi; Parables of Enoch). It seems heuristically apposite, then, to distinguish between messiahs who are *like* David and those who are *sons of* David, a distinction rarely observed by Markan interpreters.

Second, the Gospel of Mark references Davidic ancestral traditions as much as or more than every other messiah text except for Matthew and Luke-Acts. Thus to speak of "die *spärliche* Überlieferung zum Davidssohn" in Mark, as Christoph Burger did, is already to make a retrospective value judgement based almost entirely on a Synoptic comparison. Additional questions about the absence of certain patrilineal traditions in the Second Gospel are equally suspect. To make elaborate ancestral trees the conditio sine qua non of Davidic messiahship surrenders an interpretive hegemony to Matthew and Luke not just over Mark but over the whole of Second Temple literature.

Third, and most significant for our purposes, we observed that ancient authors recognized *multiple* conventions for characterizing messiahs as Davidic. To wit, the early reception history of iconic texts such as Psalm 2 and Isaiah 11 offers ample evidence that the name David is an optional feature of messiah language. Moreover, when we do encounter ancestral claims in messiah texts, these invariably occur alongside of and among a mélange of intertextual references to Davidic scriptural traditions. These observations suggest that it would be imprudent to answer Mark's *Davidssohnfrage* by isolating pericope with the name David. Rather, we must attend to the various ways in which the evangelist resources his scriptural traditions, in order to discern between the frames he actualizes and those he narcotizes (see Section 1.2).

The balance of this study attempted just such an analysis. In contrast to a dominant strand of Markan scholarship, I argued that the portrait of Christ to emerge from the first half of the narrative communicates that Jesus of Nazareth is a messiah *like* David (Chapters 3 and 4), leaving open-ended the question of the evangelist's position on Davidic descent. Mark accomplished his rhetorical aims both by way of allusions to scriptural traditions that his linguistic community typically associated with David and his ancestral line (e.g., Ps 2; Ezek 34) and by drawing his life of Jesus into intertextual conversation with iconic moments in the Deuteronomistic Historian's life of David (e.g., 1 Sam 16–17; 21). He appears to have been particularly interested in the period of David's life in which God's anointed faced rejection from his family (cf. Psalms 27; 69) and persecution from the current regime, a narrative thread that comes to a head at the first passion prediction, at which time the Markan Jesus introduces the motif of the necessity of messianic rejection vis-à-vis a scriptural intertext about a rejected-but-vindicated Davidic king, Psalm 118 (117 LXX).

In Chapter 5, I approached Mark's contentious son-of-David material with the methodological commitment that the portrait developed in the first half of the narrative provides the requisite framework for assessing the blind man's cry, "son of David, have mercy on me." Far from being a Davidic bolt from the blue, Bartimaeus's cry confirms the audience's growing suspicion that Jesus of Nazareth is the son of David and prepares the way for his entry into the city of his ancestor (cf. Gen 49:10–11; Zech 9:9), the place where the messiah must go to be rejected by the temple hierarchs (cf. Ps 118). Mark builds up to the *Davidssohnfrage* by constructing a symbolic world in which the only conceivable path to messianic enthronement is rejection, suffering, and death – motifs he consistently locates in Davidic scriptural traditions. Thus, by the time he introduces the *Davidssohnfrage*, in 12:35–37, the audience knows that the purpose of the question is not to deny what the rest of the narrative has already established. Instead, the question presses the audience to integrate what David said to and about his "lord" at God's right hand in Psalm 110 (109 LXX) with everything the narrative has communicated about Jesus.

Finally, in Chapter 6, I posited that the crucifixion and resurrection of Jesus furnished Mark with a hermeneutical guide for reading traditions about David and his descendants. In one respect, the evangelist's path is no different than his contemporaries: he constructs his messiah via creative use of the Jewish scriptures guided by ideological commitments about his messianic claimant. Yet, in another respect, Mark is quite unique: he is the first, so far as we know, to write a narrative account of the *crucified* messiah, one which bears witness to a sophisticated interpretive imagination.

7.2   Messianism and Markan Christology: Dead Ends and Future Prospects

We are now in a position to appreciate more fully the irony of Malbon's claim, cited at the opening of Chapter 1, that the Davidic sonship of Jesus is "a Christian belief that is simply assumed to be in all 'Christian' materials." *Pace* Malbon, it would appear to be the case that it is her position, a negative appraisal of the *Davidssohnfrage*, which becomes entrenched in Gospels scholarship as the direct result of a Wredean *traditionsgeschichtlich* approach to early Christianity. To be sure, one can easily locate scholars before and after Wrede who conclude that the historical Jesus rejected the notion that the messiah must be a descendant of David, typically, as I have argued, because they found certain tenants of messianism distasteful. But the interpretive tradition that sees *Mark* as anti-Davidic is unquestionably the child of Protestant New Testament scholarship, begotten of a set of a priori methodological decisions about how an evangelist like Mark should express interest in the idea of Davidic sonship. Indeed, the more one probes this tradition, the more one gets the sense that its case could be reduced to a singular point: Mark is anti-Davidic because he isn't Matthew. And once we determine that Mark has it out for David, it is remarkable – suspiciously so – how quickly the label "Davidic" becomes a convenient cipher for everything we want Jesus to reject: ideologies of violence, authoritarianism, colonialism, and the like.

How then do we avoid hedging our method to fit our interests? Rather than treat Davidic messianism as derivative of some pristine idea, the tenants of which modern interpreters are inclinded to find unsavory, I have argued that we should focus instead on the ways in which ancient writers negotiated traditions about David and his descendants in light of the realities of their respective messiahs – *Davidic* messiah language, as it were. In so doing, we quickly find that judgments about a given author's interest in Davidic messiahship cannot be reduced to passages containing the name David but must take into account the totality of the ways in which that author uses material that evoke Davidic frames in an ancient Jewish encyclopedia. This is not to say, of course, that we should give up speaking of the different ideas Second Temple Jews held about messiahs (or even, for that matter, of "the messianic idea" as a distinctive contribution of the Jewish people to the world), only that *if* we are interested in discerning which method best equips us to attend to any given author's particular brand of messianism in general or to answer Mark's *Davidssohnfrage* in particular, a sociolinguistic one is advisable and indeed superior to its competitors. Bauckham is exactly right: Christology, as with messianism, is "a tradition of exegesis, not a tradition of ideas passed on independently of exegesis."[1]

My study also makes several contributions to the debate over the extent to which the Jewish scriptures should inform the Gospel's symbolic world. If my interpretive wager that Markan Christology is best handled as one example of ancient messiah language is sound, then we should not be surprised – indeed, we should anticipate – the presence of intertextual references to traditions about David and his descendants. The results of this study suggest that the extent to which Markan messiah language resources Davidic traditions is more expansive than has typically been realized. While there will always be debate over the plausibility of particular scriptural allusions – some may find certain proposals too fanciful, while others may wish I would have gone further – it seems to me that the burden of proof is squarely on the shoulders of those who wish to claim that Mark is uninterested in, or even hostile toward, scriptural traditions about Israel's kings.

The points at which Mark tends to draw on Davidic scriptural traditions revolve around the motifs of persecution and suffering, on the one hand, and the motifs of vindication and exaltation, on the other – hardly a novel observation, to be sure (see, e.g., Juel's

---

[1] Bauckham, *Jesus and the God of Israel*, 174.

Messianic Exegesis). Yet it seems to me that these foci inform Mark's selection and refraction of iconic moments in David's life not only in the passion narrative, but also in the early stages of Jesus's messianic career. Despite the important contributions of Adela Yarbro Collins, Rikk Watts, Joel Marcus, and Richard Hays, to name but a few, there remains more work to be done on the seemingly endless reservoir of Markan hermeneutics of the Jewish scriptures.

Finally, no one would argue that Markan Christology is reducible to an affirmation of Jesus's Davidic filiation. My argument throughout, rather, has been that there is little justification for concluding that the evangelist rejects or is circumspect about this idea, since he mentions it as much as or more than virtually every other messianically inclined author in antiquity, when – and this is critical – he would have had the option to ignore or even reject it. Indeed, many of the moves Mark makes throughout the narrative are best explained when we posit that he plays his language game with the presupposition of Jesus's Davidic ancestry. The evangelist never set out to prove that his Christ was a descendant of David; he simply took the point for granted.

The challenge with assessing presuppositions, of course, is that they are almost always underdetermined. How do we measure the significance of Davidic sonship for Mark? Most interpreters conclude that its significance is minimal, since the evangelist puts the accent on divine sonship. But this seems misguided. While it is true that the *Davidssohnfrage* constructs a competitive relationship between Davidic and divine sonship, its function in the Synoptic Gospels, in Mark no less than in Matthew and Luke, is to assert that the messiah is more than the son of David: he is God's son. Wrede and his acolytes would have us believe that the path to "high" Christology is paved with the swift diminution of Davidic sonship, an idea they trace back to the pre-Pauline tradition in Rom 1:3–4. Such remains one of many hypotheses interpreters of ancient Christianity must test and weigh for themselves. But let us do so henceforth with the clear understanding that Mark is not a witness to this christological strategy.

BIBLIOGRAPHY

Primary Sources and Reference Works

Aland, Barbara, Kurt Aland, Johannes Karavidopoulos, Carlo M. Martini, and Bruce M. Metzger, eds. *Novum Testamentum Graece.* 28th edn. Stuttgart: Deutsche Bibelgesellschaft, 2012.

Johannes Karavidopoulos, Carlo M. Martin, and Bruce Metzger, eds. *The Greek New Testament.* 5th edn. Stuttgart: Deutsche Bibelgesellschaft, 2014.

Allegro, John M., ed. *Qumrân Cave 4: I (4Q158–4Q186).* DJD 5. Oxford: Clarendon, 1968.

Augustine. *Enarationes in psalmos I-L.* Edited by Eligius Dekkers and Jean Fraipont. CCL 38. Turnhout: Brepols, 1956.

Baars, Willem, ed. "Apocryphal Psalms." In *Canticles or Odes, Prayer of Manasseh, Apocryphal Psalms, Psalms of Solomon, Tobit, and 1 (3) Esdras. The Old Testament in Syriac According to the Peshiṭta Version, Part IV, Fascicle 6.* Leiden: Brill, 1972.

Barthélemy, Dominique, and J. T. Milik, eds. *Qumran Cave 1: I.* DJD 1. Oxford: Clarendon, 1955.

Bauckham, Richard, James R. Davila, and Alexander Panayotov, eds. Volume 1 of *Old Testament Pseudepigrapha: More Noncanonical Scriptures.* Grand Rapids, MI: Eerdmans, 2013.

Bensly, Robert L., ed. *The Fourth Book of Ezra: The Latin Version Edited from the MSS.* TS 3.2. Cambridge: Cambridge University Press, 1895.

Bidawid, R. J., ed. 1973. "4 Esdras." In *Apocalypse of Baruch, 4 Esdras. The Old Testament in Syriac According to the Peshiṭta Version, Part IV, Fascicle 3.* Leiden: Brill, 1973.

Blass, Friedrich, Albert Debrunner, and Robert W. Funk. *A Greek Grammar of the New Testament and Other Early Christian Literature.* Chicago: University of Chicago Press, 1961.

Bogaert, Pierre-Maurice, Jacques Cazeaux, Daniel J. Harrington, and Charles Perrot, eds. *Pseudo-Philo Les Antiquités Bibliques.* 2 vols. SC 229 and 230. Paris: Cerf, 1976.

Braude, William G., ed. *The Midrash on Psalms.* 2 vols. YJS 13. New Haven, CT: Yale University Press, 1959.

Brooke, George, John Collins, Torleif Elgvin, Peter Flint, Jonas Greenfield, Erik Larson, Carol Newsom, Émile Puech, Lawrence H. Schiffman,

Michael Stone, and Julio Trebolle Barrea., eds. *Qumran Cave 4 XVII: Parabiblical Texts, Part 3*. DJD 22. Oxford: Clarendon, 1996.

Charlesworth, James H., ed. *The Old Testament Pseudepigraph*. 2 vols. Garden City, NY: Doubleday, 1983, 1985.

Charlesworth, James H., with J. M. Baumgarten, M. T. Davis, J. Duhaime, Y. Ofer, H. W. L. Rietz, J. J. M. Roberts, D. Schwartz, B. A. Strawn, and R. E. Whitaker, eds. *The Dead Sea Scrolls: Hebrew, Aramaic, and Greek Texts with English Translations, Volume 2: Damascus Document, War Scroll, and Related Documents*. The Princeton Theological Seminary Dead Sea Scrolls Project. Tübingen: Mohr Siebeck, 1995.

Chilton, Bruce D., ed. *The Isaiah Targum*. ArBib 11. Edinburgh: T&T Clark, 1987.

Chilton, Bruce D., Darrell Bock, Daniel M. Gurtner, Jacob Neusner, Lawrence H. Schiffman and Daniel Oden., eds. *A Comparative Handbook to the Gospel of Mark: Comparisons with Pseudepigrapha, the Qumran Scrolls, and Rabbinic Literature*. New Testament Gospels in Their Judaic Contexts 1. Leiden: Brill, 2010.

Cross, Frank Moore, Donald W. Parry, Richard J. Saley, and Eugene Ulrich, eds. *Qumran Cave 4, XII: 1–2 Samuel*. DJD 17. Oxford: Clarendon, 2005.

Danby, Herbert, ed. *The Mishnah: Translated from the Hebrew with Introduction and Brief Explanatory Notes*. Oxford: Oxford University Press, 1933.

Danker, Frederick W., Walter Bauer, William F. Arndt, and F. Wilbur Gingrich, eds. *A Greek-English Lexicon of the New Testament and Other Early Christian Literature*. 3rd edn. Chicago: Chicago University Press, 2000.

Ehrman, Bart D., ed. *The Apostolic Fathers*. 2 vols. LCL. Cambridge, MA: Harvard University Press, 2003.

Elliger, Karl, and Wilhelm Rudolph, eds. *Biblia Hebraica Stuttgartensia*. Stuttgart: Deutsche Bibelgesellschaft, 1983.

Eshel, Esther, Hanan Eshel, Carol Newsom, Bilhah Nitzan, Eileen Schuller, and Ada Yardeni, eds. *Qumran Cave 4 VI: Poetical and Liturgical Texts, Part 1*. DJD 11. Oxford: Clarendon, 1998.

García Martínez, Florentino, and Eibert J. C. Tigchelaar. *The Dead Sea Scrolls Study Edition*. 2 vols. Leiden: Brill, 1997–1998.

García Martínez, Florentino, Eibert J. C. Tigchelaar, and Adam S. van der Woude, eds. *Qumran Cave 11 II: 11Q2–18, 11Q20–31*. DJD 23. Oxford: Clarendon, 1998.

Goodspeed, Edgar J., ed. *Die ältesten Apologeten: Texte mit kurzen Einleitungen*. Göttingen: Vandenhoeck & Ruprecht, 1914.

Gourdain, Jean-Louis, ed. *Jérôme Homélies sur Marc*. SC 494. Paris: Cerf, 2005.

Greenfield, Jonas C., Michael E. Stone, and Esther Eshel. *The Aramaic Levi Document: Edition, Translation, Commentary*. SVTP 19. Leiden: Brill, 2004.

Gurtner, Daniel M., ed. *Second Baruch: A Critical Edition of the Syriac Text with Greek and Latin Fragments, English Translation, Introduction, and Concordances*. Jewish and Christian Texts in Contexts and Related Studies 5. London: T&T Clark, 2009.

Homer. *Iliad, Volume 1: Books 1–12.* Edited by A. T. Murray and William F. Wyatt. LCL 170. Cambridge, MA: Harvard University Press, 1924.

Jacobson, Howard. *A Commentary on Pseudo-Philo's Liber Antiquitatum Biblicarum: With Latin Text and English Translation.* 2 vols. AGJU 31. Leiden: Brill, 1996.

Jonge, Marinus de, *The Testament of the Twelve Patriarchs: A Critical Edition of the Greek Text.* Leiden: Brill, 1978.

Josephus. Edited by Henry St. J. Thackeray, Ralph Marcus, Allen Wirkgren, and Louis H. Feldman, eds. 10 vols. LCL. Cambridge, MA: Harvard University Press, 1926–1965.

Justin Martyr. *The First and Second Apologies: Translated with Introduction and Notes.* Translated by Leslie William Barnard. ACW 56. New York: Paulist, 1997.

Dialogue with Trypho. Translated by Thomas B. Falls. Revised by Thomas P. Halton. Edited by Michael Slusser. Selections from the Fathers of the Church 3. Washington, DC: Catholic University of America Press, 2003.

Mason, Steven, ed. *Flavius Josephus: Translation and Commentary. Volume 9: Life of Josephus.* Leiden: Brill, 2001.

Metzger, Bruce M. *A Textual Commentary on the Greek New Testament.* 2nd edn. Stuttgart: Deutsche Bibelgesellschaft, 1994.

Meyer, Marvin, ed. *The Nag Hammadi Scriptures: The Revised and Updated Translation of Gnostic Texts.* New York: HaperCollins, 2007.

Muraoka, Takamitsu. *A Grammar of Qumran Aramaic.* ANESSup 38. Leuven: Peters, 2011.

Nickelsburg, George W. E., and James C. VanderKam. *1 Enoch: The Hermeneia Translation.* Minneapolis, MN: Fortress, 2012.

Petschenig, Michael, and Michaela Zelzer. *Sancti Ambrosi Opera Pars V: Exposition Psalmi CXVIII.* CSEL 62. Vienna: Österreichische Akademie der Wissenschaften, 1999.

Philo. Translated by F. H. Colson, G. H. Whitaker, and Ralph Marcus. 10 vols. with 2 supplements. LCL. Cambridge, MA: Harvard University Press, 1929–1962.

Rahlfs, Alfred, ed. *Septuaginta: Psalmi cum Odis.* 2nd edn. Septuaginta 10. Göttingen: Vandenhoeck & Ruprecht, 1979.

Rousseau, Adelin, and Louis Doutreleua, eds. *Irénée de Lyon Contre les Hérésies: Livre III.* SC 210 and 211. Paris: Cerf, 1974.

Sanders, James A., ed. *The Psalms Scroll of Qumran Cave 11 (11QPs^a).* DJD 4. Oxford: Clarendon, 1965.

Schäfer, Peter, ed., with H. J. Becker, K. Hermann, C. Rohrbacher-Sticker, and S. Siebers. *Übersetzung der Hekhalot-Literatur§§ II 81–334.* 2 vols. TSAJ 17. Tübingen: Mohr Siebeck, 1987.

Sokoloff, Michael. *A Syriac Lexicon: A Translation from the Latin, Correction, Expansion, and Update of C. Brockelmann's Lexicon Syriacum.* Winona Lake, IN: Eisenbrauns; Piscataway, NJ: Gorgias, 2009.

Stec, David M., ed. *The Targum of Psalms: Translated with a Critical Introduction, Apparatus, and Notes.* ArBib 16. London: T&T Clark, 2004.

Stegemann, Hartmut, Eileen Schuller, and Carol Newsom, eds. *1QHodayot^a with Incorporation of 1QHodayot^b and 4QHodayot^{a-f}*. DJD 40. Oxford: Clarendon, 2009.

Stone, Michael E., and Matthias Henze. *4 Ezra and 2 Baruch: Translation, Introduction, and Notes*. Minneapolis, MN: Fortress, 2013.

Tissot, Dom Gabriel, ed. *Ambroise de Milan Traité sur L'Évangile de S. Luc*. 2 vols. SC 45 and 52. Paris: Cerf, 1956–1958.

Tromp, Johannes. *The Assumption of Moses: A Critical Edition with Commentary*. SVTP 10. Leiden: Brill, 1993.

Ulrich, Eugene. *The Biblical Qumran Scrolls: Transcriptions and Textual Variants*. 3 vols. Leiden: Brill, 2013.

Vermes, Geza. *The Complete Dead Sea Scrolls in English*. Rev. edn. London: Penguin, 2004.

Walter, D. M., ed. *The Book of Psalms: The Old Testament in Syriac According to the Peshiṭta Version, Part II, Fascicle 3*. Leiden: Brill, 1980.

Wevers, John William, ed. *Genesis*. Septuaginta 1. Göttingen: Vandenhoeck & Ruprecht, 1974.

——— *Notes on the Greek Text of Genesis*. SCS 35. Atlanta, GA: Scholars Press, 1993.

Wright, Robert B. *The Psalms of Solomon: A Critical Edition of the Greek Text*. Jewish and Christian Texts in Contexts and Related Studies 1. London: T&T Clark, 2007.

Yadin, Yigael, *The Temple Scroll*. 3 vols. Rev. edn. with suppl. Jerusalem: Israel Exploration Society, The Institute of Archeology of the Hebrew University of Jerusalem, The Shrine of the Book, 1983.

Ziegler, Joseph, ed. *Isaias*. 3rd edn. Septuaginta 14. Göttingen: Vandenhoeck & Ruprecht, 1983.

Secondary Sources

Achtemeier, Paul J. "'And He Followed Him': Miracles and Discipleship in Mark 10:46–52." *Semeia* 11 (1978): 115–145.

——— "'He Taught Them Many Things': Reflections on Marcan Christology." *CBQ* 42 (1980): 465–481.

Ådna, Jostein. *Jesu Stellung zum Tempel: Die Tempelaktion und das Tempelwort als Ausdruck seiner messianischen Sendung*. WUNT 2/119. Tübingen: Mohr Siebeck, 2000.

——— "The Servant of Isaiah 53 as Triumphant and Interceding Messiah: The Reception of Isaiah 52:13–53:12 in the Targum Isaiah with Special Attention to the Concept of the Messiah." Pages 189–224 in *The Suffering Servant: Isaiah 53 in Jewish and Christian Sources*. Edited by Bernd Janowski and Peter Stuhlmacher. Translated by Daniel P. Bailey. Grand Rapids, MI: Eerdmans, 2004.

Ahearne-Kroll, Stephen P. *The Psalms of Lament in Mark's Passion: Jesus' Davidic Suffering*. SNTSMS 142. Cambridge: Cambridge University Press, 2007.

Alkier, Stefan. "Intertextualität – Annäherungen an ein texttheoretisches Paradigma." Pages 1–26 in *Heiligkeit und Herrschaft: Intertextuelle*

Studien zu Heiligkeitsvorstellungen und zu Psalm 110. Edited by Dieter Sänger. Biblisch-Theologische Studien 55. Neukirchen-Vluyn: Neukirchener, 2003.

Neues Testament. UTB 3404. Tübingen: Fracke, 2010.

Allison, Dale C. "Elijah Must Come First." *JBL* 103 (1984): 256–258.

The New Moses: A Matthean Typology. Edinburgh: T&T Clark, 1993.

Ambrozic, Aloysius. The *Hidden Kingdom: A Redaction-Critical Study of the References to the Kingdom of God in Mark's Gospel.* CBQMS 2. Washington, DC: Catholic Biblical Association of America, 1972.

Anderson, Janice Capel, and Stephen D. Moore. "Introduction: The Lives of Mark." Pages 1–27 in *Mark & Method: New Approaches in Biblical Studies.* Edited by Janice Capel Anderson and Stephen D. Moore. 2nd edn. Minneapolis, MN: Fortress, 2008.

Atkinson, Kenneth R. *An Intertextual Study of the Psalms of Solomon.* Lewiston, NY: Mellon, 2001.

Attridge, Harold W. "Giving Voice to Jesus: Use of the Psalms in the New Testament." Pages 101–112 in *Psalms in Community: Jewish and Christian Textual, Liturgical, and Artistic Traditions.* Edited by Harold W. Attridge and Margot E. Fassler. SymS 25. Atlanta, GA: SBL, 2003.

Aune, David E. "Christian Prophecy and the Messianic Status of Jesus." Pages 404–422 in *The Messiah: Developments in Earliest Judaism and Christianity.* Edited by James H. Charlesworth. Minneapolis, MN: Fortress, 1992.

Revelation. 3 vols. WBC 52. Dallas, TX: Word, 1997–1998.

"From the Idealized Past to the Imaginary Future: Eschatological Restoration in Jewish Apocalyptic Literature." Pages 147–178 in *Restoration: Old Testament, Jewish, and Christian Literature.* Edited by James M. Scott. JSJSup 72. Leiden: Brill, 2001.

Bacon, Benjamin Wisner. *The Gospel of Mark: Its Composition and Date.* New Haven, CT: Yale University Press, 1925.

Bal, Mieke. *Narratology: Introduction to the Theory of Narrative.* 2nd edn. Toronto: University of Toronto Press, 1997.

Barr, James. "'Abbā Isn't 'Daddy'." *JTS* 39 (1988): 28–47. Repr., Pages 262–280 in *Bible and Interpretation: The Collected Essays of James Barr.* 3 vols. Edited by John Barton. Oxford: Oxford University Press, 2013.

Barton, Stephen C. *Discipleship and Family Ties in Mark and Matthew.* SNTSMS 80 Cambridge: Cambridge University Press, 1994.

Bates, Matthew W. *The Birth of the Trinity: Jesus, God, and Spirit in New Testament & Early Christian Interpretation of the Old Testament.* Oxford: Oxford University Press, 2015.

"A Christology of Incarnation and Enthronement: Romans 1:3–4 as Unified, Nonadoptionist, and Nonconciliatory." *CBQ* 77 (2015): 107–127.

Bauckham, Richard. "Jesus and the Wild Animals (Mark 1:13): A Christological Image for an Ecological Age." Pages 3–21 in *Jesus of Nazareth: Lord and Christ: Essays on the Historical Jesus and New Testament Christology.* Edited by Joel B. Green and Max Turner. Grand Rapids, MI: Eerdmans, 1994.

Jesus and the God of Israel: God Crucified and Other Studies on the New Testament's Christology of Divine Identity. Grand Rapids, MI: Eerdmans, 2008.

Bauernfeind, Otto. *Die Wörte der Dämonen im Markusevangelium*. BWA(N) T 8. Stuttgart: Kohlhammer, 1927.

Baur, Ferdinand Christian, *Das Markusevangelium: Nach seinem Ursprung und Charakter, nebst einem Anhang über das Evangelium Marcion's*. Tübingen: Mohr Siebeck, 1851.

Beaton, Richard. *Isaiah's Christ in Matthew's Gospel*. SNTSMS 123. Cambridge: Cambridge University Press, 2002.

Ben-Porat, Ziva. "The Poetics of Literary Allusion." *PTL* 1 (1976): 105–128.

Berger, Klaus. "Die königlichen Messiastraditionen des Neuen Testaments." *NTS* 20 (1974): 1–44.

Best, Ernest. *The Temptation and the Passion: The Markan Soteriology*. SNTSMS 2. Cambridge: Cambridge University Press, 1965.

Disciples and Discipleship: Studies in the Gospel According to Mark. Edinburgh: T&T Clark, 1986.

Bhabha, Homi K. *The Location of Culture*. London: Routledge, 1994.

Black, C. Clifton. *Mark: Images of an Apostolic Interpreter*. Columbia, SC: University of South Carolina Press, 1994. Repr., Minneapolis, MN: Fortress, 2001.

Mark. ANTC. Nashville, TN: Abingdon Press, 2011.

The Disciples According to Mark: Markan Redaction in Current Debate. JSNTSup 27. Sheffield: Sheffield Academic Press, 1989. Repr., Grand Rapids, MI: Eerdmans, 2012.

Black, Mark C. "The Rejected and Slain Messiah Who Is Coming with the Angels: The Messianic Exegesis of Zechariah 9–14 in the Passion Narratives." PhD diss., Emory University, 1990.

Black, Matthew. "The Messianism of the Parables of Enoch: Their Date and Contributions to Christological Origins." Pages 145–168 in *The Messiah: Developments in Earliest Judaism and Christianity*. Edited by James H. Charlesworth. Minneapolis, MN: Fortress, 1992.

Blenkinsopp, Joseph A. "The Oracle of Judah and the Messianic Entry." *JBL* 80 (1961): 55–64.

Isaiah 40–55: A New Translation with Introduction and Commentary. AB 19A New York: Doubleday, 2002.

Isaiah 56–66: A New Translation with Introduction and Commentary. AB 19B. New York: Doubleday, 2003.

Opening the Sealed Book: Interpretations of the Book of Isaiah in Late Antiquity. Grand Rapids, MI: Eerdmans, 2006.

David Remembered: Kingship and National Identity in Ancient Israel. Grand Rapids, MI: Eerdmans, 2013.

Boccaccini, Gabriele, ed. *Enoch and the Messiah Son of Man: Revisiting the Book of Parables*. Grand Rapids, MI: Eerdmans, 2007.

Bockmuehl, Markus. "The Son of David and His Mother." *JTS* 62 (2011): 476–493.

Boring, M. Eugene. "Mark 1:1–15 and the Beginning of the Gospel." *Semeia* 52 (1990): 43–81.

Mark: A Commentary. NTL. Louisville, KY: Westminster John Knox, 2006.

Botner, Max. "The Role of Transcriptional Probability in the Text-Critical Debate on Mark 1:1." *CBQ* 77 (2015): 467–480.
"How Do the Seeds Land? A Note on ΕΙΣ ΑΥΤΟΝ in Mark 1:10." *JTS* 66 (2015): 547–552.
"Prophetic Script and Dramatic Enactment in Mark's Prologue." *BBR* 26 (2016): 59–70.
"The Messiah is 'the Holy One': ὁ ἅγιος τοῦ θεοῦ as a Messianic Title in Mark 1:24." *JBL* 136 (2017): 419–435.
"What Has Mark's Christ to Do with David's Son? A History of Interpretation." *CBR* 16 (2017): 50–70.
Review of *The Grammar of Messianism: An Ancient Jewish Political Idiom and Its Users*, by Matthew V. Novenson. *JSJ* 47 (2017): 591–594.
"'Then David Began to Sing This Song': Composition and Hermeneutics in Pseudo-Philo's Psalm of David (LAB 59.4)." *JSP* 28 (2018): 69–87.
"Has Jesus Read What David Did? Probing Problems in Mark 2:25–26." *JTS* 69 (2018): 484–499.
"'Whoever Does the Will of God' (Mark 3:35): Mark's Christ as the Model Son." Pages 106–117 in *Son of God: Divine Sonship in Jewish and Christian Antiquity*. Edited by Garrick V. Allen, Kai Akagi, Paul Sloan, and Madhavi Nevader. University Park: Pennsylvania State University Press, 2019.
Bousset, Wilhelm. *Kyrios Christos: A History of the Belief in Christ from the Beginnings of Christianity to Irenaeus*. Translated by John E. Steely. Nashville, TN: Abingdon, 1970. Translation of *Kyrios Christos: Geschichte des Christusglaubens von den Anfangen des Christentums bis Irenaeus*. Göttingen: Vandenhoeck & Ruprecht, 1921.
Boyarin, Daniel. "The Talmud in Jesus: How Much Jewishness in Mark's Christ?" Pages 941–964 in *Envisioning Judaism: Studies in Honor of Peter Schäfer on the Occasion of His Seventieth Birthday*. Edited by Ra'anan S. Boustan, Klaus Herrmann, Reimund Leicht, Annette Yoshiko Reed, and Giuseppe Veltri, with Alex Ramos. 2 vols. Tübingen: Mohr Siebeck, 2013.
Breytenbach, Cilliers. "Das Markusevangelium, Psalm 110,1 und 118,22f.: Folgetext und Prätext." Pages 197–222 in *The Scriptures in the Gospels*. Edited by C. M. Tuckett. BETL 131. Leuven: Leuven University Press, 1997.
Broadhead, Edwin K. "Jesus the Nazarene: Narrative Strategy and Christological Imagery in the Gospel of Mark." *JSNT* 52 (1993): 3–18.
Naming Jesus: Titular Christology in the Gospel of Mark. JSNTSup 175. Sheffield: Sheffield Academic Press, 1999.
Brooke, George J. *Exegesis at Qumran: 4QFlorilegium in its Jewish Context*. JSOTSup 29. Sheffield: JSOT Press, 1985.
"Ezekiel in Some Qumran and New Testament Texts." Pages 317–337 in *The Madrid Qumran Congress: Proceedings of the International Congress on the Dead Sea Scrolls, Madrid 18–21 March 1991*. Edited by Julio Trebolle Barrera and Luis Vegas Montaner. 2 vols. STDJ 11. Leiden: Brill, 1992.
"Kingship and Messianism in the Dead Sea Scrolls." Pages 434–455 in *King and Messiah in Israel and the Ancient Near East: Proceedings of the*

Oxford Old Testament Seminar. Edited by John Day. LHBOTS 270. Sheffield: Sheffield Academic Press, 1998.

The Dead Sea Scrolls and the New Testament. Minneapolis, MN: Fortress, 2005.

Brown, Raymond E. *The Gospel According to John (i-xii): Introduction, Translation, and Notes*. AB 29. Garden City, NY: Doubleday, 1966. Repr. London: Chapman, 1975.

The Birth of the Messiah: A Commentary on the Infancy Narratives in the Gospels of Matthew and Luke. London: Chapman, 1993.

The Death of the Messiah: From Gethsemane to the Grave: A Commentary on the Passion Narratives in the Four Gospels. 2 vols. New York: Doubleday, 1994.

Bruner, Jerome. "The Narrative Construction of Reality." *Critical Inquiry* 18 (1991): 1–21.

Bultmann, Rudolf. *The History of the Synoptic Tradition*. Translated by John Marsh. Oxford: Blackwell, 1963. Translation of *Die Geschichte der synoptischen Tradition*. Rev. edn. Göttingen: Vandenhoeck & Ruprecht, 1921.

New Testament Theology. 2 vols. Translated by Kendrick Grobel. New York: Scribner's Sons, 1951, 1955. Repr., Waco, TX: Baylor University Press, 2007.

Burger, Christoph. *Jesus als Davidssohn: Eine traditionsgeschichtliche Untersuchung*. FRLANT 98. Göttingen: Vandenhoeck & Ruprecht, 1970.

Burridge, Richard A. *What Are the Gospels? A Comparison with Greco-Roman Biography*. 2nd edn. Grand Rapids, MI: Eerdmans, 2004.

Caird, G. B. "Son by Appointment." Pages 73–81 in *The New Testament Age: Essays in Honor of Bo Reicke*. Edited by William C. Weinrich. 2 vols. Macon, GA: Mercer University Press, 1984.

Caneday, Ardel B. "Mark's Provocative Use of Scripture in Narration: 'He Was with the Wild Animals and Angels Ministered to Him.'" *BBR* 9 (1999): 19–36.

Carey, Holly J. *Jesus' Cry from the Cross: Towards a First-Century Understanding of the Intertextual Relationship between Psalm 22 and the Narrative of Mark's Gospel*. LNTS 398. London: T&T Clark, 2009.

"'Is it as Bad as All That?' The Misconception of Mark as a *Film Noir*." Pages 3–21 in *Mark, Manuscripts, and Monotheism: Essays in Honor of Larry W. Hurtado*. Edited by Chris Keith and Dieter T. Roth. LNTS 528. London: Bloomsbury T&T Clark, 2014.

Casey, Maurice. "Culture and Historicity: The Plucking of the Grain (Mark 2.23–28)." *NTS* 34 (1988): 1–23.

Catchpole, D. R. "The 'Triumphal' Entry." Pages 319–334 in *Jesus and the Politics of his Day*. Edited by Ernst Bammel and C. F. D. Moule. Cambridge: Cambridge University Press, 1984.

Chae, Young S. *Jesus as the Eschatological Shepherd: Studies in the Old Testament, Second Temple Judaism, and in the Gospel of Matthew*. WUNT 2/216. Tübingen: Mohr Siebeck, 2006.

Charlesworth, James H. "From Messianology to Christology: Problems and Prospects." Pages 3–35 in *The Messiah: Developments in Earliest*

Judaism and Christianity. Edited by James H. Charlesworth. Minneapolis, MN: Fortress, 1992.

"The Son of David: Solomon and Jesus (Mark 10.47)." Pages 72–87 in *The New Testament and Hellenistic Judaism*. Edited by Peder Borgen and Søren Giversen. Peabody, MA: Hendrickson, 1995.

"The Date and Provenance of the Parables of Enoch." Pages 37–57 in *Parables of Enoch: A Paradigm Shift*. Edited by James H. Charlesworth and Darrell L. Bock. *Jewish and Christian Texts in Context and Related Studies* 11. London: T&T Clark, 2013.

Chatman, Seymour. *Story and Discourse: Narrative Structure in Fiction and Film*. Ithaca, NY: Cornell University Press, 1978.

Chester, Andrew. *Messiah and Exaltation: Jewish Messianic and Visionary Traditions and New Testament Christology*. WUNT 207. Tübingen: Mohr Siebeck, 2007.

Childs, Brevard. "Psalm Titles and Midrashic Exegesis." *JSS* 16 (1971): 137–149.

Chilton, Bruce D. "Jesus *ben David*: Reflection on the *Davidssohnfrage*." *JSNT* 14 (1982): 88–112.

The Glory of Israel: The Theology and Provenance of the Isaiah Targum. JSOTSup 23. Sheffield: JSOT Press, 1983.

Cohn-Sherbok, D. M. "An Analysis of Jesus' Arguments Concerning the Plucking of Grain on the Sabbath." *JSNT* 2 (1979): 31–41.

Collins, John J. *Daniel: A Commentary on the Book of Daniel*. Hermeneia. Minneapolis, MN: Fortress, 1993.

"The Interpretation of Psalm 2." Pages 49–66 in *Echoes from the Caves: Qumran and the New Testament*. Edited by Florentino García Martínez. STDJ 85. Leiden: Brill, 2009.

The Scepter and the Star: Messianism in Light of the Dead Sea Scrolls. 2nd edn. Grand Rapids, MI: Eerdmans, 2010.

Cook, Edward M. "4Q246." *BBR* 5 (1995): 43–66.

Cranfield, C. E. B. *The Gospel According to Saint Mark: An Introduction and Commentary*. CGTC. Cambridge: Cambridge University Press, 1959.

Crossan, John Dominic. "Mark and the Relatives of Jesus." *NovT* 15 (1973): 81–113.

Croy, N. Clayton. *The Mutilation of Mark's Gospel*. Nashville, TN: Abingdon, 2003.

Cullmann, Oscar. *The Christology of the New Testament*. Translated by Shirley C. Guthrie and Charles A. M. Hall. Philadelphia: Westminster, 1963. Translation of *Die Christologie des Neuen Testaments*. Tübingen: Mohr Siebeck, 1957.

Dahl, Nils Alstrup. *Studies in Paul: Theology for the Early Christian Mission*. Minneapolis, MN: Augsburg, 1977.

Daly-Denton, Margaret. *David in the Fourth Gospel: The Johannine Reception of the Psalms*. AGJU 47. Leiden: Brill, 2000.

Daube, David. *The New Testament and Rabbinic Judaism*. London: Athlone, 1956.

"Responsibilities of Master and Disciples in the Gospels." *NTS* 19 (1972): 1–15.

Davenport, Gene L. "The 'Anointed of the Lord' in Psalms of Solomon 17." Pages 67–92 in *Ideal Figures in Ancient Judaism*. Edited by George W. E. Nickelsburg and John J. Collins. SCS 12. Chico, CA: Scholars Press, 1980.

Davies, W. D., and Dale C. Allison Jr. *A Critical and Exegetical Commentary on the Gospel According to Saint Matthew*. 3 vols. ICC. Edinburgh: T&T Clark, 1988–1997.

Davis, Phillip G. "Mark's Christological Paradox." *JSNT* 35 (1989): 3–18.

Derrett, J. D. M. "Judaica in St. Mark." Pages 85–100 in *Studies in the New Testament, Volume 1: Glimpses of the Legal and Social Presuppositions of the Authors*. Leiden: Brill, 1977.

Dewey, Joanna. *Markan Public Debate: Literary Technique, Concentric Structure and Theology in Mark 2:1–3:6*. SBLDS 48. Chico, CA: Scholars Press, 1980.

———. *The Oral Ethos of the Early Church: Speaking, Writing, and the Gospel of Mark*. Biblical Performance Criticism Series 8. Eugene, OR: Cascade, 2013.

Dibelius, Martin. *From Tradition to Gospel*. Translated by Betram Lee Woolf. London: James. Clark & Co., 1971. Translation of *Die Formgeschichte des Evangeliums*. 2nd edn. Tübingen: Mohr Siebeck, 1933.

Dixon, Edward P. "Descending Spirit and Descending Gods: A 'Greek' Interpretation of the Spirit's 'Descent as a Dove' in Mark 1:10." *JBL* 128 (2009): 759–780.

Doble, Peter. "The Psalms in Luke-Acts." Pages 83–117 in *The Psalms in the New Testament*. Edited by Steven Moyise and Maarten J. J. Menken. London: T&T Clark, 2004.

———. "Luke 24.26, 44 – Songs of God's Servant: David and His Psalms in Luke-Acts." *JSNT* 28 (2006): 267–283.

Dodd, C. H. *According to the Scriptures: The Sub-Structure of New Testament Theology*. New York: Scribner's Sons, 1953.

Donahue, John R. *Are You the Christ? The Trial Narrative in the Gospel of Mark*. SBLDS 10. Missoula, MT: Scholars Press, 1973.

———. "Temple, Trial and Royal Christology (Mark 14:53–65)." Pages 61–79 in *The Passion in Mark: Studies on Mark 14–16*. Edited by Werner H. Kelber. Philadelphia: Fortress, 1976.

Donahue, John and Daniel J. Harrington. *The Gospel of Mark*. SP 2. Collegeville: Liturgical, 2002.

Drawnel, Henryk. *An Aramaic Wisdom Text from Qumran: A New Interpretation of the Levi Document*. JSJSup 86. Leiden: Brill, 2004.

Duff, Paul Brooks. "The March of the Divine Warrior and the Advent of the Greco-Roman King: Mark's Account of Jesus' Entry into Jerusalem." *JBL* 111 (1992): 55–71.

Duling, Dennis C. "The Promises to David and Their Entrance into Christianity – Nailing Down a Likely Hypothesis." *NTS* 20 (1974): 55–77.

———. "Solomon, Exorcism, and the Son of David." *HTR* 68 (1975): 235–252.

Dumortier, J.-B. "Un rituel d'intronisation: le Ps. LXXXIX 2–38." *VT* 22 (1972): 176–196.

Dunn, James D. G. *Baptism in the Holy Spirit: A Re-Examination of the New Testament Teaching on the Gift of the Spirit in Relation to Pentecostalism Today*. London: SCM, 1970.

Christology in the Making: A New Testament Inquiry into the Origins of the Doctrine of the Incarnation. 2nd edn. London: SCM, 1989.

Eckstein, Hans-Joachim. "Markus 10,46–52 als Schlüsseltext des Markuse-vangeliums." *ZNW* 87 (1996): 33–50.

Eco, Umberto. *A Theory of Semiotics.* Bloomington, IN: Indiana University Press, 1976.

The Role of the Reader: Explorations in the Semiotics of Texts. Bloomington, IN: Indiana University Press, 1979.

Semiotics and the Philosophy of Language. London: Macmillan Press, 1984.

Richard Rorty, Jonathan Culler, and Christine Brooke-Rose. *Interpretation and Overinterpretation.* Edited by Stefan Collini. Cambridge: Cambridge University Press, 1992.

Kant and the Platypus: Essays on Language and Cognition. Translated by Alastair McEwen. London: Vintage, 1999.

Ehrman, Bart D. *The Orthodox Corruption of Scripture: The Effect of Early Christological Controversies on the Text of the New Testament.* Oxford: Oxford University Press, 1993.

Elledge, Casey D. *The Statutes of the King: The Temple Scroll's Legislation of Kingship (11Q19 LVI 12–LIX 21).* CahRB 56. Paris: Gabalda, 2004

Elliott, J. K. "Mark 1.1–3 – A Later Addition to the Gospel?" *NTS* 46 (2000): 584–588.

Evans, Craig A. "Patristic Interpretation of Mark 2:26: 'When Abiathar Was High Priest,'" *VC* 40 (1986): 183–186.

"David in the Dead Sea Scrolls." Pages 183–197 in *The Scrolls and the Scriptures: Qumran Fifty Years After.* Edited by Stanley E. Porter and Craig A. Evans. JSPSup 26. Sheffield: Sheffield Academic Press, 1997.

Mark 8:27–16:20. WBC 34B. Nashville, TN: Thomas Nelson, 2001.

"The Beginning of the Good News and the Fulfillment of Scripture in the Gospel of Mark." Pages 83–103 in *Hearing the Old Testament in the New Testament.* Edited by Stanley E. Porter. Grand Rapids, MI: Eerdmans, 2006.

Eve, Eric. *Behind the Gospels: Understanding the Oral Tradition.* London: SPCK, 2013.

Fairstein, M. M. "Why Do the Scribes Say That Elijah Must Come First?" *JBL* 100 (1981): 75–86.

Ferda, Tucker S. "Naming the Messiah: A Contribution to the 4Q246 'Son of God' Debate." *DSD* 21 (2014): 150–175.

Fiorenza, Elisabeth Schüssler. *In Memory of Her: A Feminist Theological Reconstruction of Christian Origins.* London: SCM, 1983.

Fishbane, Michael. *Biblical Interpretation in Ancient Israel.* Oxford: Clarendon, 1985.

Fisk, Bruce Norman. *Do You Not Remember? Scripture, Story and Exegesis in the Rewritten Bible of Pseudo-Philo.* JSPSup 37. Sheffield: Sheffield Academic Press, 2001.

Fitzmyer, Joseph A. *Essays on the Semitic Background of the New Testament.* London: Chapman, 1971.

The Gospel According to Luke (I–IX): Introduction, Translation, and Notes. AB 28 Garden City, NY: Doubleday, 1981.

"More about Elijah Coming First." *JBL* 104 (1985): 295–296.

"4Q246: The 'Son of God' Document from Qumran." *Bib* 74 (1993): 153–174.

A Wandering Aramean: Collected Aramaic Essays. Volume 2 of *The Semitic Background of the New Testament.* Missoula, MT: Scholars Press, 1979. Repr., Grand Rapids, MI: Eerdmans, 1997.

The One Who Is To Come. Grand Rapids, MI: Eerdmans, 2007.

Fletcher-Louis, Crispin H. T. "Jesus as the High Priestly Messiah: Part 1." *JSHJ* 4 (2006): 155–175.

"Jesus as the High Priestly Messiah: Part 2." *JSHJ* 5 (2007): 57–79.

Jesus Monotheism, Volume 1: Christological Origins: The Emerging Consensus and Beyond. Eugene, OR: Cascade, 2015.

Flusser, David. "The Hubris of the Antichrist in a Fragment from Qumran." *Imm* 10 (1980): 31–37.

Foster, Paul. "Echoes without Resonance: Critiquing Certain Aspects of Recent Scholarly Trends in the Study of the Jewish Scriptures in the New Testament." *JSNT* 38 (2015): 96–111.

Fowler, Robert M. *Loaves and Fishes: The Function of the Feeding Stories in the Gospel of Mark.* SBLDS 54. Chico, CA: Scholars Press, 1978.

Fraade, Steven D. "The Torah of the King (Deut 17.14–20) in the Temple Scroll and Early Rabbinic Law." Pages 25–60 in *The Dead Sea Scrolls as Background to Postbiblical Judaism and Early Christianity: Papers from an International Conference at St. Andrews in 2001.* Edited by James R. Davila. STDJ 46. Leiden: E. J. Brill, 2003.

France, R. T. *The Gospel of Mark: A Commentary on the Greek Text.* NIGTC. Grand Rapids, MI: Eerdmans, 2002.

Friedrich, Gerhard. "Beobachtungen zur messianischen Hohepriestererwartung in den Synoptikern." *ZTK* 53 (1956): 265–311.

Fuller, Reginald. *The Foundations of New Testament Christology.* London: Lutterworth, 1965.

Gamble, Harry Y. *Books and Readers in the Early Church: A History of Early Christian Texts.* New Haven, CT: Yale University Press, 1995.

García Martínez, Florentino. *Qumran and Apocalyptic: Studies on the Aramaic Texts from Qumran.* STDJ 9. Leiden: Brill, 1992.

Garrett, Susan R. *The Temptation of Jesus in Mark's Gospel.* Grand Rapids, MI: Eerdmans, 1998.

Gathercole, Simon J. *The Pre-Existent Son: Recovering the Christologies of Matthew, Mark, and Luke.* Grand Rapids, MI: Eerdmans, 2006.

Gibson, Jeffrey B. "Jesus' Wilderness Temptation According to Mark." *JSNT* 5 (1994): 3–34.

Gieschen, C. A. "Why Was Jesus with the Wild Beasts (Mark 1:13)?" *CTQ* 73 (2009): 77–80.

Glazier-McDonald, Beth. *Malachi: The Divine Messenger.* SBLDS 98. Atlanta, GA: Scholars Press, 1987.

Gnilka, Joachim. *Das Evangelium nach Markus.* 2 vols. in one. EKKNT 2. Neukirchen-Vluyn: Neukirchener, 1977–1978. Repr., Neukirchen-Vluyn: Neukirchener, 2011.

Goldingay, John. *Psalms.* 3 vols. BCOTWP. Grand Rapids, MI: Baker Academic, 2006.

Goldstein, Jonathan A. "How the Authors of 1 and 2 Maccabees Treated the 'Messianic' Promises." Pages 69–96 in *Judaisms and Their Messiahs at the Turn of the Christian Era*. Edited by Jacob Neusner, William Scott Green, and Ernest S. Frerichs. Cambridge: Cambridge University Press, 1987.

Gould, Ezra P. *A Critical and Exegetical Commentary on the Gospel According to St. Mark*. ICC. Edinburgh: T&T Clark, 1896.

Grant, Jamie. *King as Exemplar: The Function of Deuteronomy's Kingship Law in the Shaping of the Book of Psalms*. AcBib 17. Atlanta, GA: Society of Biblical Literature, 2004.

Green, William Scott. "Introduction: Messiah in Judaism: Rethinking the Question." Pages 1–13 in *Judaisms and Their Messiahs at the Turn of the Christian Era*. Edited by Jacob Neusner, William Scott Green, and Ernest S. Frerichs. Cambridge: Cambridge University Press, 1987.

Grundmann, Walter. *Das Evangelium nach Markus*. 2 vols. THKNT 2. Berlin: Evangelische Verlagsanstalt, 1965.

Guelich, Robert A. "'The Beginning of the Gospel': Mark 1:1–15." *BR* 27 (1982): 5–15.

———. *Mark 1–8:26*. WBC 34A. Dallas, TX: Word, 1989.

Gundry, Robert H. *The Use of the Old Testament in St. Matthew's Gospel, with Special Reference to the Messianic Hope*. NovTSup 18. Leiden: Brill, 1967.

———. *Mark: A Commentary on His Apology for the Cross*. Grand Rapids, MI: Eerdmans, 1993.

Hahn, Ferdinand. *Titles of Jesus in Christology: Their History in Early Christianity*. Translated by Harold Knight and George Ogg. London: Lutterworth, 1969. Repr., Cambridge: James Clarke & Co, 2002. Translation of *Christologische Hoheitstitel: ihre Geschichte im frühen Christentum*. Göttingen: Vandenhoeck & Ruprecht, 1963.

Hamerton-Kelly, R. G. "Sacred Violence and the Messiah: The Markan Passion Narrative as a Redefinition of Messianology." Pages 461–493 in *The Messiah: Developments in Earliest Judaism and Christianity*. Edited by James H. Charlesworth. Minneapolis, MN: Fortress, 1992.

Harnack, Adolf von. *History of Dogma*. Translated by Neil Buchanan et al. 7 vols. London: Williams & Norgate, 1894–1899.

Harrington, Daniel J. "The Original Language of Pseudo-Philo's *Liber Antiquitatum Biblicarum*." *HTR* 63 (1970): 503–514.

Hatina, Thomas R. *In Search of a Context: The Function of Scripture in Mark's Narrative*. JSNTSup 232. Sheffield: Sheffield Academic Press, 2002.

Hay, David M. *Glory at the Right Hand: Psalm 110 in Early Christianity*. SBLMS 18. Nashville, TX: Abingdon, 1973. Repr., Atlanta, GA: Society of Biblical Literature, 1989.

Hays, Richard B. *Echoes of Scripture in the Letters of Paul*. New Haven, CT: Yale University Press, 1989.

———. *The Conversion of the Imagination: Paul as Interpreter of Israel's Scriptures*. Grand Rapids, MI: Eerdmans, 2005.

Hays, Richard B., Stefan Alkier, and Leroy A. Huizenga, eds., *Reading the Bible Intertextually* (Waco, TX: Baylor University Press, 2009).

Reading Backwards: Figural Christology and the Fourfold Gospel Witness (Waco, TX: Baylor University Press, 2014)

Echoes of Scripture in the Gospels. Waco, TX: Baylor University Press, 2016.

Head, Peter. "A Text-Critical Study of Mark 1.1: 'The Beginning of the Gospel of Jesus Christ." *NTS* 37 (1991): 621–629.

Heim, Knut M. "The (God-)forsaken King of Psalm 89: A Historical and Intertextual Enquiry. Pages 296–322 in *King and Messiah in Israel and the Ancient Near East: Proceedings of the Oxford Old Testament Seminar.* Edited by John Day. LHBOTS 270. Sheffield: Sheffield Academic Press, 1998.

Heitmüller, Wilhelm, "Zum Problem Jesus und Paulus." *ZNW* 13 (1912): 320–337.

Henderson, Suzanne Watts. *Christology and Discipleship in the Gospel of Mark.* SNTSMS 135. Cambridge: Cambridge University Press, 2006.

Hengel, Martin. *The Son of God: The Origin of Christology and the History of Jewish-Hellenistic Religion.* Translated by John Bowden. Minneapolis, MN: Fortress, 1976. Repr., Eugene, OR: Wipf and Stock, 2007.

Studies in the Gospel of Mark. Translated by John Bowden. Minneapolis, MN: Fortress, 1985. Repr., Eugene, OR: Wipf and Stock, 2003.

Henze, Matthias. *Jewish Apocalypticism in Late First Century Israel: Reading Second Baruch in Context.* TSAJ 142. Tübingen: Mohr Siebeck, 2011.

Holladay, Carl. *Theios Anēr in Hellenistic Judaism: A Critique of the Use of This Category in New Testament Christology.* SBLDS 40. Missoula, MT: Scholars Press, 1977.

Holtzmann, Heinrich Julius. *Das messianische Bewusstsein Jesu: Ein Beitrag zur Leben-Jesu-Forschung.* Tübingen: Mohr Siebeck, 1907.

Lehrbuch der neutestamentlichen Theologie. 2 vols. Tübingen: Mohr Siebeck, 1911.

Hooker, Morna D. *The Gospel According to Mark.* BNTC 2. London: A&C Black, 1991. Repr., Peabody, MA: Hendrickson, 1995.

Horbury, William. *Jewish Messianism and the Cult of Christ.* London: SCM, 1998.

Messianism among Jews and Christians: Biblical and Historical Studies. 2nd edn. London: T&T Clark, 2016.

Horsley, Richard A. 1992. "'Messianic' Figures and Movements in First-Century Palestine. Pages 276–295 in *The Messiah: Developments in Earliest Judaism and Christianity.* Edited by James H. Charlesworth. Minneapolis, MN: Fortress.

Hearing the Whole Story: The Politics of Plot in Mark's Gospel. Louisville, KY: Westminster John Knox, 2001.

Text and Tradition in Performance and Writing. Biblical Performance Criticism 9. Eugene, OR: Cascade, 2013.

Horsley, Richard A. and John S. Hanson. 1999. *Bandits, Prophets & Messiahs: Popular Movements in the Time of Jesus,* 2nd edn. Harrisburg, PA: Trinity.

Hultgren, Arland J. "The Formation of the Sabbath Pericope in Mark 2:23–28." *JBL* 91 (1972): 38–43.

Hurtado, Larry W. *Lord Jesus Christ: Devotion to Jesus in Earliest Christianity*. Grand Rapids, MI: Eerdmans, 2003.
"Oral Fixation and New Testament Studies? 'Orality', 'Performance' and Reading Texts in Early Christianity." *NTS* 60 (2014): 321–340.
Iersel, Bas M. F. van. *Mark: A Reader-Response Commentary*. Translated by W. H. Bisscheroux. JSNTSup 164. Sheffield: Sheffield Academic Press, 1998.
Ilan, Tal. "'Man Born of Woman . . .' (Job 14:1): The Phenomenon of Men Bearing Metronymes at the Time of Jesus." *NovT* 34 (1992): 23–45.
"King David, King Herod, and Nicolaus of Damascus." *JSQ* 3 (1998): 195–240.
Incigneri, Brian J. *The Gospel to the Romans*. BibInt 65. Leiden: Brill, 2003.
Jaffee, Martin S. *Torah in the Mouth: Writing and Oral Tradition in Palestinian Judaism, 200 BCE – 400 CE*. Oxford: Oxford University Press, 2001.
Janse, Sam. *"You Are My Son": The Reception History of Psalm 2 in Early Judaism and the Early Church*. CBET 51. Leuven: Peeters, 2009.
Jassen, Alex P. *Scripture and Law in the Dead Sea Scrolls*. Cambridge: Cambridge University Press, 2014.
Jeremias, Joachim. *Abba: Studien zur neutestamentlichen Theologie und Zeitgeschichte*. Göttingen: Vandenhoeck & Ruprecht, 1966.
"παῖς θεοῦ." Pages 654–717 in volume 5 of *Theological Dictionary of the New Testament*. Edited by Gerhard Kittel and Gerhard Friedrich. Translated by Geoffrey W. Bromiley. 10 vols. Grand Rapids, MI: Eerdmans, 1967.
Jewett, Robert. "The Redaction and Use of an Early Christian Confession in Romans 1:3–4." Pages 99–122 in *The Living Text: Essays in Honor of Ernest W. Saunders*. Edited by Dennis E. Groh and Robert Jewett. Lanham, MD: University Press of America, 1985.
Jipp, Joshua W. "Luke's Scriptural Suffering Messiah: A Search for Precedent, a Search for Identity." *CBQ* 72 (2010): 255–274.
"Ancient, Modern, and Future Interpretations of Romans 1:3–4: Reception History and Biblical Interpretation," *JTI* 3 (2009): 241–259.
Johansson, Daniel. "The Identity of Jesus in the Gospel of Mark: Past and Present Proposals." *CBR* 9 (2010): 364–393.
"*Kyrios* in the Gospel of Mark." *JSNT* 33 (2010): 101–124.
"Jesus and God in the Gospel of Mark: Unity and Distinction." PhD diss., University of Edinburgh, 2011.
Johnson, Earl S. "Mark 10:46–52: Blind Bartimaeus." *CBQ* 40 (1978): 191–204, 1978.
"Is Mark 15.39 the Key to Mark's Christology?" *JSNT* 31 (1987): 3–22.
Johnson, Nathan C., Romans 1:3–4: Beyond Antithetical Parallelism. *JBL* 136 (2017): 467–490.
"Rendering David a Servant in *Psalm of Solomon* 17.21." *JSP* 26 (2017): 235–250.
Johnson, Sherman E. "The Davidic-Royal Motif in the Gospels." *JBL* 87 (1968): 136–150.
Juel, Donald H. *Messiah and Temple: The Trial of Jesus in the Gospel of Mark*. SBLDS 31 Missoula, MT: Scholars Press, 1977.

Messianic Exegesis: Christological Interpretation of the Old Testament in Early Christianity. Philadelphia: Fortress, 1988.

"The Origin of Mark's Christology." Pages 449–460 in *The Messiah: Developments in Earliest Judaism and Christianity*. Edited by James H. Charlesworth. Minneapolis, MN: Fortress, 1922.

Karrer, Martin. *Jesus Christus im Neuen Testament*. GNT 11. Göttingen: Vandenhoeck & Ruprecht, 1998.

Kazmierski, Carl. *R. Jesus, the Son of God: A Study of the Markan Tradition and Its Redaction by the Evangelist*. FB 33. Würzburg: Echter, 1979.

Kealy, Seán P. *Mark's Gospel: A History of Its Interpretation: From the Beginning Until 1979*. New York: Paulist, 1982.

Keck, Leander. "The Introduction to Mark's Gospel." *NTS* 12 (1966): 352–370.

Kee, Howard Clark. *Community of the New Age: Studies in Mark's Gospel*. Philadelphia: Westminster, 1977. Repr., Macon, GA: Mercer University Press, 1983.

"Christology in Mark's Gospel." Pages 187–208 in *Judaisms and Their Messiahs at the Turn of the Christian Era*. Edited by Jacob Neusner, William Scott Green, and Ernest S. Frerichs. Cambridge: Cambridge University Press, 1987.

Keener, Craig S. *The Gospel of John: A Commentary*. 2 vols. Peabody, MA: Hendrickson, 2003.

Kelber, Werner. *The Kingdom in Mark: A New Place and a New Time*. Philadelphia: Fortress, 1974.

Kertelge, Karl. *Die Wunder Jesu im Markusevangelium: Eine redaktions-geschichtliche Untersuchung*. SANT 23. München: Kösel-Verlag, 1970.

Kingsbury, Jack D. *The Christology of Mark's Gospel*. Philadelphia: Fortress, 1983.

Kirk, J. R. Daniel, *A Man Attested by God: The Human Jesus of the Synoptic Gospels*. Grand Rapids, MI: Eerdmans, 2016.

Kirk, J. R. Daniel, and Stephen L. Young. "'I Will Set His Hand to the Sea': Psalm 88:26 LXX and Christology in Mark." *JBL* 133 (2014): 333–340.

Kister, Menahem, "Plucking on the Sabbath and Christian-Jewish Polemic." *Imm* 24–25 (1990): 35–51.

Klawans, Jonathan. *Purity, Sacrifice, and the Temple: Symbolism and Super-sessionsim in the Study of Ancient Judaism*. Oxford: Oxford University Press, 2006.

"The Prohibition of Oaths and Contra-Scriptural Halakhot: A Response to John P. Meier," *JSHJ* 6 (2008) 33–48.

Klostermann, Erich. *Das Markusevangelium*. HNT 3. Tübingen: Mohr Siebeck, 1950.

Knoppers, Gary N. "David's Relation to Moses: The Contexts, Content and Conditions of the Davidic Promises." Pages 72–90 in *King and Messiah in Israel and the Ancient Near East: Proceedings of the Oxford Old Testament Seminar*. Edited by John Day. LHBOTS 270. Sheffield: Sheffield Academic Press, 1998.

Koester, Craig R. *Revelation: A New Translation with Introduction and Commentary*. AB 38A. New Haven, CT: Yale University Press, 2014.

Kraus, Hans-Joachim. *Psalms*. Translated by Hilton C. Oswald. 2 vols. CC. Minneapolis, MN: Fortress, 1989.

Krause, Deborah. "The One Who Comes Unbinding the Blessing of Judah: Mark 11.1–10 as Midrash on Gen 49.11, Zechariah 9.9, and Psalm 118.25–26." Pages 141–153 in *Early Christian Interpretation of the Scriptures of Israel: Investigation and Proposals*. Edited by Craig A. Evans and James A. Sanders. JSNTSup 148. Sheffield: Sheffield Academic Press, 1997.

Kugel, James. *Traditions of the Bible: A Guide to the Bible as It Was at the Start of the Common Era*. Cambridge, MA: Harvard University Press, 1998.

Kuhn, Heinz W. "Das Reittier Jesu in der Einzugsgeschichte des Markusevangelium." *ZNW* 50 (1959): 82–91.

Kümmel, Werner Georg. *The New Testament: The History of the Investigation of Its Problems*. Translated by S. McLean Gilmour and Howard C. Kee. Nashville, TN: Abingdon, 1972.

Kvanvig, Helge S. "The Son of Man in the Parables of Enoch." Pages 179–215 in *Enoch and the Messiah Son of Man: Revisiting the Book of Parables*. Edited by Gabriele Boccaccini. Grand Rapids, MI: Eerdmans, 2007.

Laato, Antti. *Josiah and David Redivivus: The Historical Josiah and the Messianic Expectations of Exilic and Postexilic Times*. ConBOT 33. Stockholm: Almqvist & Wiksell, 1992.

Lagrange, M.-J. *Évangile selon Saint Marc, with Corrections and Additions*. 6th edn. Paris: Librairie Lecoffre, 1942.

Lane, William L. *The Gospel According to Mark*. NICNT 2. Grand Rapids, MI: Eerdmans, 1974.

Le Donne, Anthony. *The Historiographical Jesus: Memory, Typology, and the Son of David*. Waco, TX: Baylor University Press, 2009.

Lentzen-Deis, Fritzleo. *Die Taufe Jesu nach den Synoptikern: Literarkritische und gattungsgeschichtliche Untersuchungen*. Frankfurter Theologische Studien 4. Frankfurt: Knecht, 1970.

Levenson, Jon D. *The Death and Resurrection of the Beloved Son: The Transformation of Child Sacrifice in Judaism and Christianity*. New Haven, CT: Yale University Press, 1993.

Levey, Samson H. *The Messiah: An Aramaic Interpretation: The Messianic Exegesis of the Targum*. HUCM 2. Cincinnati, OH: Hebrew Union College-Jewish Institute of Religion, 1974.

Levine, Baruch A. *Numbers 21–36: A New Translation with Introduction and Commentary*. AB 4A. New York: Doubleday, 2000.

Levine, Yigal. "Jesus, 'Son of God' and 'Son of David': The 'Adoption' of Jesus into the Davidic Line." *JSNT* 28 (2006): 415–442.

Liew, Tat-siong Benny. *Politics of Parousia: Reading Mark Inter(con)textually*. BibInt 42. Leiden: Brill, 1999.

"Tyranny, Boundary, and Might: Colonial Mimicry in Mark's Gospel." *JSNT* 73 (1999): 7–31.

Lindars, Barnabas. *New Testament Apologetic*. London: SCM, 1961.

Lohmeyer, Ernst. *Das Evangelium des Markus*. KEK 2. 11th edn. Göttingen: Vandenhoeck & Ruprecht, 1951.

Lohse, Eduard. "υἰὸς Δαυίδ." Pages 478–488 in volume 8 of *Theological Dictionary of the New Testament*. Edited by Gerhard Kittel and Gerhard Friedrich. Translated by Geoffrey W. Bromiley. 10 vols. Grand Rapids, MI: Eerdmans, 1972.

Lövestam, Evald. *Son and Saviour: A Study of Acts 13, 32–37, with an Appendix: "Son of God" in the Synoptic Gospels*. Translated by Michael J. Petry. CN 18. Lund: Gleerup, 1961.

"Die Davidssohnfrage." *SEÅ* 27 (1962): 72–82.

Lührmann, Dieter. *Das Markusevangelium*. HNT 3. Tübingen: Mohr Siebeck, 1987.

Mack, Burton L., and Vernon K. Robbins. *Patterns of Persuasion in the Gospels*. Sonoma, CA: Polebridge, 1989.

Macrae, George. "Messiah and Gospel." Pages 169–185 in *Judaisms and Their Messiahs at the Turn of the Christian Era*. Edited by Jacob Neusner, William Scott Green, and Ernest S. Frerichs. Cambridge: Cambridge University Press, 1987.

Malbon, Elizabeth Struthers. *In the Company of Jesus: Characters in Mark's Gospel*. Louisville, KY: Westminster John Knox, 2000.

"Narrative Criticism: How Does the Story Mean?" Pages 29–57 in *Mark & Method: New Approaches in Biblical Studies*. Edited by Janice Capel Anderson and Stephen D. Moore. 2nd edn. Minneapolis, MN: Fortress, 2008.

Mark's Jesus: Characterization as Narrative Christology. Waco, TX: Baylor University Press, 2009.

"The Jesus of Mark and the 'Son of David'." Pages 162–185 in *Between Author & Audience in Mark: Narration, Characterization, and Interpretation*. Edited by Elizabeth Struthers Malbon. New Testament Monographs 23. Sheffield: Sheffield Phoenix Press, 2009.

Marcus, Joel. "Mark 14:61: 'Are You the Messiah-Son-of-God?'" *NovT* 31 (1989): 125–141.

The Way of the Lord: Christological Exegesis of the Old Testament in the Gospel of Mark. Louisville, KY: Westminster John Knox, 1992.

"The Jewish War and the *Sitz im Leben* of Mark." *JBL* 111 (1992): 441–462.

"Authority to Forgive Sins upon the Earth: The *Shema* in the Gospel of Mark." Pages 196–211 in *The Gospels and the Scriptures of Israel*. Edited by Craig A. Evans and W. Richard Steger. JSNTSup 104. Sheffield: Sheffield Academic Press, 1994.

Mark 1–8: A New Translation with Notes and Commentary. AB 27. New Haven, CT: Yale University Press, 2000.

"Son of Man as Son of Adam." *RB* 110 (2003): 38–61, 370–386.

"Crucifixion as Parodic Exaltation." *JBL* 125 (2006): 73–87.

Mark 8–16: A New Translation with Notes and Commentary. *AB 27*. New Haven, CT: Yale University Press, 2009.

Marshak, Adam Kolman. *The Many Faces of Herod the Great*. Grand Rapids, MI: Eerdmans, 2015.

Marxsen, Willi. *Mark the Evangelist: Studies on the Redaction History of the Gospel*. Translated by James Boyce, Donald Juel, and William Poehlmann. Nashville, TN: Abingdon, 1969. Translation of *Der Evangelist*

Markus: Studien zur Redaktionsgeschichte des Evangeliums. Göttingen: Vandenhoeck & Ruprecht, 1956.

Mason, Eric F. *"You Are a Priest Forever": Second Temple Jewish Messianism and the Priestly Christology of the Epistle to the Hebrews.* STDJ 74. Leiden: Brill, 2008. Repr., Atlanta, GA: SBL.

Matera, Frank J. *The Kingship of Jesus: Composition and Theology in Mark 15.* SBLDS 66. Chico, CA: Scholars Press, 1982.

"The Prologue as the Interpretative Key to Mark's Gospel." *JSNT* 34 (1988): 3–20.

Mauser, Ulrich. *Christ in the Wilderness: The Wilderness Theme in the Second Gospel and Its Basis in the Biblical Tradition.* SBT 39. Bloomsbury: SCM, 1963.

Meier, John P. "From Elijah-Like Prophet to Royal Davidic Messiah." Pages 45–83 in *Jesus: A Colloquium in the Holy Land.* Edited by Doris Donnelly. New York: Continuum, 2001.

"The Historical Jesus and the Plucking of the Grain on the Sabbath." *CBQ* 66 (2004): 561–581.

A Marginal Jew: Rethinking the Historical Jesus, Volume 4: *Law and Love.* New Haven, CT: Yale University Press, 2009.

Menn, Esther M. "Sweet Singer of Israel: David and the Psalms in Early Judaism." Pages 61–74 in *Psalms in Community: Jewish and Christian Textual, Liturgical, and Artistic Traditions.* Edited by Harold W. Attridge and Margot E. Fassler. SymS 25. Atlanta, GA: Society of Biblical Literature, 2003.

Meyers, Carol L., and Eric M. Meyers. *Zechariah 9–14: A New Translation with Introduction and Commentary.* AB 25C. Garden City, NY: Doubleday, 1993.

Milgrom, Jacob. "Further Studies in the Temple Scroll." *JQR* 71 (1980): 89–106.

Numbers. JPSTC 4. Philadelphia: Jewish Publication Society, 1989.

Moffitt, David M. *Atonement and the Logic of Resurrection in the Epistle to the Hebrews.* NovTSup 141. Leiden: Brill, 2011.

Moloney, Francis J. *The Gospel of Mark: A Commentary.* Peabody, MA: Hendrickson, 2002.

Moo, Douglas J. *The Old Testament in the Gospel Passion Narratives.* Sheffield: Almond, 1983.

Moore, Stephen D. *Empire and Apocalypse: Postcolonialism and the New Testament.* The Bible in the Modern World 12. Sheffield: Sheffield Phoenix Press, 2006.

Morgan, C. Shannon. "When Abiathar Was High Priest." *JBL* 98 (1979): 409–410.

Morgan, Robert. *The Nature of New Testament Theology: The Contribution of William Wrede and Adolf Schlatter.* London: SCM, 1973.

Mowinckel, Sigmund. *He That Cometh: The Messiah Concept in the Old Testament and Later Judaism.* Translated by G. W. Anderson. Nashville, TN: Abingdon, 1955. Repr., Grand Rapids, MI: Eerdmans, 2005.

Moyise, Steven. "Isaiah in 1 Peter." Pages 175–188 in *Isaiah in the New Testament.* Edited by Steven Moyise and Maarten J. J. Menken. London: T&T Clark, 2005.

Moyise, Steven, and Maarten J. J. Menken, eds. *The Psalms in the New Testament*. London: T&T Clark, 2004.

Mussner, Franz. "Ein Wortspiel in Mk 1,24?" *BZ* 4 (1960): 285–286.

Myers, Ched. *Binding the Strong Man: A Political Reading of Mark's Story of Jesus*. New York: Orbis, 1988.

Myers, Jacob M. *I and II Esdras: Introduction, Translation and Commentary*. AB 42. Garden City, NY: Doubleday, 1974.

Neirynck, Frans. "Jesus and the Sabbath: Some Observations on Mark II,27." Pages 227–270 in *Jésus aux Origins de la Christologie*. Edited by J. Dupont, 2nd edn., BETL 40. Leuven: Peeters, 1989.

Newman, Judith H. "The Democratization of Kingship in Wisdom of Solomon." Pages 309–328 in *The Idea of Biblical Interpretation: Essays in Honor of James L. Kugel*. Edited by Hindy Najman and Judith H. Newman. JSJSup 83. Leiden: Brill, 2004.

Nickelsburg, George W. E. *Resurrection, Immortality, and Eternal Life in Intertestamental Judaism and Early Christianity*. HTS 56. Cambridge, MA: Harvard University Press, 2006.

Nickelsburg, George W. E., and James C. VanderKam. *1 Enoch 2: A Commentary on the Book of 1 Enoch Chapters 37–82*. Hermeneia. Minneapolis, MN: Fortress, 2012.

Noth, Martin. "Die fünf syrisch überlieferten apokryphen Psalms." *ZAW* 48 (1930): 1–23.

Novenson, Matthew V. *Christ among the Messiahs: Christ Language in Paul and Messiah Language in Ancient Judaism*. New York: Oxford University Press, 2012.

——— *The Grammar of Messianism: An Ancient Jewish Political Idiom and Its Users*. New York: Oxford University Press, 2017.

Novakovic, Lidija. *Messiah, the Healer of the Sick: A Study of Jesus as the Son of David in the Gospel of Matthew*. WUNT 2/170. Tübingen: Mohr Siebeck, 2003.

O'Brien, Kelli S. *The Use of Scripture in the Markan Passion Narrative*. LNTS 384. London: T&T Clark, 2010.

Oegema, Gerbern S. *The Anointed and His People*. JSPSup 27. Sheffield: Sheffield Academic Press, 1998.

Peirce, Charles Sanders. *Elements of Logic*. Volume 2 of *Collected Papers*. Edited by Charles Hartshorne and Paul Weiss. 8 vols. Cambridge, MA: Harvard University Press, 1932.

Peppard, Michael. *The Son of God in the Roman World: Divine Sonship in Its Social and Political Context*. Oxford: Oxford University Press, 2011.

Perrin, Norman. "The Christology of Mark: A Study in Methodology." *JR* 51 (1971): 173–187. Repr., pages 125–140 in *The Interpretation of Mark*. Edited by William R. Telford. 2nd edn. Edinburgh: T&T Clark, 1995.

Pesch, Rudolf. *Das Markusevangelium*. 2 vols. HThKNT 2. Freiburg: Herder, 1976–1977.

Pietersma, Albert. "Exegesis and Liturgy in the Superscriptions of the Greek Psalter." Pages 99–138 in *X Congress of International Organization for Septuagint and Cognate Studies*. Edited by Bernard A. Taylor. SCS 51. Atlanta, GA: Society of Biblical Literature, 2001.

"Septuagintal Exegesis and the Superscriptions of the Greek Psalter." Pages 443–475 in *The Book of Psalms: Composition and Reception.* Edited by Peter W. Flint and Patrick D. Miller. VTSup 99. Leiden: Brill, 2005.

Piotrowski, Nicholas G. *Matthew's New David at the End of Exile: A Socio-Rhetorical Study of Scriptural Quotations.* NovTSup 170. Leiden: Brill, 2016.

Pomykala, Kenneth E. *The Davidic Dynasty Tradition in Early Judaism: Its History and Significance for Messianism.* EJL 7. Atlanta, GA: Scholars Press, 1995.

Powell, Mark Allan. "Narrative Criticism: The Emergence of a Prominent Reading Strategy." Pages 19–43 in *Mark as Story: Retrospect and Prospect.* Edited by Kelly R. Iverson and Christopher W. Skinner. RBS 65. Atlanta, GA: Society of Biblical Literature, 2001.

Puech, Emile. "Préséance Sacerdotale et Messie-Roi dans la Règle de la Congrégation (*1Qsa* ii 11–22)." *RevQ* 16 (1993–1995): 351–365.

"Les psaumes davidiques du rituel d'exorcisme (11Q11)." Pages 160–181 in *Sapiential, Liturgical and Poetical Texts from Qumran: Proceedings of the Third Meeting of the International Organization for Qumran Studies (Oslo 1998).* Edited by Daniel K. Falk, Florentino García Martínez, and Eileen M. Schuller. STDJ 35. Leiden: Brill, 2000.

"Le fils de Dieu, le fils du Très-Haut, messi roi en 4Q246." Pages 271–286 in *Le jugement dans l'un et l'autre testament: Mélanges offerts à Raymond Kuntzmann.* Edited by Oliver Artus. LD 197. Paris: Cerf, 2004.

Rainbow, Paul. "Melchizedek as a Messiah at Qumran." *BBR* 7 (1997): 179–194.

Räisänen, Heikki. *The 'Messianic Secret' in Mark's Gospel.* Translated by C. M. Tuckett. Edinburgh: T&T Clark, 1990.

Rawlinson, A. E. J. *St Mark: With Introduction, Commentary, and Additional Notes.* 4th edn. London: Methuen, 1936.

Reimarus, Hermann Samuel. *Fragments.* Edited by Charles H. Talbert. Translated by Ralph S. Fraser. London: SCM Press, 1971.

Reynolds, Benjamin E. *The Apocalyptic Son of Man in the Gospel of John.* WUNT 2/249. Tübingen: Mohr Siebeck, 2008.

Rhoads, David, Joanna Dewey, and Donald Michie. *Mark as Story: An Introduction to the Narrative of a Gospel.* 3rd edn. Minneapolis, MN: Fortress, 2012.

Riffaterre, Michael. "Compulsory Reader Response: The Intertextual Drive." Pages 56–78 in *Intertextuality: Theories and Practice.* Edited by M. Worton and J. Still. Manchester: Manchester University Press, 1990.

Robbins, Vernon K. "The Healing of Blind Bartimaeus (10:46–52) in the Marcan Theology." *JBL* 92 (1973): 224–243.

Roberts, J. J. M. "The Enthronement of Yhwh and David: The Abiding Theological Significance of the Kingship Language in the Psalms." *CBQ* 64 (2002): 675–686.

Robinson, James M. *The Problem of History in Mark.* SBT 21. London: SCM, 1957.

Rösel, Martin. "Die Psalmüberschriften des Septuaginta-Psalter." Pages 125–148 in *Der Septuaginta-Psalter: Sprachliche und theologische Aspekte.* Edited by Erich Zenger. BibS(F) 32. Freiburg: Herder, 2001.

Rossé, Gérard. *The Cry of Jesus on the Cross: A Biblical and Theological Study.* New York: Paulis, 1987.

Rowe, C. Kavin. *Early Narrative Christology: The Lord in the Gospel of Luke.* BZNW 139. Berlin: De Gruyter, 2006.

Rowe, Robert D. *God's Kingdom and God's Son: The Background to Mark's Christology from Concepts of Kingship in the Psalms.* AGJU 50. Leiden: Brill, 2002.

Ruppert, Lothar. *Jesus als der leidende Gerechte? Der Weg Jesu im Licht eines alt- und zwischentestamentlichen Motivs.* Stuttgart: KBW, 1972.

Sanders, E. P. *Jewish Law from Jesus to the Mishnah: Five Studies.* London: SCM, 1990.

Sanders, James A. "A New Testament Hermeneutic Fabric: Psalm 118 in the Entrance Narrative." Pages 177–190 in *Early Jewish and Christian Exegesis: Studies in Memory of William Hugh Brownlee.* Edited by Craig A. Evans and William F. Stinespring. Atlanta, GA: Scholars Press, 1987.

Schäfer, Peter. *The Jewish Jesus: How Judaism and Christianity Shaped Each Other.* Princeton, NJ: Princeton University Press, 2012.

Schiffman, Laurence H. "The King, His Guard, and the Royal Council in the *Temple Scroll.*" *PAAJR* 54 (1987): 237–257.

"Messianic Figures and Ideas in the Qumran Scrolls." Pages 116–129 in *The Messiah: Developments in Earliest Judaism and Christianity.* Edited by James H. Charlesworth. Minneapolis, MN: Fortress, 1992.

Schlatter, Adolf. *Markus: Der Evangelist für die Griechen.* Stuttgart: Calwer, 1935.

Schneider, Gerhard. "Die Davidssohnfrage (Mark 12,35–37)." *Bib* 53 (1972): 65–90.

Schniedewind, William M. *Society and the Promise to David.* Oxford: Oxford University Press, 1999.

Schreiber, Johannes. "Die Christologie des Markusevangeliums." *ZTK* 58 (1961): 154–183.

Theologie des Vertrauens: Eine redaktionsgeschichtliche Untersuchung des Markusevangelium. Hamburg: Furche-Verlag, 1967.

Die Markuspassion: Eine redaktionsgeschichtliche Untersuchung. BZNW 68. Berlin: De Gruyter, 1993.

Schuller, Eileen M. "The Psalm of 4Q372 1 within the Context of Second Temple Prayer." *CBQ* 54 (1992): 67–79.

Schweitzer, Albert. *The Quest of the Historical Jesus: A Critical Study of Its Progress from Reimarus to Wrede.* Translated by W. Montgomery. Mineola, NY: Dover, 2005. Translation of *Geschichte der Leben-Jesu Forschung.* Tübingen: Mohr Siebeck 1913; repr. 2 vols., Hamburg: Siebenstern Taschenbuch, 1966.

The Mysticism of Paul the Apostle. Translated by William Montgomery. Baltimore: Johns Hopkins University Press, 1998. Translation of *Mystik des Apostels Paulus.* Tübingen: Mohr Siebeck, 1930.

Schweizer, Eduard. *The Good News According to Mark.* Translated by Donald H. Madvig. Louisville, KY: John Knox, 1970.

Segal, Michael. "Who Is the 'Son of God' in 4Q246? An Overlooked Example of Biblical Interpretation." *DSD* 21 (2014): 289–312.

Shekan, Patrick. "Again the Syriac Apocryphal Psalms." *CBQ* 38 (1976): 143–158.

Shively, Elizabeth E. *Apocalyptic Imagination in the Gospel of Mark: The Literary and Theological Role of Mark 3:22–30.* BZNW 189. Berlin: De Gruyter, 2012.

"Characterizing the Non-Human: Satan in the Gospel of Mark." Pages 127–151 in *Character Studies and the Gospel of Mark.* Edited by Christopher Skinner and Matthew Hauge. LNTS 483. London: T&T Clark, 2014.

Smith, Stephen H. "The Function of the Son of David Tradition in Mark's Gospel." *NTS* 42 (1996): 523–539.

Snodgrass, Klyne. *The Parable of the Wicked Tenants: An Inquiry into Parable Interpretation.* WUNT 27. Tübingen: Mohr Siebeck, 1983.

Steichele, Hans-Jörg. *Der leidende Sohn Gottes: Eine Untersuchung einiger alttestamentlicher Motive in der Christologie des Markusevangeliums.* Biblische Untersuchungen 14. Regensburg: Pustet, 1980.

Stein, Robert H. *Mark.* BECNT. Grand Rapids, MI: Baker Academic, 2008.

Sternberg, Meir. *The Poetics of Biblical Narrative: Ideological Literature and the Drama of Reading.* Bloomington, IN: Indiana University Press, 1985.

Steudel, Annette. "אחרית הימים in the Texts from Qumran." *RevQ* 16 (1993): 225–246.

Der Midrasch zur Eschatologie aus der Qumrangemeinde (4QMidrEschat ^{a,b}): Materielle Rekonstruktion, Textbestand, Gattung und traditionsgeschichtliche Einordnung des durch 4Q174 ("Florilegium") und 4Q177 ("Catena A") repräsentierten werkes aus den Qumranfunden. STDJ 13. Leiden: Brill, 1994.

"The Eternal Reign of the People of God – Collective Expectations in Qumran Texts (4Q264 and 1QM)." *RevQ* 17 (1996): 507–525.

"Psalm 2 im antiken Judentum." Pages 189–197 in *Gottessohn und Menschensohn: Exegetische Studien zu zwei Paradigmen biblischer Intertextualität.* Edited by Dieter Sänger. BibS(N) 67. Neukirchen-Vluyn: Neukirchener, 2004.

Stone, Michael E. *Fourth Ezra: A Commentary on the Book of Fourth Ezra.* Hermeneia. Minneapolis, MN: Fortress, 1990.

Strauss, David Friedrich. *The Life of Jesus Critically Examined.* Translated by George Eliot. London: Sonnenschein, 1982. Translation of *Das Leben Jesu kritisch bearbeitet.* Tübingen: Mohr Siebeck, 1835.

Strauss, Mark L. *The Davidic Messiah in Luke-Acts: The Promise and Its Fulfillment in Lukan Christology.* JSNTSup 110. Sheffield: Sheffield Academic Press, 1995.

Stuckenbruck, Loren T. "Messianic Ideas in the Apocalyptic and Related Literature of Early Judaism." Pages 90–113 in *The Messiah in the Old and New Testaments.* Edited by Stanley E. Porter. Grand Rapids, MI: Eerdmans, 2007.

Suhl, Alfred. *Die Funktion der alttestamentlichen Zitate und Anspielungen im Markusevangelium.* Gütersloh: Gütersloher, 1965.

Tannehill, Robert C. "The Disciples in Mark: The Function of a Narrative Role." *JR* 57 (1977): 386–405.

"The Gospel of Mark as Narrative Christology." *Semeia* 16 (1980): 57–96.

Taylor, Vincent. *The Gospel According to St. Mark: The Greek Text with Introduction, Notes, and Indexes.* London: Macmillan, 1952.

Telford, William R. *The Theology of the Gospel of Mark.* Cambridge: Cambridge University Press, 1999.

Theisohn, Johannes. *Der auserwählte Richter: Untersuchungen zum traditionsgeschichtlichen Ort der Menschensohngestalt der Äthiopischen Henoch.* SUNT 12. Göttingen: Vandenhoeck & Ruprecht, 1975.

Theissen, Gerd. "From the Historical Jesus to the Kerygmatic Son of God: How Role Analysis Contributes to the Understanding of New Testament Christology. Pages 235–260 in *Jesus Research: New Methodologies and Perceptions, The Second Princeton-Prague Symposium on Jesus Research.* Edited by James H. Charlesworth, with Brian Rhea and Petr Pokorný. Grand Rapids, MI: Eerdmans, 2014.

Tillesse, Georges Minette de. *Le secret messianique dans l'Évangile de Marc.* LD 47. Paris: Cerf, 1968.

Tolbert, Mary Ann. *Sowing the Gospel: Mark's World in Literary-Historical Perspective* Minneapolis, MN: Fortress, 1989.

Tooman, William A. *Gog of Magog: Reuse of Scripture and Compositional Technique in Ezekiel 38–39.* FAT 2/52. Tübingen: Mohr Siebeck, 2011.

Trocmé, Étienne. "Is There a Marcan Christology?" Pages 3–14 in *Christ and Spirit in the New Testament.* Edited by Barnabas Lindars and Stephen S. Smalley. Cambridge: Cambridge University Press, 1973.

L'Évangile selon Saint Marc. CNT 2. Genève: Labor et Fides, 2000.

Turner, Max. *Power from on High: The Spirit in Israel's Restoration and Witness in Luke-Acts.* Journal of Pentecostal Theology Supplement Series 9. Sheffield: Sheffield Academic Press, 1996.

Tyson, Joseph B. "The Blindness of the Disciples in Mark." *JBL* 80 (1961): 261–268.

van Unnik, W. C. "Jesus the Christ." *NTS* 8 (1962): 101–116.

VanderKam, James C. "Righteous One, Messiah, Chosen One, and Son of Man in 1 Enoch 37–71. Pages 169–191 in *The Messiah: Developments in Earliest Judaism and Christianity.* Edited by James H. Charlesworth. Minneapolis, MN: Fortress, 1992.

Vermes, Geza. *Scripture and Tradition in Judaism: Haggadic Studies.* StPB 4. Leiden: Brill, 1973.

Vielhauer, Philipp. "Erwägungen zur Christologie des Markusevangliums." Pages 199–214 in *Aufsätze zum Neuen Testament.* München: Chr. Kaiser, 1964.

Waddell, James A. *The Messiah: A Comparative Study of the Enochic Son of Man and the Pauline Kyrios.* Jewish and Christian Texts in Contexts and Related Studies Series 10. London: T&T Clark, 2001.

Waetjen, Herman. *A Reordering of Power: A Socio-Political Reading of Mark's Gospel.* Minneapolis, MN: Fortress, 1989.

Wagner, J. Ross. "Psalm 118 in Luke-Acts: Tracing a Narrative Thread." Pages 154–178 in *Early Christian Interpretation of the Scriptures of*

Israel: Investigation and Proposals. Edited by Craig A. Evans and James A. Sanders. JSNTSup 148. Sheffield: Sheffield Academic Press, 1997.

Heralds of the Good News: Isaiah and Paul in Concert in the Letter to the Romans. NovTSup 101. Leiden: Brill, 2002. Repr., Leiden: Brill, 2003.

Walck, Leslie W. *The Son of Man in the Parables of Enoch and in Matthew.* Jewish and Christian Texts in Contexts and Related Studies 9. London: T&T Clark, 2011.

Wasserman, Tommy. "'The Son of God' Was in the Beginning (Mark 1:1)." *JTS* 62 (2011): 20–50.

Wasserman, Tommy, and Peter J. Gurry. *A New Approach to Textual Criticism: An Introduction to the Coherence-Based Genealogical Method.* RBS 80. Atlanta, GA: SBL, 2017.

Watts, Rikki E. *Isaiah's New Exodus in Mark.* WUNT 2/88. Tübingen: Mohr Siebeck, 1997. Repr., Grand Rapids, MI: Baker Academic, 2000.

"The Lord's House and David's Lord: The Psalms and Mark's Perspective on Jesus and the Temple." *BibInt* 15 (2007): 307–322.

"Mark." Pages 111–249 in *Commentary on the New Testament Use of the Old Testament.* Edited by G. K. Beale and D. A. Carson. Grand Rapids, MI: Baker Academic, 2007.

Webb, Robert L. *John the Baptizer and Prophet: A Socio-Historical Study.* JSNTSup 62. Sheffield: JSOT Press, 1991.

Weeden, Theodore J. "The Heresy that Necessitated Mark's Gospel." *ZNW* 59 (1968): 145–158. Repr., pages 89–104 in *The Interpretation of Mark.* Edited by William R. Telford. 2nd edn. Edinburgh: T&T Clark, 1995.

Weiss, Bernhard. *Biblical Theology of the New Testament.* 2 vols. Volume 1 translated by David Eaton. Volume 2 translated by James E. Duguid. Clark's Theological Library 12 and 13. Edinburgh: T&T Clark, 1882–1883.

Weiss, Johannes. *Jesus' Proclamation of the Kingdom of God.* Translated by Richard Hyde Hiers and David Larrimore Holland. Philadelphia: Fortress, 1971. Translation of *Die Predigt Jesu vom Reiche Gottes.* Göttingen: Vandenhoeck & Ruprecht, 1892.

Wellhausen, Julius. *Das Evangelium Marci.* Berlin: Georg Reimer, 1903.

Wenham, John W. "Mark 2,26." *JTS* 1 (1950): 156.

Westermann, Claus. *Genesis 17–50.* Translated by John J. Scullion. CC. Minneapolis, MN: Augsburg, 1986.

Whitsett, Christopher G. "Son of God, Seed of David: Paul's Messianic Exegesis in Romans 2:3–4 [sic]." *JBL* 119 (2000): 661–681.

Wilson, Andrew, and Lawrence M. Wills. "Literary Sources in the Temple Scroll." *HTR* 75 (1982): 275–288.

Wilson, Gerald H. "Shaping the Psalter: A Consideration of Editorial Linkage in the Books of the Psalms." Pages 72–82 in *The Shape and Shaping of the Psalter.* Edited by J. C. McCann. JSOTSup 159. Sheffield: JSOT Press, 1993.

Woude, Adam S. van der. "Melchisedek als himmlische Erlösergestalt in den neugefundenen eschatologischen Midraschim aus Qumran Höhle XI." *OtSt* 14 (1965): 354–373.

Wrede, William. *The Messianic Secret: Das Messiasgeheimnis in den Evangelien.* Translated by J. C. G. Greig. London: James Clark & Co, 1971.

Translation of *Das Messiasgeheimnis in den Evangelien: Zugleich ein Beitrag zum Verständnis des Markusevangeliums.* Gottingen: Vandenhoeck & Ruprecht, 1901.

Vorträge und Studien. Tübingen: Mohr Siebeck, 1907.

Wright, N. T. *The New Testament and the People of God.* Volume 1 of *Christian Origins and the Question of God.* Minneapolis, MN: Fortress, 1992.

Jesus and the Victory of God. Volume 2 of *Christian Origins and the Question of God.* London: Minneapolis, MN: Fortress, 1996.

Paul and the Faithfulness of God. 2 vols. Volume 4 of *Christian Origins and the Question of God.* London: Minneapolis, MN: Fortress, 2013.

Xeravits, Géza. *King, Priest, Prophet: Positive Eschatological Protagonists of the Qumran Library.* STDJ 67. Leiden: Brill, 2003.

Yadin, Yigael. *The Temple Scroll: The Hidden Law of the Dead Sea Sect.* London: Weidenfeld & Nicolson, 1985.

Yarbro Collins, Adela. "The Influence of Daniel on the New Testament." Pages 90–112 in John J. Collins, *Daniel: A Commentary on the Book of Daniel.* Hermeneia. Minneapolis, MN: Fortress, 1993.

"Establishing the Text: Mark 1:1." Pages 111–127 in *Texts and Contexts: The Function of Biblical Texts in Their Textual and Situational Contexts: Essays in Honor of Lars Hartman.* Edited by Tord Fornberg and David Hellholm. Oslo: Scandinavian University Press, 1995.

"The Appropriation of the Psalms of Individual Lament by Mark." Pages 223–241 in *The Scriptures in the Gospels.* Edited by C. M. Tuckett. BETL 131. Leuven: University Press, 1997.

"Mark and His Readers: The Son of God among Jews." *HTR* 92 (1999): 393–408.

2000. "Mark and His Readers: The Son of God among Greeks and Romans." *HTR* 93 (2000): 85–100.

Mark: A Commentary. Hermeneia. Minneapolis, MN: Fortress, 2007.

Yarbro Collins, Adela, and John J. Collins. *King and Messiah as Son of God.* Grand Rapids, MI: Eerdmans, 2008.

Young, Frances M. *Biblical Exegesis and the Formation of Christian Culture.* Peabody, MA: Hendrickson, 2002.

Zahn, Molly M. "4QReworked Pentateuch C and the Literary Sources of the *Temple Scroll*: A New (Old) Perspective." *DSD* 19 (2012): 133–158.

Zimmermann, Johannes. *Messianische Texte aus Qumran: Königliche, priesterliche und prophetische Messiasvorstellungen in den Schriftfunden von Qumran.* WUNT 2/104. Tübingen: Mohr Siebeck, 1998.

INDEX OF ANCIENT SOURCES

Mishnah, Talmud, and Related Texts

INDEX OF MODERN AUTHORS

INDEX OF SUBJECTS

CPSIA information can be obtained
at www.ICGtesting.com
Printed in the USA
LVHW040001231020
669550LV00002B/89